Aviation Maintenance Technician Handbook–Powerplant

Volume 1

2012

U.S. Department of Transportation
FEDERAL AVIATION ADMINISTRATION
Flight Standards Service

Published by Books Express Publishing
Copyright © Books Express, 2012
ISBN 978-1-78266-021-7

Books Express publications are available from all good retail and online booksellers. For publishing proposals and direct ordering please contact us at: info@books-express.com

Volume Contents

Volume 1

Preface v

Acknowledgments vii

Table of Contents ix

Chapter 1
Aircraft Engines 1-1

Chapter 2
Engine Fuel and Fuel Metering Systems 2-1

Chapter 3
Induction and Exhaust Systems 3-1

Chapter 4
Engine Ignition and Electrical Systems 4-1

Chapter 5
Engine Starting Systems 5-1

Volume 2

Chapter 6
Lubrication and Cooling Systems 6-1

Chapter 7
Propellers 7-1

Chapter 8
Engine Removal and Replacement 8-1

Chapter 9
Engine Fire Protection Systems 9-1

Chapter 10
Engine Maintenance and Operation 10-1

Chapter 11
Light-Sport Aircraft Engines 11-1

Preface

The Aviation Maintenance Technician Handbook–Powerplant (FAA-H-8083-32) is one of a series of three handbooks for persons preparing for certification as a powerplant mechanic. It is intended that this handbook provide the basic information on principles, fundamentals, and technical procedures in the subject matter areas relating to the powerplant rating. It is designed to aid students enrolled in a formal course of instruction, as well as the individual who is studying on his or her own. Since the knowledge requirements for the airframe and powerplant ratings closely parallel each other in some subject areas, the chapters which discuss fire protection systems and electrical systems contain some material which is also duplicated in the Aviation Maintenance Technician Handbook–Airframe (FAA-H-8083-31).

This handbook contains an explanation of the units that make up each of the systems that bring fuel, air, and ignition together in an aircraft engine for combustion. It also contains information on engine construction features, lubrication systems, exhaust systems, cooling systems, cylinder removal and replacement, compression checks, and valve adjustments. Because there are so many different types of aircraft in use today, it is reasonable to expect that differences exist in airframe components and systems. To avoid undue repetition, the practice of using representative systems and units is carried out throughout the handbook. Subject matter treatment is from a generalized point of view and should be supplemented by reference to manufacturer's manuals or other textbooks if more detail is desired. This handbook is not intended to replace, substitute for, or supersede official regulations or the manufacturer's instructions. Occasionally the word "must" or similar language is used where the desired action is deemed critical. The use of such language is not intended to add to, interpret, or relieve a duty imposed by Title 14 of the Code of Federal Regulations (14 CFR).

This handbook is available for download, in PDF format, from www.faa.gov.

The subject of Human Factors is contained in the Aviation Maintenance Technician Handbook–General (FAA-H-8083-30).

This handbook is published by the United States Department of Transportation, Federal Aviation Administration, Airman Testing Standards Branch, AFS-630, P.O. Box 25082, Oklahoma City, OK 73125.

Comments regarding this publication should be sent, in email form, to the following address:

AFS630comments@faa.gov

Acknowledgments

The Aviation Maintenance Technician Handbook–Powerplant (FAA-H-8083-32) was produced by the Federal Aviation Administration (FAA) with the assistance of Safety Research Corporation of America (SRCA). The FAA wishes to acknowledge the following contributors:

Mr. Tom Wild for images used throughout this handbook

Free Images Live (www.freeimageslive.co.uk) for image used in Chapter 1

Mr. Stephen Sweet (www.stephensweet.com) for image used in Chapter 1

Pratt & Whitney for images used in Chapters 2, 3, 6, 7, and 8

Teledyne Continental Motors (www.genuinecontinental.aero) for images used in chapter 2, 3, and 11

DeltaHawk Engines, Inc. (www.deltahawkengines.com) for image used in Chapter 6

Mr. Felix Gottwald for image used in Chapter 7

Mr. Stephen Christopher (www.schristo.com) for images used in Chapter 8

Mr. Yunjin Lee for images used in Chapter 9

Aeromax Aviation, LLC (www.aeromaxaviation.com) for images used in Chapter 11

Avid Aircraft (www.avidflyeraircraft.com) for image used in Chapter 11

Flight and Safety Design (www.eco1aircraft.com) for image used in Chapter 11

Great Plains Aircraft Supply Co., Inc. (www.greatplainsas.com) for image used in Chapter 11

Lycoming Engines (www.lycoming.textron.com) for image used in Chapter 11

Revmaster LLC Aviation (revmasteraviation.com) for images used in Chapter 11

Rotech Research Canada, Ltd. (www.rotec.com) for images used in Chapter 11

Additional appreciation is extended to Mr. Gary E. Hoyle, Dean of Students, Pittsburgh Institute of Aeronautics; Mr. Tom Wild, Purdue University; Dr. Ronald Sterkenburg, Associate Professor of the Department of Aviation Technology, Purdue University; for their technical support and input.

Table of Contents

Volume Contents iii

Preface v

Acknowledgments vii

Table of Contents ix

Chapter 1
Aircraft Engines 1-1
General Requirements 1-1
   Power and Weight 1-2
   Fuel Economy 1-3
   Durability and Reliability 1-3
   Operating Flexibility 1-3
   Compactness 1-3
   Powerplant Selection 1-3
Types of Engines 1-4
   Inline Engines 1-4
   Opposed or O-Type Engines 1-4
   V-Type Engines 1-5
   Radial Engines 1-5
Reciprocating Engines 1-5
   Design and Construction 1-5
   Crankcase Sections 1-5
   Accessory Section 1-7
   Accessory Gear Trains 1-7
Crankshafts 1-8
   Crankshaft Balance 1-10
   Dynamic Dampers 1-10
Connecting Rods 1-10
   Master-and-Articulated Rod Assembly 1-11
   Knuckle Pins 1-12
   Plain-Type Connecting Rods 1-12
   Fork-and-Blade Rod Assembly 1-12
Pistons 1-12
   Piston Construction 1-12
   Piston Pin 1-13
Piston Rings 1-14
   Piston Ring Construction 1-14
   Compression Ring 1-14

Oil Control Rings 1-14
Oil Scraper Ring 1-14
Cylinders 1-14
   Cylinder Heads 1-15
   Cylinder Barrels 1-16
   Cylinder Numbering 1-16
Firing Order 1-17
   Single-Row Radial Engines 1-17
   Double-Row Radial Engines 1-17
Valves 1-17
   Valve Construction 1-17
Valve Operating Mechanism 1-18
   Cam Rings 1-19
   Camshaft 1-20
   Tappet Assembly 1-20
   Solid Lifters/Tappets 1-21
   Hydraulic Valve Tappets/Lifters 1-21
   Push Rod 1-22
   Rocker Arms 1-22
   Valve Springs 1-22
Bearings 1-22
   Plain Bearings 1-23
   Ball Bearings 1-23
   Roller Bearings 1-23
Propeller Reduction Gearing 1-24
Propeller Shafts 1-24
Reciprocating Engine Operating Principles 1-24
Operating Cycles 1-26
   Four-Stroke Cycle 1-26
      Intake Stroke 1-27
      Compression Stroke 1-27
      Power Stroke 1-27
      Exhaust Stroke 1-28
   Two-Stroke Cycle 1-28
   Rotary Cycle 1-28
   Diesel Cycle 1-28
Reciprocating Engine Power and Efficiencies ... 1-28
   Work 1-28
   Horsepower 1-28
   Piston Displacement 1-29
   Area of a Circle 1-29

Example	1-29
Compression Ratio	1-29
Indicated Horsepower	1-31
Example	1-32
Brake Horsepower	1-32
Example	1-33
Friction Horsepower	1-33
Friction and Brake Mean Effective Pressures	1-33
Thrust Horsepower	1-35
Efficiencies	1-35
Thermal Efficiency	1-35
Example	1-35
Mechanical Efficiency	1-36
Volumetric Efficiency	1-36
Propulsive Efficiency	1-36
Gas Turbine Engines	1-37
Types and Construction	1-37
Air Entrance	1-38
Accessory Section	1-39
Compressor Section	1-39
Compressor Types	1-40
Centrifugal-Flow Compressors	1-40
Axial-Flow Compressor	1-41
Diffuser	1-44
Combustion Section	1-44
Turbine Section	1-47
Exhaust Section	1-51
Gas Turbine Engine Bearings and Seals	1-52
Turboprop Engines	1-54
Turboshaft Engines	1-55
Turbofan Engines	1-55
Turbine Engine Operating Principles	1-57
Thrust	1-57
Gas Turbine Engine Performance	1-58
Ram Recovery	1-60

Chapter 2
Engine Fuel and Fuel Metering Systems......2-1

Fuel System Requirements	2-1
Vapor Lock	2-2
Basic Fuel System	2-2
Fuel Metering Devices for Reciprocating Engines	2-3
Fuel/Air Mixtures	2-4
Carburetion Principles	2-6
Venturi Principles	2-6
Application of Venturi Principle to Carburetor	2-6
Metering and Discharge of Fuel	2-7
Carburetor Systems	2-8
Carburetor Types	2-9
Carburetor Icing	2-9
Float-Type Carburetors	2-10
Float Chamber Mechanism System	2-10
Main Metering System	2-11
Idling System	2-12
Mixture Control System	2-12
Accelerating System	2-14
Economizer System	2-14
Pressure Injection Carburetors	2-15
Typical Injection Carburetor	2-15
Throttle Body	2-16
Regulator Unit	2-16
Fuel Control Unit	2-18
Automatic Mixture Control (AMC)	2-19
Stromberg PS Carburetor	2-20
Accelerating Pump	2-21
Manual Mixture Control	2-21
Fuel-Injection Systems	2-22
Bendix/Precision Fuel-Injection System	2-22
Fuel Injector	2-22
Airflow Section	2-22
Regulator Section	2-22
Fuel Metering Section	2-23
Flow Divider	2-23
Fuel Discharge Nozzles	2-24
Continental/TCM Fuel-Injection System	2-25
Fuel-Injection Pump	2-25
Fuel/Air Control Unit	2-27
Fuel Control Assembly	2-28
Fuel Manifold Valve	2-28
Fuel Discharge Nozzle	2-28
Carburetor Maintenance	2-28
Carburetor Removal	2-28
Installation of Carburetor	2-30
Rigging Carburetor Controls	2-30
Adjusting Idle Mixtures	2-30
Idle Speed Adjustment	2-31
Fuel System Inspection and Maintenance	2-32
Complete System	2-32
Fuel Tanks	2-33
Lines and Fittings	2-33
Selector Valves	2-33
Pumps	2-33
Main Line Strainers	2-33
Fuel Quantity Gauges	2-33
Fuel Pressure Gauge	2-34
Pressure Warning Signal	2-34
Water Injection Systems for Reciprocating Engines	2-34
Turbine Engine Fuel System—General Requirements	2-34
Turbine Fuel Controls	2-34
Hydromechanical Fuel Control	2-35

Hydromechanical/Electronic Fuel Control..............2-35
FADEC Fuel Control Systems 2-37
FADEC for an Auxiliary Power Unit......................2-37
FADEC Fuel Control Propulsion Engine................2-39
Fuel System Operation 2-41
Water Injection System..2-42
Fuel Control Maintenance..2-42
Engine Fuel System Components 2-43
Main Fuel Pumps (Engine Driven) 2-43
Fuel Heater 2-43
Fuel Filters..2-44
Fuel Spray Nozzles and Fuel Manifolds 2-45
Simplex Fuel Nozzle 2-45
Duplex Fuel Nozzle 2-46
Airblast Nozzles 2-46
Flow Divider 2-46
Fuel Pressurizing and Dump Valves 2-46
Combustion Drain Valves 2-47
Fuel Quantity Indicating Units...................................2-48

Chapter 3
Induction and Exhaust Systems 3-1
Reciprocating Engine Induction Systems 3-1
Basic Carburetor Induction System.........................3-2
Induction System Icing 3-4
Induction System Filtering 3-5
Induction System Inspection and Maintenance 3-5
Induction System Troubleshooting......................3-5
Supercharged Induction Systems 3-5
Turbosuperchargers 3-8
Normalizer Turbocharger 3-11
Ground-Boosted Turbosupercharger System 3-11
A Typical Turbosupercharger System 3-13
Turbocharger Controllers and System
Descriptions 3-15
Variable Absolute Pressure Controller (VAPC) ..3-16
Sloped Controller...3-16
Absolute Pressure Controller 3-17
Turbocharger System Troubleshooting 3-17
Turbine Engine Inlet Systems 3-17
Divided-Entrance Duct...3-19
Variable-Geometry Duct 3-19
Compressor Inlet Screens.......................................3-20
Bellmouth Compressor Inlets.................................3-20
Turboprop and Turboshaft Compressor Inlets 3-21
Turbofan Engine Inlet Sections...............................3-21
Reciprocating Engine Exhaust Systems......................3-22
Radial Engine Exhaust Collector Ring System........3-23
Manifold and Augmentor Exhaust Assembly 3-24
Reciprocating Engine Exhaust System

Maintenance Practices..3-24
Exhaust System Inspection.....................................3-24
Muffler and Heat Exchanger Failures 3-25
Exhaust Manifold and Stack Failures.....................3-25
Internal Muffler Failures 3-25
Exhaust Systems With Turbocharger..........................3-26
Augmentor Exhaust System 3-26
Exhaust System Repairs 3-26
Turbine Engine Exhaust Nozzles 3-26
Convergent Exhaust Nozzle 3-28
Convergent-Divergent Exhaust Nozzle...................3-28
Thrust Reversers 3-28
Afterburning/Thrust Augmentation 3-29
Thrust Vectoring 3-31
Engine Noise Supression 3-31
Turbine Engine Emissions 3-33

Chapter 4
Engine Ignition and Electrical Systems 4-1
Reciprocating Engine Ignition Systems........................4-1
Magneto-Ignition System Operating Principles............4-2
High-Tension Magneto System Theory of
Operation 4-2
The Magnetic Circuit..4-2
The Primary Electrical Circuit..............................4-4
The Secondary Electrical Circuit..........................4-6
Magneto and Distributor Venting..........................4-7
Ignition Harness...4-8
Ignition Switches...4-9
Single and Dual High-Tension System
Magnetos 4-10
Magneto Mounting Systems..................................4-10
Low-Tension Magneto System 4-12
FADEC System Description 4-12
Low-Voltage Harness...4-13
Electronic Control Unit (ECU)...............................4-14
PowerLink Ignition System...................................4-14
Booster Coil 4-16
Impulse Coupling 4-17
High-Tension Retard Breaker Vibrator...................4-18
Low-Tension Retard Breaker Vibrator....................4-20
Spark Plugs 4-21
Reciprocating Engine Ignition System
Maintenance and Inspection 4-22
Magneto-Ignition Timing Devices.............................4-23
Built-In Engine Timing Reference Marks...............4-23
Timing Disks 4-24
Piston Position Indicators......................................4-24
Timing Lights 4-25
Checking the Internal Timing of a Magneto...............4-25

High-Tension Magneto E-Gap Setting
(Bench Timing) 4-26
Timing the High-tension Magneto to the Engine 4-26
Performing Ignition System Checks 4-27
Ignition Switch Check 4-28
Maintenance and Inspection of Ignition Leads 4-28
Replacement of Ignition Harness 4-29
Checking Ignition Induction Vibrator Systems 4-30
Spark Plug Inspection and Maintenance 4-30
Carbon Fouling of Spark Plugs 4-30
Oil Fouling of Spark Plugs 4-30
Lead Fouling of Spark Plugs 4-30
Graphite Fouling of Spark Plugs 4-31
Gap Erosion of Spark Plugs 4-31
Spark Plug Removal 4-32
Spark Plug Reconditioning Service 4-33
Inspection Prior to Installation 4-33
Spark Plug Installation 4-34
Spark Plug Lead Installation 4-35
Breaker Point Inspection 4-35
Dielectric Inspection 4-38
Ignition Harness Maintenance 4-38
High-Tension Ignition Harness Faults 4-38
Harness Testing 4-39
Turbine Engine Ignition Systems 4-39
Capacitor Discharge Exciter Unit 4-41
Igniter Plugs 4-41
Turbine Ignition System Inspection and
Maintenance 4-42
Inspection 4-42
Check System Operation 4-43
Repair 4-43
Removal, Maintenance, and Installation of Ignition
System Components 4-43
Ignition System Leads 4-43
Igniter Plugs 4-44
Powerplant Electrical Systems 4-45
Wire Size 4-45
Factors Affecting the Selection of Wire Size 4-45
Factors Affecting Selection of Conductor
Material 4-47
Conductor Insulation 4-49
Identifying Wire and Cable 4-50
Electrical Wiring Installation 4-51
Wire Groups and Bundles 4-51
Twisting Wires 4-51
Spliced Connections in Wire Bundles 4-52
Slack in Wiring Bundles 4-52
Bend Radii 4-52
Routing and Installation 4-52
Protection Against Chafing 4-53

Protection Against High Temperature 4-53
Protection Against Solvents and Fluids 4-53
Protection of Wires in Wheel Well Area 4-54
Routing Precautions 4-54
Installation of Cable Clamps 4-54
Lacing and Tying Wire Bundles 4-55
Single-Cord Lacing 4-55
Double-Cord Lacing 4-56
Lacing Branch-Offs 4-56
Tying 4-56
Cutting Wire and Cable 4-57
Stripping Wire and Cable 4-57
Solderless Terminals and Splices 4-58
Copper Wire Terminals 4-59
Crimping Tools 4-59
Aluminum Wire Terminals 4-60
Splicing Copper Wires Using Preinsulated
Wires 4-60
Emergency Splicing Repairs 4-60
Splicing with Solder and Potting Compound 4-60
Connecting Terminal Lugs to Terminal Blocks 4-62
Bonding and Grounding 4-62
General Bonding and Grounding Procedures 4-62
Connectors 4-64
Types of Connectors 4-65
Connector Identification 4-66
Installation of Connectors 4-66
Conduit 4-66
Electrical Equipment Installation 4-67
Electrical Load Limits 4-67
Controlling or Monitoring the Electrical Load 4-67
Circuit Protection Devices 4-67
Switches 4-68
Relays 4-68

Chapter 5
Engine Starting Systems 5-1
Introduction 5-1
Reciprocating Engine Starting Systems 5-2
Inertia Starters 5-2
Direct Cranking Electric Starter 5-2
Direct Cranking Electric Starting System for
Large Reciprocating Engines 5-3
Direct Cranking Electric Starting System for
Small Aircraft 5-6
Reciprocating Engine Starting System
Maintenance Practices 5-8
Troubleshooting Small Aircraft Starting Systems 5-8
Gas Turbine Engine Starters 5-8
Electric Starting Systems and Starter Generator
Starting System 5-11

Troubleshooting a Starter Generator Starting
  System 5-12
Air Turbine Starters 5-13
  Air Turbine Starter Troubleshooting Guide 5-17

Glossary G-1

Index I-1

Chapter 1
Aircraft Engines

General Requirements

Aircraft require thrust to produce enough speed for the wings to provide lift or enough thrust to overcome the weight of the aircraft for vertical takeoff. For an aircraft to remain in level flight, thrust must be provided that is equal to and in the opposite direction of the aircraft drag. This thrust, or propulsive force, is provided by a suitable type of aircraft heat engine. All heat engines have in common the ability to convert heat energy into mechanical energy by the flow of some fluid mass (generally air) through the engine. In all cases, the heat energy is released at a point in the cycle where the working pressure is high relative to atmospheric pressure.

The propulsive force is obtained by the displacement of a working fluid (again, atmospheric air). This air is not necessarily the same air used within the engine. By displacing air in a direction opposite to that in which the aircraft is propelled, thrust can be developed. This is an application of Newton's third law of motion. It states that for every action there is an equal and opposite reaction. So, as air is being displaced to the rear of the aircraft the aircraft is moved forward by this principle. One misinterpretation of this principle is air is pushing against the air behind the aircraft making it move forward. This is not true. Rockets in space have no air to push against, yet, they can produce thrust by using Newton's third law. Atmospheric air is the principal fluid used for propulsion in every type of aircraft powerplant except the rocket, in which the total combustion gases are accelerated and displaced. The rocket must provide all the fuel and oxygen for combustion and does not depend on atmospheric air. A rocket carries its own oxidizer rather than using ambient air for combustion. It discharges the gaseous byproducts of combustion through the exhaust nozzle at an extremely high velocity (action) and it is propelled in the other direction (reaction).

The propellers of aircraft powered by reciprocating or turboprop engines accelerate a large mass of air at a relatively lower velocity by turning a propeller. The same amount of thrust can be generated by accelerating a small mass of air to a very high velocity. The working fluid (air) used for the propulsive force is a different quantity of air than that used within the engine to produce the mechanical energy to turn the propeller.

Turbojets, ramjets, and pulse jets are examples of engines that accelerate a smaller quantity of air through a large velocity change. They use the same working fluid for propulsive force that is used within the engine. One problem with these types of engines is the noise made by the high velocity air exiting the engine. The term turbojet was used to describe any gas turbine engine, but with the differences in gas turbines used in aircraft, this term is used to describe a type of gas turbine that passes all the gases through the core of the engine directly.

Turbojets, ramjets, and pulse jets have very little to no use in modern aircraft due to noise and fuel consumption. Small general aviation aircraft use mostly horizontally opposed reciprocating piston engines. While some aircraft still use radial reciprocating piston engines, their use is very limited. Many aircraft use a form of the gas turbine engine to produce power for thrust. These engines are normally the turboprop, turboshaft, turbofan, and a few turbojet engines. "Turbojet" is the former term for any turbine engine. Now that there are so many different types of turbine engine, the term used to describe most turbine engines is "gas turbine engine." All four of the previously mentioned engines belong to the gas turbine family.

All aircraft engines must meet certain general requirements of efficiency, economy, and reliability. Besides being economical in fuel consumption, an aircraft engine must be economical in the cost of original procurement and the cost of maintenance; and it must meet exacting requirements of efficiency and low weight-to-horsepower ratio. It must be capable of sustained high-power output with no sacrifice in reliability; it must also have the durability to operate for long periods of time between overhauls. It needs to be as compact as possible, yet have easy accessibility for maintenance. It is required to be as vibration free as possible and be able to cover a wide range of power output at various speeds and altitudes.

These requirements dictate the use of ignition systems that deliver the firing impulse to the spark plugs at the proper time in all kinds of weather and under other adverse conditions. Engine fuel delivery systems provide metered fuel at the correct proportion of fuel/air ingested by the engine regardless of the attitude, altitude, or type of weather in which the engine is operated. The engine needs a type of oil system that delivers oil under the proper pressure to lubricate and cool all of the operating parts of the engine when it is running. Also, it must have a system of damping units to damp out the vibrations of the engine when it is operating.

Power and Weight

The useful output of all aircraft powerplants is thrust, the force which propels the aircraft. Since the reciprocating engine is rated in brake horsepower (bhp), the gas turbine engine is rated in thrust horsepower (thp):

$$Thp = \frac{thrust \times aircraft\ speed\ (mph)}{375\ mile\text{-}pounds\ per\ hour}$$

The value of 375 mile-pounds per hour is derived from the basic horsepower formula as follows:

$$1\ hp = 33{,}000\ ft\text{-}lb\ per\ minute$$

$$33{,}000 \times 60 = 1{,}980{,}000\ ft\text{-}lb\ per\ hour$$

$$\frac{1{,}980{,}000}{5{,}280\ ft\ in\ a\ mile} = 375\ mile\text{-}pounds\ per\ hour$$

One horsepower equals 33,000 ft-lb per minute or 375 mile-pounds per hour. Under static conditions, thrust is figured as equivalent to approximately 2.6 pounds per hour.

If a gas turbine is producing 4,000 pounds of thrust and the aircraft in which the engine is installed is traveling at 500 mph, the thp is:

$$\frac{4{,}000 \times 500}{375} = 5{,}333.33\ thp$$

It is necessary to calculate the horsepower for each speed of an aircraft, since the horsepower varies with speed. Therefore, it is not practical to try to rate or compare the output of a turbine engine on a horsepower basis. The aircraft engine operates at a relatively high percentage of its maximum power output throughout its service life. The aircraft engine is at full power output whenever a takeoff is made. It may hold this power for a period of time up to the limits set by the manufacturer. The engine is seldom held at a maximum power for more than 2 minutes, and usually not that long. Within a few seconds after lift-off, the power is reduced to a power that is used for climbing and that can be maintained for longer periods of time. After the aircraft has climbed to cruising altitude, the power of the engine(s) is further reduced to a cruise power which can be maintained for the duration of the flight.

If the weight of an engine per brake horsepower (called the specific weight of the engine) is decreased, the useful load that an aircraft can carry and the performance of the aircraft obviously are increased. Every excess pound of weight carried by an aircraft engine reduces its performance. Tremendous improvement in reducing the weight of the aircraft engine through improved design and metallurgy has resulted in reciprocating engines with a much improved power-to-weight ratio (specific weight).

Fuel Economy
The basic parameter for describing the fuel economy of aircraft engines is usually specific fuel consumption. Specific fuel consumption for gas turbines is the fuel flow measured in (lb/hr) divided by thrust (lb), and for reciprocating engines the fuel flow (lb/hr) divided by brake horsepower. These are called thrust-specific fuel consumption and brake-specific fuel consumption, respectively. Equivalent specific fuel consumption is used for the turboprop engine and is the fuel flow in pounds per hour divided by a turboprop's equivalent shaft horsepower. Comparisons can be made between the various engines on a specific fuel consumption basis. At low speed, the reciprocating and turboprop engines have better economy than the pure turbojet or turbofan engines. However, at high speed, because of losses in propeller efficiency, the reciprocating or turboprop engine's efficiency becomes limited above 400 mph less than that of the turbofan. Equivalent specific fuel consumption is used for the turboprop engine and is the fuel flow in pounds per hour divided by a turboprop's equivalent shaft horsepower. Comparisons can be made between the various engines on a specific fuel consumption basis.

Durability and Reliability
Durability and reliability are usually considered identical factors since it is difficult to mention one without including the other. An aircraft engine is reliable when it can perform at the specified ratings in widely varying flight attitudes and in extreme weather conditions. Standards of powerplant reliability are agreed upon by the Federal Aviation Administration (FAA), the engine manufacturer, and the airframe manufacturer. The engine manufacturer ensures the reliability of the product by design, research, and testing. Close control of manufacturing and assembly procedures is maintained, and each engine is tested before it leaves the factory.

Durability is the amount of engine life obtained while maintaining the desired reliability. The fact that an engine has successfully completed its type or proof test indicates that it can be operated in a normal manner over a long period before requiring overhaul. However, no definite time interval between overhauls is specified or implied in the engine rating. The time between overhauls (TBO) varies with the operating conditions, such as engine temperatures, amount of time the engine is operated at high-power settings, and the maintenance received. Recommended TBOs are specified by the engine manufacturer.

Reliability and durability are built into the engine by the manufacturer, but the continued reliability of the engine is determined by the maintenance, overhaul, and operating personnel. Careful maintenance and overhaul methods, thorough periodical and preflight inspections, and strict observance of the operating limits established by the engine manufacturer make engine failure a rare occurrence.

Operating Flexibility
Operating flexibility is the ability of an engine to run smoothly and give desired performance at all speeds from idling to full-power output. The aircraft engine must also function efficiently through all the variations in atmospheric conditions encountered in widespread operations.

Compactness
To affect proper streamlining and balancing of an aircraft, the shape and size of the engine must be as compact as possible. In single-engine aircraft, the shape and size of the engine also affect the view of the pilot, making a smaller engine better from this standpoint, in addition to reducing the drag created by a large frontal area.

Weight limitations, naturally, are closely related to the compactness requirement. The more elongated and spread out an engine is, the more difficult it becomes to keep the specific weight within the allowable limits.

Powerplant Selection
Engine specific weight and specific fuel consumption were discussed in the previous paragraphs, but for certain design requirements, the final powerplant selection may be based

on factors other than those that can be discussed from an analytical point of view. For that reason, a general discussion of powerplant selection follows.

For aircraft whose cruising speed does not exceed 250 mph, the reciprocating engine is the usual choice of powerplant. When economy is required in the low speed range, the conventional reciprocating engine is chosen because of its excellent efficiency and relatively low cost. When high altitude performance is required, the turbo-supercharged reciprocating engine may be chosen because it is capable of maintaining rated power to a high altitude (above 30,000 feet). Gas turbine engines operate most economically at high altitudes. Although in most cases the gas turbine engine provides superior performance, the cost of gas turbine engines is a limiting factor. In the range of cruising speed of 180 to 350 mph, the turboprop engine performs very well. It develops more power per pound of weight than does the reciprocating engine, thus allowing a greater fuel load or payload for engines of a given power. From 350 mph up to Mach .8–.9, turbofan engines are generally used for airline operations. Aircraft intended to operate at Mach 1 or higher are powered by pure turbojet engines/afterburning (augmented) engines, or low-bypass turbofan engines.

Types of Engines

Aircraft engines can be classified by several methods. They can be classed by operating cycles, cylinder arrangement, or the method of thrust production. All are heat engines that convert fuel into heat energy that is converted to mechanical energy to produce thrust. Most of the current aircraft engines are of the internal combustion type because the combustion process takes place inside the engine. Aircraft engines come in many different types, such as gas turbine based, reciprocating piston, rotary, two or four cycle, spark ignition, diesel, and air or water cooled. Reciprocating and gas turbine engines also have subdivisions based on the type of cylinder arrangement (piston) and speed range (gas turbine).

Many types of reciprocating engines have been designed. However, manufacturers have developed some designs that are used more commonly than others and are, therefore, recognized as conventional. Reciprocating engines may be classified according to the cylinder arrangement (in line, V-type, radial, and opposed) or according to the method of cooling (liquid cooled or air cooled). Actually, all piston engines are cooled by transferring excess heat to the surrounding air. In air-cooled engines, this heat transfer is direct from the cylinders to the air. Therefore, it is necessary to provide thin metal fins on the cylinders of an air-cooled engine in order to have increased surface for sufficient heat transfer. Most reciprocating aircraft engines are air cooled although a few high powered engines use an efficient liquid-cooling system. In liquid-cooled engines, the heat is transferred from the cylinders to the coolant, which is then sent through tubing and cooled within a radiator placed in the airstream. The coolant radiator must be large enough to cool the liquid efficiently. The main problem with liquid cooling is the added weight of coolant, heat exchanger (radiator), and tubing to connect the components. Liquid cooled engines do allow high power to be obtained from the engine safely.

Inline Engines

An inline engine generally has an even number of cylinders, although some three-cylinder engines have been constructed. This engine may be either liquid cooled or air cooled and has only one crank shaft, which is located either above or below the cylinders. If the engine is designed to operate with the cylinders below the crankshaft, it is called an inverted engine.

The inline engine has a small frontal area and is better adapted to streamlining. When mounted with the cylinders in an inverted position, it offers the added advantages of a shorter landing gear and greater pilot visibility. With increase in engine size, the air cooled, inline type offers additional problems to provide proper cooling; therefore, this type of engine is confined to low- and medium-horsepower engines used in very old light aircraft.

Opposed or O-Type Engines

The opposed-type engine has two banks of cylinders directly opposite each other with a crankshaft in the center *Figure 1-1*. The pistons of both cylinder banks are connected to the single crankshaft. Although the engine can be either liquid cooled or air cooled, the air-cooled version is used predominantly in aviation. It is generally mounted with the cylinders in a horizontal position. The opposed-type engine has a low weight-to-horsepower ratio, and its narrow silhouette makes it ideal for horizontal installation on the aircraft wings (twin engine applications). Another advantage is its low vibration characteristics.

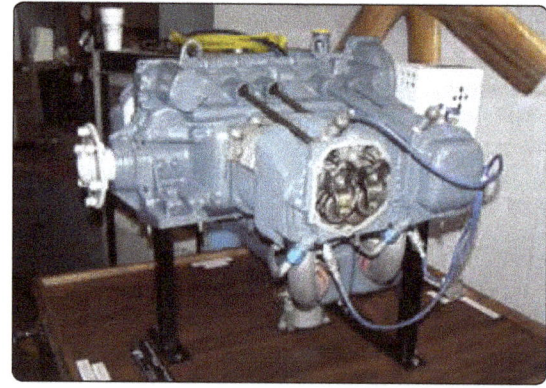

Figure 1-1. *A typical four-cylinder opposed engine.*

V-Type Engines

In V-type engines, the cylinders are arranged in two in-line banks generally set 60° apart. Most of the engines have 12 cylinders, which are either liquid cooled or air cooled. The engines are designated by a V followed by a dash and the piston displacement in cubic inches. For example, V-1710. This type of engine was used mostly during the second World War and its use is mostly limited to older aircraft.

Radial Engines

The radial engine consists of a row, or rows, of cylinders arranged radially about a central crankcase. *[Figure 1-2]* This type of engine has proven to be very rugged and dependable. The number of cylinders which make up a row may be three, five, seven, or nine. Some radial engines have two rows of seven or nine cylinders arranged radially about the crankcase, one in front of the other. These are called double-row radials. *[Figure 1-3]* One type of radial engine has four rows of cylinders with seven cylinders in each row for a total of 28 cylinders. Radial engines are still used in some older cargo planes, war birds, and crop spray planes. Although many of these engines still exist, their use is limited. The single-row, nine-cylinder radial engine is of relatively simple construction, having a one-piece nose and a two-section main crankcase. The larger twin-row engines are of slightly more complex construction than the single row engines. For example, the crankcase of the Wright R-3350 engine is composed of the crankcase front section, four crankcase main sections (front main, front center, rear center, and rear main), rear cam and tappet housing, supercharger front housing, supercharger rear housing, and supercharger rear housing cover. Pratt and Whitney engines of comparable size incorporate the same basic sections, although the construction and the nomenclature differ considerably.

Figure 1-3. *Double row radials.*

Reciprocating Engines

Design and Construction

The basic major components of a reciprocating engine are the crankcase, cylinders, pistons, connecting rods, valves, valve-operating mechanism, and crankshaft. In the head of each cylinder are the valves and spark plugs. One of the valves is in a passage leading from the induction system; the other is in a passage leading to the exhaust system. Inside each cylinder is a movable piston connected to a crankshaft by a connecting rod. *Figure 1-4* illustrates the basic parts of a reciprocating engine.

Crankcase Sections

The foundation of an engine is the crankcase. It contains the bearings and bearing supports in which the crankshaft revolves. Besides supporting itself, the crankcase must provide a tight enclosure for the lubricating oil and must support various external and internal mechanisms of the engine. It also provides support for attachment of the cylinder assemblies, and the powerplant to the aircraft. It must be sufficiently rigid and strong to prevent misalignment of the crankshaft and its bearings. Cast or forged aluminum alloy is generally used for crankcase construction because it is light and strong. The crankcase is subjected to many variations of mechanical loads and other forces. Since the cylinders are fastened to the crankcase, the tremendous forces placed on the cylinder tend to pull the cylinder off the crankcase. The unbalanced centrifugal and inertia forces of the crankshaft acting through the main bearings subject the crankcase to bending moments which change continuously in direction and magnitude. The crankcase

Figure 1-2. *Radial engine.*

Figure 1-4. *Basic parts of a reciprocating engine.*

must have sufficient stiffness to withstand these bending moments without major deflections. *[Figure 1-5]*

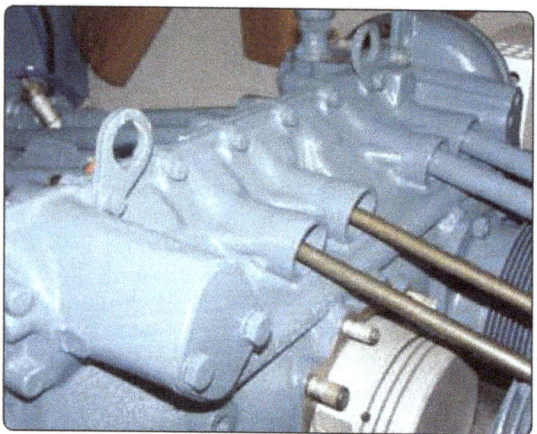

Figure 1-5. *The crankcase.*

If the engine is equipped with a propeller reduction gear, the front or drive end is subjected to additional forces. In addition to the thrust forces developed by the propeller under high power output, there are severe centrifugal and gyroscopic forces applied to the crankcase due to sudden changes in the direction of flight, such as those occurring during maneuvers of the airplane. Gyroscopic forces are particularly severe when a heavy propeller is installed. To absorb centrifugal loads, a large centrifugal bearing is used in the nose section.

The shape of the nose or front of the crankcase section varies considerably. In general, it is either tapered or round. Depending upon the type of reciprocating engine, the nose or front area of the crankcase varies somewhat. If the propeller is driven directly by the crankshaft, less area is needed for this component of the engine. The crankcases used on engines having opposed or inline cylinder arrangements vary in form for the different types of engines, but in general they are approximately cylindrical. One or more sides are surfaced to serve as a base to which the cylinders are attached by means of cap screws, bolts, or studs. These accurately machined surfaces are frequently referred to as cylinder pads.

If the propeller is driven by reduction gearing (gears that slow down the speed of the propeller less than the engine), more area is required to house the reduction gears. A tapered nose section is used quite frequently on direct-drive, low-powered engines, because extra space is not required to house the propeller reduction gears. Crankcase nose sections are usually cast of either aluminum alloy or magnesium. The crankcase nose section on engines that develop from 1,000 to 2,500 hp is usually larger to house reduction gears and sometimes ribbed to get as much strength as possible.

The governor is used to control propeller speed and blade angle. The mounting of the propeller governor varies. On some engines, it is located on the rear section, although this complicates the installation, especially if the propeller is operated or controlled by oil pressure, because of the distance between the governor and propeller. Where hydraulically operated propellers are used, it is good practice to mount the governor on the nose section as close to the propeller as possible to reduce the length of the oil passages. The governor is then driven either from gear teeth on the periphery of the bell gear or by some other suitable means. This basic arrangement is also used for turboprops.

On some of the larger radial engines, a small chamber is located on the bottom of the nose section to collect the oil. This is called the nose section oil sump. Since the nose section transmits many varied forces to the main crankcase or power section, it must be secured properly to transmit the loads efficiently.

The machined surfaces on which the cylinders are mounted are called cylinder pads. They are provided with a suitable means of retaining or fastening the cylinders to the crankcase. The general practice in securing the cylinder flange to the pad is to mount studs in threaded holes in the crankcase. The inner portion of the cylinder pads are sometimes chamfered or tapered to permit the installation of a large rubber O-ring around the cylinder skirt, which effectively seals the joint between the cylinder and the crankcase pads against oil leakage.

Because oil is thrown about the crankcase, especially on inverted inline and radial-type engines, the cylinder skirts extend a considerable distance into the crankcase sections to reduce the flow of oil into the inverted cylinders. The piston and ring assemblies must be arranged so that they throw out the oil splashed directly into them.

Mounting lugs are spaced about the periphery of the rear of the crankcase or the diffuser section of a radial engine. These are used to attach the engine assembly to the engine mount or framework provided for attaching the powerplant to the fuselage of single-engine aircraft or to the wing nacelle structure of multiengine aircraft. The mounting lugs may be either integral with the crankcase or diffuser section or detachable, as in the case of flexible or dynamic engine mounts.

The mounting arrangement supports the entire powerplant including the propeller, and therefore is designed to provide ample strength for rapid maneuvers or other loadings. Because of the elongation and contraction of the cylinders, the intake pipes which carry the mixture from the diffuser chamber through the intake valve ports are arranged to provide a slip joint which must be leak proof. The atmospheric pressure on the outside of the case of an un-supercharged engine is higher than on the inside, especially when the engine is operating at idling speed. If the engine is equipped with a supercharger and operated at full throttle, the pressure is considerably higher on the inside than on the outside of the case. If the slip joint connection has a slight leakage, the engine may idle fast due to a slight leaning of the mixture. If the leak is quite large, it may not idle at all. At open throttle, a small leak probably would not be noticeable in operation of the engine, but the slight leaning of the fuel/air mixture might cause detonation or damage to the valves and valve seats. On some radial engines, the intake pipe has considerable length and on some inline engines, the intake pipe is at right angles to the cylinders. In these cases, flexibility of the intake pipe or its arrangement eliminates the need for a slip joint. In any case, the engine induction system must be arranged so that it does not leak air and change the desired fuel/air ratio.

Accessory Section

The accessory (rear) section usually is of cast construction and the material may be either aluminum alloy, which is used most widely, or magnesium, which has been used to some extent. On some engines, it is cast in one piece and provided with means for mounting the accessories, such as magnetos, carburetors, fuel, oil, vacuum pumps, starter, generator, tachometer drive, etc., in the various locations required to facilitate accessibility. Other adaptations consist of an aluminum alloy casting and a separate cast magnesium cover plate on which the accessory mounts are arranged. Accessory drive shafts are mounted in suitable drive arrangements that are carried out to the accessory mounting pads. In this manner, the various gear ratios can be arranged to give the proper drive speed to magnetos, pumps, and other accessories to obtain correct timing or functioning.

Accessory Gear Trains

Gear trains, containing both spur- and bevel-type gears, are used in the different types of engines for driving engine components and accessories. Spur-type gears are generally used to drive the heavier loaded accessories or those requiring the least play or backlash in the gear train. Bevel gears permit angular location of short stub shafts leading to the various accessory mounting pads. On opposed, reciprocating engines, the accessory gear trains are usually simple arrangements. Many of these engines use simple gear trains to drive the engine's accessories at the proper speeds.

Crankshafts

The crankshaft is carried in a position parallel to the longitudinal axis of the crankcase and is generally supported by a main bearing between each throw. The crankshaft main bearings must be supported rigidly in the crankcase. This usually is accomplished by means of transverse webs in the crankcase, one for each main bearing. The webs form an integral part of the structure and, in addition to supporting the main bearings, add to the strength of the entire case. The crankcase is divided into two sections in a longitudinal plane. This division may be in the plane of the crankshaft so that one-half of the main bearing (and sometimes camshaft bearings) are carried in one section of the case and the other half in the opposite section. *[Figure 1-6]* Another method is to divide the case in such a manner that the main bearings are secured to only one section of the case on which the cylinders are attached, thereby providing means of removing a section of the crankcase for inspection without disturbing the bearing adjustment.

The crankshaft is the backbone of the reciprocating engine. It is subjected to most of the forces developed by the engine. Its main purpose is to transform the reciprocating motion of the piston and connecting rod into rotary motion for rotation of the propeller. The crankshaft, as the name implies, is a shaft composed of one or more cranks located at specified points along its length. The cranks, or throws, are formed by forging offsets into a shaft before it is machined. Since crankshafts must be very strong, they generally are forged from a very strong alloy, such as chromium-nickel-molybdenum steel.

A crankshaft may be of single-piece or multipiece construction. *Figure 1-7* shows two representative types of solid crankshafts used in aircraft engines. The four-throw construction may be used either on four-cylinder horizontal opposed or four-cylinder inline engines. The six-throw shaft is used on six-cylinder inline engines, 12-cylinder V-type engines, and six-cylinder opposed engines. Crankshafts of radial engines may be the single-throw, two-throw, or four-throw type, depending on whether the engine is the single-row, twin-row, or four-row type. A single-throw radial engine crankshaft is shown in *Figure 1-8*. No matter how many throws it may have, each crankshaft has three main parts—a journal, crankpin, and crank cheek. Counterweights

Figure 1-6. *Typical opposed engine exploded into component assemblies.*

1-8

Figure 1-7. *Solid types of crankshafts.*

Figure 1-8. *A single-throw radial engine crankshaft.*

and dampers, although not a true part of a crankshaft, are usually attached to it to reduce engine vibration.

The journal is supported by, and rotates in, a main bearing. It serves as the center of rotation of the crankshaft. It is surface-hardened to reduce wear. The crankpin is the section to which the connecting rod is attached. It is off-center from the main journals and is often called the throw. Two crank cheeks and a crankpin make a throw. When a force is applied to the crankpin in any direction other than parallel or perpendicular to and through the center line of the crankshaft, it causes the crankshaft to rotate. The outer surface is hardened by nitriding to increase its resistance to wear and to provide the required bearing surface. The crankpin is usually hollow. This reduces the total weight of the crankshaft and provides a passage for the transfer of lubricating oil. On early engines, the hollow crankpin also served as a chamber for collecting sludge, carbon deposits, and other foreign material. Centrifugal force threw these substances to the outside of the chamber and kept them from reaching the connecting-rod bearing surface. Due to the use of ashless dispersant oils, newer engines no longer use sludge chambers. On some engines, a passage is drilled in the crank cheek to allow oil from the hollow crankshaft to be sprayed on the cylinder walls. The crank cheek connects the crankpin to the main journal. In some designs, the cheek extends beyond the journal and carries a counterweight to balance the crankshaft. The crank cheek must be of sturdy construction to obtain the required rigidity between the crankpin and the journal.

In all cases, the type of crankshaft and the number of crankpins must correspond with the cylinder arrangement of the engine. The position of the cranks on the crankshaft in relation to the other cranks of the same shaft is expressed in degrees.

The simplest crankshaft is the single-throw or 360° type. This type is used in a single-row radial engine. It can be constructed in one or two pieces. Two main bearings (one on each end) are provided when this type of crankshaft is used. The double-throw or 180° crankshaft is used on double-row radial engines. In the radial-type engine, one throw is provided for each row of cylinders.

Crankshaft Balance

Excessive vibration in an engine not only results in fatigue failure of the metal structures, but also causes the moving parts to wear rapidly. In some instances, excessive vibration is caused by a crankshaft that is not balanced. Crankshafts are balanced for static balance and dynamic balance. A crankshaft is statically balanced when the weight of the entire assembly of crankpins, crank cheeks, and counterweights is balanced around the axis of rotation. When checked for static balance, it is placed on two knife edges. If the shaft tends to turn toward any one position during the test, it is out of static balance.

Dynamic Dampers

A crankshaft is dynamically balanced when all the forces created by crankshaft rotation and power impulses are balanced within themselves so that little or no vibration is produced when the engine is operating. To reduce vibration to a minimum during engine operation, dynamic dampers are incorporated on the crankshaft. A dynamic damper is merely a pendulum that is fastened to the crankshaft so that it is free to move in a small arc. It is incorporated in the counterweight assembly. Some crankshafts incorporate two or more of these assemblies, each being attached to a different crank cheek. The distance the pendulum moves and, thus, its vibrating frequency corresponds to the frequency of the power impulses of the engine. When the vibration frequency of the crankshaft occurs, the pendulum oscillates out of time with the crankshaft vibration, thus reducing vibration to a minimum.

The construction of the dynamic damper used in one engine consists of a movable slotted-steel counterweight attached to the crank cheek. Two spool-shaped steel pins extend into the slot and pass through oversized holes in the counterweight and crank cheek. The difference in the diameter between the pins and the holes provides a pendulum effect. An analogy of the functioning of a dynamic damper is shown in *Figure 1-9*.

Connecting Rods

The connecting rod is the link that transmits forces between the piston and the crankshaft. *[Figure 1-10]* Connecting rods must be strong enough to remain rigid under load and yet be light enough to reduce the inertia forces that are produced when the rod and piston stop, change direction, and start again at the end of each stroke.

Figure 1-10. *A connecting rod between the piston and crankshaft.*

There are four types of connecting-rod assemblies *[Figure 1-11]*:

1. Plain
2. Fork and blade
3. Master and articulated
4. Split-type

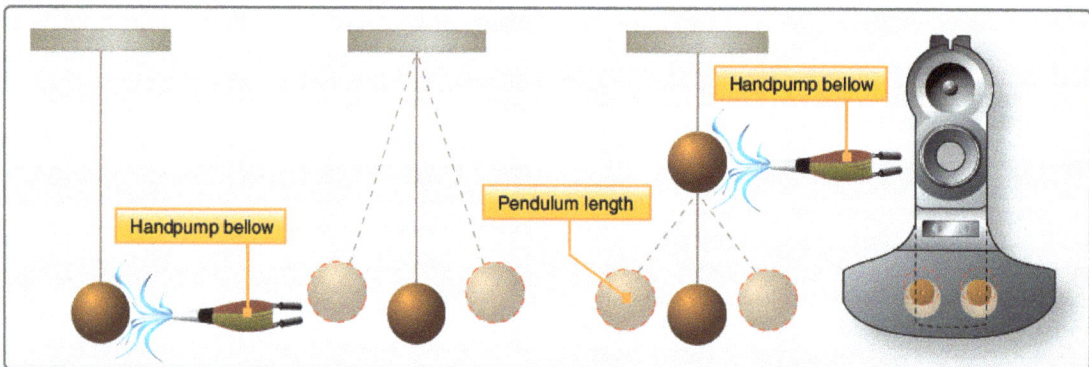

Figure 1-9. *Principles of a dynamic damper.*

Figure 1-11. *Connecting rod assembly.*

Master-and-Articulated Rod Assembly

The master-and-articulated rod assembly is commonly used in radial engines. In a radial engine, the piston in one cylinder in each row is connected to the crankshaft by a master rod. All other pistons in the row are connected to the master rod by articulated rods. In an 18-cylinder engine, which has two rows of cylinders, there are two master rods and 16 articulated rods. The articulated rods are constructed of forged steel alloy in either the I- or H-shape, denoting the cross-sectional shape. Bronze bushings are pressed into the bores in each end of the articulated rod to provide knuckle-pin and piston-pin bearings.

The master rod serves as the connecting link between the piston pin and the crankpin. The crankpin end, or the big end, contains the crankpin or master rod bearing. Flanges around the big end provide for the attachment of the articulated rods. The articulated rods are attached to the master rod by knuckle pins, which are pressed into holes in the master rod flanges during assembly. A plain bearing, usually called a piston-pin bushing, is installed in the piston end of the master rod to receive the piston pin.

When a crankshaft of the split-spline or split-clamp type is employed, a one-piece master rod is used. The master and articulated rods are assembled and then installed on the crankpin; the crankshaft sections are then joined together. In engines that use the one-piece type of crankshaft, the big end of the master rod is split, as is the master rod bearing. The main part of the master rod is installed on the crankpin; then the bearing cap is set in place and bolted to the master rod. The centers of the knuckle pins do not coincide with the center of the crankpin. Thus, while the crankpin center describes a true circle for each revolution of the crankshaft, the centers of the knuckle pins describe an elliptical path. *[Figure 1-12]* The elliptical paths are symmetrical about a center line through the master rod cylinder. It can be seen that the major diameters of the ellipses are not the same. Thus, the link rods have varying degrees of angularity relative to the center of the crank throw.

Because of the varying angularity of the link rods and the elliptical motion of the knuckle pins, all pistons do not move an equal amount in each cylinder for a given number of degrees of crank throw movement. This variation in piston position between cylinders can have considerable effect on engine operation. To minimize the effect of these factors on valve and ignition timing, the knuckle pin holes in the master rod flange are not equidistant from the center of the crankpin, thereby offsetting to an extent the effect of the link rod angularity.

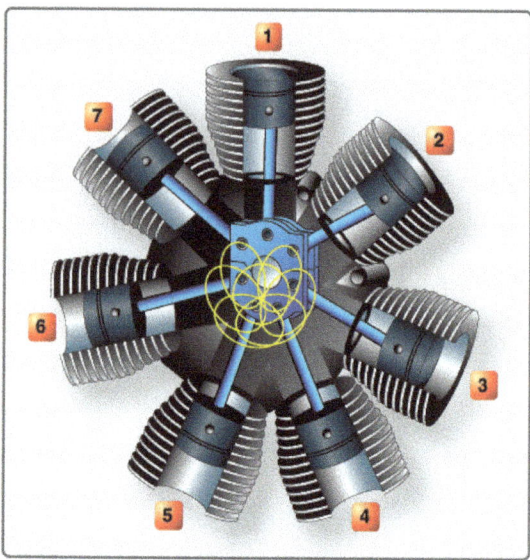

Figure 1-12. *Elliptical travel path of knuckle pins in an articulated rod assembly.*

Another method of minimizing the adverse effects on engine operation is to use a compensated magneto. In this magneto the breaker cam has a number of lobes equal to the number of cylinders on the engine. To compensate for the variation in piston position due to link rod angularity, the breaker cam lobes are ground with uneven spacing. This allows the breaker contacts to open when the piston is in the correct firing position. This is further outlined during the discussion on ignition timing in Chapter 4, Engine Ignition and Electrical Systems.

Knuckle Pins

The knuckle pins are of solid construction except for the oil passages drilled in the pins, which lubricate the knuckle pin bushings. These pins may be installed by pressing into holes in the master rod flanges so that they are prevented from turning in the master rod. Knuckle pins may also be installed with a loose fit so that they can turn in the master rod flange holes, and also turn in the articulating rod bushings. These are called full-floating knuckle pins. In either type of installation, a lock plate on each side retains the knuckle pin and prevents a lateral movement.

Plain-Type Connecting Rods

Plain-type connecting rods are used in inline and opposed engines. The end of the rod attached to the crankpin is fitted with a cap and a two-piece bearing. The bearing cap is held on the end of the rod by bolts or studs. To maintain proper fit and balance, connecting rods should always be replaced in the same cylinder and in the same relative position.

Fork-and-Blade Rod Assembly

The fork-and-blade rod assembly is used primarily in V-type engines. The forked rod is split at the crankpin end to allow space for the blade rod to fit between the prongs. A single two-piece bearing is used on the crankshaft end of the rod. This type of connecting rod is not used much on modern engines.

Pistons

The piston of a reciprocating engine is a cylindrical member which moves back and forth within a steel cylinder. *[Figure 1-13]* The piston acts as a moving wall within the combustion chamber. As the piston moves down in the cylinder, it draws in the fuel/air mixture. As it moves upward, it compresses the charge, ignition occurs, and the expanding gases force the piston downward. This force is transmitted to the crankshaft through the connecting rod. On the return upward stroke, the piston forces the exhaust gases from the cylinder and the cycle repeats.

Figure 1-13. *A piston.*

Piston Construction

The majority of aircraft engine pistons are machined from aluminum alloy forgings. Grooves are machined in the outside surface of the piston to receive the piston rings, and cooling fins are provided on the inside of the piston for greater heat transfer to the engine oil.

Pistons may be either the trunk type or the slipper type. *[Figure 1-14]* Slipper-type pistons are not used in modern, high-powered engines because they do not provide adequate strength or wear resistance. The top of the piston, or head, may be flat, convex, or concave. Recesses may be machined in the piston head to prevent interference with the valves.

Figure 1-14. *Piston assembly and types of pistons.*

Modern engines use cam ground pistons that are a larger diameter perpendicular to the piston pin. This larger diameter keeps the piston straight in the cylinder as the engine warms up from initial start up. As the piston heats up during warm up, the part of the piston in line with the pin has more mass and expands more making the piston completely round. At low temperatures, the piston is oval shaped and, when it warms to operating temperature, it becomes round. This process reduces the tendency of the piston to cock or slap in the cylinder during warm up. When the engine reaches its normal operating temperature, the piston assumes the correct dimensions in the cylinder.

As many as six grooves may be machined around the piston to accommodate the compression rings and oil rings. *[Figure 1-15]* The compression rings are installed in the three uppermost grooves; the oil control rings are installed immediately above the piston pin. The piston is usually drilled at the oil control ring grooves to allow surplus oil scraped from the cylinder walls by the oil control rings to pass back into the crankcase. An oil scraper ring is installed at the base of the piston wall or skirt to prevent excessive oil consumption. The portions of the piston walls that lie between ring grooves are called the ring lands. In addition to acting as a guide for the piston head, the piston skirt incorporates the piston-pin bosses. The piston-pin bosses are of heavy

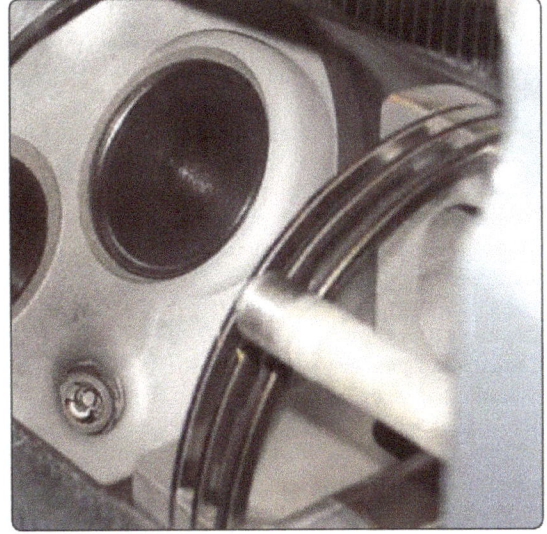

Figure 1-15. *Machined rings around a piston.*

construction to enable the heavy load on the piston head to be transferred to the piston pin.

Piston Pin

The piston pin joins the piston to the connecting rod. It is machined in the form of a tube from a nickel steel alloy forging, casehardened and ground. The piston pin is sometimes called a wristpin because of the similarity between the relative motions of the piston and the articulated rod and that of the human arm. The piston pin used in modern aircraft engines is the full-floating type, so called because the pin is free to rotate in both the piston and in the connecting rod piston-pin bearing. The piston pin must be held in place to prevent the pin ends from scoring the cylinder walls. A plug of relatively soft aluminum in the pin end provides a good bearing surface against the cylinder wall.

Piston Rings

The piston rings prevent leakage of gas pressure from the combustion chamber and reduce to a minimum the seepage of oil into the combustion chamber. *[Figure 1-15]* The rings fit into the piston grooves but spring out to press against the cylinder walls; when properly lubricated, the rings form an effective gas seal.

Piston Ring Construction

Most piston rings are made of high-grade cast iron. *[Figure 1-14]* After the rings are made, they are ground to the cross-section desired. Then they are split so that they can be slipped over the outside of the piston and into the ring grooves that are machined in the piston wall. Since their purpose is to seal the clearance between the piston and the cylinder wall, they must fit the cylinder wall snugly enough to provide a gastight fit. They must exert equal pressure at all points on the cylinder wall, and must make a gastight fit against the sides of the ring grooves.

Gray cast iron is most often used in making piston rings. In some engines, chrome-plated mild steel piston rings are used in the top compression ring groove because these rings can better withstand the high temperatures present at this point. Chrome rings must be used with steel cylinder walls. Never use chrome rings on chrome cylinders.

Compression Ring

The purpose of the compression rings is to prevent the escape of combustion gases past the piston during engine operation. They are placed in the ring grooves immediately below the piston head. The number of compression rings used on each piston is determined by the type of engine and its design, although most aircraft engines use two compression rings plus one or more oil control rings.

The cross-section of the ring is either rectangular or wedge shaped with a tapered face. The tapered face presents a narrow bearing edge to the cylinder wall, which helps to reduce friction and provide better sealing.

Oil Control Rings

Oil control rings are placed in the grooves immediately below the compression rings and above the piston pin bores. There may be one or more oil control rings per piston; two rings may be installed in the same groove, or they may be installed in separate grooves. Oil control rings regulate the thickness of the oil film on the cylinder wall. If too much oil enters the combustion chamber, it burns and leaves a thick coating of carbon on the combustion chamber walls, the piston head, the spark plugs, and the valve heads. This carbon can cause the valves and piston rings to stick if it enters the ring grooves or valve guides. In addition, the carbon can cause spark plug misfiring as well as detonation, preignition, or excessive oil consumption. To allow the surplus oil to return to the crankcase, holes are drilled in the bottom of the oil control piston ring grooves or in the lands next to these grooves.

Oil Scraper Ring

The oil scraper ring usually has a beveled face and is installed in the groove at the bottom of the piston skirt. The ring is installed with the scraping edge away from the piston head or in the reverse position, depending upon cylinder position and the engine series. In the reverse position, the scraper ring retains the surplus oil above the ring on the upward piston stroke, and this oil is returned to the crankcase by the oil control rings on the downward stroke.

Cylinders

The portion of the engine in which the power is developed is called the cylinder. *[Figure 1-16]* The cylinder provides a combustion chamber where the burning and expansion of gases take place, and it houses the piston and the connecting rod. There are four major factors that need to be considered in the design and construction of the cylinder assembly. It must:

1. Be strong enough to withstand the internal pressures developed during engine operation.

2. Be constructed of a lightweight metal to keep down engine weight.

3. Have good heat-conducting properties for efficient cooling.

4. Be comparatively easy and inexpensive to manufacture, inspect, and maintain.

The cylinder head of an air cooled engine is generally made of aluminum alloy because aluminum alloy is a good conductor of heat and its light weight reduces the overall engine weight. Cylinder heads are forged or die-cast for greater strength. The inner shape of a cylinder head is generally semispherical. The semispherical shape is stronger than conventionalist design and aids in a more rapid and thorough scavenging of the exhaust gases.

Figure 1-16. *An example of an engine cylinder.*

The cylinder used in the air cooled engine is the overhead valve type. *[Figure 1-17]* Each cylinder is an assembly of two major parts: cylinder head and cylinder barrel. At assembly, the cylinder head is expanded by heating and then screwed down on the cylinder barrel, which has been chilled. When the head cools and contracts and the barrel warms up and expands, a gastight joint results. The majority of the cylinders used are constructed in this manner using an aluminum head and a steel barrel. *[Figure 1-18]*

Cylinder Heads

The purpose of the cylinder head is to provide a place for combustion of the fuel/air mixture and to give the cylinder more heat conductivity for adequate cooling. The fuel/air mixture is ignited by the spark in the combustion chamber and commences burning as the piston travels toward top dead center (top of its travel) on the compression stroke. The ignited charge is rapidly expanding at this time, and pressure is increasing so that, as the piston travels through the top dead center position, it is driven downward on the power stroke. The intake and exhaust valve ports are located in the cylinder head along with the spark plugs and the intake and exhaust valve actuating mechanisms.

After the cylinder head is cast, the spark plug bushings, valve guides, rocker arm bushings, and valve seats are installed in the cylinder head. Spark plug openings may be fitted with bronze or steel bushings that are shrunk and screwed into

Figure 1-17. *Cutaway view of the cylinder assembly.*

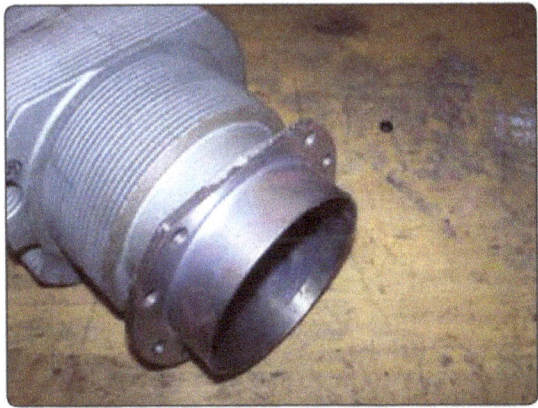

Figure 1-18. *The aluminum head and steel barrel of a cylinder.*

the openings. Stainless steel Heli-Coil spark plug inserts are used in many engines currently manufactured. Bronze or steel valve guides are usually shrunk or screwed into drilled openings in the cylinder head to provide guides for the valve stems. These are generally located at an angle to the center line of the cylinder. The valve seats are circular rings of

1-15

hardened metal that protect the relatively soft metal of the cylinder head from the hammering action of the valves (as they open and close) and from the exhaust gases.

The cylinder heads of air cooled engines are subjected to extreme temperatures; it is therefore necessary to provide adequate cooling fin area and to use metals that conduct heat rapidly. Cylinder heads of air cooled engines are usually cast or forged. Aluminum alloy is used in the construction for a number of reasons. It is well adapted for casting or for the machining of deep, closely spaced fins, and it is more resistant than most metals to the corrosive attack of tetraethyl lead in gasoline. The greatest improvement in air cooling has resulted from reducing the thickness of the fins and increasing their depth. In this way, the fin area has been increased in modern engines. Cooling fins taper from 0.090" at the base to 0.060" at the tip end. Because of the difference in temperature in the various sections of the cylinder head, it is necessary to provide more cooling-fin area on some sections than on others. The exhaust valve region is the hottest part of the internal surface; therefore, more fin area is provided around the outside of the cylinder in this section.

Cylinder Barrels

The cylinder barrel in which the piston operates must be made of a high-strength material, usually steel. It must be as light as possible, yet have the proper characteristics for operating under high temperatures. It must be made of a good bearing material and have high tensile strength. The cylinder barrel is made of a steel alloy forging with the inner surface hardened to resist wear of the piston and the piston rings which bear against it. This hardening is usually done by exposing the steel to ammonia or cyanide gas while the steel is very hot. The steel soaks up nitrogen from the gas, which forms iron nitrides on the exposed surface. As a result of this process, the metal is said to be nitrided. This nitriding only penetrates into the barrel surface a few thousands of an inch. As the cylinder barrels wear due to use, they can be repaired by chroming. This is a process that plates chromium on the surface of the cylinder barrel and brings it back to new standard dimensions. Chromium-plated cylinders should use cast iron rings. Honing the cylinder walls is a process that brings it to the correct dimensions and provides crosshatch pattern for seating the piston rings during engine break-in. Some engine cylinder barrels are choked at the top, or they are smaller in diameter to allow for heat expansion and wear.

In some instances, the barrel has threads on the outside surface at one end so that it can be screwed into the cylinder head. The cooling fins are machined as an integral part of the barrel and have limits on repair and service.

Cylinder Numbering

Occasionally, it is necessary to refer to the left or right side of the engine or to a particular cylinder. Therefore, it is necessary to know the engine directions and how cylinders of an engine are numbered. The propeller shaft end of the engine is always the front end, and the accessory end is the rear end, regardless of how the engine is mounted in an aircraft. When referring to the right side or left side of an engine, always assume the view is from the rear or accessory end. As seen from this position, crankshaft rotation is referred to as either clockwise or counterclockwise.

Inline and V-type engine cylinders are usually numbered from the rear. In V-engines, the cylinder banks are known as the right bank and the left bank, as viewed from the accessory end. *[Figure 1-19]* The cylinder numbering of the opposed engine

Figure 1-19. *Numbering of engine cylinders.*

shown begins with the right rear as No. 1 and the left rear as No. 2. The one forward of No. 1 is No. 3; the one forward of No. 2 is No. 4, and so on. The numbering of opposed engine cylinders is by no means standard. Some manufacturers number their cylinders from the rear and others from the front of the engine. Always refer to the appropriate engine manual to determine the numbering system used by that manufacturer.

Single-row radial engine cylinders are numbered clockwise when viewed from the rear. Cylinder No. 1 is the top cylinder. In double-row engines, the same system is used. The No. 1 cylinder is the top one in the rear row. No. 2 cylinder is the first one clockwise from No. 1, but No. 2 is in the front row. No. 3 cylinder is the next one clockwise to No. 2, but is in the rear row. Thus, all odd-numbered cylinders are in the rear row, and all even-numbered cylinders are in the front row.

Firing Order

The firing order of an engine is the sequence in which the power event occurs in the different cylinders. The firing order is designed to provide for balance and to eliminate vibration to the greatest extent possible. In radial engines, the firing order must follow a special pattern since the firing impulses must follow the motion of the crank throw during its rotation. In inline engines, the firing orders may vary somewhat, yet most orders are arranged so that the firing of cylinders is evenly distributed along the crankshaft. Six-cylinder inline engines generally have a firing order of 1-5-3-6-2-4. Cylinder firing order in opposed engines can usually be listed in pairs of cylinders, as each pair fires across the center main bearing. The firing order of six-cylinder opposed engines is 1-4-5-2-3-6. The firing order of one model four-cylinder opposed engine is 1-4-2-3, but on another model it is 1-3-2-4.

Single-Row Radial Engines

On a single-row radial engine, all the odd-numbered cylinders fire in numerical succession; then, the even numbered cylinders fire in numerical succession. On a five-cylinder radial engine, for example, the firing order is 1-3-5-2-4, and on a seven-cylinder radial engine it is 1-3-5-7-2-4-6. The firing order of a nine-cylinder radial engine is 1-3-5-7-9-2-4-6-8.

Double-Row Radial Engines

On a double-row radial engine, the firing order is somewhat complicated. The firing order is arranged with the firing impulse occurring in a cylinder in one row and then in a cylinder in the other row; therefore, two cylinders in the same row never fire in succession.

An easy method for computing the firing order of a 14-cylinder, double-row radial engine is to start with any number from 1 to 14, and add 9 or subtract 5 (these are called the firing order numbers), whichever gives an answer between 1 and 14, inclusive. For example, starting with 8, 9 cannot be added since the answer would then be more than 14; therefore, subtract 5 from 8 to get 3, add 9 to 3 to get 12, subtract 5 from 12 to get 7, subtract 5 from 7 to get 2, and so on.

The firing order numbers of an 18-cylinder, double-row radial engine are 11 and 7; that is, begin with any number from 1 to 18 and add 11 or subtract 7. For example, beginning with 1, add 11 to get 12; 11 cannot be added to 12 because the total would be more than 18, so subtract 7 to get 5, add 11 to 5 to get 16, subtract 7 from 16 to get 9, subtract 7 from 9 to get 2, add 11 to 2 to get 13, and continue this process for 18 cylinders.

Valves

The fuel/air mixture enters the cylinders through the intake valve ports, and burned gases are expelled through the exhaust valve ports. The head of each valve opens and closes these cylinder ports. The valves used in aircraft engines are the conventional poppet type. The valves are also typed by their shape and are called either mushroom or tulip because of their resemblance to the shape of these plants. *Figure 1-20* illustrates various shapes and types of these valves.

Figure 1-20. *Various valve types.*

Valve Construction

The valves in the cylinders of an aircraft engine are subjected to high temperatures, corrosion, and operating stresses; thus, the metal alloy in the valves must be able to resist all these factors. Because intake valves operate at lower temperatures than exhaust valves, they can be made of chromic-nickel steel. Exhaust valves are usually made of nichrome, silchrome, or cobalt-chromium steel because these materials are much more heat resistant.

The valve head has a ground face that forms a seal against the ground valve seat in the cylinder head when the valve is closed. The face of the valve is usually ground to an angle of either 30° or 45°. In some engines, the intake-valve face is ground to an angle of 30°, and the exhaust-valve face is ground to a 45° angle. Valve faces are often made more durable by the application of a material called stellite. About ¹⁄₁₆ inch of this alloy is welded to the valve face and ground to the correct angle. Stellite is resistant to high-temperature corrosion and also withstands the shock and wear associated with valve operation. Some engine manufacturers use a nichrome facing on the valves. This serves the same purpose as the stellite material.

The valve stem acts as a pilot for the valve head and rides in the valve guide installed in the cylinder head for this purpose. *[Figure 1-21]* The valve stem is surface hardened to resist wear. The neck is the part that forms the junction between the head and the stem. The tip of the valve is hardened to withstand the hammering of the valve rocker arm as it opens the valve. A machined groove on the stem near the tip receives the split-ring stem keys. These stem keys form a lock ring to hold the valve spring retaining washer in place. *[Figure 1-22]*

Figure 1-21. *View of valve guide installed on a cylinder head.*

Some intake and exhaust valve stems are hollow and partially filled with metallic sodium. This material is used because it is an excellent heat conductor. The sodium melts

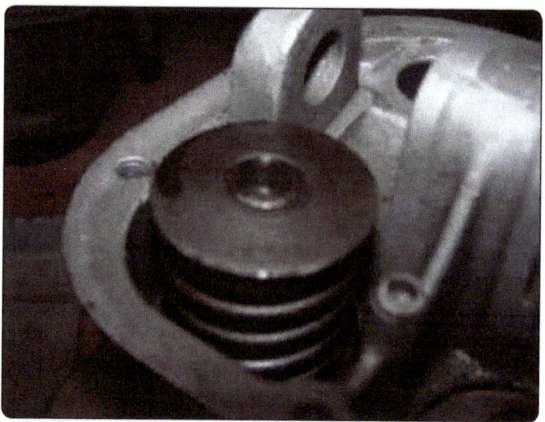

Figure 1-22. *Stem keys forming a lock ring to hold valve spring retaining washers in place.*

at approximately 208 °F and the reciprocating motion of the valve circulates the liquid sodium, allowing it to carry away heat from the valve head to the valve stem where it is dissipated through the valve guide to the cylinder head and the cooling fins. Thus, the operating temperature of the valve may be reduced as much as 300° to 400 °F. Under no circumstances should a sodium-filled valve be cut open or subjected to treatment which may cause it to rupture. Exposure of the sodium in these valves to the outside air results in fire or explosion with possible personal injury.

The most commonly used intake valves have solid stems, and the head is either flat or tulip shaped. Intake valves for low-power engines are usually flat headed. In some engines, the intake valve may be the tulip type and have a smaller stem than the exhaust valve or it may be similar to the exhaust valve but have a solid stem and head. Although these valves are similar, they are not interchangeable since the faces of the valves are constructed of different material. The intake valve usually has a flat milled on the tip to identify it.

Valve Operating Mechanism

For a reciprocating engine to operate properly, each valve must open at the proper time, stay open for the required length of time, and close at the proper time. Intake valves are opened just before the piston reaches top dead center, and exhaust valves remain open after top dead center. At a particular instant, therefore, both valves are open at the same time (end of the exhaust stroke and beginning of the intake stroke). This valve overlap permits better volumetric efficiency and lowers the cylinder operating temperature. This timing of the valves is controlled by the valve-operating mechanism and is referred to as the valve timing.

The valve lift (distance that the valve is lifted off its seat) and the valve duration (length of time the valve is held open) are both determined by the shape of the cam lobes. Typical cam lobes are illustrated in *Figure 1-23*. The portion of the lobe that gently starts the valve operating mechanism moving is called a ramp, or step. The ramp is machined on each side of the cam lobe to permit the rocker arm to be eased into contact with the valve tip and thus reduce the shock load which would otherwise occur. The valve operating mechanism consists of a cam ring or camshaft equipped with lobes that work against a cam roller or a cam follower. *[Figures 1-24 and 1-25]* The cam follower pushes a push rod and ball socket, actuating a rocker arm, which in turn opens the valve. Springs, which slip over the stem of the valves and are held in place by the valve-spring retaining washer and stem key, close each valve and push the valve mechanism in the opposite direction. *[Figure 1-26]*

Figure 1-23. *Typical cam lobes.*

Figure 1-24. *Valve-operating mechanism (radial engine).*

Cam Rings

The valve mechanism of a radial engine is operated by one or two cam rings, depending upon the number of rows of cylinders. In a single-row radial engine, one ring with a double cam track is used. One track operates the intake valves, the other operates the exhaust valves. The cam ring is a circular piece of steel with a series of cams or lobes on the outer surface. The surface of these lobes and the space between them (on which the cam rollers ride) is known as the cam track. As the cam ring revolves, the lobes cause the cam roller to raise the tappet in the tappet guide, thereby transmitting the force through the push rod and rocker arm to open the valve. In a single-row radial engine, the cam ring is usually located between the propeller reduction gearing and the front end of the power section. In a twin-row radial engine, a second cam for the operation of the valves in the rear row is installed between the rear end of the power section and the supercharger section.

The cam ring is mounted concentrically with the crankshaft and is driven by the crankshaft at a reduced rate of speed through the cam intermediate drive gear assembly. The cam ring has two parallel sets of lobes spaced around the outer periphery, one set (cam track) for the intake valves and the other for the exhaust valves. The cam rings used may have four or five lobes on both the intake and the exhaust tracks. The timing of the valve events is determined by the spacing of these lobes and the speed and direction at which the cam rings are driven in relation to the speed and direction of the crankshaft. The method of driving the cam varies on different makes of engines. The cam ring can be designed with teeth on either the inside or outside periphery. If the reduction gear meshes with the teeth on the outside of the ring, the cam turns in the direction of rotation of the crankshaft. If the ring is driven from the inside, the cam turns in the opposite direction from the crankshaft. *[Figure 1-24]*

Figure 1-25. *Valve-operating mechanism (opposed engine).*

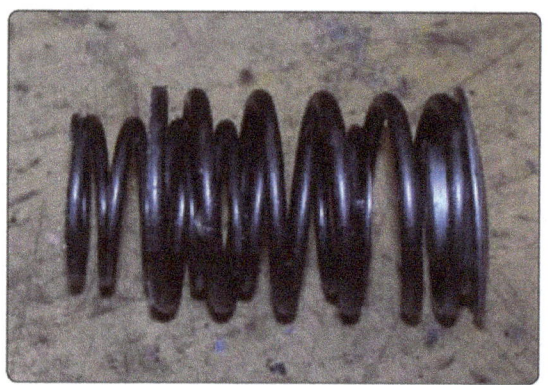

Figure 1-26. *A typical set of valve springs used to dampen oscillations. Multiple springs are used to protect against breakage.*

A four-lobe cam may be used on either a seven-cylinder or nine-cylinder engine. *[Figure 1-27]* On the seven cylinder, it rotates in the same direction as the crankshaft, and on the nine cylinder, opposite the crankshaft rotation. On the nine-cylinder engine, the spacing between cylinders is 40° and the firing order is 1-3-5-7-9-2-4-6-8. This means that there is a space of 80° between firing impulses. The spacing on the four lobes of the cam ring is 90°, which is greater than the spacing between impulses. Therefore, to obtain proper relation of valve operations and firing order, it is necessary to drive the cam opposite the crankshaft rotation. Using the four-lobe cam on the seven-cylinder engine, the spacing between the firing of the cylinders is greater than the spacing of the cam lobes. Therefore, it is necessary for the cam to rotate in the same direction as the crankshaft.

Camshaft

The valve mechanism of an opposed engine is operated by a camshaft. The camshaft is driven by a gear that mates with another gear attached to the crankshaft. *[Figure 1-28]* The camshaft always rotates at one-half the crankshaft speed. As the camshaft revolves, the lobes cause the tappet assembly to rise in the tappet guide, transmitting the force through the push rod and rocker arm to open the valve. *[Figure 1-29]*

Tappet Assembly

The tappet assembly consists of:

1. A cylindrical tappet, which slides in and out in a tappet guide installed in one of the crankcase sections around the cam ring;
2. A tappet roller, which follows the contour of the cam ring and lobes;
3. A tappet ball socket or push rod socket; and
4. A tappet spring.

5 Cylinders		7 Cylinders		9 Cylinders		Direction of Rotation
Number of Lobes	Speed	Number of Lobes	Speed	Number of Lobes	Speed	
3	1/6	4	1/8	5	1/10	with crankshaft
2	1/4	3	1/6	4	1/8	opposite crankshaft

Figure 1-27. *Radial engines, cam ring table.*

Figure 1-28. *Cam drive mechanism opposed-type aircraft engine.*

Figure 1-29. *Cam load on lifter body.*

The function of the tappet assembly is to convert the rotational movement of the cam lobe into reciprocating motion and to transmit this motion to the push rod, rocker arm, and then to the valve tip, opening the valve at the proper time. The purpose of the tappet spring is to take up the clearance between the rocker arm and the valve tip to reduce the shock load when the valve is opened. A hole is drilled through the tappet to allow engine oil to flow to the hollow push rods to lubricate the rocker assemblies.

Solid Lifters/Tappets

Solid lifters or cam followers generally require the valve clearance to be adjusted manually by adjusting a screw and lock nut. Valve clearance is needed to assure that the valve has enough clearance in the valve train to close completely. This adjustment or inspection was a continuous maintenance item until hydraulic lifters were used.

Hydraulic Valve Tappets/Lifters

Some aircraft engines incorporate hydraulic tappets that automatically keep the valve clearance at zero, eliminating the necessity for any valve clearance adjustment mechanism. A typical hydraulic tappet (zero-lash valve lifter) is shown in *Figure 1-30*.

When the engine valve is closed, the face of the tappet body (cam follower) is on the base circle or back of the cam.

Figure 1-30. *Hydraulic valve tappets.*

[Figure 1-30] The light plunger spring lifts the hydraulic plunger so that its outer end contacts the push rod socket, exerting a light pressure against it, thus eliminating any clearance in the valve linkage. As the plunger moves outward, the ball check valve moves off its seat. Oil from the supply chamber, which is directly connected with the engine lubrication system, flows in and fills the pressure chamber. As the camshaft rotates, the cam pushes the tappet body and the hydraulic lifter cylinder outward. This action forces the ball check valve onto its seat; thus, the body of oil trapped in the pressure chamber acts as a cushion. During the interval when the engine valve is off its seat, a predetermined leakage occurs between plunger and cylinder bore, which compensates for any expansion or contraction in the valve train. Immediately after the engine valve closes, the amount of oil required to fill the pressure chamber flows in from the supply chamber, preparing for another cycle of operation.

Hydraulic valve lifters are normally adjusted at the time of overhaul. They are assembled dry (no lubrication), clearances checked, and adjustments are usually made by using push rods of different lengths. A minimum and maximum valve clearance is established. Any measurement between these extremes is acceptable, but approximately half way between the extremes is desired. Hydraulic valve lifters require less maintenance, are better lubricated, and operate more quietly than the screw adjustment type.

Push Rod

The push rod, tubular in form, transmits the lifting force from the valve tappet to the rocker arm. A hardened-steel ball is pressed over or into each end of the tube. One ball end fits into the socket of the rocker arm. In some instances, the balls are on the tappet and rocker arm, and the sockets are on the push rod. The tubular form is employed because of its lightness and strength. It permits the engine lubricating oil under pressure to pass through the hollow rod and the drilled ball ends to lubricate the ball ends, rocker-arm bearing, and valve-stem guide. The push rod is enclosed in a tubular housing that extends from the crankcase to the cylinder head, referred to as push rod tubes.

Rocker Arms

The rocker arms transmit the lifting force from the cams to the valves. *[Figure 1-31]* Rocker arm assemblies are supported by a plain, roller, or ball bearing, or a combination of these, which serves as a pivot. Generally, one end of the arm bears against the push rod and the other bears on the valve stem. One end of the rocker arm is sometimes slotted to accommodate a steel roller. The opposite end is constructed with either a threaded split clamp and locking bolt or a tapped hole. The arm may have an adjusting screw, for adjusting the clearance between the rocker arm and the valve stem tip.

Figure 1-31. *Rocker opposed engine arms.*

The screw can be adjusted to the specified clearance to make certain that the valve closes fully.

Valve Springs

Each valve is closed by two or three helical springs. If a single spring were used, it would vibrate or surge at certain speeds. To eliminate this difficulty, two or more springs (one inside the other) are installed on each valve. Each spring vibrates at a different engine speed and rapid damping out of all spring-surge vibrations during engine operation results. Two or more springs also reduce danger of weakness and possible failure by breakage due to heat and metal fatigue. The springs are held in place by split locks installed in the recess of the valve spring upper retainer or washer, and engage a groove machined into the valve stem. The functions of the valve springs are to close the valve and to hold the valve securely on the valve seat.

Bearings

A bearing is any surface which supports, or is supported by, another surface. A good bearing must be composed of material that is strong enough to withstand the pressure imposed on it and should permit the other surface to move with a minimum of friction and wear. The parts must be held in position within very close tolerances to provide efficient and quiet operation, and yet allow freedom of motion. To accomplish this, and at the same time reduce friction of moving parts so that power loss is not excessive, lubricated bearings of many types are used. Bearings are required to take radial loads, thrust loads, or a combination of the two. An example of a radial load would be a rotating shaft being held or contained in one position on a radial plane. Thrust load would be the rotating shaft being contained from moving axially along the shafts axis. These radial and thrust loads are illustrated in *Figure 1-32*. There are two ways in which bearing surfaces move in relation to each other. One is by

Figure 1-32. *Radial and thrust loads.*

the sliding movement of one metal against the other (sliding friction), and the second is for one surface to roll over the other (rolling friction). The three different types of bearings in general use are plain, roller, and ball. *[Figure 1-33]*

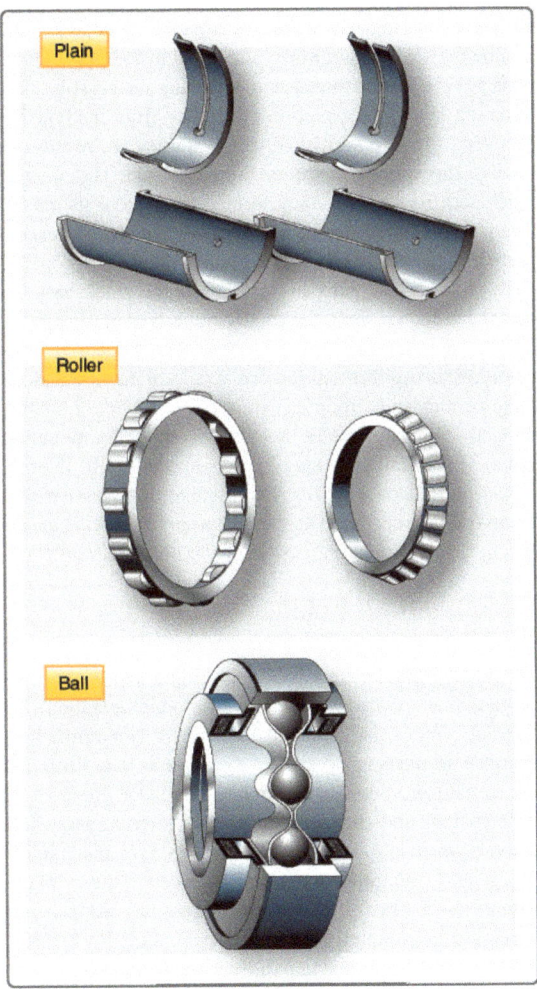

Figure 1-33. *Bearings.*

Plain Bearings

Plain bearings are generally used for the crankshaft, cam ring, camshaft, connecting rods, and the accessory drive shaft bearings. Such bearings are usually subjected to radial loads only, although some have been designed to take thrust loads. Plain bearings are usually made of nonferrous (having no iron) metals, such as silver, bronze, aluminum, and various alloys of copper, tin, or lead. Master rod or crankpin bearings in some engines are thin shells of steel, plated with silver on both the inside and the outside surfaces and with lead-tin plated over the silver on the inside surface only. Smaller bearings, such as those used to support various shafts in the accessory section, are called bushings. Porous Oilite bushings are widely used in this instance. They are impregnated with oil so that the heat of friction brings the oil to the bearing surface during engine operation.

Ball Bearings

A ball bearing assembly consists of grooved inner and outer races, one or more sets of balls, in bearings designed for disassembly, and a bearing retainer. They are used for shaft bearings and rocker arm bearings in some reciprocating engines. Special deep-groove ball bearings are used to transmit propeller thrust and radial loads to the engine nose section of radial engines. Since this type of bearing can accept both radial and thrust loads, it is used in gas turbine engines to support one end of a shaft (radial loads)and to keep the shaft from moving axially (thrust loads).

Roller Bearings

Roller bearings are made in many types and shapes, but the two types generally used in the aircraft engine are the straight roller and the tapered roller bearings. Straight roller bearings are used where the bearing is subjected to radial loads only. In tapered roller bearings, the inner- and outer-race bearing surfaces are cone-shaped. Such bearings withstand both radial and thrust loads. Straight roller bearings are used in high power reciprocating aircraft engines for the crankshaft main bearings. They are also used in gas turbine applications where radial loads are high. Generally, a rotating shaft in a gas turbine engine is supported by a deep-groove ball bearing (radial and thrust loads) on one end and a straight roller bearing (radial loads only) on the other end.

Propeller Reduction Gearing

The increased brake horsepower delivered by a high horsepower engine results partly from increased crankshaft rpm. It is therefore necessary to provide reduction gears to limit the propeller rotation speed to a value at which efficient operation is obtained. Whenever the speed of the blade tips approaches the speed of sound, the efficiency of the propeller decreases rapidly. Reduction gearing for engines allows the engine to operate at a higher rpm, developing more power while slowing down the propeller rpm. This prevents the propeller efficiency from decreasing. Since reduction gearing must withstand extremely high stresses, the gears are machined from steel forgings. Many types of reduction gearing systems are in use. The three types most commonly used are spur planetary, bevel planetary, and spur and pinion. [*Figure 1-34*]

The spur planetary reduction gearing consists of a large driving gear or sun gear splined (and sometimes shrunk) to the crankshaft, a large stationary gear, called a bell gear, and a set of small spur planetary pinion gears mounted on a carrier ring. The ring is fastened to the propeller shaft and the planetary gears mesh with both the sun gear and the stationary bell or ring gear. The stationary gear is bolted or splined to the front section housing. When the engine is operating, the sun gear rotates. Because the planetary gears are meshed with this ring, they also must rotate. Since they also mesh with the stationary gear, they walk or roll around it as they rotate, and the ring in which they are mounted rotates the propeller shaft in the same direction as the crankshaft but at a reduced speed.

In some engines, the bell gear is mounted on the propeller shaft, and the planetary pinion gear cage is held stationary. The sun gear is splined to the crankshaft and acts as a driving gear. In such an arrangement, the propeller travels at a reduced speed but in opposite direction to the crankshaft.

In the bevel planetary reduction gearing system, the driving gear is machined with beveled external teeth and is attached to the crankshaft. A set of mating bevel pinion gears is mounted in a cage attached to the end of the propeller shaft. The pinion gears are driven by the drive gear and walk around the stationary gear, which is bolted or splined to the front section housing. The thrust of the bevel pinion gears is absorbed by a thrust ball bearing of special design. The drive and the fixed gears are generally supported by heavy-duty ball bearings. This type of planetary reduction assembly is more compact than the other one described and, therefore, can be used where a smaller propeller gear step-down is desired. In the case of gas turbine turboprop engines, more than one stage of reduction gearing is used do to the high output speeds of the engine. Several types of lower powered engines can use the spur and pinion reduction gear arrangement.

Propeller Shafts

Propeller shafts may be of three major types: tapered, splined, or flanged. Tapered shafts are identified by taper numbers. Splined and flanged shafts are identified by SAE numbers. The propeller shaft of most low power output engines is forged as part of the crankshaft. It is tapered and a milled slot is provided so that the propeller hub can be keyed to the shaft. The keyway and key index of the propeller are in relation to the No. 1 cylinder top dead center. The end of the shaft is threaded to receive the propeller retaining nut. Tapered propeller shafts are common on older and smaller engines.

The propeller shaft of high-output radial engines is generally splined. It is threaded on one end for a propeller hub nut. The thrust bearing, which absorbs propeller thrust, is located around the shaft and transmits the thrust to the nose section housing. The shaft is threaded for attaching the thrust-bearing retaining nut. On the portion protruding from the housing (between the two sets of threads), splines are located to receive the splined propeller hub. The shaft is generally machined from a steel-alloy forging throughout its length. The propeller shaft may be connected by reduction gearing to the engine crankshaft, but in smaller engines the propeller shaft is simply an extension of the engine crankshaft. To turn the propeller shaft, the engine crankshaft must revolve.

Flanged propeller shafts are used on most modern reciprocating and turboprop engines. One end of the shaft is flanged with drilled holes to accept the propeller mounting bolts. The installation may be a short shaft with internal threading to accept the distributor valve to be used with a controllable propeller. The flanged propeller shaft is a very common installation on most propeller driven aircraft.

Reciprocating Engine Operating Principles

The relationships between pressure, volume, and temperature of gases are the basic principles of engine operation. An internal combustion engine is a device for converting heat energy into mechanical energy. Gasoline is vaporized and mixed with air, forced or drawn into a cylinder, compressed by a piston, and then ignited by an electric spark. The conversion of the resultant heat energy into mechanical energy and then into work is accomplished in the cylinder. *Figure 1-35* illustrates the various engine components necessary to accomplish this conversion and also presents the principal terms used to indicate engine operation.

The operating cycle of an internal combustion reciprocating engine includes the series of events required to induct,

Figure 1-34. *Reduction gears.*

compress, ignite, and burn, causing expansion of the fuel/air charge in the cylinder and to scavenge or exhaust the byproducts of the combustion process. When the compressed mixture is ignited, the resultant gases of combustion expand very rapidly and force the piston to move away from the cylinder head. This downward motion of the piston, acting on the crankshaft through the connecting rod, is converted to a circular or rotary motion by the crankshaft. A valve in the top or head of the cylinder opens to allow the burned gases to escape, and the momentum of the crankshaft and the propeller forces the piston back up in the cylinder where it is ready for the next event in the cycle. Another valve in the cylinder

Figure 1-35. *Components and terminology of engine operation.*

cycle after its originator, a German physicist. The four-stroke cycle engine has many advantages for use in aircraft. One advantage is that it lends itself readily to high performance through supercharging.

In this type of engine, four strokes are required to complete the required series of events or operating cycle of each cylinder. *[Figure 1-36]* Two complete revolutions of the crankshaft (720°) are required for the four strokes; thus, each cylinder in an engine of this type fires once in every two revolutions of the crankshaft. In the following discussion of the four-stroke cycle engine operation, note that the timing of the ignition and the valve events vary considerably in different engines. Many factors influence the timing of a specific engine, and it is most important that the engine manufacturer's recommendations in this respect be followed in maintenance and overhaul. The timing of the valve and ignition events is always specified in degrees of crankshaft travel. It should be remembered that a certain amount of crankshaft travel is required to open a valve fully; therefore, the specified timing represents the start of opening rather than the full-open position of the valve. An example valve timing chart can be seen in *Figure 1-37*.

head then opens to let in a fresh charge of the fuel/air mixture. The valve allowing for the escape of the burning exhaust gases is called the exhaust valve, and the valve which lets in the fresh charge of the fuel/air mixture is called the intake valve. These valves are opened and closed mechanically at the proper times by the valve-operating mechanism.

The bore of a cylinder is its inside diameter. The stroke is the distance the piston moves from one end of the cylinder to the other, specifically from top dead center (TDC) to bottom dead center (BDC), or vice versa. *[Figure 1-35]*

Operating Cycles

There are several operating cycles in use:

1. Four stroke
2. Two stroke
3. Rotary
4. Diesel

Four-Stroke Cycle

The vast majority of certified aircraft reciprocating engines operate on the four-stroke cycle, sometimes called the Otto

Figure 1-36. *Four-stroke cycle.*

Figure 1-37. *Valve timing chart.*

Intake Stroke

During the intake stroke, the piston is pulled downward in the cylinder by the rotation of the crankshaft. This reduces the pressure in the cylinder and causes air under atmospheric pressure to flow through the carburetor, which meters the correct amount of fuel. The fuel/air mixture passes through the intake pipes and intake valves into the cylinders. The quantity or weight of the fuel/air charge depends upon the degree of throttle opening.

The intake valve is opened considerably before the piston reaches TDC on the exhaust stroke, in order to induce a greater quantity of the fuel/air charge into the cylinder and thus increase the horsepower. The distance the valve may be opened before TDC, however, is limited by several factors, such as the possibility that hot gases remaining in the cylinder from the previous cycle may flash back into the intake pipe and the induction system.

In all high-power aircraft engines, both the intake and the exhaust valves are off the valve seats at TDC at the start of the intake stroke. As mentioned above, the intake valve opens before TDC on the exhaust stroke (valve lead), and the closing of the exhaust valve is delayed considerably after the piston has passed TDC and has started the intake stroke (valve lag). This timing is called valve overlap and is designed to aid in cooling the cylinder internally by circulating the cool incoming fuel/air mixture, to increase the amount of the fuel/air mixture induced into the cylinder, and to aid in scavenging the byproducts of combustion from the cylinder.

The intake valve is timed to close about 50° to 75° past BDC on the compression stroke, depending upon the specific engine, to allow the momentum of the incoming gases to charge the cylinder more completely. Because of the comparatively large volume of the cylinder above the piston when the piston is near BDC, the slight upward travel of the piston during this time does not have a great effect on the incoming flow of gases. This late timing can be carried too far because the gases may be forced back through the intake valve and defeat the purpose of the late closing.

Compression Stroke

After the intake valve is closed, the continued upward travel of the piston compresses the fuel/air mixture to obtain the desired burning and expansion characteristics. The charge is fired by means of an electric spark as the piston approaches TDC. The time of ignition varies from 20° to 35° before TDC, depending upon the requirements of the specific engine to ensure complete combustion of the charge by the time the piston is slightly past the TDC position.

Many factors affect ignition timing, and the engine manufacturer has expended considerable time in research and testing to determine the best setting. All engines incorporate devices for adjusting the ignition timing, and it is most important that the ignition system be timed according to the engine manufacturer's recommendations.

Power Stroke

As the piston moves through the TDC position at the end of the compression stroke and starts down on the power stroke, it is pushed downward by the rapid expansion of the burning gases within the cylinder head with a force that can be greater than 15 tons (30,000 psi) at maximum power output of the engine. The temperature of these burning gases may be between 3,000° and 4,000 °F. As the piston is forced downward during the power stroke by the pressure of the burning gases exerted upon it, the downward movement of the connecting rod is changed to rotary movement by the crankshaft. Then, the rotary movement is transmitted to the propeller shaft to drive the propeller. As the burning gases are expanded, the temperature drops to within safe limits before the exhaust gases flow out through the exhaust port.

The timing of the exhaust valve opening is determined by, among other considerations, the desirability of using as much of the expansive force as possible and of scavenging the cylinder as completely and rapidly as possible. The valve is opened considerably before BDC on the power stroke (on some engines at 50° and 75° before BDC) while there is still some pressure in the cylinder. This timing is used so that the pressure can force the gases out of the exhaust port as soon as possible. This process frees the cylinder of waste heat after the desired expansion has been obtained and avoids overheating the cylinder and the piston. Thorough scavenging is very important, because any exhaust products remaining in the cylinder dilute the incoming fuel/air charge at the start of the next cycle.

Exhaust Stroke

As the piston travels through BDC at the completion of the power stroke and starts upward on the exhaust stroke, it begins to push the burned exhaust gases out the exhaust port. The speed of the exhaust gases leaving the cylinder creates a low pressure in the cylinder. This low or reduced pressure speeds the flow of the fresh fuel/air charge into the cylinder as the intake valve is beginning to open. The intake valve opening is timed to occur at 8° to 55° before TDC on the exhaust stroke on various engines.

Two-Stroke Cycle

The two-stroke-cycle engine has re-emerged being used in ultra-light, light sport, and many experimental aircraft. As the name implies, two-stroke cycle engines require only one upstroke and one down stroke of the piston to complete the required series of events in the cylinder. Thus, the engine completes the operating cycle in one revolution of the crankshaft. The intake and exhaust functions are accomplished during the same stroke. These engines can be either air or water cooled and generally require a gear reduction housing between the engine and propeller.

Rotary Cycle

The rotary cycle has a three-sided rotor that turns inside an elliptical housing, completing three of the four cycles for each revolution. These engines can be single rotor or multi rotor and can be air or water cooled. They are used mostly with experimental and light aircraft. Vibration characteristics are also very low for this type of engine.

Diesel Cycle

The diesel cycle depends on high compression pressures to provide for the ignition of the fuel/air charge in the cylinder. As air is drawn in the cylinder, it is compressed by a piston and, at maximum pressure, fuel is sprayed in the cylinder. At this point, the high pressure and temperature in the cylinder causes the fuel to burn increasing the internal pressure of the cylinder. This drives the piston down, turning or driving the crankshaft. Water and air cooled engines that can operate on JETA fuel (kerosene) use a version of the diesel cycle. There are many types of diesel cycles, in use including two-stroke and four-stroke diesels.

Reciprocating Engine Power and Efficiencies

All aircraft engines are rated according to their ability to do work and produce power. This section presents an explanation of work and power and how they are calculated. Also discussed are the various efficiencies that govern the power output of a reciprocating engine.

Work

A physicist defines work as force times distance. Work done by a force acting on a body is equal to the magnitude of the force multiplied by the distance through which the force acts.

$$\text{Work (W)} = \text{Force (F)} \times \text{Distance (D)}$$

Work is measured by several standards. The most common unit is called foot-pound (ft-lb). If a one-pound mass is raised one foot, one ft-lb of work has been performed. The greater the mass is and/or the greater the distance is, the greater the work performed.

Horsepower

The common unit of mechanical power is the horsepower (hp). Late in the 18th century, James Watt, the inventor of the steam engine, found that an English workhorse could work at the rate of 550 ft-lb per second, or 33,000 ft-lb per minute, for a reasonable length of time. From his observations came the unit of horsepower, which is the standard unit of mechanical power in the English system of measurement. To calculate the hp rating of an engine, divide the power developed in ft-lb per minute by 33,000, or the power in ft-lb per second by 550.

$$\text{One hp} = \frac{\text{ft-lb per min}}{33,000}$$
$$\text{or}$$
$$\frac{\text{ft-lb per sec}}{550}$$

As stated above, work is the product of force and distance, and power is work per unit of time. Consequently, if a 33,000-lb weight is lifted through a vertical distance of 1 foot in 1 minute, the power expended is 33,000 ft-lb per minute, or exactly 1 hp.

Work is performed not only when a force is applied for lifting; force may be applied in any direction. If a 100-lb weight is dragged along the ground, a force is still being applied to perform work, although the direction of the resulting motion is approximately horizontal. The amount of this force would depend upon the roughness of the ground.

If the weight were attached to a spring scale graduated in pounds, then dragged by pulling on the scale handle, the amount of force required could be measured. Assume that the force required is 90 lb, and the 100-lb weight is dragged 660 feet in 2 minutes. The amount of work performed in the 2 minutes is 59,400 ft-lb or 29,700 ft-lb per minute. Since 1 hp is 33,000 ft-lb per minute, the hp expended in this case is 29,700 divided by 33,000, or 0.9 hp.

Piston Displacement

When other factors remain equal, the greater the piston displacement, the greater the maximum horsepower an engine is capable of developing. When a piston moves from BDC to TDC, it displaces a specific volume. The volume displaced by the piston is known as piston displacement and is expressed in cubic inches for most American-made engines and cubic centimeters for others.

The piston displacement of one cylinder may be obtained by multiplying the area of the cross-section of the cylinder by the total distance the piston moves in the cylinder in one stroke. For multicylinder engines, this product is multiplied by the number of cylinders to get the total piston displacement of the engine.

Since the volume (V) of a geometric cylinder equals the area (A) of the base multiplied by the height (h), it is expressed mathematically as:

$$V = A \times h$$

The area of the base is the area of the cross-section of the cylinder.

Area of a Circle

To find the area of a circle, it is necessary to use a number called pi (π). This number represents the ratio of the circumference to the diameter of any circle. Pi cannot be stated exactly because it is a never-ending decimal. It is 3.1416 expressed to four decimal places, which is accurate enough for most computations.

The area of a circle, as in a rectangle or triangle, must be expressed in square units. The distance that is one-half the diameter of a circle is known as the radius. The area of any circle is found by squaring the radius (r) and multiplying by π. The formula is:

$$A = \pi r^2$$

The radius of a circle is equal to ½ the diameter:

$$r = \frac{d}{2}$$

Example

Compute the piston displacement of the PWA 14 cylinder engine having a cylinder with a 5.5 inch diameter and a 5.5 inch stroke. Formulas required are:

$$r = \frac{d}{2}$$
$$A = \pi r^2$$
$$V = A \times h$$

Total $V = V \times n$ (number of cylinders)

Substitute values into these formulas and complete the calculation.

$$r = \frac{d}{2} = 5.5 \text{ inches (in)} \div 2 = 2.75 \text{ in}$$

$A = \pi r^2 = 3.1416 (2.75 \text{ in} \times 2.75 \text{ in})$

$A = 3.1416 \times 7.5625$ square inches (in^2) = 23.7584 in^2

$V = A \times h = 23.7584$ in$^2 \times 5.5$ in = 130.6712 cubic inches (in^3)

Total $V = V \times n = 130.6712$ in$^3 \times 14$

Total $V = 1829.3968$ in^3

Rounded off to the next whole number, total piston displacement equals 1,829 cubic inches.

Another method of calculating the piston displacement uses the diameter of the piston instead of the radius in the formula for the area of the base.

$$A = \tfrac{1}{4}(\pi)(d^2)$$

Substituting $A = \tfrac{1}{4} \times 3.1416 \times 5.5$ in $\times$ 5.5 in

$A = 0.7854 \times 30.25$ in^2

$A = 23.758$ in^2

From this point on, the calculations are identical to the preceding example.

Compression Ratio

All internal combustion engines must compress the fuel/air mixture to receive a reasonable amount of work from each power stroke. The fuel/air charge in the cylinder can be compared to a coil spring in that the more it is compressed, the more work it is potentially capable of doing.

The compression ratio of an engine is a comparison of the volume of space in a cylinder when the piston is at the bottom of the stroke to the volume of space when the piston is at the top of the stroke. *[Figure 1-38]* This comparison is expressed as a ratio, hence the term compression ratio. Compression ratio is a controlling factor in the maximum horsepower developed by an engine, but it is limited by present day fuel grades and the high engine speeds and manifold pressures required for takeoff. For example, if there are 140 cubic inches of space in the cylinder when the piston is at the bottom and there are 20 cubic inches of space when the piston is at the top of the stroke, the compression ratio would be 140 to 20. If this ratio is expressed in fraction form, it would be 140/20 or 7 to 1, usually represented as 7:1.

The limitations placed on compression ratios, manifold pressure, and the manifold pressure's effect on compression pressures has a major effect on engine operation. Manifold pressure is the average absolute pressure of the air or fuel/air charge in the intake manifold and is measured in units of inches of mercury ("Hg). Manifold pressure is dependent on engine speed (throttle setting) and the degree supercharging. The operation of the supercharger increases the weight of the charge entering the cylinder. When a true supercharger is used with the aircraft engine, the manifold pressure may be considerably higher than the pressure of the outside atmosphere. The advantage of this condition is that a greater amount of charge is forced into a given cylinder volume, and a greater output of horsepower results.

Compression ratio and manifold pressure determine the pressure in the cylinder in that portion of the operating cycle when both valves are closed. The pressure of the charge before compression is determined by manifold pressure, while the pressure at the height of compression (just prior to ignition) is determined by manifold pressure times the compression ratio. For example, if an engine were operating at a manifold pressure of 30 "Hg with a compression ratio of 7:1, the pressure at the instant before ignition would be approximately 210 "Hg. However, at a manifold pressure of 60 "Hg, the pressure would be 420 "Hg.

Without going into great detail, it has been shown that the compression event magnifies the effect of varying the manifold pressure, and the magnitude of both affects the pressure of the fuel charge just before the instant of ignition. If the pressure at this time becomes too high, pre-ignition or detonation occur and produce overheating. Pre-ignition is

Figure 1-38. *Compression ratio.*

when the fuel air charge starts to burn before the spark plug fires. Detonation occurs when the fuel air charge is ignited by the spark plug, but instead of burning at a controlled rate, it explodes causing cylinder temperatures and pressures to spike very quickly. If this condition exists for very long, the engine can be damaged or destroyed.

One of the reasons for using engines with high compression ratios is to obtain long-range fuel economy, to convert more heat energy into useful work than is done in engines of low compression ratio. Since more heat of the charge is converted into useful work, less heat is absorbed by the cylinder walls. This factor promotes cooler engine operation, which in turn increases the thermal efficiency. Here again, a compromise is needed between the demand for fuel economy and the demand for maximum horsepower without detonation. Some manufacturers of high compression engines suppress detonation at high manifold pressures by using high octane fuel and limiting maximum manifold pressure.

Indicated Horsepower

The indicated horsepower produced by an engine is the horsepower calculated from the indicated mean effective pressure and the other factors which affect the power output of an engine. Indicated horsepower is the power developed in the combustion chambers without reference to friction losses within the engine. This horsepower is calculated as a function of the actual cylinder pressure recorded during engine operation.

To facilitate the indicated horsepower calculations, a mechanical indicating device, such as is attached to the engine cylinder scribes the actual pressure existing in the cylinder during the complete operating cycle. This pressure variation can be represented by the kind of graph shown in *Figure 1-39*. Notice that the cylinder pressure rises on the compression stroke, reaches a peak after top center, and decreases as the piston moves down on the power stroke. Since the cylinder pressure varies during the operating cycle, an average pressure (line AB) is computed. This average pressure, if applied steadily during the time of the power stroke, would do the same amount of work as the varying pressure during the same period. This average pressure is known as indicated mean effective pressure and is included in the indicated horsepower calculation with other engine specifications. If the characteristics and the indicated mean effective pressure of an engine are known, it is possible to calculate the indicated horsepower rating.

The indicated horsepower for a four-stroke cycle engine can be calculated from the following formula, in which the letter symbols in the numerator are arranged to spell the word "PLANK" to assist in memorizing the formula:

$$\text{Indicated horsepower} = \frac{\text{PLANK}}{33{,}000}$$

Where:

P = Indicated mean effective pressure, in psi

L = Length of the stroke, in feet or in fractions of a foot

A = Area of the piston head or cross-sectional area of the cylinder, in square inches

N = Number of power strokes per minute: $\frac{\text{rpm}}{2}$

K = Number of cylinders

In the formula above, the area of the piston multiplied by the indicated mean effective pressure gives the force acting on the piston in pounds. This force multiplied by the length of the stroke in feet gives the work performed in one power stroke, which, multiplied by the number of power strokes per minute, gives the number of ft-lb per minute of work produced by one cylinder. Multiplying this result by the number of cylinders in the engine gives the amount of work performed, in ft-lb,

Figure 1-39. *Compression ratio.*

by the engine. Since hp is defined as work done at the rate of 33,000 ft-lb per minute, the total number of ft-lb of work performed by the engine is divided by 33,000 to find the indicated horsepower.

Example
Given:

Indicated mean
effective pressure (P) = 1.65 lb/in²

Stroke (L) = 6 in or .5 ft

Bore = .5 in

rpm = 3,000

No. of cylinders (K) = 12

Indicated hp = $\dfrac{PLANK}{33,000 \text{ ft-lb/min}}$

Find indicated hp.

A is found by using the equation

$A = \frac{1}{4}\pi D^2$

$A = \frac{1}{4} \times 3.1416 \times 5.5 \text{ in} \times 5.5 \text{ in}$

$= 23.76 \text{ in}^2$

N is found by multiplying the rpm by ½:

N = ½ × 3,000 = 1,500 rpm

Now, substituting in the formula:

Indicated hp = $\dfrac{1.65 \text{ lb/in}^2 \times .5 \text{ in} \times 23.76 \text{ in}^2 \times 1,500 \text{ rpm} \times 12}{33,000 \text{ ft-lb/min}}$

Indicated hp = 1069.20

Brake Horsepower

The indicated horsepower calculation discussed in the preceding paragraph is the theoretical power of a frictionless engine. The total horsepower lost in overcoming friction must be subtracted from the indicated horsepower to arrive at the actual horsepower delivered to the propeller. The power delivered to the propeller for useful work is known as brake horsepower (bhp). The difference between indicated and brake horsepower is known as friction horsepower, which is the horsepower required to overcome mechanical losses, such as the pumping action of the pistons, the friction of the pistons, and the friction of all other moving parts.

The measurement of an engine's bhp involves the measurement of a quantity known as torque or twisting moment. Torque is the product of a force and the distance of the force from the axis about which it acts, or

Torque = force × distance
(at right angles to the force)

Torque is a measure of load and is properly expressed in pound-inches (lb-in) or pound-feet (lb-ft). Torque should not be confused with work, which is expressed in inch-pounds (in-lb) or foot-pounds (ft-lb).

There are numerous devices for measuring torque, such as a dynamometer or a torque meter. One very simple type of device that can be used to demonstrate torque calculations is the Prony brake. *[Figure 1-40]* All of these torque-measuring devices are usable to calculate power output of an engine on a test stand. It consists essentially of a hinged collar, or brake, which can be clamped to a drum splined to the propeller shaft. The collar and drum form a friction brake, which can be adjusted by a wheel. An arm of a known length is rigidly attached to or is a part of the hinged collar and terminates at a point that rests on a set of scales. As the propeller shaft rotates, it tends to carry the hinged collar of the brake with it and is prevented from doing so only by the arm that rests on the scale. The scale indicates the force necessary to arrest the motion of the arm. If the resulting force registered on the scale is multiplied by the length of the arm, the resulting product is the torque exerted by the rotating shaft. For example, if the scale registers 200 pounds and the length of the arm is 3.18 feet, the torque exerted by the shaft is:

200 lb × 3.18 ft = 636 lb-ft

Once the torque is known, the work done per revolution of the propeller shaft can be computed without difficulty by the equation:

Work per revolution = 2π × torque

If work per revolution is multiplied by the rpm, the result is work per minute, or power. If the work is expressed in ft-lb per minute, this quantity is divided by 33,000. The result is the brake horsepower of the shaft.

Power = Work per revolution × rpm
and
bhp = $\dfrac{\text{Work per revolution} \times \text{rpm}}{33,000}$

$\dfrac{2\pi r \times \text{force on the scales (lb)} \times \text{length of arm (ft)} \times \text{rpm}}{33,000}$

Figure 1-40. *Typical prony brake.*

Example

Given:

Force on scales	= 200 lb
Length of arm	= 3.18 ft
rpm	= 3,000
π	= 3.1416

Find bhp substituting in equation:

$$bhp = \frac{6.2832 \times 200 \times 3.18 \times 3,000}{33,000}$$

$$= 363.2$$
$$= 363$$

As long as the friction between the brake collar and propeller shaft drum is great enough to impose an appreciable load on the engine, but is not great enough to stop the engine, it is not necessary to know the amount of friction between the collar and drum to compute the bhp. If there were no load imposed, there would be no torque to measure, and the engine would "run away." If the imposed load is so great that the engine stalls, there may be considerable torque to measure, but there is no rpm. In either case, it is impossible to measure the bhp of the engine. However, if a reasonable amount of friction exists between the brake drum and the collar and the load is then increased, the tendency of the propeller shaft to carry the collar and arm about with it becomes greater, thus imposing a greater force upon the scales. As long as the torque increase is proportional to the rpm decrease, the horsepower delivered at the shaft remains unchanged. This can be seen from the equation in which 2πr and 33,000 are constants and torque and rpm are variables. If the change in rpm is inversely proportional to the change in torque, their product remains unchanged, and bhp remains unchanged. This is important. It shows that horsepower is the function of both torque and rpm, and can be changed by changing either torque, rpm, or both.

Friction Horsepower

Friction horsepower is the indicated horsepower minus brake horsepower. It is the horsepower used by an engine in overcoming the friction of moving parts, drawing in fuel, expelling exhaust, driving oil and fuel pumps, and other engine accessories. On modern aircraft engines, this power loss through friction may be as high as 10 to 15 percent of the indicated horsepower.

Friction and Brake Mean Effective Pressures

The indicated mean effective pressure (**IMEP**), discussed previously, is the average pressure produced in the combustion chamber during the operating cycle and is an expression of the theoretical, frictionless power known as indicated horsepower. In addition to completely disregarding power lost to friction, indicated horsepower gives no indication of how much actual power is delivered to the propeller shaft for doing useful work. However, it is related to actual pressures that occur in the cylinder and can be used as a measure of these pressures.

To compute the friction loss and net power output, the indicated horsepower of a cylinder may be thought of as two separate powers, each producing a different effect. The first power overcomes internal friction, and the horsepower thus consumed is known as friction horsepower. The second power, known as brake horsepower, produces useful work at the propeller. That portion of IMEP that produces brake horsepower is called brake mean effective pressure (BMEP). The remaining pressure used to overcome internal friction is called friction mean effective pressure (FMEP). *[Figure 1-41]* IMEP is a useful expression of total cylinder power output, but is not a real physical quantity; likewise, FMEP and BMEP are theoretical but useful expressions of friction losses and net power output.

Although **BMEP** and **FMEP** have no real existence in the cylinder, they provide a convenient means of representing pressure limits or rating engine performance throughout its entire operating range. There is an operating relationship between IMEP, BMEP, and FMEP.

One of the basic limitations placed on engine operation is the pressure developed in the cylinder during combustion. In the discussion of compression ratios and indicated mean effective pressure, it was found that, within limits, increased pressure resulted in increased power. It was also noted that if the cylinder pressure were not controlled within close limits, it would impose dangerous internal loads that might result in engine failure. Therefore, it is important to have a means of determining these cylinder pressures as a protective measure and for efficient application of power.

If the bhp is known, the BMEP can be computed by means of the following equation:

$$BMEP = \frac{bhp \times 33{,}000}{LANK}$$

Given:

bhp = 1,000

Stroke = 6 in

Bore = 5.5 in

rpm = 3,000

Number of cycles = 12

Find BMEP:

Find length of stroke (in ft) :

L = 6 in = .5 ft

Figure 1-41. *Power and pressure.*

Find area of cylinder bore:

$A = \frac{1}{4}\pi D^2$

$A = \frac{1}{4} \times 3.1416 \times 5.5 \text{ in} \times 5.5 \text{ in}$

$A = 23.76 \text{ in}^2$

Find number of power strokes per min:

$N = \frac{1}{2} \times rpm$

$N = \frac{1}{2} \times 3{,}000 \text{ rpm}$

$N = 1{,}500$

Then, substituting in the equation:

$$\text{BMEP} = \frac{1{,}000 \text{ bhp} \times 33{,}000 \text{ ft-lb/min}}{.5 \text{ ft} \times 23.76 \text{ in}^2 \times 1{,}500 \text{ strokes/min} \times 12}$$

$$= 154.32 \text{ lb/in}^2$$

Thrust Horsepower

Thrust horsepower can be considered the result of the engine and the propeller working together. If a propeller could be designed to be 100 percent efficient, the thrust and the bph would be the same. However, the efficiency of the propeller varies with the engine speed, attitude, altitude, temperature, and airspeed. Thus, the ratio of the thrust horsepower and the bhp delivered to the propeller shaft will never be equal. For example, if an engine develops 1,000 bhp, and it is used with a propeller having 85 percent efficiency, the thrust horsepower of that engine-propeller combination is 85 percent of 1,000 or 850 thrust hp. Of the four types of horsepower discussed, it is the thrust horsepower that determines the performance of the engine-propeller combination.

Efficiencies

Thermal Efficiency

Any study of engines and power involves consideration of heat as the source of power. The heat produced by the burning of gasoline in the cylinders causes a rapid expansion of the gases in the cylinder, and this, in turn, moves the pistons and creates mechanical energy. It has long been known that mechanical work can be converted into heat and that a given amount of heat contains the energy equivalent of a certain amount of mechanical work. Heat and work are theoretically interchangeable and bear a fixed relation to each other. Heat can therefore be measured in work units (for example, ft-lb) as well as in heat units. The British thermal unit (BTU) of heat is the quantity of heat required to raise the temperature of 1 pound of water by 1 °F. It is equivalent to 778 ft-lb of mechanical work. A pound of petroleum fuel, when burned with enough air to consume it completely, gives up about 20,000 BTU, the equivalent of 15,560,000 ft-lb of mechanical work. These quantities express the heat energy of the fuel in heat and work units, respectively.

The ratio of useful work done by an engine to the heat energy of the fuel it uses, expressed in work or heat units, is called the thermal efficiency of the engine. If two similar engines use equal amounts of fuel, the engine that converts into work the greater part of the energy in the fuel (higher thermal efficiency) delivers the greater amount of power. Furthermore, the engine that has the higher thermal efficiency has less waste heat to dispose of to the valves, cylinders, pistons, and cooling system of the engine. A high thermal efficiency also means low specific fuel consumption and, therefore, less fuel for a flight of a given distance at a given power. Thus, the practical importance of a high thermal efficiency is threefold, and it constitutes one of the most desirable features in the performance of an aircraft engine.

Of the total heat produced, 25 to 30 percent is utilized for power output, 15 to 20 percent is lost in cooling (heat radiated from cylinder head fins), 5 to 10 percent is lost in overcoming friction of moving parts; and 40 to 45 percent is lost through the exhaust. Anything that increases the heat content going into mechanical work on the piston, which reduces the friction and pumping losses, or which reduces the quantity of unburned fuel or the heat lost to the engine parts, increases the thermal efficiency.

The portion of the total heat of combustion that is turned into mechanical work depends to a great extent upon the compression ratio. The compression ratio is the ratio of the piston displacement plus combustion chamber space to the combustion chamber space, as mentioned earlier. Other things being equal, the higher the compression ratio is, the larger is the proportion of the heat energy of combustion turned into useful work at the crankshaft. On the other hand, increasing the compression ratio increases the cylinder head temperature. This is a limiting factor because the extremely high temperature created by high compression ratios causes the material in the cylinder to deteriorate rapidly and the fuel to detonate instead of burning at a controlled rate.

The thermal efficiency of an engine may be based on either bhp or indicated horsepower (ihp) and is represented by the formula:

Indicated thermal efficiency =
$$\frac{\text{ihp} \times 33{,}000}{\text{weight of fuel burned/min.} \times \text{heat value} \times 778}$$

The formula for brake thermal efficiency is the same as shown above, except the value for bhp is inserted instead of the value for ihp.

Example

An engine delivers 85 bhp for a period of 1 hour and during that time consumes 50 pounds of fuel. Assuming the fuel has a heat content of 18,800 BTU per pound, find the thermal efficiency of the engine:

$$\frac{85 \text{ ihp} \times 33{,}000}{.833 \times 18{,}800 \text{ BTU} \times 778} = \frac{2{,}805{,}000}{12{,}184{,}569}$$

Brake thermal efficiency = 0.23 or 23 percent

Reciprocating engines are only about 34 percent thermally efficient; that is, they transform only about 34 percent of the total heat potential of the burning fuel into mechanical energy. The remainder of the heat is lost through the exhaust gases, the cooling system, and the friction within the engine. Thermal distribution in a reciprocating engine is illustrated in *Figure 1-42*.

Mechanical Efficiency

Mechanical efficiency is the ratio that shows how much of the power developed by the expanding gases in the cylinder is actually delivered to the output shaft. It is a comparison between the bhp and the ihp. It can be expressed by the formula:

$$\text{Mechanical efficiency} = \frac{\text{bhp}}{\text{ihp}}$$

Brake horsepower is the useful power delivered to the propeller shaft. Indicated horsepower is the total hp developed in the cylinders. The difference between the two is friction horsepower (fhp), the power lost in overcoming friction. The factor that has the greatest effect on mechanical efficiency is the friction within the engine itself. The friction between moving parts in an engine remains practically constant throughout an engine's speed range. Therefore, the mechanical efficiency of an engine is highest when the engine is running at the rpm at which maximum bhp is developed. Mechanical efficiency of the average aircraft reciprocating engine approaches 90 percent.

Volumetric Efficiency

Volumetric efficiency is a ratio expressed in terms of percentages. It is a comparison of the volume of fuel/air charge (corrected for temperature and pressure) inducted into the cylinders to the total piston displacement of the engine. Various factors cause departure from a 100 percent volumetric efficiency. The pistons of an naturally aspirated engine displace the same volume each time they travel from top center to bottom center of the cylinders. The amount of charge that fills this volume on the intake stroke depends on the existing pressure and temperature of the surrounding atmosphere. Therefore, to find the volumetric efficiency of an engine, standards for atmospheric pressure and temperature had to be established. The U.S. standard atmosphere was established in 1958 and provides the necessary pressure and temperature values to calculate volumetric efficiency.

The standard sea level temperature is 59 °F, or 15 °C. At this temperature, the pressure of one atmosphere is 14.69 lb/in^2, and this pressure supports a column of mercury (Hg) 29.92 inches high, or 29.92 "Hg. These standard sea level conditions determine a standard density, and if the engine draws in a volume of charge of this density exactly equal to its piston displacement, it is said to be operating at 100 percent volumetric efficiency. An engine drawing in less volume than this has a volumetric efficiency lower than 100 percent. An engine equipped with true supercharging (boost above 30.00 "Hg) may have a volumetric efficiency greater than 100 percent. The equation for volumetric efficiency is:

$$\text{Volumetric Efficiency} = \frac{\text{Volume of charge (corrected for temperature and pressure)}}{\text{Piston displacement}}$$

Many factors decrease volumetric efficiency, including:

- Part-throttle operation
- Long intake pipes of small diameter
- Sharp bends in the induction system
- Carburetor air temperature too high
- Cylinder-head temperature too high
- Incomplete scavenging
- Improper valve timing

Propulsive Efficiency

A propeller is used with an engine to provide thrust. The engine supplies bhp through a rotating shaft, and the

Figure 1-42. *Thermal distribution in an engine.*

propeller absorbs the bhp and converts it into thrust hp. In this conversion, some power is wasted. Since the efficiency of any machine is the ratio of useful power output to the power input, propulsive efficiency (in this case, propeller efficiency) is the ratio of thrust hp to bhp. On the average, thrust hp constitutes approximately 80 percent of the bhp. The other 20 percent is lost in friction and slippage. Controlling the blade angle of the propeller is the best method of obtaining maximum propulsive efficiency for all conditions encountered in flight.

During takeoff, when the aircraft is moving at low speeds and when maximum power and thrust are required, a low propeller blade angle gives maximum thrust. For high-speed flying or diving, the blade angle is increased to obtain maximum thrust and efficiency. The constant-speed propeller is used to give required thrust at maximum efficiency for all flight conditions.

Gas Turbine Engines
Types and Construction
In a reciprocating engine, the functions of intake, compression, combustion, and exhaust all take place in the same combustion chamber. Consequently, each must have exclusive occupancy of the chamber during its respective part of the combustion cycle. A significant feature of the gas turbine engine is that separate sections are devoted to each function, and all functions are performed simultaneously without interruption.

A typical gas turbine engine consists of:

1. An air inlet,
2. Compressor section,
3. Combustion section,
4. Turbine section,
5. Exhaust section,
6. Accessory section, and
7. The systems necessary for starting, lubrication, fuel supply, and auxiliary purposes, such as anti-icing, cooling, and pressurization.

The major components of all gas turbine engines are basically the same; however, the nomenclature of the component parts of various engines currently in use varies slightly due to the difference in each manufacturer's terminology. These differences are reflected in the applicable maintenance manuals. One of the greatest single factors influencing the construction features of any gas turbine engine is the type of compressor or compressors for which the engine is designed.

Four types of gas turbine engines are used to propel and power aircraft. They are the turbofan, turboprop, turboshaft, and turbojet. The term "turbojet" was used to describe any gas turbine engine used in aircraft. As gas turbine technology evolved, these other engine types were developed to take the place of the pure turbojet engine. The turbojet engine has problems with noise and fuel consumption in the speed range that airliners fly (.8 Mach). Due to these problems, use of pure turbojet engines is very limited. So, almost all airliner-type aircraft use a turbofan engine. It was developed to turn a large fan or set of fans at the front of the engine and produces about 80 percent of the thrust from the engine. This engine was quieter and has better fuel consumption in this speed range. Turbofan engines have more than one shaft in the engine; many are two-shaft engines. This means that there is a compressor and a turbine that drives it and another compressor and turbine that drives it. These two shafted engines use two spools (a spool is a compressor and a shaft and turbines that driven that compressor). In a two-spool engine, there is a high-pressure spool and a low-pressure spool. The low-pressure spool generally contains the fan(s) and the turbine stages it takes to drive them. The high-pressure spool is the high-pressure compressor, shaft, and turbines. This spool makes up the core of the engine, and this is where the combustion section is located. The high-pressure spool is also referred to as the gas generator because it contains the combustion section.

Turbofan engines can be low bypass or high bypass. The amount of air that is bypassed around the core of the engine determines the bypass ratio. As can be seen in *Figure 1-43*, the air generally driven by the fan does not pass through the internal working core of the engine. The amount of air flow in lb/sec from the fan bypass to the core flow of the engine is the bypass ratio.

$$\text{Bypass ratio} = \frac{100 \text{ lb/sec flow fan}}{20 \text{ lb/sec flowcore}} = 5:1 \text{ bypass ratio}$$

Some low-bypass turbofan engines are used in speed ranges above .8 Mach (military aircraft). These engines use augmenters or afterburners to increase thrust. By adding more fuel nozzles and a flame holder in the exhaust system extra fuel can be sprayed and burned which can give large increases in thrust for short amounts of time.

The turboprop engine is a gas turbine engine that turns a propeller through a speed reduction gear box. This type of engine is most efficient in the 300 to 400 mph speed range and can use shorter runways that other aircraft. Approximately 80 to 85 percent of the energy developed by the gas turbine engine is used to drive the propeller. The rest of the available energy exits the exhaust as thrust. By adding the horsepower developed by the engine shaft and the horsepower in the exiting thrust, the answer is equivalent shaft horsepower.

Figure 1-43. *Turbofan engine with separate nozzles fan and core.*

With regard to aircraft, the turboshaft engine is a gas turbine engine made to transfer horsepower to a shaft that turns a helicopter transmission or is an onboard auxiliary power unit (APU). An APU is used on turbine-powered aircraft to provide electrical power and bleed air on the ground and a backup generator in flight. Turboshaft engines can come in many different styles, shapes, and horsepower ranges.

Air Entrance

The air entrance is designed to conduct incoming air to the compressor with a minimum energy loss resulting from drag or ram pressure loss; that is, the flow of air into the compressor should be free of turbulence to achieve maximum operating efficiency. Proper inlet design contributes materially to aircraft performance by increasing the ratio of compressor discharge pressure to duct inlet pressure.

This is also referred to as the compressor pressure ratio. This ratio is the outlet pressure divided by the inlet pressure. The amount of air passing through the engine is dependent upon three factors:

1. The compressor speed (rpm)
2. The forward speed of the aircraft
3. The density of the ambient (surrounding) air

Turbine inlet type is dictated by the type of gas turbine engine. A high-bypass turbofan engine inlet is completely different from a turboprop or turboshaft inlet. Large gas turbine-powered aircraft almost always have a turbofan engine. The inlet on this type of engine is bolted to the front (A flange) of the engine. These engines are mounted on the wings, or nacelles, on the aft fuselage, and a few are in the vertical fin. A typical turbofan inlet can be seen in *Figure 1-44*. Since on most modern turbofan engines the huge fan is the first part of the aircraft the incoming air comes into contact with, icing protection must be provided. This prevents chucks of ice from forming on the leading edge of the inlet, breaking loose, and damaging the fan. Warm air is bled from the engine's compressor and is ducted through the inlet to prevent ice from forming. If inlet guide vanes are used to straighten the air flow, then they also have anti-icing air flowing through them. The inlet also contains some sound-reducing materials that absorb the fan noise and make the engine quieter.

Figure 1-44. *Typical turbofan inlet.*

Turboprops and turboshafts can use an inlet screen to help filter out ice or debris from entering the engine. A deflector vane and a heated inlet lip are used to prevent ice or large chunks from entering the engine.

On military aircraft, the divided entrance permits the use of very short ducts with a resultant small pressure drop through skin friction. Military aircraft can fly at speeds above Mach 1, but the airflow through the engine must always stay below Mach 1. Supersonic air flow in the engine would destroy the engine. By using convergent and divergent shaped ducts, the air flow is controlled and dropped to subsonic speeds before entering the engine. Supersonic inlets are used to slow the incoming engine air to less than Mach 1 before it enters the engine.

Accessory Section

The accessory section of the gas turbine engine has various functions. The primary function is to provide space for the mounting of accessories necessary for operation and control of the engine. Generally, it also includes accessories concerned with the aircraft, such as electric generators and hydraulic pumps. Secondary functions include acting as an oil reservoir and/or oil sump and housing the accessory drive gears and reduction gears.

The arrangement and driving of accessories has always been a major problem on gas turbine engines. Driven accessories on turbofans are usually mounted on the accessory gear box, which is on the bottom of the engine. The location of the accessory gear box varies somewhat, but most turboprops and turboshafts have the accessory cases mounted to the back section of the engine.

The components of the accessory section of all gas turbine engines have essentially the same purpose, even though they often differ quite extensively in construction details and nomenclature.

The basic elements of the accessory section are:

1. The accessory case, which has machined mounting pads for the engine-driven accessories, and
2. The gear train, which is housed within the accessory case.

The accessory case may be designed to act as an oil reservoir. If an oil tank is utilized, a sump is usually provided below the front bearing support for the drainage and scavenging of oil used to lubricate bearings and drive gears. The accessory case is also provided with adequate tubing or cored passages for spraying, lubricating oil on the gear train and supporting bearings.

The gear train is driven by the engine high-pressure compressor through an accessory drive shaft (tower shaft) gear coupling, which splines with a gear box gear and the high-pressure compressor. The reduction gearing within the case provides suitable drive speeds for each engine accessory or component. Because the rotor operating rpm is so high, the accessory reduction gear ratios are relatively high. The accessory drives are supported by ball bearings assembled in the mounting pad bores of the accessory case. *[Figure 1-45]*

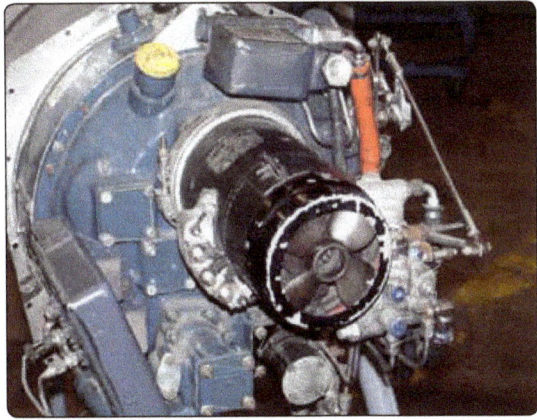

Figure 1-45. *Typical turboprop accessory case.*

Compressor Section

The compressor section of the gas turbine engine has many functions. Its primary function is to supply air in sufficient quantity to satisfy the requirements of the combustion burners. Specifically, to fulfill its purpose, the compressor must increase the pressure of the mass of air received from the air inlet duct, and then, discharge it to the burners in the quantity and at the pressures required.

A secondary function of the compressor is to supply bleed-air for various purposes in the engine and aircraft. The bleed-air is taken from any of the various pressure stages of the compressor. The exact location of the bleed ports is, of course, dependent on the pressure or temperature required for a particular job. The ports are small openings in the compressor case adjacent to the particular stage from which the air is to be bled; thus, varying degrees of pressure are available simply by tapping into the appropriate stage. Air is often bled from the final or highest pressure stage since, at this point, pressure and air temperature are at a maximum. At times it may be necessary to cool this high-pressure air. If it is used for cabin pressurization or other purposes to which excess heat would be uncomfortable or detrimental, the air is sent through an air conditioning unit before it enters the cabin.

1-39

Bleed air is utilized in a wide variety of ways. Some of the current applications of bleed air are:

1. Cabin pressurization, heating, and cooling;
2. Deicing and anti-icing equipment;
3. Pneumatic starting of engines; and
4. Auxiliary drive units (ADU).

Compressor Types

The two principal types of compressors currently being used in gas turbine aircraft engines are centrifugal flow and axial flow. The centrifugal-flow compressor achieves its purpose by picking up the entering air and accelerating it outwardly by centrifugal action. The axial-flow compressor compresses air while the air continues in its original direction of flow, thus avoiding the energy loss caused by turns. The components of each of these two types of compressor have their individual functions in the compression of air for the combustion section. A stage in a compressor is considered to be a rise in pressure.

Centrifugal-Flow Compressors

The centrifugal-flow compressor consists of an impeller (rotor), a diffuser (stator), and a compressor manifold. *[Figure 1-46]* Centrifugal compressors have a high pressure rise per stage that can be around 8:1. Generally centrifugal compressors are limited to two stages due to efficiency concerns. The two main functional elements are the impeller and the diffuser. Although the diffuser is a separate unit and is placed inside and bolted to the manifold, the entire assembly (diffuser and manifold) is often referred to as the diffuser. For clarification during compressor familiarization, the units are treated individually. The impeller is usually made from forged aluminum alloy, heat treated, machined, and smoothed for minimum flow restriction and turbulence.

In most types, the impeller is fabricated from a single forging. This type impeller is shown in *Figure 1-46*. The impeller, whose function is to pick up and accelerate the air outwardly to the diffuser, may be either of two types—single entry or double entry. The principal differences between the two types of impellers are size and ducting arrangement. The double-entry type has a smaller diameter, but is usually operated at a higher rotational speed to assure sufficient airflow. The single-entry impeller, shown in *Figure 1-47*, permits convenient ducting directly to the impeller eye (inducer vanes) as opposed to the more complicated ducting necessary to reach the rear side of the double-entry type. Although slightly more efficient in receiving air, the single-entry impeller must be large in diameter to deliver the same quantity of air as the double-entry type. This, of course, increases the overall diameter of the engine.

Figure 1-47. *Single-entry impeller.*

Included in the ducting for double-entry compressor engines is the plenum chamber. This chamber is necessary for a double-entry compressor because the air must enter the

Figure 1-46. *(A) Components of a centrifugal-flow compressor; (B) Air outlet elbow with turning vanes for reducing air pressure losses.*

engine at almost right angles to the engine axis. Therefore, in order to give a positive flow, the air must surround the engine compressor at a positive pressure before entering the compressor. Included in some installations as necessary parts of the plenum chamber are the auxiliary air-intake doors (blow-in doors). These blow-in doors admit air to the engine compartment during ground operation, when air requirements for the engine are in excess of the airflow through the inlet ducts. The doors are held closed by spring action when the engine is not operating. During operation, however, the doors open automatically whenever engine compartment pressure drops below atmospheric pressure. During takeoff and flight, ram air pressure in the engine compartment aids the springs in holding the doors closed.

The diffuser is an annular chamber provided with a number of vanes forming a series of divergent passages into the manifold. The diffuser vanes direct the flow of air from the impeller to the manifold at an angle designed to retain the maximum amount of energy imparted by the impeller. They also deliver the air to the manifold at a velocity and pressure satisfactory for use in the combustion chambers. Refer to *Figure 1-46A* and note the arrow indicating the path of airflow through the diffuser, then through the manifold.

The compressor manifold shown in *Figure 1-46A* diverts the flow of air from the diffuser, which is an integral part of the manifold, into the combustion chambers. The manifold has one outlet port for each chamber so that the air is evenly divided. A compressor outlet elbow is bolted to each of the outlet ports. These air outlets are constructed in the form of ducts and are known by a variety of names, such as air outlet ducts, outlet elbows, or combustion chamber inlet ducts. Regardless of the terminology used, these outlet ducts perform a very important part of the diffusion process; that is, they change the radial direction of the airflow to an axial direction, in which the diffusion process is completed after the turn. To help the elbows perform this function in an efficient manner, turning vanes (cascade vanes) are sometimes fitted inside the elbows. These vanes reduce air pressure losses by presenting a smooth, turning surface. *[Figure 1-46B]*

Axial-Flow Compressor

The axial-flow compressor has two main elements: a rotor and a stator. The rotor has blades fixed on a spindle. These blades impel air rearward in the same manner as a propeller because of their angle and airfoil contour. The rotor, turning at high speed, takes in air at the compressor inlet and impels it through a series of stages. From inlet to exit, the air flows along an axial path and is compressed at a ratio of approximately 1.25:1 per stage. The action of the rotor increases the compression of the air at each stage and accelerates it rearward through several stages. With this increased velocity, energy is transferred from the compressor to the air in the form of velocity energy. The stator blades act as diffusers at each stage, partially converting high velocity to pressure. Each consecutive pair of rotor and stator blades constitutes a pressure stage. The number of rows of blades (stages) is determined by the amount of air and total pressure rise required. Compressor pressure ratio increases with the number of compression stages. Most engines utilize up to 16 stages and more.

The stator has rows of vanes, which are in turn attached inside an enclosing case. The stator vanes, which are stationary, project radially toward the rotor axis and fit closely on either side of each stage of the rotor blades. In some cases, the compressor case, into which the stator vanes are fitted, is horizontally divided into halves. Either the upper or lower half may be removed for inspection or maintenance of rotor and stator blades.

The function of the stator vanes is to receive air from the air inlet duct or from each preceding stage and increase the pressure of the air and deliver it to the next stage at the correct velocity and pressure. They also control the direction of air to each rotor stage to obtain the maximum possible compressor blade efficiency. Shown in *Figure 1-48* are the rotor and stator elements of a typical axial-flow compressor. The first stage rotor blades can be preceded by an inlet guide vane assembly that can be fixed or variable.

The guide vanes direct the airflow into the first stage rotor blades at the proper angle and impart a swirling motion to the air entering the compressor. This preswirl, in the direction of engine rotation, improves the aerodynamic characteristics of the compressor by reducing drag on the first stage rotor blades. The inlet guide vanes are curved steel vanes usually welded to steel inner and outer shrouds.

At the discharge end of the compressor, the stator vanes are constructed to straighten the airflow to eliminate turbulence. These vanes are called straightening vanes or the outlet vane assembly. The casings of axial-flow compressors not only support the stator vanes and provide the outer wall of the axial path the air follows, but they also provide the means for extracting compressor air for various purposes. The stator vanes are usually made of steel with corrosion- and erosion-resistant qualities. Quite frequently, they are shrouded (enclosed) by a band of suitable material to simplify the fastening problem. The vanes are welded into the shrouds, and the outer shroud is secured to the compressor housing inner wall by radial retaining screws.

The rotor blades are usually made of stainless steel with the latter stages being made of titanium. The design of

Figure 1-48. *Rotor and stator elements of a typical axial-flow compressor.*

blade attachment to the rotor disk rims varies, but they are commonly fitted into disks by either bulb-type or fir-tree methods. *[Figure 1-49]* The blades are then locked into place by differing methods. Compressor blade tips are reduced in thickness by cutouts, referred to as blade profiles. These profiles prevent serious damage to the blade or housing should the blades contact the compressor housing. This condition can occur if rotor blades become excessively loose or if rotor support is reduced by a malfunctioning bearing. Even though blade profiles greatly reduce such possibilities, occasionally a blade may break under stress of rubbing and cause considerable damage to compressor blades and stator vane assemblies. The blades vary in length from entry to discharge because the annular working space (drum to casing) is reduced progressively toward the rear by the decrease in the casing diameter. *[Figure 1-50]* This feature provides for a fairly constant velocity through the compressor, which helps to keep the flow of air constant.

The rotor features either drum-type or disk-type construction. The drum-type rotor consists of rings that are flanged to fit one against the other, wherein the entire assembly can then be held together by through bolts. This type of construction is satisfactory for low-speed compressors where centrifugal stresses are low. The disk-type rotor consists of a series of disks machined from aluminum forgings, shrunk over a steel shaft, with rotor blades dovetailed into the disk rims. Another method of rotor construction is to machine the disks and shaft from a single aluminum forging, and then to bolt steel stub shafts on the front and rear of the assembly to provide bearing support surfaces and splines for joining the turbine shaft. The drum-type and disk-type rotors are illustrated in *Figures 1-50* and *1-51*, respectively.

Figure 1-49. *Common designs of compressor blade attachment to the rotor disk.*

Figure 1-50. *Drum-type compressor rotor.*

Figure 1-51. *Disk-type compressor rotor.*

The combination of the compressor stages and turbine stages on a common shaft is an engine referred to as an engine spool. The common shaft is provided by joining the turbine and compressor shafts by a suitable method. The engine's spool is supported by bearings, which are seated in suitable bearing housings.

As mentioned earlier, there are two configurations of the axial compressor currently in use: the single rotor/spool and the dual rotor/spool, sometimes referred to as solid spool and split spool (two spool, dual spool).

One version of the solid-spool (one spool) compressor uses variable inlet guide vanes. Also, the first few rows of stator vanes are variable. The main difference between variable inlet guide vane (VIGV) and a variable stator vane (VSV) is their position with regard to the rotor blades. VIGV are in front of the rotor blades, and VSV are behind the rotor blades. The angles of the inlet guide vanes and the first several stages of the stator vanes are can be variable. During operation, air enters the front of the engine and is directed into the compressor at the proper angle by the variable inlet guide and directed by the VSV. The air is compressed and forced into the combustion section. A fuel nozzle that extends into each combustion liner atomizes the fuel for combustion. These variables are controlled in direct relation to the amount of power the engine is required to produce by the power lever position.

Most turbofan engines are of the split-spool compressor type. Most large turbofan engines use a large fan with a few stages of compression called the low-pressure spool. These turbofans incorporate two compressors with their respective turbines and interconnecting shafts, which form two physically independent rotor systems. Many dual rotor systems have rotors turning in opposite directions and with no mechanical connection to each other. The second spool, referred to as the high-pressure spool and is the compressor for the gas generator and core of the engine, supplies air to the combustion section of the engine.

The advantages and disadvantages of both types of compressors are included in the following list. Even though each type has advantages and disadvantages, each has its use by type and size of engine.

The centrifugal-flow compressor's advantages are:

- High pressure rise per stage,
- Efficiency over wide rotational speed range,
- Simplicity of manufacture and low cost,
- Low weight, and
- Low starting power requirements.

The centrifugal-flow compressor's disadvantages are:

- Its large frontal area for a given airflow and
- Losses in turns between stages.

The axial-flow compressor's advantages are:

- High peak efficiencies;
- Small frontal area for given airflow;
- Straight-through flow, allowing high ram efficiency; and
- Increased pressure rise by increasing number of stages, with negligible losses.

The axial-flow compressor's disadvantages are:

- Good efficiencies over only narrow rotational speed range,
- Difficulty of manufacture and high cost,
- Relatively high weight, and
- High starting power requirements (partially overcome by split compressors).

Diffuser

The diffuser is the divergent section of the engine after the compressor and before the combustion section. It has the all-important function of reducing high-velocity compressor discharge air to increased pressure at a slower velocity. This prepares the air for entry into the flame burning area of the combustion section at a lower velocity so that the flame of combustion can burn continuously. If the air passed through the flame area at a high velocity, it could extinguish the flame.

Combustion Section

The combustion section houses the combustion process, which raises the temperature of the air passing through the engine. This process releases energy contained in the air/fuel mixture. The major part of this energy is required at the turbine or turbine stages to drive the compressor. About ⅔ of the energy is used to drive the gas generator compressor. The remaining energy passes through the remaining turbine stages that absorb more of the energy to drive the fan, output shaft, or propeller. Only the pure turbojet allows the air to create all the thrust or propulsion by exiting the rear of the engine in the form of a high-velocity jet. These other engine types have some jet velocity out the rear of the engine but most of the thrust or power is generated by the additional turbine stages driving a large fan, propeller, or helicopter rotor blades.

The primary function of the combustion section is, of course, to burn the fuel/air mixture, thereby adding heat energy to the air. To do this efficiently, the combustion chamber must:

- Provide the means for proper mixing of the fuel and air to assure good combustion,
- Burn this mixture efficiently,
- Cool the hot combustion products to a temperature that the turbine inlet guide vanes/blades can withstand under operating conditions, and
- Deliver the hot gases to the turbine section.

The location of the combustion section is directly between the compressor and the turbine sections. The combustion chambers are always arranged coaxially with the compressor and turbine regardless of type, since the chambers must be in a through-flow position to function efficiently. All combustion chambers contain the same basic elements:

1. Casing
2. Perforated inner liner
3. Fuel injection system
4. Some means for initial ignition
5. Fuel drainage system to drain off unburned fuel after engine shutdown

There are currently three basic types of combustion chambers, variations within type being in detail only. These types are:

1. Can type
2. Can-annular type
3. Annular type

The can-type combustion chamber is typical of the type used on turboshaft and APUs. *[Figure 1-52]* Each of the can-type combustion chambers consists of an outer case or housing, within which there is a perforated stainless steel (highly heat resistant) combustion chamber liner or inner liner. *[Figure 1-53]* The outer case is removed to facilitate liner replacement.

Figure 1-52. *Can-type combustion chamber.*

Older engines with several combustion cans had each can with interconnector (flame propagation) tube, which was a necessary part of the can-type combustion chambers. Since each can is a separate burner operating independently of the other cans, there must be some way to spread combustion during the initial starting operation. This is accomplished by interconnecting all the chambers. As the flame is started by the spark igniter plugs in two of the lower chambers, it passes through the tubes and ignites the combustible mixture

Figure 1-53. *Inside view of a combustion chamber liner.*

in the adjacent chamber, and continues until all the chambers are burning.

The flame tubes vary in construction details from one engine to another, although the basic components are almost identical. *[Figure 1-54]* The spark igniters previously mentioned are normally two in number, and are located in two of the can-type combustion chambers.

Another very important requirement in the construction of combustion chambers is providing the means for draining unburned fuel. This drainage prevents gum deposits in the fuel manifold, nozzles, and combustion chambers. These deposits are caused by the residue left when the fuel evaporates. Probably most important is the danger of afterfire if the fuel is allowed to accumulate after shutdown. If the fuel is not drained, a great possibility exists that, at the next starting attempt, the excess fuel in the combustion chamber will ignite and exhaust gas temperature will exceed safe operating limits.

The liners of the can-type combustors have perforations of various sizes and shapes, each hole having a specific purpose and effect on flame propagation within the liner. *[Figure 1-52]* The air entering the combustion chamber is divided by the proper holes, louvers, and slots into two main streams—primary and secondary air. The primary or combustion air is directed inside the liner at the front end, where it mixes with the fuel and is burned. Secondary or cooling air passes between the outer casing and the liner and joins the combustion gases through larger holes toward the rear of the liner, cooling the combustion gases from about 3,500 °F to near 1,500 °F. To aid in atomization of the fuel, holes are provided around the fuel nozzle in the dome or inlet end of the can-type combustor liner. Louvers are also provided along the axial length of the liners to direct a cooling layer of air along the inside wall of the liner. This layer of air also tends to control the flame pattern by keeping it centered in the liner, thereby preventing burning of the liner walls. *Figure 1-55* illustrates the flow of air through the louvers in the annular combustion chamber.

Some provision is always made in the combustion chamber case for installation of a fuel nozzle. The fuel nozzle delivers the fuel into the liner in a finely atomized spray. The more the spray is atomized, the more rapid and efficient the burning process is.

Two types of fuel nozzle currently being used in the various types of combustion chambers are the simplex nozzle and the duplex nozzle. The construction features of these nozzles are covered in greater detail in Chapter 3, Engine Fuel and Fuel Metering Systems.

Figure 1-54. *Interconnecting flame tubes for can-type combustion chambers.*

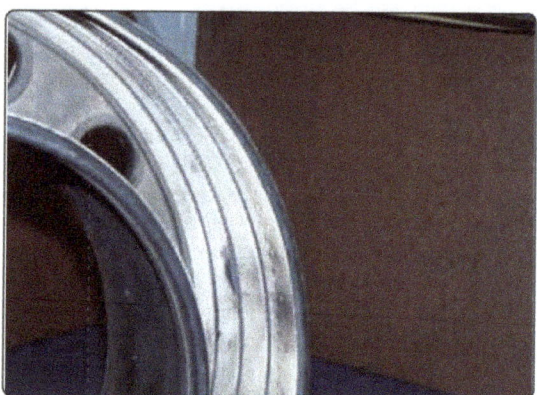

Figure 1-55. *Annular combustion chamber liner.*

The spark igniter plugs of the annular combustion chamber are the same basic type used in the can-type combustion chambers, although construction details may vary. There are usually two igniters mounted on the boss provided on each of the chamber housings. The igniters must be long enough to protrude from the housing into the combustion chamber.

The burners are interconnected by projecting flame tubes which facilitate the engine-starting process as mentioned previously in the can-type combustion chamber familiarization. The flame tubes function identically to those previously discussed, differing only in construction details.

This type of combustion chamber is not used in modern engines. The forward face of each chamber presents six apertures, which align with the six fuel nozzles of the corresponding fuel nozzle cluster. *[Figure 1-56]* These nozzles are the dual-orifice (duplex) type requiring the use of a flow-divider (pressurizing valve), as mentioned in the can-type combustion chamber discussion. Around each nozzle are preswirl vanes for imparting a swirling motion to the fuel spray, which results in better atomization of the fuel, better burning, and efficiency. The swirl vanes function to provide two effects imperative to proper flame propagation:

1. High flame speed—better mixing of air and fuel, ensuring spontaneous burning.

2. Low air velocity axially—swirling eliminates overly rapid flame movement axially.

The swirl vanes greatly aid flame propagation, since a high degree of turbulence in the early combustion and cooling stages is desirable. The vigorous mechanical mixing of the fuel vapor with the primary air is necessary, since mixing by diffusion alone is too slow. This same mechanical mixing is also established by other means, such as placing coarse screens in the diffuser outlet, as is the case in most axial-flow engines.

Figure 1-56. *Can-annular combustion chamber components and arrangement.*

The can-annular combustion chambers also must have the required fuel drain valves located in two or more of the bottom chambers, assuring proper drainage and elimination of residual fuel burning at the next start.

The flow of air through the holes and louvers of the can-annular chambers, is almost identical with the flow through other types of burners. *[Figure 1-56]* Special baffling is used to swirl the combustion airflow and to give it turbulence. *Figure 1-57* shows the flow of combustion air, metal cooling air, and the diluent or gas cooling air. The air flow direction is indicated by the arrows.

Figure 1-57. *Airflow through a can-annular combustion chamber.*

The basic components of an annular combustion chamber are a housing and a liner, as in the can type. The liner consists of an undivided circular shroud extending all the way around the outside of the turbine shaft housing. The chamber may be constructed of heat-resistant materials, which are sometimes coated with thermal barrier materials, such as ceramic materials. The annular combustion chamber is illustrated in *Figure 1-58*. Modern turbine engines usually have an annular combustion chamber. As can be seen in *Figure 1-59*, the annular combustion chamber also uses louvers and holes to prevent the flame from contacting the side of the combustion chamber.

Figure 1-58. *Annular combustion with chamber ceramic coating.*

Figure 1-59. *Combustion chamber louvers and holes.*

Turbine Section

The turbine transforms a portion of the kinetic (velocity) energy of the exhaust gases into mechanical energy to drive the gas generator compressor and accessories. The sole purpose of the gas generator turbine is to absorb approximately 60 to 70 percent of the total pressure energy from the exhaust gases. The exact amount of energy absorption at the turbine is determined by the load the turbine is driving (i.e., compressor size and type, number of accessories, and the load applied by the other turbine stages). These turbine stages can be used to drive a low-pressure compressor (fan), propeller, and shaft. The turbine section of a gas turbine engine is located aft, or downstream, of the combustion chamber. Specifically, it is directly behind the combustion chamber outlet.

The turbine assembly consists of two basic elements: turbine inlet guide vanes and turbine blades. *[Figures 1-60* and *1-61]* The stator element is known by a variety of names, of which turbine inlet nozzle vanes, turbine inlet guide vanes, and nozzle diaphragm are three of the most commonly used. The turbine inlet nozzle vanes are located directly aft of the combustion chambers and immediately forward of the turbine wheel. This is the highest or hottest temperature that comes in contact with metal components in the engine. The turbine inlet temperature must be controlled or damage will occur to the turbine inlet vanes.

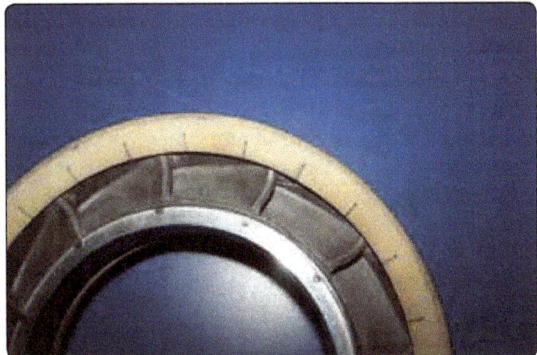

Figure 1-60. *Turbine inlet guide vanes.*

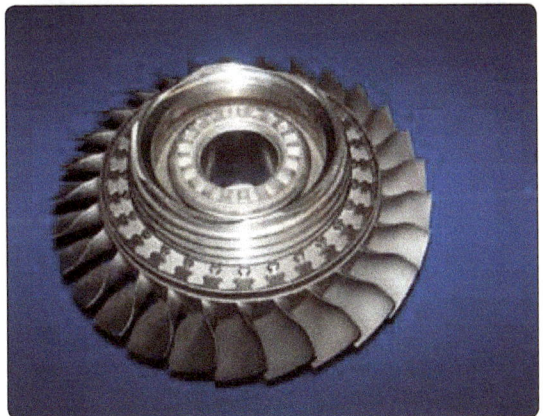

Figure 1-61. *Turbine blades.*

After the combustion chamber has introduced the heat energy into the mass airflow and delivered it evenly to the turbine inlet nozzles, the nozzles must prepare the mass air flow to drive the turbine rotor. The stationary vanes of the turbine inlet nozzles are contoured and set at such an angle that they form a number of small nozzles discharging gas at extremely high speed; thus, the nozzle converts a varying portion of the heat and pressure energy to velocity energy that can then be converted to mechanical energy through the turbine blades.

The second purpose of the turbine inlet nozzle is to deflect the gases to a specific angle in the direction of turbine wheel rotation. Since the gas flow from the nozzle must enter the turbine blade passageway while it is still rotating, it is essential to aim the gas in the general direction of turbine rotation.

The turbine inlet nozzle assembly consists of an inner shroud and an outer shroud between which the nozzle vanes are fixed. The number and size of inlet vanes employed vary with different types and sizes of engines. *Figure 1-62* illustrates typical turbine inlet nozzles featuring loose and welded vanes. The vanes of the turbine inlet nozzle may be assembled between the outer and inner shrouds or rings in a variety of ways. Although the actual elements may vary slightly in configuration and construction features, there is one characteristic peculiar to all turbine inlet nozzles: the nozzle vanes must be constructed to allow thermal expansion. Otherwise, there would be severe distortion or warping of the metal components because of rapid temperature changes. The thermal expansion of turbine nozzles is accomplished by one of several methods. One method necessitates loose assembly of the supporting inner and outer vane shrouds. *[Figure 1-62A]*

Each vane fits into a contoured slot in the shrouds, which conforms to the airfoil shape of the vane. These slots are slightly larger than the vanes to give a loose fit. For further support, the inner and outer shrouds are encased by inner and outer support rings, which provide increased strength and rigidity. These support rings also facilitate removal of the nozzle vanes as a unit. Without the rings, the vanes could fall out as the shrouds were removed.

Another method of thermal expansion construction is to fit the vanes into inner and outer shrouds; however, in this method the vanes are welded or riveted into position. *[Figure 1-62B]* Some means must be provided to allow thermal expansion; therefore, either the inner or the outer shroud ring is cut into segments. The saw cuts separating the segments allow sufficient expansion to prevent stress and warping of the vanes.

The rotor element of the turbine section consists essentially of a shaft and a wheel. *[Figure 1-63]* The turbine wheel is a dynamically balanced unit consisting of blades attached to a rotating disk. The disk, in turn, is attached to the main power-transmitting shaft of the engine. The exhaust gases leaving the turbine inlet nozzle vanes act on the blades of the turbine wheel, causing the assembly to rotate at a very high rate of speed. The high rotational speed imposes severe centrifugal loads on the turbine wheel, and at the same time the elevated temperatures result in a lowering of the strength of the material. Consequently, the engine speed and temperature must be controlled to keep turbine operation within safe limits.

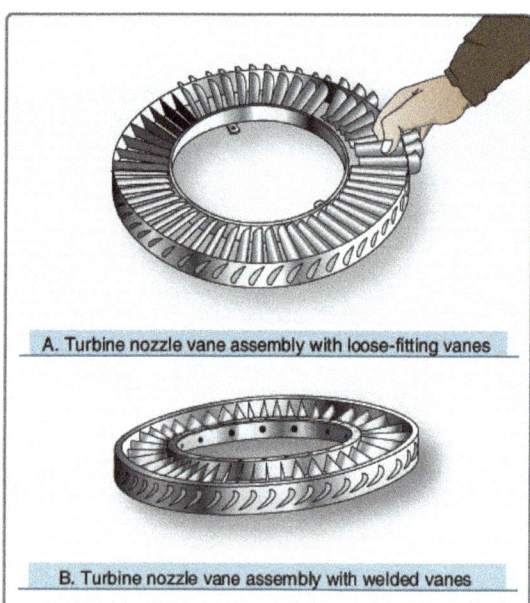

Figure 1-62. *Typical turbine nozzle vane assemblies.*

Figure 1-63. *Rotor elements of the turbine assembly.*

The turbine disk is referred to as such without blades. When the turbine blades are installed, the disk then becomes the turbine wheel. The disk acts as an anchoring component for the turbine blades. Since the disk is bolted or welded to the shaft, the blades can transmit to the rotor shaft the energy they extract from the exhaust gases.

The disk rim is exposed to the hot gases passing through the blades and absorbs considerable heat from these gases. In addition, the rim also absorbs heat from the turbine blades by conduction. Hence, disk rim temperatures are normally high and well above the temperatures of the more remote inner portion of the disk. As a result of these temperature gradients, thermal stresses are added to the rotational stresses. There are various methods to relieve, at least partially, the aforementioned stresses. One such method is to bleed cooling air back onto the face of the disk.

Another method of relieving the thermal stresses of the disk is incidental to blade installation. A series of grooves or notches, conforming to the blade root design, are broached in the rim of the disk. These grooves allow attachment of the turbine blades to the disk; at the same time, space is provided by the notches for thermal expansion of the disk. Sufficient clearance exists between the blade root and the notch to permit movement of the turbine blade when the disk is cold. During engine operation, expansion of the disk decreases the clearance. This causes the blade root to fit tightly in the disk rim.

The turbine shaft is usually fabricated from alloy steel. *[Figure 1-63]* It must be capable of absorbing the high torque loads that are exerted on it.

The methods of connecting the shaft to the turbine disk vary. In one method, the shaft is welded to the disk, which has a butt or protrusion provided for the joint. Another method is by bolting. This method requires that the shaft have a hub that fits a machined surface on the disk face. Then, the bolts are inserted through holes in the shaft hub and anchored in tapped holes in the disk. Of the two connection methods, bolting is more common.

The turbine shaft must have some means for attachment to the compressor rotor hub. This is usually accomplished by a spline cut on the forward end of the shaft. The spline fits into a coupling device between the compressor and turbine shafts. If a coupling is not used, the splined end of the turbine shaft may fit into a splined recess in the compressor rotor hub. This splined coupling arrangement is used almost exclusively with centrifugal compressor engines, while axial compressor engines may use either of these described methods.

There are various ways of attaching turbine blades, some similar to compressor blade attachment. The most satisfactory method utilizes the fir-tree design. *[Figure 1-64]*

Figure 1-64. *Turbine blade with fir-tree design and lock-tab method of blade retention.*

The blades are retained in their respective grooves by a variety of methods, the more common of which are peening, welding, lock tabs, and riveting. *Figure 1-65* shows a typical turbine wheel using rivets for blade retention.

Figure 1-65. *Rivet method of turbine blade retention.*

The peening method of blade retention is used frequently in various ways. One of the most common applications of peening requires a small notch to be ground in the edge of the blade fir-tree root prior to the blade installation. After the blade is inserted into the disk, the notch is filled by the disk metal, which is "flowed" into it by a small punch-mark made in the disk adjacent to the notch. The tool used for this job is similar to a center punch.

1-49

Another method of blade retention is to construct the root of the blade so that it contains all the elements necessary for its retention. This method uses the blade root as a stop made on one end of the root so that the blade can be inserted and removed in one direction only, while on the opposite end is a tang. This tang is bent to secure the blade in the disk.

Turbine blades may be either forged or cast, depending on the composition of the alloys. Most blades are precision cast and finish ground to the desired shape. Many turbine blades are cast as a single crystal, which gives the blades better strength and heat properties. Heat barrier coating, such as ceramic coating, and air flow cooling help keep the turbine blades and inlet nozzles cooler. This allows the exhaust temperature to be raised, increasing the efficiency of the engine. *Figure 1-66* shows a turbine blade with air holes for cooling purposes.

Figure 1-66. *Turbine blade with cooling holes.*

Most turbines are open at the outer perimeter of the blades; however, a second type called the shrouded turbine is sometimes used. The shrouded turbine blades, in effect, form a band around the outer perimeter of the turbine wheel. This improves efficiency and vibration characteristics, and permits lighter stage weights. On the other hand, it limits turbine speed and requires more blades. *[Figure 1-67]*

Figure 1-67. *Shrouded turbine blades.*

In turbine rotor construction, it occasionally becomes necessary to utilize turbines of more than one stage. A single turbine wheel often cannot absorb enough power from the exhaust gases to drive the components dependent on the turbine for rotative power; thus, it is necessary to add additional turbine stages.

A turbine stage consists of a row of stationary vanes or nozzles, followed by a row of rotating blades. In some models of turboprop engine, as many as five turbine stages have been utilized successfully. It should be remembered that, regardless of the number of wheels necessary for driving engine components, there is always a turbine nozzle preceding each wheel.

As was brought out in the preceding discussion of turbine stages, the occasional use of more than one turbine wheel is warranted in cases of heavy rotational loads. It should also be pointed out that the same loads that necessitate multistage turbines often make it advantageous to incorporate multiple compressor rotors.

In the single-stage rotor turbine, the power is developed by one turbine rotor, and all engine-driven parts are driven by this single wheel. *[Figure 1-68]* This arrangement is used on engines where the need for low weight and compactness predominates. This is the simplest version of the pure turbojet engine. A multistage turbine is shown in *Figure 1-69*.

Figure 1-68. *Single-stage rotor turbine.*

Figure 1-69. *Multirotor turbine.*

In multiple spool engines, each spool has its own set of turbine stages. Each set of turbine stages turns the compressor attached to it. Most turbofan engines have two spools: low pressure (fan shaft a few stages of compression and the turbine to drive it) and high pressure (high pressure compressor shaft and high pressure turbine). *[Figure 1-70]*

Figure 1-70. *Dual-rotor turbine for split-spool compressor.*

The remaining element to be discussed concerning turbine familiarization is the turbine casing or housing. The turbine casing encloses the turbine wheel and the nozzle vane assembly, and at the same time gives either direct or indirect support to the stator elements of the turbine section. It always has flanges provided front and rear for bolting the assembly to the combustion chamber housing and the exhaust cone assembly, respectively. A turbine casing is illustrated in *Figure 1-71*.

Figure 1-71. *Turbine casing assembly.*

Exhaust Section

The exhaust section of the gas turbine engine consists of several components. Although the components have individual purposes, they also have one common function: they must direct the flow of hot gases rearward in such a manner as to prevent turbulence and, at the same time, impart a high final or exit velocity to the gases. In performing the various functions, each of the components affects the flow of gases in different ways. The exhaust section is located directly behind the turbine section and ends when the gases are ejected at the rear in the form of a high-velocity exhaust gases. The components of the exhaust section include the exhaust cone, tailpipe (if required), and the exhaust nozzle. The exhaust cone collects the exhaust gases discharged from the turbine section and gradually converts them into a solid flow of gases. In performing this, the velocity of the gases is decreased slightly and the pressure increased. This is due to the diverging passage between the outer duct and the inner cone; that is, the annular area between the two units increases rearward. The exhaust cone assembly consists of an outer shell or duct, an inner cone, three or four radial hollow struts or fins, and the necessary number of tie rods to aid the struts in supporting the inner cone from the outer duct.

The outer shell or duct is usually made of stainless steel and is attached to the rear flange of the turbine case. This element collects the exhaust gases and delivers them directly to the exhaust nozzle. The duct must be constructed to include such features as a predetermined number of thermocouple bosses for installing exhaust temperature thermocouples, and there must also be insertion holes for the supporting tie rods. In some cases, tie rods are not used for supporting the inner cone. If such is the case, the hollow struts provide the sole support of the inner cone, the struts being spot-welded in position to the inside surface of the duct and to the inner cone, respectively. *[Figure 1-72]* The radial struts actually have a twofold function. They not only support the inner cone in the exhaust duct, but they also perform the important function of straightening the swirling exhaust gases that would otherwise leave the turbine at an angle of approximately 45°.

Figure 1-72. *Exhaust collector with welded support struts.*

The centrally located inner cone fits rather closely against the rear face of the turbine disk, preventing turbulence of the gases as they leave the turbine wheel. The cone is supported by the radial struts. In some configurations, a small hole is located in the exit tip of the cone. This hole allows cooling air to be circulated from the aft end of the cone, where the pressure of the gases is relatively high, into the interior of the cone and consequently against the face of the turbine wheel. The flow of air is positive, since the air pressure at the turbine wheel is relatively low due to rotation of the wheel; thus air circulation is assured. The gases used for cooling the turbine wheel return to the main path of flow by passing through the clearance between the turbine disk and the inner cone. The exhaust cone assembly is the terminating component of the basic engine. The remaining component (the exhaust nozzle) is usually considered an airframe component.

The tailpipe is usually constructed so that it is semiflexible. On some tailpipes, a bellows arrangement is incorporated in its construction, allowing movement in installation, maintenance, and in thermal expansion. This eliminates stress and warping which would otherwise be present.

The heat radiation from the exhaust cone and tailpipe could damage the airframe components surrounding these units. For this reason, some means of insulation had to be devised. There are several suitable methods of protecting the fuselage structure; two of the most common are insulation blankets and shrouds.

The insulation blanket, illustrated in *Figures 1-73* and *1-74*, consists of several layers of aluminum foil, each separated by a layer of fiberglass or some other suitable material. Although these blankets protect the fuselage from heat radiation, they are used primarily to reduce heat loss from the exhaust system. The reduction of heat loss improves engine performance.

Figure 1-73. *Exhaust system insulation blanket.*

There are two types of exhaust nozzle designs: the converging design for subsonic gas velocities and the converging-diverging design for supersonic gas velocities. These exhaust nozzle designs are discussed in greater detail in Chapter 2, Induction and Exhaust Systems.

The exhaust nozzle opening may be of either fixed or variable area. The fixed-area type is the simpler of the two exhaust nozzles since there are no moving parts. The outlet area of the fixed exhaust nozzle is very critical to engine performance. If the nozzle area is too large, thrust is wasted; if the area is too small, the engine could choke or stall. A variable-area exhaust nozzle is used when an augmenter or afterburner is used due to the increased mass of flow when the afterburner is activated. It must increase its open area when the afterburner is selected. When the afterburner is off, the exhaust nozzle closes to a smaller area of opening.

Gas Turbine Engine Bearings and Seals

The main bearings have the critical function of supporting the main engine rotor. The number of bearings necessary for proper engine support is, for the most part, determined by the length and weight of the engine rotor. The length and weight are directly affected by the type of compressor used in the engine. Naturally, a two-spool compressor requires more bearing support. The minimum number of bearings required to support one shaft is one deep groove ball bearing (thrust and radial loads) and one straight roller bearing (radial load only). Sometimes, it is necessary to use more than one roller bearing if the shaft is subject to vibration or its length is excessive. The gas turbine rotors are supported by ball and roller bearings, which are antifriction bearings. *[Figure 1-75]* Many newer engines use hydraulic bearings, in which the outside race is surrounded by a thin film of oil. This reduces vibrations transmitted to the engine.

In general, antifriction bearings are preferred largely because they:

- Offer little rotational resistance,
- Facilitate precision alignment of rotating elements,
- Are relatively inexpensive,
- Are easily replaced,
- Withstand high momentary overloads,
- Are simple to cool, lubricate, and maintain,
- Accommodate both radial and axial loads, and
- Are relatively resistant to elevated temperatures.

The main disadvantages are their vulnerability to foreign matter and tendency to fail without appreciable warning. Usually the ball bearings are positioned on the compressor or turbine shaft so that they can absorb any axial (thrust) loads or radial loads. Because the roller bearings present a larger working surface, they are better equipped to support radial loads than thrust loads. Therefore, they are used primarily for this purpose. A typical ball or roller bearing assembly

Figure 1-74. *Insulation blanket with the temperatures obtained at the various locations shown.*

includes a bearing support housing, which must be strongly constructed and supported in order to carry the radial and axial loads of the rapidly rotating rotor. The bearing housing usually contains oil seals to prevent the oil leaking from its normal path of flow. It also delivers the oil to the bearing for its lubrication, usually through spray nozzles. The oil seals may be the labyrinth or thread (helical) type. These seals also may be pressurized to minimize oil leaking along the compressor shaft. The labyrinth seal is usually pressurized, but the helical seal depends solely on reverse threading to stop oil leakage. These two types of seals are very similar, differing only in thread size and the fact that the labyrinth seal is pressurized.

Another type of oil seal used on some of the later engines is the carbon seal. These seals are usually spring loaded and are similar in material and application to the carbon brushes used in electrical motors. Carbon seals rest against a surface provided to create a sealed bearing cavity or void; thus, the oil is prevented from leaking out along the shaft into the compressor airflow or the turbine section. *[Figure 1-76]*

The ball or roller bearing is fitted into the bearing housing and may have a self-aligning feature. If a bearing is self-aligning, it is usually seated in a spherical ring. This allows the shaft a certain amount of radial movement without transmitting stress to the bearing inner race.

The bearing surface is usually provided by a machined journal on the appropriate shaft. The bearing is usually locked in position by a steel snap ring or other suitable locking device. The rotor shaft also provides the matching surface for the oil seals in the bearing housing. These machined surfaces are called lands and fit in rather close to the oil seal.

Figure 1-75. *Types of main bearings used for gas turbine rotor support.*

Turboprop Engines

The turbopropeller (turboprop) engine is a combination of a gas turbine engine, reduction gear box, and a propeller. *[Figure 1-77]* Turboprops are basically gas turbine engines that have a compressor, combustion chamber(s), turbine, and an exhaust nozzle (gas generator), all of which operate in the same manner as any other gas engine. However, the difference is that the turbine in the turboprop engine usually has extra stages to extract energy to drive the propeller. In addition to operating the compressor and accessories, the turboprop turbine transmits increased power forward through a shaft and a gear train to drive the propeller. The increased power is generated by the exhaust gases passing through additional stages of the turbine.

Some engines use a multirotor turbine with coaxial shafts for independent driving of the compressor and propeller. Although there are three turbines utilized in this illustration, as many as five turbine stages have been used for driving the two rotor elements, propeller, and accessories.

The exhaust gases also contribute to engine power output through thrust production, although the amount of energy available for thrust is considerably reduced. Two basic types of turboprop engine are in use: fixed turbine and free turbine. The fixed turbine has a mechanical connection from the gas generator (gas-turbine engine) to the reduction gear box

Figure 1-76. *Carbon oil seal.*

and propeller. The free turbine has only an air link from gas generator to the power turbines. There is no mechanical link from the propeller to the gas turbine engine (gas generator).

1-54

Figure 1-77. *PT6 turboprop engine.*

There are advantages and disadvantages of each system, with the airframe generally dictating the system used.

Since the basic components of normal gas-turbine and turboprop engines differ slightly only in design features, it should be fairly simple to apply acquired knowledge of the basic gas turbine to the turboprop.

The typical turboprop engine can be broken down into assemblies as follows:

1. The power section assembly—contains the usual major components of a gas turbine engine (i.e., compressor, combustion chamber, turbine, and exhaust sections).
2. The reduction gear or gearbox assembly—contains those sections unique to turboprop configurations.
3. The torquemeter assembly—transmits the torque from the engine to the gearbox of the reduction section.
4. The accessory drive housing assembly—mounted on the bottom of the compressor air inlet housing. It includes the necessary gear trains for driving all power section driven accessories at their proper rpm in relation to engine rpm.

Turboshaft Engines

A gas-turbine engine that delivers power through a shaft to operate something other than a propeller is referred to as a turboshaft engine. *[Figure 1-78]* The output shaft may be coupled directly to the engine turbine, or the shaft may be driven by a turbine of its own (free turbine) located in the exhaust stream. As mentioned with the turboprop, the free turbine rotates independently. This principle is used extensively in current production of turboshaft engines. The turboshaft engine's output is measured in horsepower instead of thrust because the power output is a turning shaft.

Turbofan Engines

The turbofan gas turbine engine is, in principle, the same as a turboprop, except that the propeller is replaced by a duct-enclosed axial-flow fan. *[Figure 1-79]* The fan can be a part of the first-stage compressor blades or can be mounted as a separate set of fan blades. The blades can be mounted forward of the compressor.

The general principle of the fan engine is to convert more of the fuel energy into pressure. With more of the energy converted to pressure, a greater product of pressure times area can be achieved. One of the major advantages is turbofan production of this additional thrust without increasing fuel flow. The end result is fuel economy with the consequent increase in range. Because more of the fuel energy is turned into pressure in the turbofan engine, additional stages must be added in the turbine section to provide the power to drive the fan. This means there is less energy left over and less thrust from the core exhaust gases. Also, in a mixed-exhaust nozzle (where fan air and core air mix in a common nozzle before entering ambient conditions) the exhaust nozzle must be larger in area. The result is that the fan develops most of the thrust. The thrust produced by the fan more than makes up for the decrease in thrust of the core (gas generator) of the engine. Depending on the fan design and bypass ratio, it produces 80 percent of the turbofan engine's total thrust.

1-55

Figure 1-78. *Turboshaft engine.*

Figure 1-79. *Turbofan engine.*

Two different exhaust nozzle designs are used with turbofan engines. The air leaving the fan can be ducted overboard by a separate fan nozzle *[Figure 1-43]*, or it can be ducted along the outer case of the basic engine to be discharged through the mixed nozzle (core and fan exhaust together). The fan air is either mixed with the exhaust gases before it is discharged (mixed or common nozzle), or it passes directly to the atmosphere without prior mixing (separate nozzle). Turbofans are the most widely used gas turbine engine for air transport aircraft. The turbofan is a compromise between the good operating efficiency and high thrust capability of a turboprop and the high speed, high altitude capability of a turbojet.

Turbine Engine Operating Principles

The principle used by a gas turbine engine as it provides force to move an airplane is based on Newton's law of momentum. This law states that for every action there is an equal and opposite reaction; therefore, if the engine accelerates a mass of air (action), it applies a force on the aircraft (reaction). The turbofan generates thrust by giving a relatively slower acceleration to a large quantity of air. The old pure turbojet engine achieves thrust by imparting greater acceleration to a smaller quantity of air. This was its main problem with fuel consumption and noise.

The mass of air is accelerated within the engine by the use of a continuous-flow cycle. Ambient air enters the inlet diffuser where it is subjected to changes in temperature, pressure, and velocity due to ram effect. The compressor then increases pressure and temperature of the air mechanically. The air continues at constant pressure to the burner section where its temperature is increased by combustion of fuel. The energy is taken from the hot gas by expanding through a turbine which drives the compressor, and by expanding through an exhaust nozzle designed to discharge the exhaust gas at high velocity to produce thrust.

The high velocity gases from the engine may be considered continuous, imparting this force against the aircraft in which it is installed, thereby producing thrust. The formula for thrust can be derived from Newton's second law, which states that force is proportional to the product of mass and acceleration. This law is expressed in the formula:

$$F = M \times A$$

where;

F = force in pounds

M = mass in pounds per seconds

A = acceleration in feet per seconds

In the above formula, mass is similar to weight, but it is actually a different quantity. Mass refers to the quantity of matter, while weight refers to the pull of gravity on that quantity of matter. At sea level under standard conditions, 1 pound of mass has a weight of 1 pound. To calculate the acceleration of a given mass, the gravitational constant is used as a unit of comparison. The force of gravity is 32.2 feet per second squared (ft/sec^2). This means that a free falling 1 pound object accelerates at the rate of 32.2 feet per second each second that gravity acts on it. Since the object mass weighs 1 pound, which is also the actual force imparted to it by gravity, it can be assumed that a force of 1 pound accelerates a 1-1 object at the rate of 32.2 ft/sec^2.

Also, a force of 10 pound accelerates a mass of 10 pound at the rate of 32.2 ft/sec^2. This is assuming there is no friction or other resistance to overcome. It is now apparent that the ratio of the force (in pounds) is to the mass (in pounds) as the acceleration in ft/sec^2 is to 32.2. Using M to represent the mass in pounds, the formula may be expressed thus:

$$\frac{F}{M} = \frac{A}{G} \quad \text{or} \quad F = \frac{MA}{G}$$

where:

F = force

M = mass

A = acceleration

G = gravity

In any formula involving work, the time factor must be considered. It is convenient to have all time factors in equivalent units (i.e., seconds, minutes, or hours). In calculating jet thrust, the term "pounds of air per second" is convenient, since the second is the same unit of time used for the force of gravity.

Thrust

Using the formula below, compute the force necessary to accelerate a mass of 50 pounds by 100 ft/sec^2.

$$F = \frac{MA}{G}$$

$$F = \frac{50 \text{ lb} \times 100 \text{ ft/sec}^2}{32.2 \text{ ft/sec}^2}$$

$$F = \frac{5{,}000 \text{ lb-ft/sec}^2}{32.2 \text{ ft/sec}^2}$$

$$F = 155 \text{ lb}$$

This illustrates that if the velocity mass per second is increased by 100, the resulting thrust is 155 pounds.

Since the turbojet engine accelerates air, the following formula can be used to determine jet thrust:

$$F = \frac{M_s (V_2 - V_1)}{G}$$

where:

- F = force in pounds
- M_s = mass flow in lb/sec
- V_1 = inlet velocity
- V_2 = jet velocity (exhaust)
- $V_2 - V_1$ = change in velocity; difference between inlet velocity and jet velocity
- G = Acceleration of gravity or 32.2 ft/sec²

As an example, to use the formula for changing the velocity of 100 pounds of mass airflow per second from 600 ft/sec to 800 ft/sec, the formula can be applied as follows:

$$F = \frac{100 \text{ lb/sec } (800 \text{ ft/sec} - 600 \text{ ft/sec})}{32.2 \text{ ft/sec}^2}$$

$$F = \frac{20,000 \text{ lb/sec}}{32.2 \text{ ft/sec}^2}$$

$$F = 621 \text{ lb}$$

As shown by the formula, if the mass airflow per second and the difference in the velocity of the air from the intake to the exhaust are known, it is easy to compute the force necessary to produce the change in the velocity. Therefore, the thrust of the engine must be equal to the force required to accelerate the air mass through the engine. Then, by using the symbol "Fn" for thrust pounds, the formula becomes:

$$F_n = \frac{M_s (V_2 - V_1)}{G}$$

Thrust of a gas turbine engine can be increased by two methods: increasing the mass flow of air through the engine or increasing the gas velocity. If the velocity of the turbojet engine remains constant with respect to the aircraft, the thrust decreases if the speed of the aircraft is increased. This is because V_1 increases in value. This does not present a serious problem, however, because as the aircraft speed increases, more air enters the engine, and jet velocity increases. The resultant net thrust is almost constant with increased airspeed.

The Brayton cycle is the name given to the thermodynamic cycle of a gas turbine engine to produce thrust. This is a variable volume constant-pressure cycle of events and is commonly called the constant-pressure cycle. A more recent term is "continuous combustion cycle." The four continuous and constant events are intake, compression, expansion (includes power), and exhaust. These cycles are discussed as they apply to a gas-turbine engine. In the intake cycle, air enters at ambient pressure and a constant volume. It leaves the intake at an increased pressure and a decrease in volume. At the compressor section, air is received from the intake at an increased pressure, slightly above ambient, and a slight decrease in volume. Air enters the compressor where it is compressed. It leaves the compressor with a large increase in pressure and decrease in volume, created by the mechanical action of the compressor. The next step, expansion, takes place in the combustion chamber by burning fuel, which expands the air by heating it. The pressure remains relatively constant, but a marked increase in volume takes place. The expanding gases move rearward through the turbine assembly and are converted from velocity energy to mechanical energy by the turbine. The exhaust section, which is a convergent duct, converts the expanding volume and decreasing pressure of the gases to a final high velocity. The force created inside the engine to keep this cycle continuous has an equal and opposite reaction (thrust) to move the aircraft forward.

Bernoulli's principle (whenever a stream of any fluid has its velocity increased at a given point, the pressure of the stream at that point is less than the rest of the stream) is applied to gas turbine engines through the design of convergent and divergent air ducts. The convergent duct increases velocity and decreases pressure. The divergent duct decreases velocity and increases pressure. The convergent principle is usually used for the exhaust nozzle. The divergent principle is used in the compressor and diffuser where the air is slowing and pressurizing.

Gas Turbine Engine Performance

Thermal efficiency is a prime factor in gas turbine performance. It is the ratio of net work produced by the engine to the chemical energy supplied in the form of fuel. The three most important factors affecting the thermal efficiency are turbine inlet temperature, compression ratio, and the component efficiencies of the compressor and turbine. Other factors that affect thermal efficiency are compressor inlet temperature and combustion efficiency. *Figure 1-80* shows the effect that changing compression ratio (compressor pressure ratio) has on thermal efficiency when compressor inlet temperature and the component efficiencies of the compressor and turbine remain constant. The effects that compressor and turbine component efficiencies have on thermal efficiency when turbine and compressor inlet temperatures remain constant are shown in *Figure 1-81*. In actual operation, the turbine engine exhaust temperature varies directly with turbine inlet temperature at a constant compression ratio.

Figure 1-80. *The effect of compression ratio on thermal efficiency.*

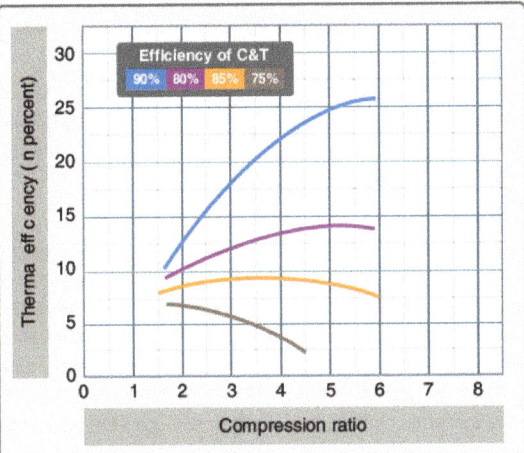

Figure 1-81. *Turbine and compressor efficiency vs. thermal efficiency.*

Rpm is a direct measure of compression ratio; therefore, at constant rpm, maximum thermal efficiency can be obtained by maintaining the highest possible exhaust temperature. Since engine life is greatly reduced at high turbine inlet temperatures, the operator should not exceed the exhaust temperatures specified for continuous operation. *Figure 1-82* illustrates the effect of turbine inlet temperature on turbine blade life. In the previous discussion, it was assumed that the state of the air at the inlet to the compressor remains constant. Since this is a practical application of a turbine engine, it becomes necessary to analyze the effect of varying inlet conditions on the thrust or power produced. The three principal variables that affect inlet conditions are the speed of the aircraft, the altitude of the aircraft, and the ambient temperature. To make the analysis simpler, the combination of these three variables can be represented by a single variable called stagnation density.

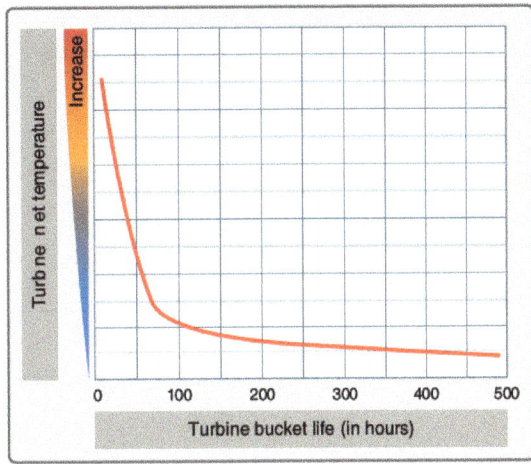

Figure 1-82. *Effect of turbine inlet temperature on turbine bucket life.*

The power produced by a turbine engine is proportional to the stagnation density at the inlet. The next three illustrations show how changing the density by varying altitude, airspeed, and outside air temperature affects the power level of the engine. *Figure 1-83* shows that the thrust output improves rapidly with a reduction in outside air temperature (OAT) at constant altitude, rpm, and airspeed. This increase occurs partly because the energy required per pound of airflow to drive the compressor varies directly with the temperature, leaving more energy to develop thrust. In addition, the thrust output increases since the air at reduced temperature has an increased density. The increase in density causes the mass flow through the engine to increase. The altitude effect on thrust, as shown in *Figure 1-84*, can also be discussed as a density and temperature effect. In this case, an increase in altitude causes a decrease in pressure and temperature.

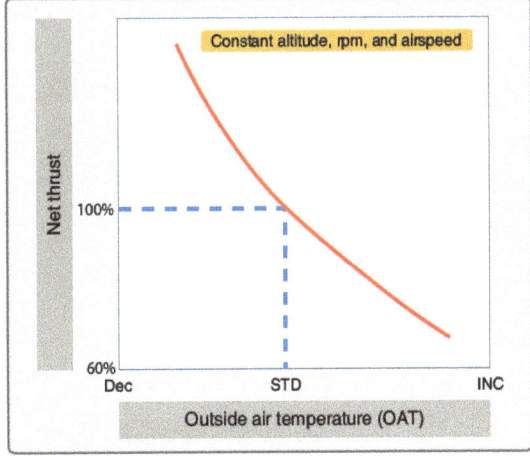

Figure 1-83. *Effect of OAT on thrust output.*

1-59

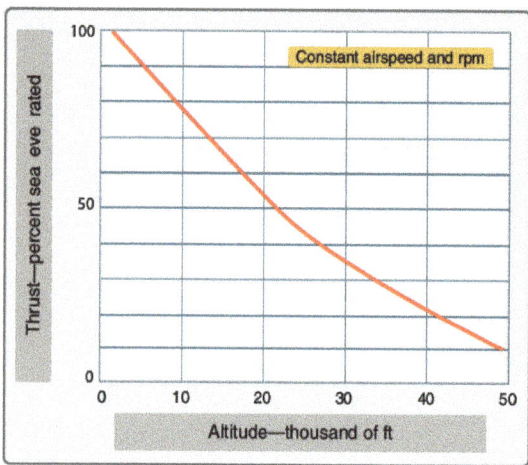

Figure 1-84. *Effect of altitude on thrust output.*

Since the temperature lapse rate is lower than the pressure lapse rate as altitude is increased, the density is decreased. Although the decreased temperature increases thrust, the effect of decreased density more than offsets the effect of the colder temperature. The net result of increased altitude is a reduction in the thrust output.

The effect of airspeed on the thrust of a gas-turbine engine is shown in *Figure 1-85*. To explain the airspeed effect, it is necessary to understand first the effect of airspeed on the factors that combine to produce net thrust: specific thrust and engine airflow. Specific thrust is the net thrust in pounds developed per pound of airflow per second. It is the remainder of specific gross thrust minus specific ram drag. As airspeed is increased, ram drag increases rapidly. The exhaust velocity remains relatively constant; thus, the effect of the increase in airspeed results in decreased specific thrust. *[Figure 1-85]* In the low-speed range, the specific thrust decreases faster than the airflow increases and causes a decrease in net thrust. As the airspeed increases into the higher range, the airflow increases faster than the specific thrust decreases and causes the net thrust to increase until sonic velocity is reached. The effect of the combination on net thrust is illustrated in *Figure 1-86*.

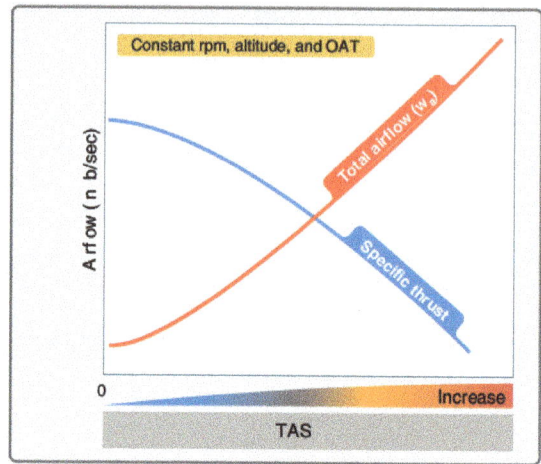

Figure 1-86. *Effect of airspeed on specific thrust and total engine airflow.*

Ram Recovery

A rise in pressure above existing outside atmospheric pressure at the engine inlet, as a result of the forward velocity of an aircraft, is referred to as ram pressure. Since any ram effect causes an increase in compressor entrance pressure over atmospheric, the resulting pressure rise causes an increase in the mass airflow and gas velocity, both of which tend to increase thrust. Although ram effect increases engine thrust, the thrust being produced by the engine decreases for a given throttle setting as the aircraft gains airspeed. Therefore, two opposing trends occur when an aircraft's speed is increased. What actually takes place is the net result of these two different effects.

An engine's thrust output temporarily decreases as aircraft speed increases from static, but soon ceases to decrease. Moving toward higher speeds, thrust output begins to increase again due to the increased pressure of ram recovery.

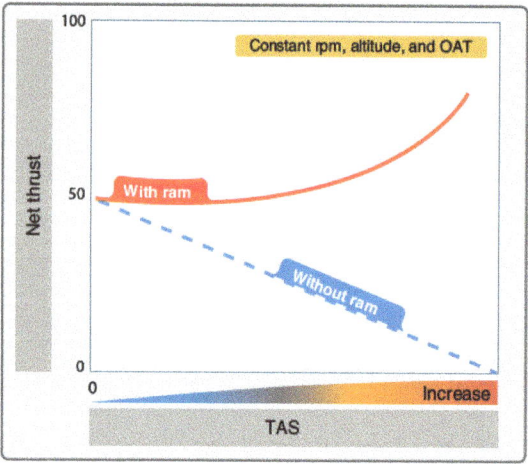

Figure 1-85. *Effect of airspeed on net thrust.*

Chapter 2
Engine Fuel and Fuel Metering Systems

Fuel System Requirements

The engine fuel system must supply fuel to the engine's fuel metering device under all conditions of ground and air operation. It must function properly at constantly changing altitudes and in any climate. The most common fuels are AVGAS for reciprocating engines and Jet A for turbine engines. AVGAS is generally either 80 (red) or 100LL (blue) octane. The LL stands for low lead although it contains four times the lead of 80 octane AVGAS. Jet A is a kerosene-based fuel that is clear to straw in color.

Electronic engine controls have allowed great increases in controlling the metered fuel flow to the engine. Engine fuel systems have become very accurate at providing the correct mixture of fuel and air to the engines. Gas turbine fuel controls have also greatly improved the ability to schedule (meter) the fuel correctly during all flight regimes. Improvements in electronics and the use of digital computers have enabled the aircraft and engines to be electronically interfaced together. By the use of electronic sensors and computer logic built in to electronic controls, the engines can be controlled with much more accuracy. Fuel cost and availability have also become factors in providing engines with fuel systems that are efficient and very precise in scheduling fuel flow to the engine. Many engines use an interactive system that senses engine parameters and feeds the information to the onboard computer (electronic engine control). The computer determines the amount of fuel needed and then sends a signal to the metering device. This signal sent to the metering device determines the correct amount of fuel needed by the engine. Electronic controls have become quite common with gas turbines and have increased the capabilities of the fuel system, making it less complicated for the technician and decreasing maintenance problems.

Engine fuel systems can be fairly complicated, yet some are quite simple, such as on small aircraft with a simple gravity-feed fuel system. This system, consisting of a tank to supply fuel to the engine, is often installed in the overhead wing and feeds a small float-type carburetor. On multiengine aircraft, complex systems are necessary so that fuel can be pumped from any combination of tanks to any combination of engines through a crossfeed system. Provisions for transferring fuel from one tank to another may also be included on large aircraft.

Vapor Lock

All fuel systems should be designed so that vapor lock cannot take place. Older gravity-feed systems were more prone to vapor lock. The fuel system should be free of tendency to vapor lock, which can result from changes in ground and in-flight climatic conditions. Normally, the fuel remains in a liquid state until it is discharged into the air stream and then instantly changes to a vapor. Under certain conditions, the fuel may vaporize in the lines, pumps, or other units. The vapor pockets formed by this premature vaporization restrict the fuel flow through units which are designed to handle liquids rather than gases. The resulting partial or complete interruption of the fuel flow is called vapor lock. The three general causes of vapor lock are the lowering of the pressure on the fuel, high fuel temperatures, and excessive fuel turbulence.

At high altitudes, the pressure on the fuel in the tank is low. This lowers the boiling point of the fuel and causes vapor bubbles to form. This vapor trapped in the fuel may cause vapor lock in the fuel system.

Transfer of heat from the engine tends to cause boiling of the fuel in the lines and the pump. This tendency is increased if the fuel in the tank is warm. High fuel temperatures often combine with low pressure to increase vapor formation. This is most apt to occur during a rapid climb on a hot day. As the aircraft climbs, the outside temperature drops, but the fuel does not lose temperature rapidly. If the fuel is warm enough at takeoff, it retains enough heat to boil easily at high altitude. The chief causes of fuel turbulence are sloshing of the fuel in the tanks, the mechanical action of the engine-driven pump, and sharp bends or rises in the fuel lines. Sloshing in the tank tends to mix air with the fuel. As this mixture passes through the lines, the trapped air separates from the fuel and forms vapor pockets at any point where there are abrupt changes in direction or steep rises. Turbulence in the fuel pump often combines with the low pressure at the pump inlet to form a vapor lock at this point.

Vapor lock can become serious enough to block the fuel flow completely and stop the engine. Even small amounts of vapor in the inlet line restrict the flow to the engine-driven pump and reduce its output pressure. To reduce the possibility of vapor lock, fuel lines are kept away from sources of heat; also, sharp bends and steep rises are avoided. In addition, the volatility of the fuel is controlled in manufacture so that it does not vaporize too readily. The major improvement in reducing vapor lock, however, is the incorporation of booster pumps in the fuel system. These booster pumps, which are used widely in most modern aircraft, keep the fuel in the lines to the engine-driven pump under pressure. The pressure on the fuel reduces vapor formation and aids in moving a vapor pocket along. The boost pump also releases vapor from the fuel as it passes through the pump. The vapor moves upward through the fuel in the tank and out the tank vents. To prevent the small amount of vapor that remains in the fuel from upsetting its metering action, vapor eliminators are installed in some fuel systems ahead of the metering device or are built into this unit.

Basic Fuel System

The basic parts of a fuel system include tanks, boost pumps, lines, selector valves, strainers, engine-driven pumps, and pressure gauges. A review of fuel systems in the Aviation Maintenance Technician—General Handbook provides some information concerning these components.

Generally, there are several tanks, even in a simple system, to store the required amount of fuel. The location of these tanks depends on both the fuel system design and the structural design of the aircraft. From each tank, a line leads to the selector valve. This valve is set from the cockpit to select the tank from which fuel is to be delivered to the engine. The boost pump forces fuel through the selector valve to the main line strainer. This filtering unit, located in the lowest part of the system, removes water and dirt from the fuel. During starting, the boost pump forces fuel through a bypass in the engine-driven pump to the metering device. Once the engine-driven pump is rotating at sufficient speed, it takes over and delivers fuel to the metering device at the specified pressure.

The airframe fuel system begins with the fuel tank and ends at the engine fuel system. The engine fuel system usually includes the engine-driven pumps and the fuel metering systems. In aircraft powered with a reciprocating engine, the engine-driven fuel pump and metering system consists of the main components from the point at which the fuel enters the first control unit until the fuel is injected into the intake pipe or cylinder. For example, the engine fuel system of a typical engine has an engine-driven fuel pump, the fuel/air control unit (metering device), the fuel manifold valve, and the fuel discharge nozzles. The fuel metering system on current reciprocating engines meters the fuel at a predetermined ratio to airflow. The airflow to the engine is controlled by the carburetor or fuel/air control unit.

The fuel metering system of the typical gas turbine engine consists of an engine-driven pump, fuel flow transmitter, fuel control with an electronic engine control, a distribution system or manifold, flow divider, and fuel discharge nozzles. On some turboprop engines, a fuel heater and a start control is a part of the engine fuel system. The rate of fuel delivery can be a function of air mass flow, compressor inlet temperature, compressor discharge pressure, compressor revolutions per minute (rpm), exhaust gas temperature, and combustion chamber pressure.

Fuel Metering Devices for Reciprocating Engines

Basic principles of operation are discussed here with no attempt being made to give detailed maintenance instructions. For the specific information needed to inspect or maintain a particular installation or unit, consult the manufacturer's instructions.

The basic requirement of a reciprocating fuel metering system is the same, regardless of the type of system used or the model engine on which the equipment is installed. It must meter fuel proportionately to air to establish the proper fuel/air mixture ratio for the engine at all speeds and altitudes at which the engine may be operated. In the fuel/air mixture curves shown in *Figure 2-1*, note that the basic best power and best economy fuel/air mixture requirements for reciprocating engines are approximately the same. The fuel metering system must atomize and distribute the fuel from the carburetor into the mass airflow. This must be accomplished so that the fuel/air charges going to all cylinders holds equal amounts of fuel. Each one of the engine's cylinders should receive the same quantity of fuel/air mixture and at the same fuel/air ratio.

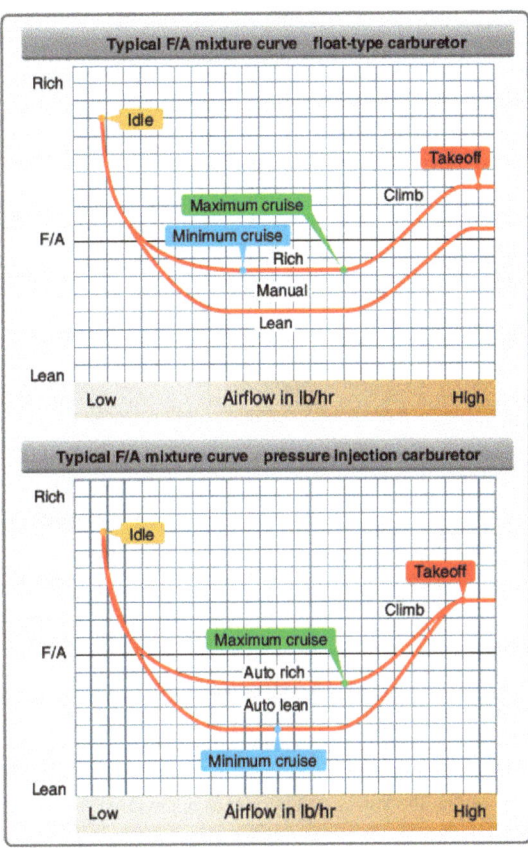

Figure 2-1. *Fuel/air mixture curves.*

Due to the drop in atmospheric pressure as altitude is increased, the density of the air also decreases. A normally-aspirated engine has a fixed amount or volume of air that it can draw in during the intake stroke, therefore less air is drawn into the engine as altitude increases. Less air tends to make carburetors run richer at altitude than at ground level, because of the decreased density of the airflow through the carburetor throat for a given volume of air. Thus, it is necessary that a mixture control be provided to lean the mixture and compensate for this natural enrichment. Some aircraft use carburetors in which the mixture control is operated manually. Other aircraft employ carburetors which automatically lean the carburetor mixture at altitude to maintain the proper fuel/air mixture.

The rich mixture requirements for an aircraft engine are established by running a power curve to determine the fuel/air mixture for obtaining maximum usable power. This curve is plotted at 100 rpm intervals from idle speed to takeoff speed. *[Figure 2-2]* Since it is necessary in the power range to add fuel to the basic fuel/air mixture requirements to keep cylinder-head temperatures in a safe range, the fuel mixture must become gradually richer as powers above cruise are used. *[Figure 2-1]* In the power range, the engine runs on a much leaner mixture, as indicated in the curves. However, on the leaner mixture, cylinder-head temperature would exceed the maximum permissible temperatures and detonation would occur.

Figure 2-3. *Specific fuel consumption curve.*

Figure 2-2. *Power versus fuel/air mixture curve.*

The best economy setting is established by running a series of curves through the cruise range, as shown in the graph in *Figure 2-3*, the low point (auto-lean) in the curve being the fuel/air mixture where the minimum fuel per horsepower is used. In this range the engine operates normally on slightly leaner mixtures and obviously operates on richer mixtures than the low-point mixture. If a mixture leaner than that specified for the engine is used, the leanest cylinder of the engine is apt to backfire because the slower burning rate of the lean mixture results in a continued burning in the cylinder when the next intake stroke starts.

Fuel/Air Mixtures

Gasoline and other liquid fuels do not burn at all unless they are mixed with air. If the mixture is to burn properly within the engine cylinder, the ratio of air to fuel must be kept within a certain range. It would be more accurate to state that the fuel is burned with the oxygen in the air. Seventy-eight percent of air by volume is nitrogen, which is inert and does not participate in the combustion process, and 21 percent is oxygen. Heat is generated by burning the mixture of gasoline and oxygen. Nitrogen and gaseous byproducts of combustion absorb this heat energy and turn it into power by expansion. The mixture proportion of fuel and air by weight is of extreme importance to engine performance. The characteristics of a given mixture can be measured in terms of flame speed and combustion temperature.

The composition of the fuel/air mixture is described by the mixture ratio. For example, a mixture with a ratio of 12 to 1 (12:1) is made up of 12 pounds of air and 1 pound of fuel. The ratio is expressed in weight because the volume of air varies greatly with temperature and pressure. The mixture ratio can also be expressed as a decimal. Thus, a fuel/air ratio of 12:1 and a fuel/air ratio of 0.083 describe the same mixture ratio. Mixtures of air and gasoline as rich as 8:1 and as lean as 16:1 will burn in an engine cylinder, but beyond these mixtures, either lean or rich blow out could occur. The engine develops maximum power with a mixture of approximately 12 parts of air and 1 part of gasoline by weight.

From a chemist's point of view, the perfect mixture for combustion of fuel and air would be 0.067 pounds of fuel to 1 pound of air (mixture ratio of 15:1). The scientist calls this chemically correct combination a stoichiometric mixture (pronounced stoy-key-o-metric). With this mixture (given sufficient time and turbulence), all the fuel and all the oxygen in the air is completely used in the combustion process. The stoichiometric mixture produces the highest combustion temperatures because the proportion of heat released to a mass of charge (fuel and air) is the greatest. If more fuel is added to the same quantity of air charge than the amount giving a chemically perfect mixture, changes of power and temperature occur. The combustion gas temperature is lowered as the mixture is enriched, and the power increases until the fuel/air ratio is approximately 0.0725. For mixtures from 0.0725 fuel/air ratio to 0.080 fuel/air ratio, the power remains essentially constant even though the combustion temperature continues downward. Mixtures from 0.0725 fuel/air ratio to 0.080 fuel/air ratio are called best power mixtures, since their use results in the greatest power for a given airflow or manifold pressure. In this fuel/air ratio range, there is no increase in the total heat released, but the weight of nitrogen and combustion products is augmented by the vapor formed with the excess fuel. Thus, the working mass of the charge is increased. In addition, the extra fuel in the charge (over the stoichiometric mixture) speeds up the combustion process, which provides a favorable time factor in converting fuel energy into power.

If the fuel/air ratio is enriched above 0.080, there is loss of power and a reduction in temperature. The cooling effects of excess fuel overtake the favorable factor of increased mass. This reduced temperature and slower rate of burning lead to an increasing loss of combustion efficiency. If, with constant airflow, the mixture is leaned below 0.067, fuel/air ratio power and temperature decrease together. This time, the loss of power is not a liability but an asset. The purpose in leaning is to save fuel. Air is free and available in limitless quantities. The object is to obtain the required power with the least fuel flow. A measure of the economical use of fuel is called specific fuel consumption (SFC), which is the fuel weight in pounds per hour per horsepower.

$$SFC = \frac{pounds\ fuel/hour}{horsepower}$$

By using this ratio, the engine's use of fuel at various power settings can be compared. When leaning below 0.067 fuel/air ratio with constant airflow, even though the power diminishes, the cost in fuel to support each horsepower hour (SFC) also is lowered. While the mixture charge is becoming weaker, this loss of strength occurs at a rate lower than that of the reduction of fuel flow. This favorable tendency continues until a mixture strength known as best economy is reached. With this fuel/air ratio, the required hp is developed with the least fuel flow or, to put it another way, the greatest power produced by a given fuel flow. The best economy fuel/air ratio varies somewhat with rpm and other conditions, but for cruise powers on most reciprocating engines, it is sufficiently accurate to define this range of operation as being from 0.060 to 0.065 fuel/air ratios on aircraft where manual leaning is practiced.

Below the best economical mixture strength, power and temperature continue to fall with constant airflow while the SFC increases. As the fuel/air ratio is reduced further, combustion becomes so cool and slow that power for a given manifold pressure gets so low as to be uneconomical. The cooling effect of rich or lean mixtures results from the excess fuel or air over that needed for combustion. Internal cylinder cooling is obtained from unused fuel when fuel/air ratios above 0.067 are used. The same function is performed by excess air when fuel/air ratios below 0.067 are used.

Varying the mixture strength of the charge produces changes in the engine operating condition affecting power, temperature, and spark-timing requirements. The best power fuel/air ratio is desirable when the greatest power from a given airflow is required. The best economy mixture results from obtaining the given power output with the least fuel flow. The fuel/air ratio which gives most efficient operation varies with engine speed and power output.

In the graph showing this variation in fuel/air ratio, note that the mixture is rich at both idling and high-speed operation and is lean through the cruising range. *[Figure 2-1]* At idling speed, some air or exhaust gas is drawn into the cylinder through the exhaust port during valve overlap. The mixture that enters the cylinder through the intake port must be rich enough to compensate for this gas or additional air. At cruising power, lean mixtures save fuel and increase the range of the airplane. An engine running near full power requires a rich mixture to prevent overheating and detonation. Since the engine is operated at full power for only short periods, the high fuel consumption is not a serious matter. If an engine is operating on a mixture that is too lean, and adjustments are made to increase the amount of fuel, the power output of the engine increases rapidly at first, then gradually until maximum power is reached. With a further increase in the amount of fuel, the power output drops gradually at first, then more rapidly as the mixture is further enriched.

There are specific instructions concerning mixture ratios for each type of engine under various operating conditions. Failure to follow these instructions results in poor performance and often in damage to the engine. Excessively rich mixtures result in loss of power and waste of fuel. With the engine operating near its maximum output, very lean mixtures cause a loss of power and, under certain conditions, serious overheating. When the engine is operated on a lean mixture, the cylinder head temperature gauge should be watched closely. If the mixture is excessively lean, the engine may backfire through the induction system or stop completely. Backfire results from slow burning of the lean mixture. If the charge is still burning when the intake valve opens, it ignites the fresh mixture and the flame travels back through the combustible mixture in the induction system.

Carburetion Principles

Venturi Principles

The carburetor must measure the airflow through the induction system and use this measurement to regulate the amount of fuel discharged into the airstream. The air measuring unit is the venturi, which makes use of a basic law of physics: as the velocity of a gas or liquid increases, the pressure decreases. As shown in *Figure 2-4*, simple venturi is a passageway or tube in which there is a narrow portion called the throat. As the velocity of the air increases to get through the narrow portion, its pressure drops. Note that the pressure in the throat is lower than that in any other part of the venturi. This pressure drop is proportional to the velocity and is, therefore, a measure of the airflow. The basic operating principle of most carburetors depends on the differential pressure between the inlet and the venturi throat.

Application of Venturi Principle to Carburetor

The carburetor is mounted on the engine so that air to the cylinders passes through the barrel, the part of the carburetor which contains the venturi. The size and shape of the venturi depends on the requirements of the engine for which the carburetor is designed. A carburetor for a high-powered engine may have one large venturi or several small ones. The air may flow either up or down the venturi, depending on the design of the engine and the carburetor. Those in which the air passes downward are known as downdraft carburetors, and those in which the air passes upward are called updraft carburetors. Some carburetors are made to use a side draft or horizontal air entry into the engine induction system, as shown in *Figure 2-5*.

Air flows through the induction system covered in Chapter 3. When a piston moves toward the crankshaft (down) on the intake stroke, the pressure in the cylinder is lowered.

Figure 2-5. *Side draft horizontal flow carburator.*

Air rushes through the carburetor and intake manifold to the cylinder to replace the air displaced by the piston as it moved down on the intake stroke. Due to this low pressure area caused by the piston moving down, the higher pressure air in the atmosphere flows in to fill the low pressure area. As it does, the airflow must pass through the carburetor venturi. The throttle valve is located between the venturi and the engine. Mechanical linkage connects this valve with the throttle lever in the cockpit. By means of the throttle, airflow to the cylinders is regulated and controls the power output of the engine. Actually, more air is admitted to the engine, and the carburetor automatically supplies enough additional gasoline to maintain the correct fuel/air ratio. This is because as the volume of airflow increases, the velocity in the venturi increases, lowering the pressure and allowing more fuel to be forced into the airstream. The throttle valve obstructs the passage of air very little when it is parallel with the flow, in the wide open throttle position. Throttle action is illustrated in *Figure 2-6*. Note how it restricts the airflow more and more as it rotates toward the closed position.

Figure 2-4. *Simple venturi.*

Figure 2-6. *Wide open throttle position.*

Metering and Discharge of Fuel

In *Figure 2-7,* showing the discharge of fuel into the airstream, locate the inlet through which fuel enters the carburetor from the engine-driven pump. The float-operated needle valve regulates the flow through the inlet, which maintains the correct level in the fuel float chamber. *[Figures 2-8* and *2-9]* This level must be slightly below the outlet of the discharge nozzle to prevent overflow when the engine is not running.

The discharge nozzle is located in the throat of the venturi at the point where the lowest drop in pressure occurs as

Figure 2-8. *Needle valve and seat.*

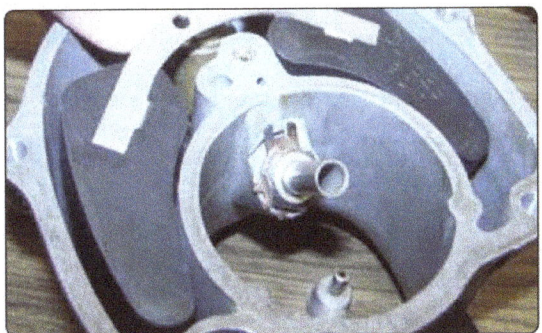

Figure 2-9. *Float chamber discharge nozzle and float.*

Figure 2-7. *Fuel discharge.*

2-7

air passes through the carburetor to the engine cylinders. There are two different pressures acting on the fuel in the carburetor—a low pressure at the discharge nozzle and a higher (atmospheric) pressure in the float chamber. The higher pressure in the float chamber forces the fuel through the discharge nozzle into the airstream. If the throttle is opened wider to increase the airflow to the engine, there is a greater drop in pressure at the venturi throat. Because of the higher differential pressure, the fuel discharge increases in proportion to the increase in airflow. If the throttle is moved toward the "closed" position, the airflow and fuel flow decrease.

The fuel must pass through the metering jet to reach the discharge nozzle. *[Figure 2-7]* A metering jet is really a certain size hole that the fuel passes through. The size of this jet determines the rate of fuel discharge at each differential pressure. If the jet is replaced with a larger one, the fuel flow increases, resulting in a richer mixture. If a smaller jet is installed, there is a decrease in fuel flow and a leaner mixture.

Carburetor Systems

To provide for engine operation under various loads and at different engine speeds, each carburetor has six systems:

1. Main metering
2. Idling
3. Accelerating
4. Mixture control
5. Idle cutoff
6. Power enrichment or economizer

Each of these systems has a definite function. It may act alone or with one or more of the others.

The main metering system supplies fuel to the engine at all speeds above idling. The fuel discharged by this system is determined by the drop in pressure in the venturi throat.

A separate system is necessary for idling because the main metering system can be erratic at very low engine speeds. At low speeds the throttle is nearly closed. As a result, the velocity of the air through the venturi is low and there is little drop in pressure. Consequently, the differential pressure is not sufficient to operate the main metering system, and no fuel is discharged from this system. Therefore, most carburetors have an idling system to supply fuel to the engine at low engine speeds.

The accelerating system supplies extra fuel during sudden increases in engine power. When the throttle is opened, the airflow through the carburetor increases to obtain more power from the engine. The main metering system then increases the fuel discharge. During sudden acceleration, however, the increase in airflow is so rapid that there is a slight time lag before the increase in fuel discharge is sufficient to provide the correct mixture ratio with the new airflow. By supplying extra fuel during this period, the accelerating system prevents a temporary leaning out of the mixture and gives smooth acceleration.

The mixture control system determines the ratio of fuel to air in the mixture. By means of a cockpit control, the manual mixture control can select the mixture ratio to suit operating conditions. In addition to these manual controls, many carburetors have automatic mixture controls so that the fuel/air ratio, once it is selected, does not change with variations in air density. This is necessary because as the airplane climbs and the atmospheric pressure decreases, there is a corresponding decrease in the weight of air passing through the induction system. The volume, however, remains constant. Since it is the volume of airflow that determines the pressure drop at the throat of the venturi, the carburetor tends to meter the same amount of fuel to this thin air as to the dense air at sea level. Thus, the natural tendency is for the mixture to become richer as the airplane gains altitude. The automatic mixture control prevents this by decreasing the rate of fuel discharge to compensate for the decrease in air density.

The carburetor has an idle cutoff system so that the fuel can be shut off to stop the engine. This system, incorporated in the manual mixture control, stops the fuel discharge from the carburetor completely when the mixture control lever is set to the "idle cutoff" position. An aircraft engine is stopped by shutting off the fuel rather than by turning off the ignition. If the ignition is turned off with the carburetor still supplying fuel, fresh fuel/air mixture continues to pass through the induction system to the cylinders. As the engine is coasting to a stop and if it is excessively hot, this combustible mixture may be ignited by local hot spots within the combustion chambers. This can cause the engine to continue running or kick backward. Also, the mixture may pass through the cylinders unburned, but be ignited in the hot exhaust manifold. Or, the engine comes to an apparently normal stop but a combustible mixture remains in the induction passages, the cylinders, and the exhaust system. This is an unsafe condition since the engine may kick over after it has been stopped and seriously injure anyone near the propeller. When the engine is shut down by means of the idle cutoff system, the spark plugs continue to ignite the fuel/air mixture until the fuel discharge from the carburetor ceases. This alone should prevent the engine from coming to a stop with a combustible mixture in the cylinders. Some engine manufacturers suggest that just before the propeller stops turning, the throttle be opened wide so that the pistons can pump fresh air through the induction system, the cylinders, and the exhaust system as an added precaution against accidental kick-over. After the engine has come to a complete stop, the ignition switch is turned to the "off" position.

The power enrichment system automatically increases the richness of the mixture during high power operation. It makes possible the variation in fuel/air ratio necessary to fit different operating conditions. Remember that at cruising speeds, a lean mixture is desirable for economy reasons, while at high power output, the mixture must be rich to obtain maximum power and to aid in cooling the engine cylinders. The power enrichment system automatically brings about the necessary change in the fuel/air ratio. Essentially, it is a valve that is closed at cruising speeds and opened to supply extra fuel to the mixture during high power operation. Although it increases the fuel flow at high power, the power enrichment system is actually a fuel saving device. Without this system, it would be necessary to operate the engine on a rich mixture over the complete power range. The mixture would then be richer than necessary at cruising speed to ensure safe operation at maximum power. The power enrichment system is sometimes called an economizer or a power compensator.

Although the various systems have been discussed separately, the carburetor functions as a unit. The fact that one system is in operation does not necessarily prevent another from functioning. At the same time that the main metering system is discharging fuel in proportion to the airflow, the mixture control system determines whether the resultant mixture is rich or lean. If the throttle is suddenly opened wide, the accelerating and power enrichment systems act to add fuel to that already being discharged by the main metering system.

Carburetor Types

The float-type carburetor, the most common of all carburetor types, has several distinct disadvantages. The effect that abrupt maneuvers have on the float action and the fact that its fuel must be discharged at low pressure leads to incomplete vaporization and difficulty in discharging fuel into some types of supercharged systems. The chief disadvantage of the float carburetor, however, is its icing tendency. Since the float carburetor must discharge fuel at a point of low pressure, the discharge nozzle must be located at the venturi throat, and the throttle valve must be on the engine side of the discharge nozzle. This means that the drop in temperature due to fuel vaporization takes place within the venturi. As a result, ice readily forms in the venturi and on the throttle valve.

A pressure-type carburetor discharges fuel into the airstream at a pressure well above atmospheric. This results in better vaporization and permits the discharge of fuel into the airstream on the engine side of the throttle valve. With the discharge nozzle located at this point, the drop in temperature due to fuel vaporization takes place after the air has passed the throttle valve and at a point where engine heat tends to offset it. Thus, the danger of fuel vaporization icing is practically eliminated. The effects of rapid maneuvers and rough air on the pressure-type carburetors are negligible since its fuel chambers remain filled under all operating conditions. Pressure carburetors have been replaced mostly by fuel injection systems and have limited use on modern aircraft engines.

Carburetor Icing

There are three general classifications of carburetor icing:

1. Fuel evaporation ice
2. Throttle ice
3. Impact ice

Fuel evaporation ice or refrigeration ice is formed because of the decrease in air temperature resulting from the evaporation of fuel after it is introduced into the airstream. As the fuel evaporates, the temperature is lowered in the area where the evaporation takes place. Any moisture in the incoming air can form ice in this area. It frequently occurs in those systems in which fuel is injected into the air upstream from the carburetor throttle, as in the case of float-type carburetors. It occurs less frequently in systems in which the fuel is injected into the air downstream from the carburetor. Refrigeration ice can be formed at carburetor air temperatures as high as 100 °F over a wide range of atmospheric humidity conditions, even at relative humidities well below 100 percent. Generally, fuel evaporation ice tends to accumulate on the fuel distribution nozzle in the carburetor. This type of ice can lower manifold pressure, interfere with fuel flow, and affect mixture distribution.

Throttle ice is formed on the rear side of the throttle, usually when the throttle is in a partially "closed" position. The rush of air across and around the throttle valve causes a low pressure on the rear side; this sets up a pressure differential across the throttle, which has a cooling effect on the fuel/air charge. Moisture freezes in this low pressure area and collects as ice on the low pressure side. Throttle ice tends to accumulate in a restricted passage. The occurrence of a small amount of ice may cause a relatively large reduction in airflow and manifold pressure. A large accumulation of ice may jam the throttles and cause them to become inoperable. Throttle ice seldom occurs at temperatures above 38 °F.

Impact ice is formed either from water present in the atmosphere as snow, sleet, or from liquid water which impinges on surfaces that are at temperatures below 32 °F.

Because of inertia effects, impact ice collects on or near a surface that changes the direction of the airflow. This type of ice may build up on the carburetor elbow, as well as the carburetor screen and metering elements. The most dangerous impact ice is that which collects on the carburetor screen and causes a very rapid reduction of airflow and power. In general, danger from impact ice normally exists only when ice forms on the leading edges of the aircraft structure. Under some conditions, ice may enter the carburetor in a comparatively dry state and will not adhere to the inlet screen or walls or affect engine airflow or manifold pressure. This ice may enter the carburetor and gradually build up internally in the carburetor air metering passages and affect carburetor metering characteristics.

Float-Type Carburetors

A float-type carburetor consists essentially of six subsystems that control the quantity of fuel discharged in relation to the flow of air delivered to the engine cylinders. These systems work together to provide the engine with the correct fuel flow during all engine operating ranges.

The essential subsystems of a float-type carburetor are illustrated in *Figure 2-10*. These systems are:

1. Float chamber mechanism system
2. Main metering system
3. Idling system
4. Mixture control system
5. Accelerating system
6. Economizer system

Float Chamber Mechanism System

A float chamber is provided between the fuel supply and the main metering system of the carburetor. The float chamber, or bowl, serves as a reservoir for fuel in the carburetor. *[Figure 2-11]* This chamber provides a nearly constant level of fuel to the main discharge nozzle which is usually about

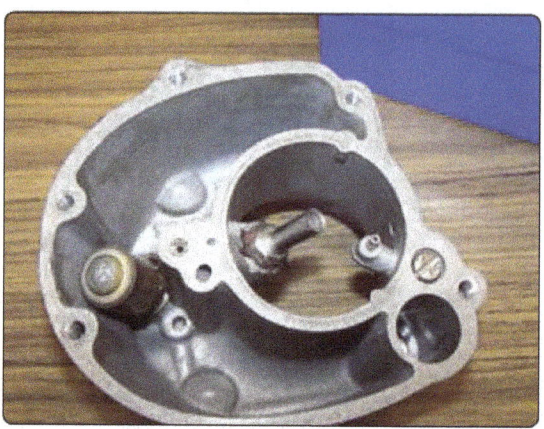

Figure 2-11. *Float chamber (bowl) with float removed.*

Figure 2-10. *A float-type carburetor.*

⅛" below the holes in the main discharge nozzle. The fuel level must be maintained slightly below the discharge nozzle outlet holes to provide the correct amount of fuel flow and to prevent fuel leakage from the nozzle when the engine is not operating.

The level of fuel in the float chamber is kept nearly constant by means of a float-operated needle valve and a seat. The needle seat is usually made of bronze. The needle valve is constructed of hardened steel, or it may have a synthetic rubber section which fits the seat. With no fuel in the float chamber, the float drops toward the bottom of the chamber and allows the needle valve to open wide. As fuel is admitted from the supply line, the float rises (floats in the fuel) and closes the needle valve when the fuel reaches a predetermined level. When the engine is running and fuel is being drawn out of the float chamber, the valve assumes an intermediate position so that the valve opening is just sufficient to supply the required amount of fuel and keep the level constant. *[Figure 2-10]*

With the fuel at the correct level (float chamber), the discharge rate is controlled accurately by the air velocity through the carburetor venturi where a pressure drop at the discharge nozzle causes fuel to flow into the intake airstream. Atmospheric pressure on top of the fuel in the float chamber forces the fuel out the discharge nozzle. A vent or small opening in the top of the float chamber allows air to enter or leave the chamber as the level of fuel rises or falls.

Main Metering System

The main metering system supplies fuel to the engine at all speeds above idling and consists of:

1. Venturi
2. Main metering jet
3. Main discharge nozzle
4. Passage leading to the idling system
5. Throttle valve

Since the throttle valve controls the mass airflow through the carburetor venturi, it must be considered a major unit in the main metering system as well as in other carburetor systems. A typical main metering system is illustrated in *Figure 2-12*. The venturi performs three functions:

1. Proportions the fuel/air mixture
2. Decreases the pressure at the discharge nozzle
3. Limits the airflow at full throttle

The fuel discharge nozzle is located in the carburetor barrel so that its open end is in the throat or narrowest part of the venturi. A main metering orifice, or jet, is placed in the fuel

Figure 2-12. *Main metering system.*

passage between the float chamber and the discharge nozzle to limit the fuel flow when the throttle valve is wide open.

When the engine crankshaft is revolved with the carburetor throttle open, the low pressure created in the intake manifold acts on the air passing through the carburetor barrel. Due to the difference in pressure between the atmosphere and the intake manifold, air flows from the air intake through the carburetor barrel into the intake manifold. The volume of airflow depends upon the degree of throttle opening. As the air flows through the venturi, its velocity increases. This velocity increase creates a low pressure area in the venturi throat. The fuel discharge nozzle is exposed to this low pressure. Since the float chamber is vented to atmospheric pressure, a pressure drop across the discharge nozzle is created. It is this pressure difference, or metering force, that causes fuel to flow from the discharge nozzle. The fuel comes out of the nozzle in a fine spray, and the tiny particles of fuel in the spray quickly vaporize in the air.

The metering force (pressure differential) in most carburetors increases as the throttle opening is increased. The fuel must be raised in the discharge nozzle to a level at which it discharges into the airstream. To accomplish this, a pressure differential of 0.5 "Hg is required. When the metering force is considerably reduced at low engine speeds, the fuel

2-11

delivery from the discharge nozzle decreases if an air bleed (air metering jet) is not incorporated in the carburetor. The decrease in fuel flow in relation to airflow is due to two factors:

1. The fuel tends to adhere to the walls of the discharge nozzle and break off intermittently in large drops instead of forming a fine spray, and
2. A part of the metering force is required to raise the fuel level from the float chamber level to the discharge nozzle outlet.

The basic principle of the air bleed can be explained by simple diagrams, as shown in *Figure 2-13*. In each case, the same degree of suction is applied to a vertical tube placed in the container of liquid. As shown in A, the suction applied on the upper end of the tube is sufficient to lift the liquid a distance of about 1 inch above the surface. If a small hole is made in the side of the tube above the surface of the liquid, as in B, and suction is applied, bubbles of air enter the tube and the liquid is drawn up in a continuous series of small slugs or drops. Thus, air "bleeds" into the tube and partially reduces the forces tending to retard the flow of liquid through the tube. However, the large opening at the bottom of the tube effectively prevents any great amount of suction from being exerted on the air bleed hole or vent. Similarly, an air bleed hole that is too large in proportion to the size of the tube would reduce the suction available to lift the liquid. If the system is modified by placing a metering orifice in the bottom of the tube and air is taken in below the fuel level by means of an air bleed tube, a finely divided mixture of air and liquid is formed in the tube, as shown in C.

In a carburetor, a small air bleed is bled into the fuel nozzle slightly below the fuel level. The open end of the air bleed is in the space behind the venturi wall where the air is relatively motionless and at approximately atmospheric pressure. The low pressure at the tip of the nozzle not only draws fuel from the float chamber but also draws air from behind the venturi. Air bled into the main metering fuel system decreases the fuel density and destroys surface tension. This results in better vaporization and control of fuel discharge, especially at lower engine speeds. The throttle, or butterfly valve, is located in the carburetor barrel near one end of the venturi. It provides a means of controlling engine speed or power output by regulating the airflow to the engine. This valve is a disk that can rotate on an axis, so that it can be turned to open or close the carburetor air passage.

Idling System

With the throttle valve closed at idling speeds, air velocity through the venturi is so low that it cannot draw enough fuel from the main discharge nozzle; in fact, the spray of fuel may stop altogether. However, low pressure (piston suction) exists on the engine side of the throttle valve. In order to allow the engine to idle, a fuel passageway is incorporated to discharge fuel from an opening in the low pressure area near the edge of the throttle valve. *[Figure 2-14]* This opening is called the idling jet. With the throttle open enough so that the main discharge nozzle is operating, fuel does not flow out of the idling jet. As soon as the throttle is closed far enough to stop the spray from the main discharge nozzle, fuel flows out the idling jet. A separate air bleed, known as the idle air bleed, is included as part of the idling system. It functions in the same manner as the main air bleed. An idle mixture adjusting device is also incorporated. A typical idling system is illustrated in *Figure 2-15*.

Mixture Control System

As altitude increases, the air becomes less dense. At an altitude of 18,000 feet, the air is only half as dense as it is at sea level. This means that a cubic foot of space contains only half as much air at 18,000 feet as at sea level. An engine

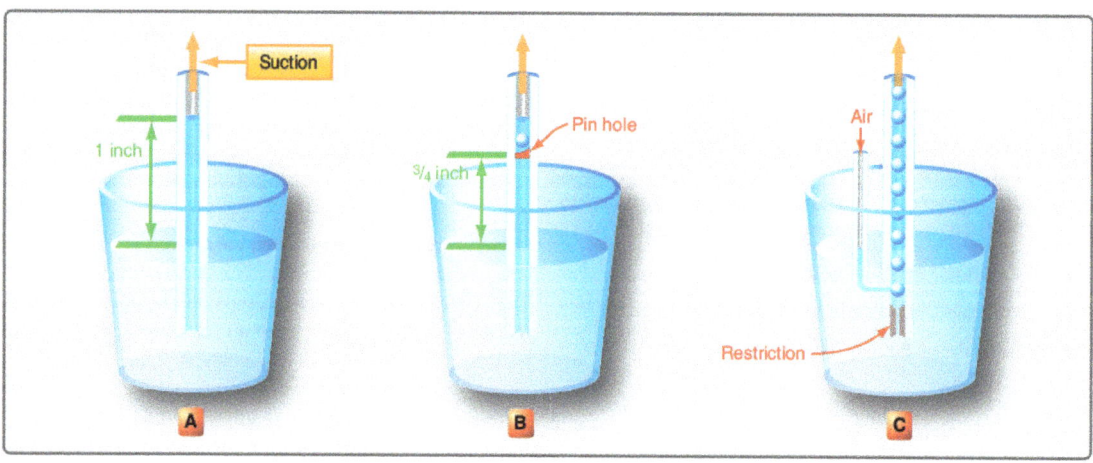

Figure 2-13. *Air bleed principle.*

Figure 2-14. *Throttle action in idle position.*

On float-type carburetors, two types of purely manual or cockpit controllable devices are in general use for controlling fuel/air mixtures, the needle type and the back-suction type. *[Figures 2-16 and 2-17]*

With the needle-type system, manual control is provided by a needle valve in the base of the float chamber. *[Figure 2-16]* This can be raised or lowered by adjusting a control in the cockpit. Moving the control to "rich," opens the needle valve wide, which permits the fuel to flow unrestricted

Figure 2-15. *Idling system.*

Figure 2-16. *Needle-type mixture control system.*

Figure 2-17. *Back-suction-type mixture control system.*

cylinder full of air at 18,000 feet contains only half as much oxygen as a cylinder full of air at sea level.

The low pressure area created by the venturi is dependent upon air velocity rather than air density. The action of the venturi draws the same volume of fuel through the discharge nozzle at a high altitude as it does at a low altitude. Therefore, the fuel mixture becomes richer as altitude increases. This can be overcome either by a manual or an automatic mixture control.

to the nozzle. Moving the control to "lean," partially closes the valve and restricts the flow of fuel to the nozzle.

The back-suction-type mixture control system is the most widely used. *[Figure 2-17]* In this system, a certain amount of venturi low pressure acts upon the fuel in the float chamber so that it opposes the low pressure existing at the main discharge nozzle. An atmospheric line, incorporating an adjustable valve, opens into the float chamber. When the valve is completely closed, pressures on the fuel in the float chamber and at the discharge nozzle are almost equal, and fuel flow is reduced to maximum lean. With the valve wide open, pressure on the fuel in the float chamber is greatest and fuel mixture is richest. Adjusting the valve to positions between these two extremes controls the mixture. The quadrant in the cockpit is usually marked "lean" near the back end and "rich" at the forward end. The extreme back position is marked "idle cutoff" and is used when stopping the engine.

On float carburetors equipped with needle-type mixture control, placing the mixture control in idle cutoff seats the needle valve, thus shutting off fuel flow completely. On carburetors equipped with back-suction mixture controls, a separate idle cutoff line, leading to the extreme low pressure on the engine side of the throttle valve, is incorporated. (See the dotted line in *Figure 2-17.*) The mixture control is so linked that when it is placed in the "idle cutoff" position, it opens another passage that leads to piston suction. When placed in other positions, the valve opens a passage leading to the atmosphere. To stop the engine with such a system, close the throttle and place the mixture in the "idle cutoff" position. Leave the throttle until the engine has stopped running and then open the throttle completely.

Accelerating System
When the throttle valve is opened quickly, a large volume of air rushes through the air passage of the carburetor; the amount of fuel that is mixed with the air is less than normal due to the slow response rate of the main metering system. As a result, after a quick opening of the throttle, the fuel/air mixture leans out momentarily. This can cause the engine to accelerate slowly or stumble as it tries to accelerate.

To overcome this tendency, the carburetor is equipped with a small fuel pump called an accelerating pump. A common type of accelerating system used in float carburetors is illustrated in *Figure 2-18*. It consists of a simple piston pump operated through linkage by the throttle control and a passageway opening into the main metering system or the carburetor barrel near the venturi. When the throttle is closed, the piston moves back and fuel fills the cylinder. If the piston is pushed forward slowly, the fuel seeps past it back into the float chamber; if pushed rapidly, it sprays fuel in the venturi and

Figure 2-18. *Accelerating system.*

enriches the mixture. An example of a cutaway accelerator pump is shown in *Figure 2-19*.

Figure 2-19. *Accelerating pump shown in cutaway.*

Economizer System
For an engine to develop maximum power at full throttle, the fuel mixture must be richer than for cruise. The additional fuel is used for cooling the engine combustion chambers to prevent detonation. An economizer is essentially a valve that is closed at throttle settings below approximately 60–70 percent of rated power. This system, like the accelerating system, is operated by the throttle control.

A typical economizer system consists of a needle valve which begins to open when the throttle valve reaches a predetermined point near the wide-open position. *[Figure 2-20]* As the throttle continues to open, the needle

Figure 2-20. *A needle-valve type economizer system.*

valve is opened further and additional fuel flows through it. This additional fuel supplements the flow from the main metering jet direct to the main discharge nozzle.

A pressure-operated economizer system is shown in *Figure 2-21*. This type has a sealed bellows located in an enclosed compartment. The compartment is vented to engine manifold pressure. When the manifold pressure reaches a certain value, the bellows is compressed and opens a valve in a carburetor fuel passage, supplementing the normal quantity of fuel being discharged through the main nozzle.

Figure 2-21. *A pressure operated economizer system.*

Another type of economizer is the back-suction system. *[Figure 2-22]* Fuel economy in cruising is provided by reducing the effective pressure acting on the fuel level in the float compartment. With the throttle valve in cruising position, suction is applied to the float chamber through an economizer hole and back-suction economizer channel and jet. The suction applied to the float chamber opposes the nozzle suction applied by the venturi. Fuel flow is reduced, leaning the mixture for cruising economy.

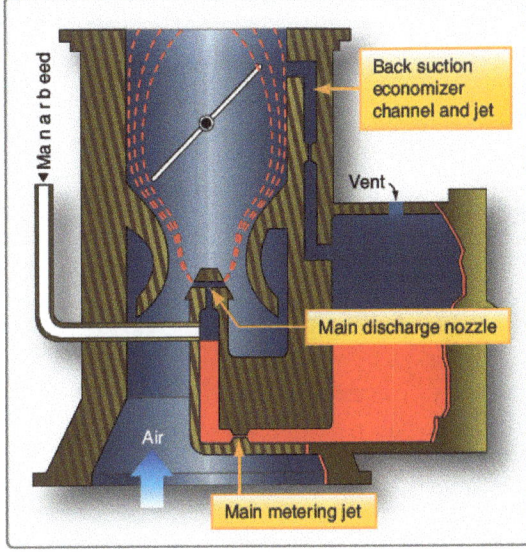

Figure 2-22. *Pressure-type carburetor.*

Another type of mixture control system uses a metering valve that is free to rotate in a stationary metering sleeve. Fuel enters the main and idling systems through a slot cut in the mixture sleeve. Fuel metering is accomplished by the relative position between one edge of the slot in the hollow metering valve and one edge of the slot in the metering sleeve. Moving the mixture control to reduce the size of the slot provides a leaner mixture for altitude compensation.

Pressure Injection Carburetors

Pressure injection carburetors are distinctly different from float-type carburetors as they do not incorporate a vented float chamber or suction pickup from a discharge nozzle located in the venturi tube. Instead, they provide a pressurized fuel system that is closed from the engine fuel pump to the discharge nozzle. The venturi serves only to create pressure differentials for controlling the quantity of fuel to the metering jet in proportion to airflow to the engine.

Typical Injection Carburetor

The injection carburetor is a hydromechanical device employing a closed feed system from the fuel pump to the discharge nozzle. It meters fuel through fixed jets according to the mass airflow through the throttle body and discharges it under a positive pressure.

The illustration in *Figure 2-23* represents a pressure-type carburetor simplified so that only the basic parts are shown. Note the two small passages, one leading from the carburetor air inlet to the left side of the flexible diaphragm and the other from the venturi throat to the right side of the diaphragm.

Figure 2-23. *Pressure-type carburetor.*

When air passes through the carburetor to the engine, the pressure on the right of the diaphragm is lowered because of the drop in pressure at the venturi throat. As a result, the diaphragm moves to the right, opening the fuel valve. Pressure from the engine-driven pump then forces fuel through the open valve to the discharge nozzle, where it sprays into the airstream. The distance the fuel valve opens is determined by the difference between the two pressures acting on the diaphragm. This difference in pressure is proportional to the airflow through the carburetor. Thus, the volume of airflow determines the rate of fuel discharge.

The pressure injection carburetor is an assembly of the following units:

1. Throttle body
2. Automatic mixture control
3. Regulator unit
4. Fuel control unit (some are equipped with an adapter)

Throttle Body

The throttle body contains the throttle valves, main venturi, boost venturi, and the impact tubes. All air entering the cylinders must flow through the throttle body; therefore, it is the air control and measuring device. The airflow is measured by volume and by weight so that the proper amount of fuel can be added to meet the engine demands under all conditions.

As air flows through the venturi, its velocity is increased and its pressure is decreased (Bernoulli's principle). This low pressure is vented to the low pressure side of the air diaphragm *[Figure 2-24 chamber B]* in the regulator assembly. The impact tubes sense carburetor inlet air pressure and direct it to the automatic mixture control, which measures the air density. From the automatic mixture control, the air is directed to the high pressure side of the air diaphragm (chamber A). The pressure differential of the two chambers acting upon the air diaphragm is known as the air metering force which opens the fuel poppet valve.

Figure 2-24. *Regulator unit.*

The throttle body controls the airflow with the throttle valves. The throttle valves may be either rectangular or disk shaped, depending on the design of the carburetor. The valves are mounted on a shaft, which is connected by linkage to the idle valve and to the throttle control in the cockpit. A throttle stop limits the travel of the throttle valve and has an adjustment which sets engine idle speed.

Regulator Unit

The regulator is a diaphragm-controlled unit divided into five chambers and contains two regulating diaphragms and a poppet valve assembly. *[Figure 2-24]* Chamber A is regulated air-inlet pressure from the air intake. Chamber B is boost venturi pressure. Chamber C contains metered fuel pressure controlled by the discharge nozzle or fuel feed valve. Chamber D contains unmetered fuel pressure controlled by the opening of the poppet valve. Chamber E is fuel pump pressure controlled by the fuel pump pressure relief valve. The poppet valve assembly is connected by a stem to the two main control diaphragms. The purpose of the regulator unit is to regulate the fuel pressure to the inlet side of the metering jets in the fuel control unit. This pressure is automatically regulated according to the mass airflow to the engine.

The carburetor fuel strainer, located in the inlet to chamber E, is a fine mesh screen through which all the fuel must pass as it enters chamber D. The strainer must be removed and cleaned at scheduled intervals.

Referring to *Figure 2-24*, assume that for a given airflow in lb/hr through the throttle body and venturi, a negative pressure of ¼ psi is established in chamber B. This tends to move the diaphragm assembly and the poppet valve in a direction to open the poppet valve permitting more fuel to enter chamber D. The pressure in chamber C is held constant at 5 psi (10 psi on some installations) by the discharge nozzle or impeller fuel feed valve. Therefore, the diaphragm assembly and poppet valve moves in the open direction until the pressure in chamber D is 5¼ psi. Under these pressures, there is a balanced condition of the diaphragm assembly with a pressure drop of ¼ psi across the jets in the fuel control unit (auto-rich or auto-lean).

If nozzle pressure (chamber C pressure) rises to 5½ psi, the diaphragm assembly balance is upset, and the diaphragm assembly moves to open the poppet valve to establish the necessary 5¾ psi pressure in chamber D. Thus, the ¼ psi differential between chamber C and chamber D is re-established, and the pressure drop across the metering jets remains the same.

If the fuel inlet pressure is increased or decreased, the fuel flow into chamber D tends to increase or decrease with the pressure change causing the chamber D pressure to do likewise. This upsets the balanced condition previously established, and the poppet valve and diaphragm assembly respond by moving to increase or decrease the flow to re-establish the pressure at the ¼ psi differential.

The fuel flow changes when the mixture control plates are moved from auto-lean to auto-rich, thereby selecting a different set of jets or cutting one or two in or out of the system. When the mixture position is altered, the diaphragm and poppet valve assembly repositions to maintain the established pressure differential of ¼ psi between chambers C and D, maintaining the established differential across the jets. Under low power settings (low airflows), the difference in pressure created by the boost venturi is not sufficient to accomplish consistent regulation of the fuel. Therefore, an idle spring, shown in *Figure 2-24*, is incorporated in the regulator. As the poppet valve moves toward the closed position, it contacts the idle spring. The spring holds the poppet valve off its seat far enough to provide more fuel than is needed for idling. This potentially overrich mixture is regulated by the idle valve. At idling speed, the idle valve restricts the fuel flow to the proper amount. At higher speeds, it is withdrawn from the fuel passage and has no metering effect.

Vapor vent systems are provided in these carburetors to eliminate fuel vapor created by the fuel pump, heat in the engine compartment, and the pressure drop across the poppet valve. The vapor vent is located in the fuel inlet (chamber E) or, on some models of carburetors, in both chambers D and E.

The vapor vent system operates in the following way. When air enters the chamber in which the vapor vent is installed, the air rises to the top of the chamber, displacing the fuel and lowering its level. When the fuel level has reached a predetermined position, the float (which floats in the fuel) pulls the vapor vent valve off its seat, permitting the vapor in the chamber to escape through the vapor vent seat, its connecting line, and back to the fuel tank.

If the vapor vent valve sticks in a closed position or the vent line from the vapor vent to the fuel tank becomes clogged, the vapor-eliminating action is stopped. This causes the vapor to build up within the carburetor to the extent that vapor passes through the metering jets with the fuel. With a given size carburetor metering jet, the metering of vapor reduces the quantity of fuel metered. This causes the fuel/air mixture to lean out, usually intermittently.

If the vapor vent valve sticks open or the vapor vent float becomes filled with fuel and sinks, a continuous flow of fuel and vapor occurs through the vent line. It is important to detect this condition, as the fuel flow from the carburetor to the fuel supply tank may cause an overflowing tank with resultant increased fuel consumption.

To check the vent system, disconnect the vapor vent line where it attaches to the carburetor, and turn the fuel booster pump on while observing the vapor vent connection at the carburetor. Move the carburetor mixture control to auto-rich; then return it to idle cutoff. When the fuel booster pump is turned on, there should be an initial ejection of fuel and air followed by a cutoff with not more than a steady drip from the vent connection. Installations with a fixed bleed from the D chamber connected to the vapor vent in the fuel inlet by a short external line should show an initial ejection of fuel and air followed by a continuing small stream of fuel. If there is no flow, the valve is sticking closed; if there is a steady flow, it is sticking open.

Fuel Control Unit

The fuel control unit is attached to the regulator assembly and contains all metering jets and valves. *[Figure 2-25]* The idle and power enrichment valves, together with the mixture control plates, select the jet combinations for the various settings (i.e., auto-rich, auto-lean, and idle cutoff).

Figure 2-25. *Fuel control unit.*

The purpose of the fuel control unit is to meter and control the fuel flow to the discharge nozzle. The basic unit consists of three jets and four valves arranged in series, parallel, and series-parallel hookups. *[Figure 2-25]* These jets and valves receive fuel under pressure from the regulator unit and then meter the fuel as it flows to the discharge nozzle. The manual mixture control valve controls the fuel flow. By using proper size jets and regulating the pressure differential across the jets, the right amount of fuel is delivered to the discharge nozzle, giving the desired fuel/air ratio in the various power settings. It should be remembered that the inlet pressure to the jets is regulated by the regulator unit and the outlet pressure is controlled by the discharge nozzle.

The jets in the basic fuel control unit are the auto-lean jet, the auto-rich jet, and power enrichment jet. The basic fuel flow is the fuel required to run the engine with a lean mixture and is metered by the auto-lean jet. The auto-rich jet adds enough fuel to the basic flow to give a slightly richer mixture than best power mixture when the manual mixture control is in the auto-rich position.

The four valves in the basic fuel control unit are:

1. Idle needle valve
2. Power enrichment valve
3. Regulator fill valve
4. Manual mixture control

The functions of these valves are:

1. The idle needle valve meters the fuel in the idle range only. It is a round, contoured needle valve, or a cylinder valve placed in series with all other metering devices of the basic fuel control unit. The idle needle valve is connected by linkage to the throttle shaft so that it restricts the fuel flowing at low power settings (idle range).

2. The manual mixture control is a rotary disk valve consisting of a round stationary disk with ports leading from the auto-lean jet, the auto-rich jet, and two smaller ventholes. Another rotating part, resembling a cloverleaf, is held against the stationary disk by spring tension and rotated over the ports in that disk by the manual mixture control lever. All ports and vents are closed in the idle cutoff position. In the auto-lean position, the ports from the auto-lean jet and the two ventholes are open. The port from the auto-rich jet remains closed in this position. In the auto-rich position, all ports are open. The valve plate positions are illustrated in *Figure 2-26.* The three positions of the manual mixture control lever make it possible to select a lean mixture a rich mixture, or to stop fuel flow entirely. The idle cutoff position is used for starting or stopping the engine. During starting, fuel is supplied by the primer.

3. The regulator fill valve is a small poppet-type valve located in a fuel passage which supplies chamber C of the regulator unit with metered fuel pressure. In idle cutoff, the flat portion of the cam lines up with the valve stem, and a spring closes the valve. This provides a means of shutting off the fuel flow to chamber C and thus provides for a positive idle cutoff.

4. The power enrichment valve is another poppet-type valve. It is in parallel with the auto-lean and auto-rich jets, but it is in series with the power enrichment jet. This valve starts to open at the beginning of the power range. It is opened by the unmetered fuel pressure overcoming metered fuel pressure and spring tension. The power enrichment valve continues to open wider during the power range until the combined flow through the valve and the auto-rich jet exceeds that of the power enrichment jet. At this point the power

Figure 2-26. *Manual mixture control valve plate positions.*

enrichment jet takes over the metering and meters fuel throughout the power range.

5. Carburetors equipped for water injection are modified by the addition of a derichment valve and a derichment jet. The derichment valve and derichment jet are in series with each other and parallel with the power enrichment jet.

The carburetor controls fuel flow by varying two basic factors. The fuel control unit, acting as a pressure-reducing valve, determines the metering pressure in response to the metering forces. The regulator unit, in effect, varies the size of the orifice through which the metering pressure forces the fuel. It is a basic law of hydraulics that the amount of fluid that passes through an orifice varies with the size of the orifice and the pressure drop across it. The internal automatic devices and mixture control act together to determine the effective size of the metering passage through which the fuel passes. The internal devices, fixed jets, and variable power enrichment valve are not subject to direct external control.

Automatic Mixture Control (AMC)

The automatic mixture control unit consists of a bellows assembly, calibrated needle, and seat. *[Figure 2-27]* The purpose of the automatic mixture control is to compensate for changes in air density due to temperature and altitude changes.

The automatic mixture control contains a metallic bellows, which is sealed at 28 "Hg absolute pressure. This bellows responds to changes in pressure and temperature. In the illustration, the automatic mixture control is located at the carburetor air inlet. As the density of the air changes, the expansion and contraction of the bellows moves the tapered needle in the atmospheric line. At sea level, the bellows is contracted and the needle is not in the atmospheric passage. As the aircraft climbs and the atmospheric pressure decreases, the bellows expands, inserting the tapered needle farther and farther into the atmospheric passage and restricting the flow of air to chamber A of the regulator unit. *[Figure 2-24]* At the same time, air leaks slowly from chamber A to chamber B through the small bleed (often referred to as the back-suction bleed or mixture control bleed). The rate at which air leaks through this bleed is about the same at high altitude as it is at sea level. As the tapered needle restricts the flow of air into chamber A, the pressure on the left side of the air diaphragm decreases. As a result, the poppet valve moves toward its seat, reducing the fuel flow to compensate for the decrease in air density. The automatic mixture control

Figure 2-27. *Automatic mixture control and throttle body.*

can be removed and cleaned if the lead seal at the point of adjustment is not disturbed.

Stromberg PS Carburetor

The PS series carburetor is a low-pressure, single-barrel, injection-type carburetor. The carburetor consists basically of the air section, the fuel section, and the discharge nozzle mounted together to form a complete fuel metering system. This carburetor is similar to the pressure-injection carburetor; therefore, its operating principles are the same.

In this type carburetor, metering is accomplished on a mass airflow basis. *[Figure 2-28]* Air flowing through the main venturi creates suction at the throat of the venturi, which is transmitted to the B chamber in the main regulating part of the carburetor and to the vent side of the fuel discharge nozzle diaphragm. The incoming air pressure is transmitted to a chamber A of the regulating part of the carburetor and to the main discharge bleed in the main fuel discharge jet. The discharge nozzle consists of a spring-loaded diaphragm connected to the discharge nozzle valve, which controls the flow of fuel injected into the main discharge jet. Here, it is mixed with air to accomplish distribution and atomization into the airstream entering the engine.

In the PS series carburetor, as in the pressure-injection carburetor, the regulator spring has a fixed tension, which tends to hold the poppet valve open during idling speeds or until the D chamber pressure equals approximately 4 psi. The discharge nozzle spring has a variable adjustment which, when tailored to maintain 4 psi, results in a balanced pressure condition of 4 psi in chamber C of the discharge nozzle assembly and 4 psi in chamber D. This produces a zero drop across the main jets at zero fuel flow.

At a given airflow, if the suction created by the venturi is equivalent to ¼ pound, the pressure decrease is transmitted to chamber B and to the vent side of the discharge nozzle. Since the area of the air diaphragm between chambers A and B is twice as great as that between chambers B and D, the ¼ pound decrease in pressure in chamber B moves the diaphragm assembly to the right to open the poppet valve.

Figure 2-28. *Schematic of the PS series carburetor.*

Meanwhile, the decreased pressure on the vent side of the discharge nozzle assembly causes a lowering of the total pressure from 4 pounds to 3¾ pounds. The greater pressure of the metered fuel (4¼ pounds) results in a differential across the metering head of ¼ pound (for the ¼ pound pressure differential created by the venturi).

The same ratio of pressure drop across the jet to venturi suction applies throughout the range. Any increase or decrease in fuel inlet pressure tends to upset the balance in the various chambers in the manner already described. When this occurs, the main fuel regulator diaphragm assembly repositions to restore the balance.

The mixture control, whether operated manually or automatically, compensates for enrichment at altitude by bleeding impact air pressure into chamber B, thereby increasing the pressure (decreasing the suction) in chamber B. Increasing the pressure in chamber B tends to move the diaphragm and poppet valve more toward the closed position, restricting fuel flow to correspond proportionately to the decrease in air density at altitude.

The idle valve and economizer jet can be combined in one assembly. The unit is controlled manually by the movement of the valve assembly. At low airflow positions, the tapered section of the valve becomes the predominant jet in the system, controlling the fuel flow for the idle range. As the valve moves to the cruise position, a straight section on the valve establishes a fixed orifice effect which controls the cruise mixture. When the valve is pulled full-open by the throttle valve, the jet is pulled completely out of the seat, and the seat side becomes the controlling jet. This jet is calibrated for takeoff power mixtures.

An airflow-controlled power enrichment valve can also be used with this carburetor. It consists of a spring-loaded, diaphragm-operated metering valve. Refer to *Figure 2-29* for a schematic view of an airflow power enrichment valve. One side of the diaphragm is exposed to unmetered fuel pressure and the other side to venturi suction plus spring tension. When the pressure differential across the diaphragm establishes a force strong enough to compress the spring, the valve opens and supplies an additional amount of fuel to the metered fuel circuit in addition to the fuel supplied by the main metering jet.

Accelerating Pump

The accelerating pump of the Stromberg PS carburetor is a spring-loaded diaphragm assembly located in the metered fuel channel with the opposite side of the diaphragm vented to the engine side of the throttle valve. With this arrangement, opening the throttle results in a rapid decrease in suction. This decrease in suction permits the spring to extend and move the accelerating pump diaphragm. The diaphragm and spring action displace the fuel in the accelerating pump and force it out the discharge nozzle.

Vapor is eliminated from the top of the main fuel chamber D through a bleed hole, then through a vent line back to the main fuel tank in the aircraft.

Manual Mixture Control

A manual mixture control provides a means of correcting for enrichment at altitude. It consists of a needle valve and seat that form an adjustable bleed between chamber A and chamber B. The valve can be adjusted to bleed off the venturi suction to maintain the correct fuel/air ratio as the aircraft gains altitude.

Figure 2-29. *Airflow power enrichment valve.*

When the mixture control lever is moved to the idle cutoff position, a cam on the linkage actuates a rocker arm which moves the idle cutoff plunger inward against the release lever in chamber A. The lever compresses the regulator diaphragm spring to relieve all tension on the diaphragm between chambers A and B. This permits fuel pressure plus poppet valve spring force to close the poppet valve, stopping the fuel flow. Placing the mixture control lever in idle cutoff also positions the mixture control needle valve off its seat and allows metering suction within the carburetor to bleed off.

Fuel-Injection Systems

The fuel-injection system has many advantages over a conventional carburetor system. There is less danger of induction system icing, since the drop in temperature due to fuel vaporization takes place in or near the cylinder. Acceleration is also improved because of the positive action of the injection system. In addition, fuel injection improves fuel distribution. This reduces the overheating of individual cylinders often caused by variation in mixture due to uneven distribution. The fuel-injection system also gives better fuel economy than a system in which the mixture to most cylinders must be richer than necessary so that the cylinder with the leanest mixture operates properly.

Fuel-injection systems vary in their details of construction, arrangement, and operation. The Bendix and Continental fuel-injection systems are discussed in this section. They are described to provide an understanding of the operating principles involved. For the specific details of any one system, consult the manufacturer's instructions for the equipment involved.

Bendix/Precision Fuel-Injection System

The Bendix inline stem-type regulator injection system (RSA) series consists of an injector, flow divider, and fuel discharge nozzle. It is a continuous-flow system which measures engine air consumption and uses airflow forces to control fuel flow to the engine. The fuel distribution system to the individual cylinders is obtained by the use of a fuel flow divider and air bleed nozzles.

Fuel Injector

The fuel injector assembly consists of:

1. An airflow section,
2. A regulator section, and
3. A fuel metering section. Some fuel injectors are equipped with an automatic mixture control unit.

Airflow Section

The airflow consumption of the engine is measured by sensing impact pressure and venturi throat pressure in the throttle body. These pressures are vented to the two sides of an air diaphragm. A cutaway view of the airflow measuring section is shown in *Figure 2-30*. Movement of the throttle valve causes a change in engine air consumption. This results in a change in the air velocity in the venturi. When airflow through the engine increases, the pressure on the left of the diaphragm is lowered due to the drop in pressure at the venturi throat. *[Figure 2-31]* As a result, the diaphragm moves to the left, opening the ball valve. Contributing to this force is the impact pressure that is picked up by the impact tubes. *[Figure 2-32]* This pressure differential is referred to as the "air metering force." This force is accomplished by channeling the impact and venturi suction pressures to opposite sides of a diaphragm. The difference between these two pressures becomes a usable force that is equal to the area of the diaphragm times the pressure difference.

Figure 2-30. *Cutaway view of airflow measuring section.*

Regulator Section

The regulator section consists of a fuel diaphragm that opposes the air metering force. Fuel inlet pressure is applied to one side of the fuel diaphragm and metered fuel pressure is applied to the other side. The differential pressure across the fuel diaphragm is called the fuel metering force. The fuel pressure shown on the ball side of the fuel diaphragm is the pressure after the fuel has passed through the fuel strainer and the manual mixture control rotary plate and is referred to as metered fuel pressure. Fuel inlet pressure is applied to the opposite side of the fuel diaphragm. The ball valve attached to the fuel diaphragm controls the orifice opening and fuel flow through the forces placed on it. *[Figure 2-33]*

The distance the ball valve opens is determined by the difference between the pressures acting on the diaphragms. This difference in pressure is proportional to the airflow through the injector. Thus, the volume of airflow determines the rate of fuel flow.

Figure 2-31. *Airflow section of a fuel injector.*

Figure 2-32. *Impact tubes for inlet air pressure.*

Figure 2-33. *Fuel diaphragm with ball valve attached.*

Under low power settings, the difference in pressure created by the venturi is insufficient to accomplish consistent regulation of the fuel. A constant-head idle spring is incorporated to provide a constant fuel differential pressure. This allows an adequate final flow in the idle range.

Fuel Metering Section

The fuel metering section is attached to the air metering section and contains an inlet fuel strainer, a manual mixture control valve, an idle valve, and the main metering jet. *[Figure 2-34]* The idle valve is connected to the throttle valve by means of an external adjustable link. In some injector models, a power enrichment jet is also located in this section.

The purpose of the fuel metering section is to meter and control the fuel flow to the flow divider. *[Figure 2-35]* The manual mixture control valve produces full rich condition when the lever is against the rich stop, and a progressively leaner mixture as the lever is moved toward idle cutoff. Both idle speed and idle mixture may be adjusted externally to meet individual engine requirements.

Flow Divider

The metered fuel is delivered from the fuel control unit to a pressurized flow divider. This unit keeps metered fuel under pressure, divides fuel to the various cylinders at all engine

Figure 2-34. *Fuel metering section of the injector.*

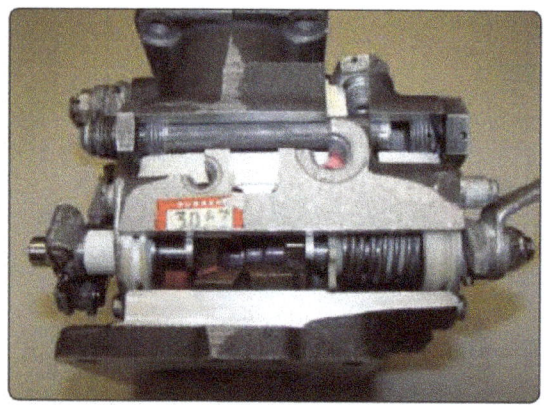

Figure 2-35. *Fuel inlet and metering.*

speeds, and shuts off the individual nozzle lines when the control is placed in idle cutoff.

Referring to the diagram in *Figure 2-36*, metered fuel pressure enters the flow divider through a channel that permits fuel to pass through the inside diameter of the flow divider needle. At idle speed, the fuel pressure from the regulator must build up to overcome the spring force applied to the diaphragm and valve assembly. This moves the valve upward until fuel can pass out through the annulus of the valve to the fuel nozzle. *[Figure 2-37]* Since the regulator meters and delivers a fixed amount of fuel to the flow divider, the valve opens only as far as necessary to pass this amount to the nozzles. At idle,

the opening required is very small; the fuel for the individual cylinders is divided at idle by the flow divider.

As fuel flow through the regulator is increased above idle requirements, fuel pressure builds up in the nozzle lines. This pressure fully opens the flow divider valve, and fuel distribution to the engine becomes a function of the discharge nozzles.

A fuel pressure gauge, calibrated in pounds per hour fuel flow, can be used as a fuel flow meter with the Bendix RSA injection system. This gauge is connected to the flow divider and senses the pressure being applied to the discharge nozzle. This pressure is in direct proportion to the fuel flow and indicates the engine power output and fuel consumption.

Fuel Discharge Nozzles

The fuel discharge nozzles are of the air bleed configuration. There is one nozzle for each cylinder located in the cylinder head. *[Figure 2-38]* The nozzle outlet is directed into the intake port. Each nozzle incorporates a calibrated jet. The jet size is determined by the available fuel inlet pressure and the maximum fuel flow required by the engine. The fuel is discharged through this jet into an ambient air pressure chamber within the nozzle assembly. Before entering the individual intake valve chambers, the fuel is mixed with air to aid in atomizing the fuel. Fuel pressure, before the individual nozzles, is in direct proportion to fuel flow; therefore, a simple pressure gauge can be calibrated in fuel flow in gallons per

Figure 2-36. *Flow divider.*

Figure 2-37. *Flow divider cutaway.*

Figure 2-38. *Fuel nozzle assembly.*

hour and be employed as a flowmeter. Engines modified with turbosuperchargers must use shrouded nozzles. By the use of an air manifold, these nozzles are vented to the injector air inlet pressure.

Continental/TCM Fuel-Injection System

The Continental fuel-injection system injects fuel into the intake valve port in each cylinder head. *[Figure 2-39]* The system consists of a fuel injector pump, a control unit, a fuel manifold, and a fuel discharge nozzle. It is a continuous-flow type, which controls fuel flow to match engine airflow. The continuous-flow system permits the use of a rotary vane pump which does not require timing to the engine.

Fuel-Injection Pump

The fuel pump is a positive-displacement, rotary-vane type with a splined shaft for connection to the accessory drive system of the engine. *[Figure 2-40]* A spring-loaded, diaphragm-type relief valve is provided. The relief valve diaphragm chamber is vented to atmospheric pressure. A sectional view of a fuel-injection pump is shown in *Figure 2-41*.

Fuel enters at the swirl well of the vapor separator. Here, vapor is separated by a swirling motion so that only liquid fuel is delivered to the pump. The vapor is drawn from the top center of the swirl well by a small pressure jet of fuel and is directed into the vapor return line. This line carries the vapor back to the fuel tank.

2-25

Figure 2-39. *Continental/TCM Fuel-Injection System.*

Figure 2-40. *Fuel pump.*

Figure 2-41. *Fuel injection pump.*

Ignoring the effect of altitude or ambient air conditions, the use of a positive-displacement, engine-driven pump means that changes in engine speed affect total pump flow proportionally. Since the pump provides greater capacity than is required by the engine, a recirculation path is required. By arranging a calibrated orifice and relief valve in this path, the pump delivery pressure is also maintained in proportion to engine speed. These provisions assure proper pump pressure and fuel delivery for all engine operating speeds.

A check valve is provided so that boost pump pressure to the system can bypass the engine-driven pump for starting. This feature also suppresses vapor formation under high ambient temperatures of the fuel, and permits use of the auxiliary pump as a source of fuel pressure in the event of engine-driven pump failure.

Fuel/Air Control Unit

The function of the fuel/air control assembly is to control engine air intake and to set the metered fuel pressure for proper fuel/air ratio. The air throttle is mounted at the manifold inlet and its butterfly valve, positioned by the throttle control in the aircraft, controls the flow of air to the engine. *[Figure 2-42]*

The air throttle assembly is an aluminum casting which contains the shaft and butterfly-valve assembly. The casting bore size is tailored to the engine size, and no venturi or other restriction is used.

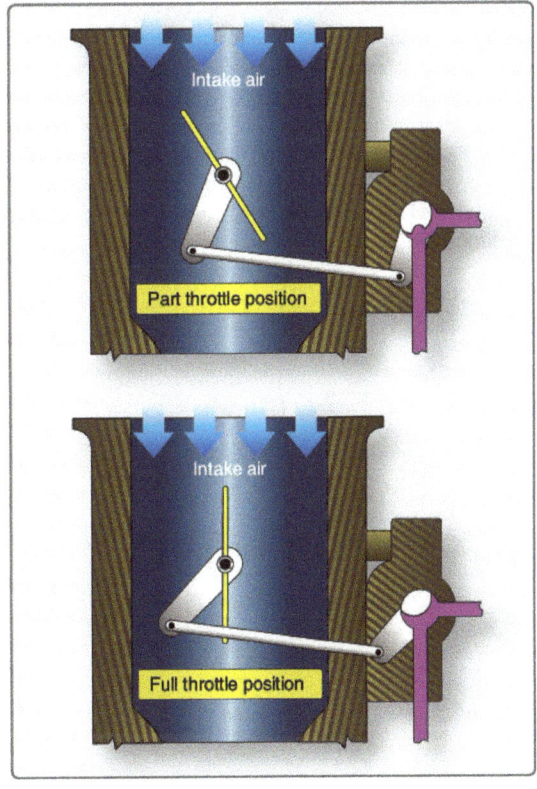

Figure 2-42. *Fuel air control unit.*

Fuel Control Assembly

The fuel control body is made of bronze for best bearing action with the stainless steel valves. Its central bore contains a metering valve at one end and a mixture control valve at the other end. Each stainless steel rotary valve includes a groove which forms a fuel chamber.

Fuel enters the control unit through a strainer and passes to the metering valve. *[Figure 2-43]* This rotary valve has a cam-shaped edge on the outer part of the end face. The position of the cam at the fuel delivery port controls the fuel passed to the manifold valve and the nozzles. The fuel return port connects to the return passage of the center metering plug. The alignment of the mixture control valve with this passage determines the amount of fuel returned to the fuel pump.

By connecting the metering valve to the air throttle, the fuel flow is properly proportioned to airflow for the correct fuel/air ratio. A control level is mounted on the mixture control valve shaft and connected to the cockpit mixture control.

Fuel Manifold Valve

The fuel manifold valve contains a fuel inlet, a diaphragm chamber, and outlet ports for the lines to the individual nozzles. *[Figure 2-44]* The spring-loaded diaphragm operates a valve in the central bore of the body. Fuel pressure provides the force for moving the diaphragm. The diaphragm is enclosed by a cover that retains the diaphragm loading spring. When the valve is down against the lapped seat in the body, the fuel lines to the cylinders are closed off. The valve is drilled for passage of fuel from the diaphragm chamber to its base, and a ball valve is installed within the valve. All incoming fuel must pass through a fine screen installed in the diaphragm chamber.

From the fuel-injection control valve, fuel is delivered to the fuel manifold valve, which provides a central point for dividing fuel flow to the individual cylinders. In the fuel manifold valve, a diaphragm raises or lowers a plunger valve to open or close the individual cylinder fuel supply ports simultaneously.

Fuel Discharge Nozzle

The fuel discharge nozzle is located in the cylinder head with its outlet directed into the intake port. The nozzle body contains a drilled central passage with a counterbore at each end. *[Figure 2-45]* The lower end is used as a chamber for fuel/air mixing before the spray leaves the nozzle. The upper bore contains a removable orifice for calibrating the nozzles. Nozzles are calibrated in several ranges, and all nozzles furnished for one engine are of the same range and are identified by a letter stamped on the hex of the nozzle body.

Drilled radial holes connect the upper counterbore with the outside of the nozzle body. These holes enter the counterbore above the orifice and draw air through a cylindrical screen fitted over the nozzle body. A shield is press-fitted on the nozzle body and extends over the greater part of the filter screen, leaving an opening near the bottom. This provides both mechanical protection and an abrupt change in the direction of airflow which keeps dirt and foreign material out of the nozzle interior.

Carburetor Maintenance

Carburetor Removal

The removal procedures vary with both the type of carburetor concerned and the type of engine on which it is used. Always refer to the applicable manufacturer's technical instructions for a particular installation. Generally, the procedures are much the same, regardless of the type of carburetor concerned.

Before removing a carburetor, make sure the fuel shutoff (or selector) valve is closed. Disconnect the throttle and mixture

Figure 2-43. *Dual fuel control assembly.*

Figure 2-44. *Fuel manifold valve assembly.*

Figure 2-45. *Fuel discharge nozzles.*

control linkages, and lockwire the throttle valve in the closed position. Disconnect the fuel inlet line and all vapor return, gauge, and primer lines. If the same carburetor is to be re-installed, do not alter the rigging of the throttle and mixture controls. Remove the airscoop or airscoop adapter. Remove the air screens and gaskets from the carburetor. Remove the nuts and washers securing the carburetor to the engine. When removing a downdraft carburetor, use extreme care to ensure that nothing is dropped into the engine. Remove the carburetor. Immediately install a protective cover on the carburetor mounting flange of the engine to prevent small parts or foreign material from falling into the engine. When there is danger of foreign material entering open fuel lines during removal or installation of the carburetor, plug them using the proper cover fittings.

Installation of Carburetor

Check the carburetor for proper lockwiring before installation on an engine. Be sure that all shipping plugs have been removed from the carburetor openings.

Remove the protective cover from the carburetor mounting flange on the engine. Place the carburetor mounting flange gasket in position. On some engines, bleed passages are incorporated in the mounting pad. The gasket must be installed so that the bleed hole in the gasket is aligned with the passage in the mounting flange.

Inspect the induction passages for the presence of any foreign material before installing the carburetor. As soon as the carburetor is placed in position on the engine, close and lockwire the throttle valves in the closed position until the remainder of the installation is completed. Place the carburetor deck screen, when feasible, in position to further eliminate the possibility of foreign objects entering the induction system.

When installing a carburetor that uses diaphragms for controlling fuel flow, connect the fuel lines and fill the carburetor with fuel. To do this, turn on the fuel boost pump and move the mixture control from the idle cutoff position to rich position. Continue the flow until oil-free fuel flows from the drain valve. This indicates that the preservative oil has been flushed from the carburetor. Turn off the fuel flow, plug the fuel inlet and vapor vent outlet, and then allow the carburetor, filled with fuel, to stand for a minimum of 8 hours. This is necessary in order to soak the diaphragms and render them pliable to the same degree as when the unit was originally calibrated. Tighten the carburetor mounting bolts to the value specified in the table of torque limits in the applicable maintenance manual. Tighten and safety any other nuts and bolts incidental to the installation of the carburetor before connecting the throttle and mixture-control levers.

After the carburetor has been bolted to the engine, check the throttle and mixture-control lever on the unit for freedom of movement before connecting the control cables or linkage. Check the vapor vent lines or return lines from the carburetor to the aircraft fuel tank for restriction.

Rigging Carburetor Controls

Connect and adjust carburetor or fuel metering equipment throttle controls so that full movement of the throttle is obtained from corresponding full movement of the control in the cockpit. In addition, check and adjust the throttle control linkages so that springback on the throttle quadrant in the aircraft is equal in both the full-open and full-closed positions. Correct any excess play or looseness of control linkage or cables. Controls should be checked so that they go stop-to-stop on the carburetor. Check for complete and full travel of each control.

When installing carburetors or fuel metering equipment incorporating manual-type mixture controls that do not have marked positions, adjust the mixture control mechanism to provide an equal amount of springback at both the rich and lean ends of the control quadrant in the cockpit when the mixture control on the carburetor or fuel metering equipment is moved through the full range. Where mixture controls with detents are used, rig the control mechanism so that the designated positions on the control quadrant in the aircraft agree with the corresponding positions on the carburetor or fuel metering equipment. Controls should move freely and smoothly without binding throughout their total travel. In all cases, check the controls for proper positioning in both the advance and retard positions. Correct excess play or looseness of control linkage or cables. Safety all controls properly to eliminate the possibility of loosening from vibration during operation.

Adjusting Idle Mixtures

Excessively rich or lean idle mixtures result in incomplete combustion within the engine cylinder, with resultant formation of carbon deposits on the spark plugs and subsequent spark plug fouling. In addition, excessively rich or lean idle mixtures make it necessary to taxi at high idle speeds with resultant fast taxi speeds and excessive brake wear. Each engine must have the carburetor idle mixture tailored for the particular engine and installation if best operation is to be obtained.

Engines that are properly adjusted, insofar as valve operation, cylinder compression, ignition, and carburetor idle mixture are concerned, idle at the prescribed rpm for indefinite periods without loading up, overheating, or spark plug fouling. If an engine does not respond to idle mixture adjustment with the resultant stable idling characteristics previously outlined, some other phase of engine operation is not correct. In such cases, determine and correct the cause of the difficulty. A general guide to check and adjust the idle mixture and speed on many types of reciprocating engine is discussed in the following paragraphs. Always refer to the appropriate manual for specific information.

Before checking the idle mixture on any engine, warm up the engine until oil and cylinder head temperatures are normal. Keep the propeller control in the increase rpm setting throughout the entire process of warming up the engine. Always make idle mixture adjustments with cylinder head temperatures at normal values. The idle mixture adjustment is made on the idle mixture fuel control valve. *[Figure 2-46]* It should not be confused with the adjustment of the idle speed stop. The importance of idle mixture adjustment cannot be overstressed. Optimum engine operation at low speeds can be obtained only when proper fuel/air mixtures are delivered to every cylinder of the engine. Excessively rich idle mixtures and the resultant incomplete combustion are responsible for more spark plug fouling than any other single cause. Excessively lean idle mixtures result in faulty acceleration. Furthermore, the idle mixture adjustment affects the fuel/air mixture and engine operation well up into the cruise range.

Figure 2-46. *Idle mixture adjustment for carburetor.*

On an engine with a conventional carburetor, the idle mixture is checked by manually leaning the mixture with the cockpit mixture control. Move the carburetor mixture control slowly and smoothly toward the idle cutoff position. On installations that do not use a manifold pressure gauge, it is necessary to observe the tachometer for an indication of an rpm change. With most installations, the idle mixture should be adjusted to provide an rpm rise prior to decreasing as the engine ceases to fire. This rpm increase varies from 10 to 50 rpm, depending on the installation. Following the momentary increase in rpm, the engine speed starts to drop. Immediately move the mixture control back to rich to prevent the engine from stopping completely.

On RSA fuel-injection engines, the optimum idle setting is one that is rich enough to provide a satisfactory acceleration under all conditions and lean enough to prevent spark plug fouling or rough operation. A rise of 25–50 rpm as the mixture control is moved to the idle cutoff position usually satisfies both of these conditions. The actual idle mixture adjustment is made by the lengthening or shortening of the linkage between the throttle lever and the idle lever. *[Figure 2-47]*

If the check of the idle mixture reveals it to be too lean or too rich, increase or decrease the idle fuel flow as required. Then, repeat the check. Continue checking and adjusting the idle mixture until it checks out properly. During this process, it may be desirable to move the idle speed stop completely out of the way and to hold the engine speed at the desired rpm by means of the throttle. This eliminates the need for frequent readjustments of the idle stop as the idle mixture is improved and the idle speed picks up. After each adjustment, clear the engine by briefly running it at higher rpm. This prevents fouling of the plugs which might otherwise be caused by incorrect idle mixture. After adjusting the idle mixture, recheck it several times to determine definitively that the mixture is correct and remains constant on repeated changes from high power back to idle. Correct any inconsistency in engine idling before releasing the aircraft for service.

Setting the idle mixture on the continental TCM fuel injection system consist of a conventional spring loaded screw located in the air throttle lever. *[Figure 2-48]* The fuel pump pressure is part of the basic calibration and requires servicing to make sure the pump pressure are set correctly before making idle adjustments. The idle mixture adjustment is the locknut at the metering valve end of the linkage between the metering valve and the air throttle levers. Tightening the nut to shorten the linkage provides a richer mixture. A leaner mixture is obtained by backing off the nut to lengthen the linkage. Adjust to obtain a slight and momentary gain in idle speed as the mixture control is slowly moved toward idle cut off. If the idle mixture is set too lean, the idle speed drops with no gain in speed.

Idle Speed Adjustment

After adjusting the idle mixture, reset the idle stop to the idle rpm specified in the aircraft maintenance manual. The engine must be warmed up thoroughly and checked for ignition system malfunctioning. Throughout any carburetor adjustment procedure, periodically run the engine up to approximately half of normal rated speed to clear the engine.

Figure 2-47. *Bendix adjustment of idle mixture linkage.*

Figure 2-48. *TCM adjustment points.*

Some carburetors are equipped with an eccentric screw to adjust idle rpm. Others use a spring-loaded screw to limit the throttle valve closing. In either case, adjust the screw as required to increase or decrease rpm with the throttle retarded against the stop. Open the throttle to clear the engine; close the throttle and allow the rpm to stabilize. Repeat this operation until the desired idling speed is obtained.

Fuel System Inspection and Maintenance

The inspection of a fuel system installation consists basically of an examination of the system for conformity to design requirements together with functional tests to prove correct operation. Since there are considerable variations in the fuel systems used on different aircraft, no attempt has been made to describe any particular system in detail. It is important that the manufacturer's instructions for the aircraft concerned be followed when performing inspection or maintenance functions.

Complete System

Inspect the entire system for wear, damage, or leaks. Make sure that all units are securely attached and properly safetied. The drain plugs or valves in the fuel system should be opened to check for the presence of sediment or water. The filter and sump should also be checked for sediment, water, or slime. The filters or screens, including those provided for flowmeters and auxiliary pumps, must be clean and free from corrosion. The controls should be checked for freedom of movement, security of locking, and freedom from damage due to chafing. The fuel vents should be checked for correct positioning and freedom from obstruction; otherwise, fuel flow or pressure fueling may be affected. Filler neck drains should be checked for freedom from obstruction.

If booster pumps are installed, the system should be checked for leaks by operating the pumps. During this check, the ammeter or load meter should be read and the readings of all the pumps, where applicable, should be approximately the same.

Fuel Tanks

All applicable panels in the aircraft skin or structure should be removed and the tanks inspected for corrosion on the external surfaces, for security of attachment, and for correct adjustment of straps and slings. Check the fittings and connections for leaks or failures.

Some fuel tanks manufactured of light alloy materials are provided with inhibitor cartridges to reduce the corrosive effects of combined leaded fuel and water. Where applicable, the cartridge should be inspected and renewed at the specified periods.

Lines and Fittings

Be sure that the lines are properly supported and that the nuts and clamps are securely tightened. To tighten hose clamps to the proper torque, use a hose-clamp torque wrench. If this wrench is not available, tighten the clamp finger-tight plus the number of turns specified for the hose and clamp. If the clamps do not seal at the specified torque, replace the clamps, the hose, or both. After installing a new hose, check the clamps daily and tighten if necessary. When this daily check indicates that cold flow has ceased, inspect the clamps at less frequent intervals.

Replace the hose if the plys have separated, if there is excessive cold flow, or if the hose is hard and inflexible. Permanent impressions from the clamp and cracks in the tube or cover stock indicate excessive cold flow. Replace any hose that has collapsed at the bends or as a result of misaligned fittings or lines. Some hoses tend to flare at the ends beyond the clamps. This is not an unsatisfactory condition unless leakage is present.

Blisters may form on the outer synthetic rubber cover of the hose. These blisters do not necessarily affect the serviceability of the hose. When a blister is discovered on a hose, remove the hose from the aircraft and puncture the blister with a pin. The blister should then collapse. If fluid (oil, fuel, or hydraulic) emerges from the pinhole in the blister, reject the hose. If only air emerges, then test the hose pressure at $1\frac{1}{2}$ times the working pressure. If no fluid leakage occurs, the hose can be regarded as serviceable.

Puncturing the outer cover of the hose may permit the entry of corrosive elements, such as water, which could attack the wire braiding and ultimately result in failure. For this reason, puncturing the outer covering of hoses exposed to the elements should be avoided.

The external surface of hose may develop fine cracks, usually short in length, which are caused by surface aging. The hose assembly may be regarded as serviceable, provided these cracks do not penetrate to the first braid.

Selector Valves

Rotate selector valves and check for free operation, excessive backlash, and accurate pointer indication. If the backlash is excessive, check the entire operating mechanism for worn joints, loose pins, and broken drive lugs. Replace any defective parts. Inspect cable control systems for worn or frayed cables, damaged pulleys, or worn pulley bearings.

Pumps

During an inspection of booster pumps, check for the following conditions:

1. Proper operation
2. Leaks and condition of fuel and electrical connections
3. Wear of motor brushes

Be sure the drain lines are free of traps, bends, or restrictions. Check the engine-driven pump for leaks and security of mounting. Check the vent and drain lines for obstructions.

Main Line Strainers

Drain water and sediment from the main line strainer at each preflight inspection. Remove and clean the screen at the periods specified in the airplane maintenance manual. Examine the sediment removed from the housing. Particles of rubber are often early warnings of hose deterioration. Check for leaks and damaged gaskets.

Fuel Quantity Gauges

If a sight gauge is used, be sure that the glass is clear and that there are no leaks at the connections. Check the lines leading to it for leaks and security of attachment. Check the mechanical gauges for free movement of the float arm and for proper synchronization of the pointer with the position of the float.

On the electrical and electronic gauges, be sure that both the indicator and the tank units are securely mounted and that their electrical connections are tight.

Fuel Pressure Gauge

Check the pointer for zero tolerance and excessive oscillation. Check the cover glass for looseness and for proper range markings. Check the lines and connections for leaks. Be sure that there is no obstruction in the vent. Replace the instrument if it is defective.

Pressure Warning Signal

Inspect the entire installation for security of mounting and condition of the electrical, fuel, and air connections. Check the lamp by pressing the test switch to see that it lights. Check the operation by turning the battery switch on, building up pressure with the booster pump, and observing the pressure at which the light goes out. If necessary, adjust the contact mechanism.

Water Injection Systems for Reciprocating Engines

These systems have very limited use in modern aircraft engines. Water injection was used mostly on large radial engines. The water injection system enabled more power to be obtained from the engine at takeoff than is possible without water injection. The carburetor (operating at high power settings) delivers more fuel to the engine than it actually needs. A leaner mixture would produce more power; however, the additional fuel is necessary to prevent overheating and detonation. With the injection of the antidetonant fluid, the mixture can be leaned out to that which produces maximum power, and the vaporization of the water-alcohol mixture then provides the cooling formerly supplied by the excess fuel.

Turbine Engine Fuel System—General Requirements

The fuel system is one of the more complex aspects of the gas turbine engine. It must be possible to increase or decrease the power at will to obtain the thrust required for any operating condition. In turbine-powered aircraft, this control is provided by varying the flow of fuel to the combustion chambers. However, some turboprop aircraft also use variable-pitch propellers; thus, the selection of thrust is shared by two controllable variables, fuel flow and propeller blade angle.

The quantity of fuel supplied must be adjusted automatically to correct for changes in ambient temperature or pressure. If the quantity of fuel becomes excessive in relation to mass airflow through the engine, the limiting temperature of the turbine blades can be exceeded, or it will produce compressor stall and a condition referred to as rich blowout. Rich blowout occurs when the amount of oxygen in the air supply is insufficient to support combustion and when the mixture is cooled below the combustion temperature by the excess fuel. The other extreme, lean flame-out, occurs if the fuel quantity is reduced proportionally below the air quantity. The engine must operate through acceleration and deceleration without any fuel-control-related problems.

The fuel system must deliver fuel to the combustion chambers not only in the right quantity, but also in the right condition for satisfactory combustion. The fuel nozzles form part of the fuel system and atomize or vaporize the fuel so that it ignites and burns efficiently. The fuel system must also supply fuel so that the engine can be easily started on the ground and in the air. This means that the fuel must be injected into the combustion chambers in a combustible condition during engine starting, and that combustion must be sustained while the engine is accelerating to its normal idling speed. Another critical condition to which the fuel system must respond occurs during a rapid acceleration. When the engine is accelerated, energy must be furnished to the turbine in excess of that necessary to maintain a constant rpm. However, if the fuel flow increases too rapidly, an over rich mixture can be produced, with the possibility of a rich blowout or compressor stall.

Turbofan, turbojet, turboshaft, and turboprop engines are equipped with a fuel control unit which automatically satisfies the requirements of the engine. Although the basic requirements apply generally to all gas turbine engines, the way in which individual fuel controls meet these needs cannot be conveniently generalized.

Turbine Fuel Controls

Gas turbine engine fuel controls can be divided into three basic groups:

1. Hydromechanical
2. Hydromechanical/electronic
3. Full Authority Digital Engine (or Electronics) Control (FADEC)

The hydromechanical/electronic fuel control is a hybrid of the two types of fuel control, but can function solely as a hydromechanical control. In the dual mode, inputs and outputs are electronic, and fuel flow is set by servo motors. The third type, FADEC, uses electronic sensors for its inputs and controls fuel flow with electronic outputs. The FADEC-type control gives the electronic controller (computer) complete control. The computing section of the FADEC system depends completely on sensor inputs to the electronic engine control (EEC) to meter the fuel flow. The fuel metering device meters the fuel using only outputs from the EEC. Most turbine fuel controls are quickly going to the FADEC type of control. This electronically controlled fuel control is very accurate in scheduling fuel by sensing many of the engine parameters.

Regardless of the type, all fuel controls accomplish essentially the same function. That function is to schedule the fuel flow to match the power required by the pilot. Some sense more engine variables than others. The fuel control can sense many different inputs, such as power lever position, engine rpm for each spool, compressor inlet pressure and temperature, burner pressure, compressor discharge pressure, and many more parameters as needed by the specific engine. These variables affect the amount of thrust that an engine produces for a given fuel flow. By sensing these parameters, the fuel control has a clear picture of what is happening in the engine and can adjust fuel flow as needed. Each type of turbine engine has its own specific needs for fuel delivery and control.

Hydromechanical Fuel Control

Hydromechanical fuel controls were used and are still used on many engines, but their use is becoming limited giving way to electronic based controls. Fuel controls have two sections, computing and metering, to provide the correct fuel flow for the engine. A pure hydromechanical fuel control has no electronic interface assisting in computing or metering the fuel flow. It also is generally driven by the gas generator gear train of the engine to sense engine speed. Other mechanical engine parameters that are sensed are compressor discharge pressure, burner pressure, exhaust temperature, and inlet air temperature and pressure. Once the computing section determines the correct amount of fuel flow, the metering section through cams and servo valves delivers the fuel to the engine fuel system. Actual operating procedures for a hydromechanical fuel control is very complicated and still the fuel metering is not as accurate as with an electronic type of interface or control. Electronic controls can receive more inputs with greater accuracy than hydromechanical controls. Early electronic controls used a hydromechanical control with an electronic system added on the system to fine tune the metering of the fuel. This arrangement also used the hydromechanical system as a backup if the electronic system failed. *[Figure 2-49]*

Hydromechanical/Electronic Fuel Control

The addition of the electronic control to the basic hydromechanical fuel control was the next step in the development of turbine engine fuel controls. Generally, this type of system used a remotely located EEC to adjust the fuel flow. A description of a typical system is explained in the following information. The basic function of the engine fuel system is to pressurize the fuel, meter fuel flow, and deliver atomized fuel to the combustion section of the engine. Fuel flow is controlled by a hydromechanical fuel control assembly, which contains a fuel shutoff section and a fuel metering section.

Figure 2-49. *Fuel control assembly schematic hydomechanical/electronic.*

This fuel control unit is sometimes mounted on the vane fuel pump assembly. It provides the power lever connection and the fuel shutoff function. The unit provides mechanical overspeed protection for the gas generator spool during normal (automatic mode) engine operation. In automatic mode, the EEC is in control of metering the fuel. In manual mode, the hydromechanical control takes over.

During normal engine operation, a remotely mounted electronic fuel control unit (EFCU) (same as an EEC) performs the functions of thrust setting, speed governing and acceleration, and deceleration limiting through EFCU outputs to the fuel control assembly in response to power lever inputs. In the event of electrical or EFCU failure, or at the option of the pilot, the fuel control assembly functions in manual mode to allow engine operation at reduced power under control of the hydromechanical portion of the controller only.

The total engine fuel and control system consists of the following components and provides the functions as indicated:

1. The vane fuel pump assembly is a fixed displacement fuel pump that provides high pressure fuel to the engine fuel control system. *[Figure 2-50]*

Figure 2-50. *Fuel pump and filter.*

2. The filter bypass valve in the fuel pump allows fuel to bypass the fuel filter when the pressure drop across the fuel filter is excessive. An integral differential pressure indicator visually flags an excessive differential pressure condition before bypassing occurs, by extending a pin from the fuel filter bowl. Fuel pump discharge flow in excess of that required by the fuel control assembly is returned from the control to the pump interstage.

3. The hydromechanical fuel control assembly provides the fuel metering function of the EFCU.

Fuel is supplied to the fuel control through a 200-micron inlet filter screen and is metered to the engine by the servo-operated metering valve. It is a fuel flow/compressor discharge pressure (Wf/P3) ratio device that positions the metering valve in response to engine compressor discharge pressure (P3). Fuel pressure differential across the servo valve is maintained by the servo-operated bypass valve in response to commands from the EFCU. *[Figure 2-49]* The manual mode solenoid valve is energized in the automatic mode. The automatic mode restricts operation of the mechanical speed governor. It is restricted to a single overspeed governor setting above the speed range controlled electronically. Deenergizing the manual mode valve enables the mechanical speed governor to function as an all speed governor in response to power lever angle (PLA). The fuel control system includes a low power sensitive torque motor which may be activated to increase or decrease fuel flow in the automatic mode (EFCU mode). The torque motor provides an interface to an electronic control unit that senses various engine and ambient parameters and activates the torque motor to meter fuel flow accordingly. This torque motor provides electromechanical conversion of an electrical signal from the EFCU. The torque motor current is zero in the manual mode, which establishes a fixed Wf/P3 ratio.

This fixed wf/P3 ratio is such that the engine operates surge free and is capable of producing a minimum of 90 percent thrust up to 30,000 feet for this example system. All speed governing of the high-pressure spool (gas generator) is achieved by the flyweight governor. The flyweight governor modulates a pneumatic servo, consistent with the speed set point as determined by the power lever angle (PLA) setting. The pneumatic servo accomplishes Wf/P3 ratio modulation to govern the gas generator speed by bleeding down the P3 acting on the metering valve servo. The P3 limiter valve bleeds down the P3 pressure acting in the metering valve servo when engine structural limits are encountered in either control mode. The start fuel enrichment solenoid valve provides additional fuel flow in parallel with the metering valve when required for engine cold starting or altitude restarts. The valve is energized by the EFCU when enrichment is required. It is always deenergized in the manual mode to prevent high altitude sub-idle operation.

Located downstream of the metering valve are the manual shutoff and pressurizing valves. The shutoff valve is a rotary unit connected to the power lever. It allows the pilot to direct fuel to the engine manually. The pressurizing valve acts as a discharge restrictor to the hydromechanical control. It functions to maintain minimum operating pressures throughout the control. The pressurizing valve also provides a positive leak-tight fuel shutoff to the engine fuel nozzles when the manual valve is closed.

4. The flow divider and drain valve assembly proportions fuel to the engine primary and secondary fuel nozzles. It drains the nozzles and manifolds at engine shutdown. It also incorporates an integral solenoid for modifying the fuel flow for cold-starting conditions.

During an engine start, the flow divider directs all flow through the primary nozzles. After start, as the engine fuel demand increases, the flow divider valve opens to allow the secondary nozzles to function. During all steady-state engine operation, both primary and secondary nozzles are flowing fuel. A 74-micron, self-bypassing screen is located under the fuel inlet fitting and provides last chance filtration of the fuel prior to the fuel nozzles.

5. The fuel manifold assembly is a matched set consisting of both primary and secondary manifolds and the fuel nozzle assemblies.

Twelve fuel nozzles direct primary and secondary fuel through the nozzles causing the fuel to swirl and form a finely atomized spray. The manifold assembly provides fuel routing and atomizing to ensure proper combustion.

The EEC system consists of the hydromechanical fuel control, EFCU, and aircraft mounted power lever angle potentiometer. Aircraft-generated control signals include inlet pressure, airstream differential pressure, and inlet temperature plus pilot selection of either manual or auto mode for the EFCU operation. Engine-generated control signals include fan spool speed, gas generator spool speed, inner turbine temperature, fan discharge temperature, and compressor discharge pressure. Aircraft- and engine-generated control signals are directed to the EFCU where these signals are interpreted. The PLA potentiometer is aircraft mounted in the throttle quadrant. The PLA potentiometer transmits an electrical signal to the EFCU, which represents engine thrust demand in relation to throttle position. If the EFCU determines a power change is required, it commands the torque motor to modulate differential pressure at the head sensor. This change in differential pressure causes the metering valve to move, varying fuel flow to the engine as required. The EFCU receives electrical signals which represent engine operating variables. It also receives a pilot-initiated signal (by power-lever position) representing engine thrust demand. The EFCU computes electrical output signals for use by the engine fuel control for scheduling engine operation within predetermined limits. The EFCU is programmed to recognize predetermined engine operating limits and to compute output signals such that these operating limits are not exceeded. The EFCU is remotely located and airframe mounted. An interface between the EFCU and aircraft/engine is provided through the branched wiring harness assembly. *[Figure 2-51]*

FADEC Fuel Control Systems

A full authority digital electronic control (FADEC) has been developed to control fuel flow on most new turbine engine models. A true FADEC system has no hydromechanical fuel control backup system. The system uses electronic sensors that feed engine parameter information into the EEC. The EEC gathers the needed information to determine the amount of fuel flow and transmits it to a fuel metering valve. The fuel metering valve simply reacts to the commands from the EEC. The EEC is a computer that is the computing section of the fuel delivery system and the metering valve meters the fuel flow. FADEC systems are used on many types of turbine engines from APUs to the largest propulsion engines.

FADEC for an Auxiliary Power Unit

The first example system is an APU engine that uses the aircraft fuel system to supply fuel to the fuel control. An electric boost pump may be used to supply fuel under pressure to the control. The fuel usually passes through an aircraft shutoff valve that is tied to the fire detecting/extinguishing system. An aircraft furnished in-line fuel filter may also be used. Fuel entering the fuel control unit first passes through a 10-micron filter. If the filter becomes contaminated, the resulting pressure drop opens the filter bypass valve and unfiltered fuel then is supplied to the APU. Shown in *Figure 2-52* is a pump with an inlet pressure access plug so that a fuel pressure gauge might be installed for troubleshooting purposes. Fuel then enters a positive displacement, gear-type pump. Upon discharge from the pump, the fuel passes through a 70-micron screen. The screen is installed at this point to filter any wear debris that might be discharged from the pump element. From the screen, fuel branches to the metering valve, differential pressure valve, and the ultimate relief valve. Also shown at this point is a pump discharge pressure access plug, another point where a pressure gauge might be installed.

The differential pressure valve maintains a constant pressure drop across the metering valve by bypassing fuel to the pump inlet so that metered flow is proportional to metering valve area. The metering valve area is modulated by the

Figure 2-51. *Engine control system.*

torque motor, which receives variable current from the ECU. The ultimate relief valve opens to bypass excess fuel back to the pump inlet whenever system pressure exceeds a predetermined pressure. This occurs during each shutdown since all flow is stopped by the shutoff valve and the differential pressure valve, is unable to bypass full pump capacity. Fuel flows from the metering valve out of the FCU, through the solenoid shutoff valve and on to the atomizer. Initial flow is through the primary nozzle tip only. The flow divider opens at higher pressure and adds flow through the secondary path.

Figure 2-52. *APU fuel system schematic.*

FADEC Fuel Control Propulsion Engine

Many large high-bypass turbofan engines use the FADEC type of fuel control system. The EEC is the primary component of the FADEC engine fuel control system. The EEC is a computer that controls the operation of the engine. The EEC housing contains two electronic channels (two separate computers) that are physically separated internally and is naturally cooled by convection. The EEC is generally placed in an area of the engine nacelle that is cool during engine operation. It attaches to the lower-left fan case with shock mounts. *[Figure 2-53]*

The EEC computer uses data it receives from many engine sensors and airplane systems to control the engine operation. It receives electronic signals from the flight deck to set engine power or thrust. The throttle lever angle resolver supplies the EEC with a signal in proportion to the thrust lever position. The EEC controls most engine components and receives feedback from them. Many components supply the EEC with data for engine operation.

Power for the EEC comes from the aircraft electrical system or the permanent magnet alternator (PMA). When the engine is running, the PMA supplies power to the EEC directly. The EEC is a two channel computer that controls every aspect of engine operation. Each channel, which is an independent computer, can completely control the operation of the engine. The processor does all of the control calculations and supplies all the data for the control signals for the torque motors and solenoids. The cross-talk logic compares data from channels A and B and uses the cross-talk logic to find which EEC channel is the best to control the output driver for a torque motor or solenoid bank. The primary channel controls all of the output drivers. If the cross-talk logic finds that the other channel is better for control of a specific bank, the EEC changes control of that one bank to the other channel. The EEC has output driver banks that supply the control signals to engine components. Each channel of the EEC supplies the driver banks with control signals. The EEC has both volatile and nonvolatile memory to store performance and maintenance data.

The EEC can control the engine thrust in two modes, which can be selected by use of a mode selection switch. In the normal mode, engine thrust is set with EPR; in the alternate mode, thrust is set by N1. When the fuel control switch is moved from run to cutoff, the EEC resets. During this reset, all fault data is recorded in the nonvolatile memory. The EEC controls the metering valve in the fuel metering unit to supply fuel flow for combustion. *[Figure 2-54]* The fuel metering unit is mounted on the front face of the gearbox and is attached to the front of the fuel pump. *[Figure 2-55]* The EEC

Figure 2-53. *EEC and programming plug.*

Figure 2-54. *Fuel metering unit.*

Figure 2-55. *Fuel pump.*

also sends a signal to the minimum pressure and shutoff valve in the fuel metering unit to start or stop fuel flow. The EEC receives position feedback for several engine components by using rotary differential transformer, linear variable differential transformer, and thermocouples. These sensors feed engine parameter information from several systems back to the EEC. The fuel control run cutoff switch controls the high pressure fuel shut off valve that allows or cuts off fuel flow. The fuel temperature sensor thermocouple attaches to the fuel outlet line on the rear of the fuel/oil cooler and sends this information to the EEC. The EEC uses a torque motor driver to control the position of the metering valve in the fuel metering unit. The EEC uses solenoid drivers to control the other functions of the FMU. The EEC also controls several other subsystems of the engine, as shown in *Figure 2-56*, through torque motors and solenoids, such as fuel and air oil coolers, bleed valves, variable stator vanes, turbine cooling air valves, and the turbine case cooling system.

Figure 2-56. *Systems controlled by EEC.*

Each channel of the EEC has seven electrical connections, three on each side and one on the bottom. Both channels share the inputs of the two connections on the top of the EEC. These are the programming plug and test connector. The programming plug selects the proper software in the EEC for the thrust rating of the engine. The plug attaches to the engine fan case with a lanyard. When removing the EEC, the plug remains with the engine. Each channel of the EEC has three pneumatic connections on the bottom of the EEC. Transducers inside the EEC supply the related and opposite EEC channel with a signal in proportion to the pressure. The pressures that are read by the EEC are ambient pressure, burner pressure, LPC exit pressure, and fan inlet pressure. Each channel has its own wire color that connects the EEC to its sensors. Channel A wiring is blue and channel B sensor signals are green. The non-EEC circuit wire is gray while the thermocouple signals are yellow. This color coding helps simplify which sensors are used with each channel.

Fuel System Operation

The fuel pump receives fuel from the airplane fuel system. The low pressure boost stage of the pump pressurizes the fuel and sends it to the fuel/oil cooler (FOC). The fuel flows from the FOC, through the fuel pump filter element, and then to the high pressure main stage of the pump. The high pressure main stage increases the fuel pressure and sends it to the fuel metering unit (FMU). It also supplies servo fuel to the servo fuel heater and engine components. Fuel for combustion (metered fuel) goes through the fuel flow transmitter to the distribution valve. *[Figure 2-57]* The fuel distribution valve supplies metered fuel to the fuel supply manifolds. *[Figure 2-58]* The fuel injectors get the metered fuel from the fuel supply manifolds and spray the fuel into the engine for combustion. *[Figure 2-59]* The fuel pump housing contains a disposable fuel filter element. The fuel filter differential

Figure 2-57. *Fuel flow transmitter.*

Figure 2-58. *Fuel distribution valve.*

Figure 2-59. *Fuel manifolds.*

pressure switch supplies a signal to the EEC that indicates an almost clogged filter condition. Unfiltered fuel can then bypass the filter element if the element becomes clogged.

Water Injection System

On warm days, thrust is reduced because of the decrease in air density. This can be compensated for by injecting water at the compressor inlet or diffuser case. This lowers the air temperature and increases air density. A microswitch in the fuel control is actuated by the control shaft when the power lever is moved toward the maximum power position.

A water injection speed reset servo resets the speed adjustment to a higher value during water injection. Without this adjustment, the fuel control would decrease rpm so that no additional thrust would be realized during water injection. The servo is a shuttle valve that is acted upon by water pressure during water injection. Movement of the servo displaces a lever on the cam-operated lever linkage to the speed governor speeder spring, increasing the force of the speeder spring and increasing the set speed. Because the resulting rpm is usually higher while water is flowing, increased thrust during water injection is ensured. If the water injection system is not armed in the cockpit or if there is no water available, nothing happens when the water injection switch in the fuel control unit is actuated. When water is available, a portion of it is directed to the water injection speed re-set servo. Water injection systems are not normally used on high-bypass turbofan engines.

Fuel Control Maintenance

The field repair of the turbine engine fuel control is very limited. The only repairs permitted in the field are the replacement of the control and adjustments afterwards. These adjustments are limited to the idle rpm and the maximum speed adjustment, commonly called trimming the engine.

Both adjustments are made in the normal range of operation. During engine trimming, the fuel control is checked for idle rpm, maximum rpm, acceleration, and deceleration. The procedures used to check the fuel control vary depending on the aircraft and engine installation.

The engine is trimmed in accordance with the procedures in the maintenance or overhaul manual for a particular engine. In general, the procedure consists of obtaining the ambient air temperature and the field barometric pressure (not sea level) immediately preceding the trimming of the engine. Care must be taken to obtain a true temperature reading comparable to that of the air that enters the engine. Using these readings, the desired turbine discharge pressure or EPR (engine pressure ratio) reading is computed from charts published in the maintenance manual.

The engine is operated at full throttle (or at the part power control trim stop) for a sufficient period of time to ensure that it has completely stabilized. Five minutes is the usual recommended stabilization period. A check should be made to ensure that the compressor air-bleed valves have fully closed and that all accessory drive air bleed for which the trim curve has not been corrected (such as a cabin air-conditioning unit) has been turned off. When the engine has stabilized, a comparison is made of the observed and the computed turbine discharge pressure Pt_7 (or EPR) to determine the approximate amount of trimming required. If a trim is necessary, the engine fuel control is then adjusted to obtain the target turbine discharge pressure Pt_7 or EPR on the gauge. Immediately following the fuel control adjustment, the tachometer reading is observed and recorded. Fuel flow and exhaust gas temperature readings should also be taken. On Pratt and Whitney engines, using a dual-spool compressor, the observed N_2 tachometer reading is next corrected for speed bias by means of temperature/rpm curve. The observed tachometer reading is divided by the percent trim speed obtained from the curve. The result is the new engine trim speed in percent, corrected to standard day (59 °F or 15 °C) temperature. The new trim speed in rpm may be calculated when the rpm at which the tachometer reads 100 percent is known. This value may be obtained from the appropriate engine manual. If all these procedures have been performed satisfactorily, the engine has been properly trimmed.

Engine trimming should always be carried out under precisely controlled conditions with the aircraft headed into the wind. Precise control is necessary to ensure maintenance of a minimum thrust level upon which the aircraft performance is based. In addition, precise control of engine trimming contributes to better engine life in terms of both maximum time between overhaul and minimum out-of-commission time due to engine maintenance requirements. Engines should never be trimmed if icing conditions exist.

Most electronic control fuel control systems do not require trimming or mechanical adjustments. Changes to the EEC in the FADEC system is normally accomplished through software changes or changing the EEC.

Engine Fuel System Components

Main Fuel Pumps (Engine Driven)

Main fuel pumps deliver a continuous supply of fuel at the proper pressure and at all times during operation of the aircraft engine. The engine-driven fuel pump must be capable of delivering the maximum needed flow at appropriate pressure to obtain satisfactory nozzle spray and accurate fuel regulation.

These engine driven fuel pumps may be divided into two distinct system categories:

1. Constant displacement
2. Nonconstant displacement

Their use depends on where in the engine fuel system they are used. Generally, a nonpositive displacement (centrifugal pump) is used at the inlet of the engine-driven pump to provide positive flow to the second stage of the pump. The output of a centrifugal pump can be varied as needed and is sometimes referred to as a boost stage of the engine-driven pump.

The second or main stage of the engine-driven fuel pump for turbine engines is generally a positive displacement type of pump. The term "positive displacement" means that the gear supplies a fixed quantity of fuel to the engine for every revolution of the pump gears. Gear-type pumps have approximately straight line flow characteristics, whereas fuel requirements fluctuate with flight or ambient air conditions. Hence, a pump of adequate capacity at all engine operating conditions has excess capacity over most of the range of operation. This is the characteristic that requires the use of a pressure relief valve for bypassing excess fuel back to the inlet. A typical two-stage turbine engine driven pump is illustrated in *Figure 2-60*. The impeller, which is driven at a greater speed than the high pressure elements, increases the fuel pressure depending upon engine speed.

The fuel is discharged from the boost element (impeller) to the two high-pressure gear elements. A relief valve is incorporated in the discharge port of the pump. This valve opens at a predetermined pressure and is capable of bypassing the total fuel flow. This allows fuel in excess of that required for engine operation at the time to be recirculated. The bypass

Figure 2-60. *Dual element fuel pump.*

fuel is routed to the inlet side of the second stage pump. Fuel flows from the pump to the fuel metering unit or fuel control. The fuel control is often attached to the fuel pump. The fuel pump is also lubricated by the fuel passing through the pump, and it should never be turned without fuel flow supplied to the inlet of the pump. As the engine coasts down at shutdown, the fuel pump should be provided with fuel until it comes to a stop.

Fuel Heater

Gas turbine engine fuel systems are very susceptible to the formation of ice in the fuel filters. When the fuel in the aircraft fuel tanks cools to 32 °F or below, residual water in the fuel tends to freeze, forming ice crystals. When these ice crystals in the fuel become trapped in the filter, they block fuel flow to the engine, which causes a very serious problem. To prevent this problem, the fuel is kept at a temperature above freezing. Warmer fuel also can improve combustion, so some means of regulating the fuel temperature is needed.

One method of regulating fuel temperature is to use a fuel heater which operates as a heat exchanger to warm the fuel. The heater can use engine bleed air or engine lubricating oil as a source of heat. The bleed air type is called an air-to-liquid exchanger and the oil type is known as a liquid-to-liquid heat exchanger. The function of a fuel heater is to protect the engine fuel system from ice formation. However, should ice form in the filter, the heater can also be used to thaw ice on the fuel screen to allow fuel to flow freely again. On most installations, the fuel filter is fitted with a pressure-drop warning switch, which illuminates a warning light on the cockpit instrument panel. If ice begins to collect on the filter surface, the pressure across the filter slowly decreases. When the pressure reaches a predetermined value, the warning light alerts the flight deck personnel.

Fuel deicing systems are designed to be used intermittently. The control of the system may be manual, by a switch in the cockpit, or automatic, using a thermostatic sensing element in the fuel heater to open or close the air or oil shutoff valve. A fuel heater system is shown in *Figure 2-61*. In a FADEC system, the computer controls the fuel temperature by sensing the fuel temperature and heating it as needed.

Fuel Filters

A low-pressure filter is installed between the supply tanks and the engine fuel system to protect the engine-driven fuel pump and various control devices. An additional high-pressure fuel filter is installed between the fuel pump and the fuel control to protect the fuel control from contaminants that could come from the low pressure pump.

The three most common types of filters in use are the micron filter, the wafer screen filter, and the plain screen mesh filter. The individual use of each of these filters is dictated by the filtering treatment required at a particular location. The micron filter has the greatest filtering action of any present-day filter type and, as the name implies, is rated in microns. *[Figure 2-62]* (A micron is one thousandth of 1 millimeter.) The porous cellulose material frequently used in construction of the filter cartridges is capable of removing foreign matter measuring from 10–25 microns. The minute openings make this type of filter susceptible to clogging; therefore, a bypass valve is a necessary safety factor.

Figure 2-62. *Aircraft fuel filter.*

Since the micron filter does such a thorough job of removing foreign matter, it is especially valuable between the fuel tank and engine. The cellulose material also absorbs water, preventing it from passing through the pumps. If water does seep through the filter, which happens occasionally when filter elements become saturated with water, the water can and does quickly damage the working elements of the fuel pump

Figure 2-61. *Fuel heater.*

and control units, since these elements depend solely on the fuel for their lubrication. To reduce water damage to pumps and control units, periodic servicing and replacement of filter elements is imperative. Daily draining of fuel tank sumps and low-pressure filters eliminates much filter trouble and undue maintenance of pumps and fuel control units.

The most widely used filters are the 200-mesh and the 35-mesh micron filters. They are used in fuel pumps, fuel controls, and between the fuel pump and fuel control where removal of micronic particles is needed. These filters, usually made of fine-mesh steel wire, are a series of layers of wire.

The wafer screen type of filter has a replaceable element, which is made of layers of screen disks of bronze, brass, steel, or similar material. *[Figure 2-63]* This type of filter is capable of removing micronic particles. It also has the strength to withstand high pressure.

Fuel Spray Nozzles and Fuel Manifolds

Although fuel spray nozzles are an integral part of the fuel system, their design is closely related to the type of combustion chamber in which they are installed. The fuel nozzles inject fuel into the combustion area in a highly atomized, precisely patterned spray so that burning is completed evenly, in the shortest possible time, and in the smallest possible space. It is very important that the fuel be evenly distributed and well centered in the flame area within the liners. This is to preclude the formation of any hot spots in the combustion chambers and to prevent the flame burning through the liner.

Fuel nozzle types vary considerably between engines, although for the most part fuel is sprayed into the combustion area under pressure through small orifices in the nozzles. The two types of fuel nozzles generally used are the simplex and the duplex configurations. The duplex nozzle usually requires a dual manifold and a pressurizing valve or flow divider for dividing primary and secondary (main) fuel flow, but the simplex nozzle requires only a single manifold for proper fuel delivery.

The fuel nozzles can be constructed to be installed in various ways. The two methods used quite frequently are:

1. External mounting wherein a mounting pad is provided for attachment of the nozzles to the case or the inlet air elbow, with the nozzle near the dome; or
2. Internal mounting at the liner dome, in which the chamber cover must be removed for replacement or maintenance of the nozzle.

The nozzles used in a specific engine should be matched so that they flow equal amounts of fuel. Even fuel distribution is important to efficient combustion in the burner section. The fuel nozzle must present a fine spray with the correct pattern and optimum atomization.

Simplex Fuel Nozzle

The simplex fuel nozzle was the first nozzle type used in turbine engines and was replaced in most installations with the duplex nozzle, which gave better atomization at starting and idling speeds. The simplex nozzle is still being used

Figure 2-63. *Wafer screen filter.*

in several installations. *[Figure 2-64]* Each of the simplex nozzles consists of a nozzle tip, an insert, and a strainer made up of fine-mesh screen and a support.

Figure 2-65. *Duplex nozzle spray pattern.*

Figure 2-64. *Simplex airblast nozzle cutaway.*

Duplex Fuel Nozzle

The duplex fuel nozzle is widely used in present day gas turbine engines. As mentioned previously, its use requires a flow divider, but at the same time it offers a desirable spray pattern for combustion over a wide range of operating pressures. *[Figure 2-65]* A nozzle typical of this type is illustrated in *Figure 2-66*.

Airblast Nozzles

Airblast nozzles are used to provide improved mixing of the fuel and airflow to provide a optimum spray for combustion. As can be seen in *Figure 2-64*, squirrel vanes are used to mix the air and fuel at the nozzle opening. By using a proportion of the primary combustion airflow in the fuel spray, locally rich fuel concentrations can be reduced. This type of fuel nozzle can be either simplex or duplex, depending upon the engine. This nozzle type can operate at lower working pressures than other nozzles which allows for lighter pumps. This airblast nozzle also helps in reducing the tendency of the nozzle to carbon up which can disturb the flow pattern.

Flow Divider

A flow divider creates primary and secondary fuel supplies that are discharged through separate manifolds, providing two separate fuel flows. *[Figure 2-67]* Metered fuel from the fuel control enters the inlet of the flow divider and passes through an orifice and then on to the primary nozzles. A passage in the flow divider directs fuel flow from both sides of the orifice to a chamber. This chamber contains a differential pressure bellows, a viscosity compensated restrictor (VCR), and a surge dampener. During engine start, fuel pressure is applied to the inlet port and across the VCR, surge dampener, and on to the primary side of the nozzles. Fuel is also applied under pressure to the outside of the flow divider bellows and through the surge dampener to the inside of the flow divider bellows. This unequal pressure causes the flow divider valve to remain closed. When fuel flow increases, the differential pressure on the bellows also increases. At a predetermined pressure, the bellows compresses, allowing the flow divider valve to open. This action starts fuel flow to the secondary manifold, which increases the fuel flow to the engine. This fuel flows out of the secondary opening in the nozzles.

Fuel Pressurizing and Dump Valves

The fuel pressurizing valve is usually required on engines incorporating duplex fuel nozzles to divide the flow into

Figure 2-66. *Duplex fuel nozzle.*

Figure 2-67. *Flow divider.*

primary and secondary manifolds. At the fuel flows required for starting and altitude idling, all the fuel passes through the primary line. As the fuel flow increases, the valve begins to open the main line until at maximum flow the secondary line is passing approximately 90 percent of the fuel.

Fuel pressurizing valves usually trap fuel forward of the manifold, giving a positive cutoff. This cutoff prevents fuel from dribbling into the manifold and through the fuel nozzles, limiting afterfires and carbonization of the fuel nozzles. Carbonization occurs because combustion chamber temperatures are lowered and the fuel is not completely burned.

A flow divider performs essentially the same function as a pressurizing valve. It is used, as the name implies, to divide flow to the duplex fuel nozzles. It is not unusual for units performing identical functions to have different nomenclature between engine manufacturers.

Combustion Drain Valves

The drain valves are units used for draining fuel from the various components of the engine where accumulated fuel is most likely to present operating problems. The possibility of combustion chamber accumulation with the resultant fire hazard is one problem. A residual problem is the deposit of lead and/or gum, after evaporation, in such places as fuel manifolds and fuel nozzles.

In some instances, the fuel manifolds are drained by an individual unit known as a drip or dump valve. This type of valve may operate by pressure differential, or it may be solenoid operated.

The combustion chamber drain valve drains fuel that accumulates in the combustion chamber after each shutdown and fuel that may have accumulated during a false start. If the combustion chambers are the can type, fuel drains by gravity down through the flame tubes or interconnecter tubes until it gathers in the lower chambers, which are fitted with drain lines to the drain valve. If the combustion chamber is of the basket or annular type, the fuel merely drains through the air holes in the liner and accumulates in a trap in the bottom of the chamber housing, which is connected to the drain line.

After the fuel accumulates in the bottom of the combustion chamber or drain lines, the drain valve allows the fuel to be drained whenever pressure within the manifold or the burner(s) has been reduced to near atmospheric pressure. A small spring holds the valve off its seat until pressure in the combustion chamber during operation overcomes the spring and closes the valve. The valve is closed during engine operation. It is imperative that this valve be in good working condition to drain accumulated fuel after each shutdown. Otherwise, a hot start during the next starting attempt or an afterfire after shutdown is likely to occur.

Fuel Quantity Indicating Units

Fuel quantity units vary from one installation to the next. A fuel counter or indicator, mounted on the instrument panel, is electrically connected to a flowmeter installed in the fuel line to the engine.

The fuel counter, or totalizer, is used to keep record of fuel use. When the aircraft is serviced with fuel, the counter is manually set to the total number of pounds of fuel in all tanks. As fuel passes through the measuring element of the flowmeter, it sends electrical impulses to the fuel counter. These impulses actuate the fuel counter mechanism so that the number of pounds passing to the engine is subtracted from the original reading. Thus, the fuel counter continually shows the total quantity of fuel, in pounds, remaining in the aircraft. However, there are certain conditions that cause the fuel counter indication to be inaccurate. Any jettisoned fuel is indicated on the fuel counter as fuel still available for use. Any fuel that leaks from a tank or a fuel line upstream of the flowmeter is not counted.

Chapter 3
Induction and Exhaust Systems

Reciprocating Engine Induction Systems

The basic induction system of an aircraft reciprocating engine consists of an air scoop used to collect the inlet air and ducting that transfers the air to the inlet filter. The air filter is generally housed in the carburetor heat box or other housing close by that is attached to the carburetor or fuel injection controller. The engine used in light aircraft is usually equipped with either a carburetor or a fuel-injection system. After air passes through the fuel metering device, an intake manifold with long curved pipes or passages is used to send the fuel/air mixture to the cylinders. An induction air scoop is shown in *Figure 3-1*. The air scoop is located on the engine cowling to allow maximum airflow into the engine's induction system. The air filter, shown in *Figure 3-2*, prevents dirt and other foreign matter from entering the engine. Filtered air enters the fuel metering device (carburetor/fuel injector) where the throttle plate controls the amount of air flowing to the engine. The air coming out of the throttle is referred to as manifold pressure. This pressure is measured in inches of mercury ("Hg) and controls engine power output.

Figure 3-1. *Inlet scoop in engine cowling.*

Induction systems can consist of several different arrangements. Two that are used are the updraft and downdraft induction systems. An updraft induction system consists of two runners and a balance tube with intake pipes for each cylinder to deliver induction air to each cylinder's intake port. *[Figure 3-3]* The balance tube is used to reduce pressure imbalances between the two side induction runners. With carbureted engines, it is important to maintain a constant and even pressure in the induction system so that each cylinder receives equal amounts of fuel. On fuel-injected engines, the fuel is injected at the intake port just before the intake valve. It is important with this system to keep the pressure consistent at each intake port.

A downdraft balanced induction system provides optimum airflow to each of the individual cylinders throughout a wide operational range. *[Figure 3-4]* Better matched fuel-to-air ratios provide a much smoother and more efficient engine operation. Air from the induction manifold flows into the intake ports where it is mixed with fuel from the fuel nozzles and then enters the cylinders as a combustible mixture as the intake valve opens.

Basic Carburetor Induction System

Figure 3-2 is a diagram of an induction system used in an engine equipped with a carburetor. In this induction system, carburetor normal flow air is admitted at the lower front nose cowling below the propeller spinner, and is passed through an air filter into air ducts leading to the carburetor. A carburetor heat air valve is located below the carburetor for selecting an alternate warm air source (carburetor heat) to prevent carburetor icing. *[Figure 3-5]* Carburetor icing occurs when the temperature is lowered in the throat of the carburetor and enough moisture is present to freeze and block the flow of air to the engine. The carburetor heat valve admits air from the outside air scoop for normal operation, and it admits warm air from the engine compartment for operation during icing conditions. The carburetor heat is operated by a push-pull control in the cockpit. When the carburetor heat air door is closed, warm ducted air from around the exhaust is directed into the carburetor. This raises the intake air temperature. An alternate air door can be opened by engine suction if the normal route of airflow should be blocked by something. The valve is spring loaded closed and is sucked open by the engine if needed.

The carburetor air filter, shown in *Figure 3-6*, is installed in the air scoop in front of the carburetor air duct. Its purpose is

Figure 3-2. *Nonsupercharged induction system using a carburetor.*

Figure 3-3. *Updraft induction system.*

Figure 3-4. *Downdraft balanced induction system.*

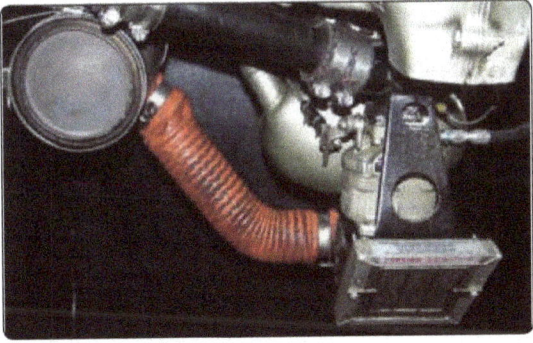

Figure 3-5. *Location of a carburetor heat air valve.*

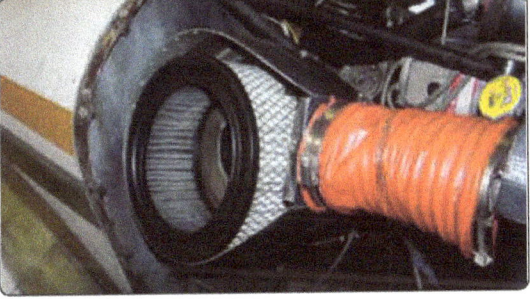

Figure 3-6. *Location of air filter.*

to stop dust and other foreign matter from entering the engine through the carburetor. The screen consists of an aluminum alloy frame and a deeply crimped screen, arranged to present maximum screen area to the airstream. There are several types of air filters in use including paper, foam, and other types of filters. Most air filters require servicing at regular intervals and the specific instructions for the type of filter must be followed. *[Figure 3-6]*

The carburetor air ducts consist of a fixed duct riveted to the nose cowling and a flexible duct between the fixed duct and the carburetor air valve housing. The carburetor air ducts normally provide a passage for outside air to the carburetor. Air enters the system through the ram-air intake. The intake opening is located in the slipstream so the air is forced into the induction system giving a ram effect to the incoming airflow. The air passes through the air ducts to the carburetor. The carburetor meters the fuel in proportion to the air and mixes the air with the correct amount of fuel. The throttle plate of the carburetor can be controlled from the cockpit to regulate the flow of air (manifold pressure), and in this way, power output of the engine can be controlled.

Although many newer aircraft are not so-equipped, some engines are equipped with carburetor air temperature indicating systems which shows the temperature of the air at the carburetor inlet. If the bulb is located at the engine side of the carburetor, the system measures the temperature of the fuel/air mixture.

Induction System Icing

A short discussion concerning the formation and location of induction system ice is helpful, even though a technician's not normally concerned with operations that occur when the aircraft is in flight. *[Figure 3-7]* Technicians should know something about induction system icing because of its effect on engine performance and troubleshooting. Even when an inspection shows that everything is in proper working order and the engine performs perfectly on the ground, induction system ice can cause an engine to act erratically and lose power in the air. Many engine troubles commonly attributed to other sources are actually caused by induction system icing.

Induction system icing is an operating hazard because it can cut off the flow of the fuel/air charge or vary the fuel/air ratio. Ice can form in the induction system while an aircraft is flying in clouds, fog, rain, sleet, snow, or even clear air that has high moisture content (high humidity). Induction system icing is generally classified in three types:

- Impact ice
- Fuel evaporation ice
- Throttle ice

Chapter 2 discusses types of icing in more detail.

Induction system ice can be prevented or eliminated by raising the temperature of the air that passes through the system, using a carburetor heat system located upstream near the induction system inlet and well ahead of the dangerous icing zones. This air is collected by a duct surrounding the exhaust manifold. Heat is usually obtained through a control valve that opens

Figure 3-7. *Location of a carburetor heat air valve.*

the induction system to the warm air circulating in the engine compartment and around the exhaust manifold.

Improper or careless use of carburetor heat can be just as dangerous as the most advanced stage of induction system ice. Increasing the temperature of the air causes it to expand and decrease in density. This action reduces the weight of the charge delivered to the cylinder and causes a noticeable loss in power because of decreased volumetric efficiency. In addition, high intake air temperature may cause detonation and engine failure, especially during takeoff and high power operation. Therefore, during all phases of engine operation, the carburetor temperature must afford the greatest protection against icing and detonation.

When there is danger of induction system icing, the cockpit carburetor heat control is moved to the hot position. Throttle ice or any ice that restricts airflow or reduces manifold pressure can best be removed by using full carburetor heat. If the heat from the engine compartment is sufficient and the application has not been delayed, it is only a matter of a few minutes until the ice is cleared.

When there is no danger of icing, the heat control is normally kept in the "cold" position. It is best to leave the control in this position if there are particles of dry snow or ice in the air. The use of heat may melt the ice or snow, and the resulting moisture may collect and freeze on the walls of the induction system. To prevent damage to the heater valves in the case of backfire, carburetor heat should not be used while starting the engine. Also, during ground operation only enough carburetor heat should be used to give smooth engine operation.

Part-throttle operation can lead to icing in the throttle area. When the throttle is placed in a partly closed position, it, in effect, limits the amount of air available to the engine. When the aircraft is in a glide, a fixed-pitch propeller windmills, causing the engine to consume more air than it normally would at this same throttle setting, thus adding to the lack of air behind the throttle. The partly closed throttle, under these circumstances, establishes a much higher than normal air velocity past the throttle, and an extremely low-pressure area is produced. The low-pressure area lowers the temperature of the air surrounding the throttle valve. If the temperature in this air falls below freezing and moisture is present, ice forms on the throttles and nearby units restricting the airflow to the engine causing it to quit. Throttle ice may be minimized on engines equipped with controllable-pitch propellers by the use of a higher than normal brake mean effective pressure (BMEP) at this low power. The high BMEP decreases the icing tendency because a large throttle opening at low engine revolutions per minute (rpm) partially removes the temperature-reducing obstruction that part-throttle operation offers.

Induction System Filtering

Dust and dirt can be a serious source of trouble to an aircraft engine. Dust consists of small particles of hard, abrasive material that can be carried by the air and drawn into the engine cylinders. It can also collect on the fuel-metering elements of the carburetor, upsetting the proper relation between airflow and fuel flow at all engine power settings. It acts on the cylinder walls by grinding down these surfaces and the piston rings. Then, it contaminates the oil and is carried through the engine, causing further wear on the bearings and gears. In extreme cases, an accumulation may clog an oil passage and cause oil starvation. Although dust conditions are most critical at ground level, continued operation under such conditions without engine protection results in extreme engine wear and can produce excessive oil consumption. When operation in a dusty atmosphere is necessary, the engine can be protected by an alternate induction system air inlet which incorporates a dust filter. This type of air filter system normally consists of a filter element, a door, and an electrically operated actuator. When the filter system is operating, air is drawn through a louvered access panel that does not face directly into the airstream. With this entrance location, considerable dust is removed as the air is forced to turn and enter the duct. Since the dust particles are solid, they tend to continue in a straight line, and most of them are separated at this point. Those that are drawn into the louvers are easily removed by the filter.

In flight, with air filters operating, consideration must be given to possible icing conditions which may occur from actual surface icing or from freezing of the filter element after it becomes rain soaked. Some installations have a spring-loaded filter door which automatically opens when the filter is excessively restricted. This prevents the airflow from being cut off when the filter is clogged with ice or dirt. Other systems use an ice guard in the filtered-air entrance.

The ice guard consists of a coarse-mesh screen located a short distance from the filtered-air entrance. In this location, the screen is directly in the path of incoming air so that the air must pass through or around the screen. When ice forms on the screen, the air, which has lost its heavy moisture particles, passes around the iced screen and into the filter element. The efficiency of any filter system depends upon proper maintenance and servicing. Periodic removal and cleaning of the filter element is essential to satisfactory engine protection.

Induction System Inspection and Maintenance

The induction system should be checked for cracks and leaks during all regularly scheduled engine inspections. The units of the system should be checked for security of mounting. The system should be kept clean at all times, since pieces of rags or paper can restrict the airflow if allowed to enter the air intakes or ducts. Loose bolts and nuts can cause serious damage if they pass into the engine.

On systems equipped with a carburetor air filter, the filter should be checked regularly. If it is dirty or does not have the proper oil film, the filter element should be removed and cleaned. After it has dried, it is usually immersed in a mixture of oil and rust-preventive compound. The excess fluid should be allowed to drain off before the filter element is reinstalled. Paper-type filters should be inspected and replaced as needed.

Induction System Troubleshooting

Figure 3-8 provides a general guide to the most common induction system troubles.

Supercharged Induction Systems

Since aircraft operate at altitudes where the air pressure is lower, it is useful to provide a system for compressing the fuel/air mixture. Some systems are used to normalize the air pressure entering the engine. These systems are used to regain the air pressure lost by the increase in altitude. This

Probable Cause	Isolation Procedure	Correction
1 Engine fails to start		
a Induction system obstructed	Inspect air scoop and air ducts	Remove obstructions
b Air leaks	Inspect carburetor mounting and intake pipes	Tighten carburetor and repair or replace intake pipe
2 Engine runs rough		
a Loose air ducts	Inspect air ducts	Tighten air ducts
b Leaking intake pipes	Inspect intake pipe packing nuts	Tighten nuts
c Engine valves sticking	Remove rocker arm cover and check valve action	Lubricate and free sticking valves
d Bent or worn valve push rods	Inspect push rods	Replace worn or damaged push rods
3 Low power		
a Restricted intake duct	Examine intake duct	Remove restrictions
b Broken door in carburetor air valve	Inspect air valve	Replace air valve
c Dirty air filter	Inspect air filter	Clear air filter
4 Engine idles improperly		
a Shrunken intake packing	Inspect packing for proper fit	Replace packing
b Hole in intake pipe	Inspect intake pipe	Replace defective intake pipes
c Loose carburetor mounting	Inspect mount bolts	Tighten mount bolts

Figure 3-8. *Common problems for troubleshooting induction systems.*

type of system is not a ground boost system and it is not used to ever boost the manifold pressure above 30 inches of mercury. A true supercharged engine, called ground boosted engines, can boost the manifold pressure above 30 inches of mercury. In other words, a true supercharger boosts the manifold pressure above ambient pressure.

Since many engines installed in light aircraft do not use any type of compressor or supercharging device, induction systems for reciprocating engines can be broadly classified as supercharged or nonsupercharged. *[Figure 3-9]* Supercharging systems used in reciprocating engine induction systems are normally classified as either internally driven or externally driven (turbosupercharged). Internally driven superchargers compress the fuel/air mixture after it leaves the carburetor, while externally driven superchargers (turbochargers) compress the air before it is mixed with the metered fuel from the carburetor.

Internally Driven Superchargers
Internally driven superchargers were used almost exclusively in high horsepower radial reciprocating engines and are engine driven through a mechanical connection. Although their use is very limited, some are still used in cargo carriers and spray planes. Except for the construction and arrangement of the various types of superchargers, all induction systems with internally driven superchargers were very similar. Aircraft engines require the same air temperature control to produce good combustion in the engine cylinders. For example, the charge must be warm enough to ensure complete fuel vaporization and, thus, even distribution. At the same time, it must not be so hot that it reduces volumetric efficiency or causes detonation. All reciprocating engines must guard against intake air that is too hot. As with any type of supercharging (compressing intake air), the air gains heat as it is compressed. Sometimes this air requires cooling before it is routed to the engine's intake ports. With these requirements, most induction systems that use internally driven superchargers must include pressure and temperature-sensing devices and the necessary units required to warm or cool the air.

The simple internally driven supercharger induction system is used to explain the location of units and the path of the air and fuel/air mixture. *[Figure 3-10]* Air enters the system through the ram air intake. The intake opening is located so that the air is forced into the induction system, giving a ram effect caused by the aircraft moving through the air. The air passes through ducts to the carburetor. The carburetor meters the fuel in proportion to the air and mixes the air with the correct amount of fuel. The carburetor can be controlled from the cockpit to regulate the flow of air. In this way, the power output of the engine can be controlled. The manifold pressure gauge measures the pressure of the fuel/air mixture before it enters the cylinders. It is an indication of the performance that can be expected of the engine. The carburetor air temperature indicator measures either the temperature of the inlet air or of the fuel/air mixture. Either the air inlet or the mixture temperature indicator serves as a guide so that the temperature of the incoming charge may be kept within safe limits. If

Figure 3-9. *An example of a naturally aspirated reciprocating engine.*

Figure 3-10. *Internally driven supercharger induction system.*

the temperature of the incoming air at the entrance to the carburetor scoop is 100 °F, there is approximately a 50 °F drop in temperature because of the partial vaporization of the fuel at the carburetor discharge nozzle. Partial vaporization takes place and the air temperature falls due to absorption of the heat by vaporization. The final vaporization takes place as the mixture enters the cylinders where higher temperatures exist. The fuel, as atomized into the airstream that flows in the induction system, is in a globular form. The problem, then, becomes one of uniformly breaking up and distributing the fuel, remaining in globular form to the various cylinders. On engines equipped with a large number of cylinders, the uniform distribution of the mixture becomes a greater problem, especially at high engine speeds when full advantage is taken of large air capacity.

One method, used mainly on radial reciprocating engines, of improving fuel distribution is shown in *Figure 3-11.* This device is known as a distribution impeller. The impeller is attached directly to the end of the rear shank of the crankshaft by bolts or studs. Since the impeller is attached to the end of the crankshaft and operates at the same speed, it does not materially boost or increase the pressure on the mixture flowing into the cylinders. But, the fuel remaining in the globular form is broken up into finer particles as it strikes the impeller, thereby coming in contact with more air. This creates a more homogeneous mixture with a consequent improvement in distribution to the various cylinders, especially on acceleration of the engine or when low temperatures prevail.

To obtain greater pressure of the fuel/air mixture within the cylinders, the diffuser or blower section contains a high speed impeller. Unlike the distribution impeller, which is connected directly to the crankshaft, the supercharger, or blower impeller, is driven through a gear train from the crankshaft.

Turbosuperchargers

Externally driven superchargers (turbosuperchargers) are designed to deliver compressed air to the inlet of the carburetor or fuel/air control unit of an engine. Externally driven superchargers derive their power from the energy of engine exhaust gases directed against a turbine that drives an impeller that compresses the incoming air. For this reason, they are commonly called turbosuperchargers or turbochargers. To be a true supercharger, it must boost the manifold pressure above 30 "Hg.

The typical turbosupercharger, shown in *Figure 3-12,* is composed of three main parts:

1. Compressor assembly
2. Turbine wheel assembly
3. A full floating shaft bearing assembly

Detail examples of a turbosupercharger are shown in *Figure 3-13.* In addition to the major assemblies, there is a baffle between the compressor casing and the exhaust-gas turbine that directs cooling air to the pump and bearing casing, and also shields the compressor from the heat radiated by the turbine. In installations where cooling air is limited, the baffle is replaced by a regular cooling shroud that receives its air directly from the induction system.

The compressor assembly is made up of an impeller, a diffuser, and a casing. The air for the induction system enters through a circular opening in the center of the compressor casing, where it is picked up by the blades of the impeller, which gives it high velocity as it travels outward toward the diffuser. The diffuser vanes direct the airflow as it leaves the impeller and also converts the high velocity of the air to high-pressure.

Motive power for the impeller is furnished through the impeller's attachment to the turbine wheel shaft of the exhaust-gas turbine. This complete assembly is referred to as the rotor. (The rotor revolves on the oil feed bearings.) The exhaust gas turbine assembly consists of the turbocharger and waste gate valve. *[Figure 3-14]* The turbine wheel, driven by exhaust gases, drives the impeller. The turbo housing collects and directs the exhaust gases onto the turbine wheel, and the

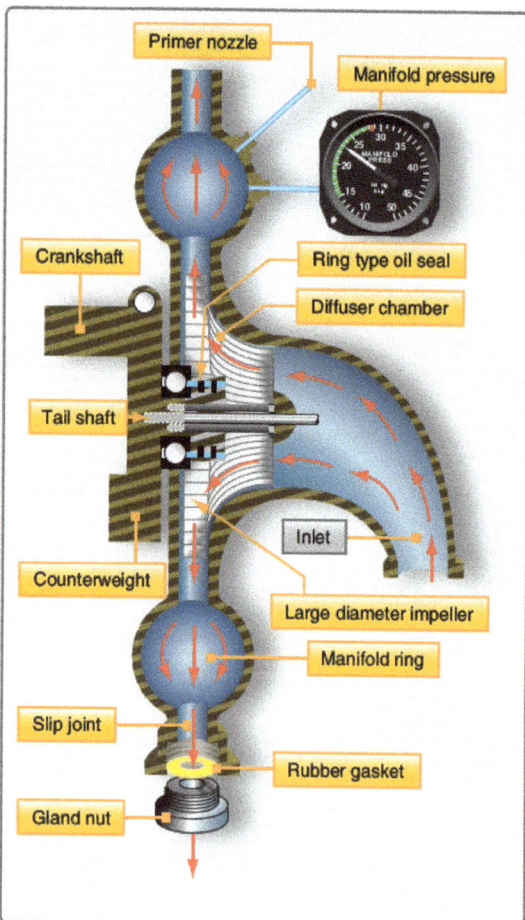

Figure 3-11. *Location of a carb heat air valve.*

Figure 3-12. *A typical turbosupercharger and its main parts.*

Figure 3-13. *Detail examples of the main components of a turbosupercharger.*

Figure 3-14. *Exhaust gas turbine assembly.*

waste gate regulates the amount of exhaust gases directed to the turbine. The waste gate controls the volume of the exhaust gas that is directed onto the turbine and thereby regulates the speed of the rotor (turbine and impeller). *[Figure 3-15]*

If the waste gate is completely closed, all the exhaust gases are "backed up" and forced through the turbine wheel. If the waste gate is partially closed, a corresponding amount of exhaust gas is directed to the turbine. The exhaust gasses, thus

Figure 3-15. *Waste gate control of exhaust.*

directed, strike the turbine blades, arranged radially around the outer edge of the turbine, and cause the rotor (turbine and impeller) to rotate. The gases, having exhausted most of their energy, are then exhausted overboard. When the waste gate is fully open, nearly all of the exhaust gases pass overboard providing little or no boost.

Normalizer Turbocharger

Some engines used in light aircraft are equipped with an externally driven normalizing system. These systems are powered by the energy of exhaust gases and are usually referred to as "normalizing turbocharger" systems. These systems were not designed to be used as a true supercharger (boost manifold pressure over 30 "Hg). They compensate for the power lost due to the pressure drop resulting from increased altitude. On many small aircraft engines, the turbocharger (normalizing) system is designed to be operated only above a certain altitude, 5,000 feet for example, since maximum power without normalizing is available below that altitude. The location of the air induction and exhaust systems of a typical normalizing turbocharger system for a small aircraft is shown in *Figure 3-16*.

Ground-Boosted Turbosupercharger System

Some ground-boosted (sea level) turbosupercharged systems are designed to operate from sea level up to their critical altitude. These engines, sometimes referred to as sea level-boosted engines, can develop more power at sea level than an engine without turbosupercharging. As was mentioned earlier, an engine must be boosted above 30 "Hg to truly be supercharged. This type of turbocharger accomplishes this by increasing the manifold pressure above 30 "Hg to around 40 "Hg.

The turbosupercharger air induction system consists of a filtered ram-air intake located on the side of the nacelle. *[Figure 3-17]* An alternate air door within the nacelle permits compressor suction automatically to admit alternate air (heated engine compartment air) if the induction air filter becomes clogged. In many cases, the alternate air door can be operated manually in the event of filter clogging.

Almost all turbocharger systems use engine oil as the control fluid for controlling the amount of boost (extra manifold pressure) provided to the engine. The waste-gate actuator and controllers use pressurized engine oil for their power supply. The turbocharger is controlled by the waste gate and waste gate actuator. The waste gate actuator, which is physically connected to the waste gate by mechanical linkage, controls the position of the waste gate butterfly valve. The waste gate bypasses the engine exhaust gases around the turbocharger turbine inlet. By controlling the amount of exhaust gases

Figure 3-16. *Typical location of the air induction and exhaust systems of a normalizing turbocharger system.*

Figure 3-17. *A turbocharger air induction system.*

that pass through the turbine of the turbocharger, the speed of the compressor and the amount of intake boost (upper deck pressure) is controlled. Engine oil is also used to cool and lubricate the bearings that support the compressor and turbine in the turbocharger. Turbocharger lubricating oil is engine oil supplied through the engine oil system. An oil supply hose from the rear of the oil cooler directs oil to the turbocharger center housings and bearings. Oil hoses return oil from the turbochargers to the oil scavenge pump located on the rear of the engine. The one-way check valve in the oil supply line prevents oil from draining into the turbocharger while the engine is not operating. Piston ring-like oil seals are used on the compressor wheel shaft to prevent the lubricating oil from entering the turbine and compressor housings from the center housing.

The position of the waste gate is controlled by adjusting the oil pressure in the waste gate actuator. Several different types of controllers are used to provide the correct pressure in the waste gate actuator. This is done either by restricting the oil flow or by allowing the oil to return to the engine. The more the oil is restricted, the more pressure is in the waste gate actuator and the more closed the waste gate is. This causes the exhaust gases to pass through the turbine, increasing the speed of the compressor raising the inlet pressure. The reverse happens if the oil is not restricted by the controllers and boost is reduced. The pressure from the outlet of the compressor of the turbocharger to the throttle is referred to as deck pressure or upper deck pressure.

A Typical Turbosupercharger System

Figure 3-18 is a schematic of a sea level booster turbosupercharger system. This system used widely is automatically regulated by three components:

- Exhaust bypass valve assembly
- Density controller
- Differential pressure controller

By regulating the waste gate position and the "fully open" and "closed" positions, a constant power output can be maintained. When the waste gate is fully open, all the exhaust gases are directed overboard to the atmosphere, and no air is compressed and delivered to the engine air inlet. Conversely, when the waste gate is fully closed, a maximum volume of exhaust gases flows into the turbocharger turbine, and maximum supercharging is accomplished. Between these two extremes of waste gate position, constant power output can be achieved below the maximum altitude at which the system is designed to operate. An engine with a critical altitude of 16,000 feet cannot produce 100 percent of its rated manifold pressure above 16,000 feet. Critical altitude means the maximum altitude at which, in standard atmosphere, it is possible to maintain, at a specified rotational speed, a specified power or a specified manifold pressure.

Figure 3-18. *Sea level booster turbosupercharger system.*

A critical altitude exists for every possible power setting below the maximum operating ceiling. If the aircraft is flown above this altitude without a corresponding change in the power setting, the waste gate is automatically driven to the fully closed position in an effort to maintain a constant power output. Thus, the waste gate is almost fully open at sea level and continues to move toward the closed position as the aircraft climbs, in order to maintain the preselected manifold pressure setting. When the waste gate is fully closed (leaving only a small clearance to prevent sticking), the manifold pressure begins to drop if the aircraft continues to climb. If a higher power setting cannot be selected, the turbocharger's critical altitude has been reached. Beyond this altitude, the power output continues to decrease.

The position of the waste gate valve, which determines power output, is controlled by oil pressure. Engine oil pressure acts on a piston in the waste gate assembly, which is connected by linkage to the waste gate valve. When oil pressure is increased on the piston, the waste gate valve moves toward the closed position, and engine output power increases. Conversely, when the oil pressure is decreased, the waste gate valve moves toward the open position, and output power is decreased as described earlier.

The position of the piston attached to the waste gate valve is dependent on bleed oil, which controls the engine oil pressure applied to the top of the piston. Oil is returned to the engine crankcase through two control devices, the density controller and the differential pressure controller. These two controllers, acting independently, determine how much oil is bled back to the crankcase and establishes the oil pressure on the piston.

The density controller is designed to limit the manifold pressure below the turbocharger's critical altitude and regulates bleed oil only at the full throttle position. The pressure- and temperature-sensing bellows of the density controller react to pressure and temperature changes between the fuel injector inlet and the turbocharger compressor. The bellows, filled with dry nitrogen, maintain a constant density by allowing the pressure to increase as the temperature increases. Movement of the bellows repositions the bleed valve, causing a change in the quantity of bleed oil, which changes the oil pressure on top of the waste gate piston. *[Figure 3-18]*

The differential pressure controller functions during all positions of the waste gate valve other than the fully open position, which is controlled by the density controller. One side of the diaphragm in the differential pressure controller senses air pressure upstream from the throttle; the other side samples pressure on the cylinder side of the throttle valve. *[Figure 3-18]* At the "wide open" throttle position when the density controller controls the waste gate, the pressure across the differential pressure controller diaphragm is at a minimum and the controller spring holds the bleed valve closed. At "part throttle" position, the air differential is increased, opening the bleed valve to bleed oil to the engine crankcase and reposition the waste gate piston. Thus, the two controllers operate independently to control turbocharger operation at all positions of the throttle. Without the overriding function of the differential pressure controller during part-throttle operation, the density controller would position the waste gate valve for maximum power. The differential pressure controller reduces injector entrance pressure and continually repositions the valve over the whole operating range of the engine.

The differential pressure controller reduces the unstable condition known as "bootstrapping" during part-throttle operation. Bootstrapping is an indication of unregulated power change that results in the continual drift of manifold pressure. This condition can be illustrated by considering the operation of a system when the waste gate is fully closed. During this time, the differential pressure controller is not modulating the waste gate valve position. Any slight change in power caused by a change in temperature or rpm fluctuation is magnified and results in manifold pressure change since the slight change causes a change in the amount of exhaust gas flowing to the turbine. Any change in exhaust gas flow to the turbine causes a change in power output and is reflected in manifold pressure indications. Bootstrapping, then, is an undesirable cycle of turbocharging events causing the manifold pressure to drift in an attempt to reach a state of equilibrium.

Bootstrapping is sometimes confused with the condition known as overboost, but bootstrapping is not a condition that is detrimental to engine life. An overboost condition is one in which manifold pressure exceeds the limits prescribed for a particular engine and can cause serious damage. A pressure relief valve when used in some systems, set slightly in excess of maximum deck pressure, is provided to prevent damaging over boost in the event of a system malfunction.

The differential pressure controller is essential to smooth functioning of the automatically controlled turbocharger, since it reduces bootstrapping by reducing the time required to bring a system into equilibrium. There is still extra throttle sensitivity with a turbocharged engine than with a naturally aspirated engine. Rapid movement of the throttle can cause a certain amount of manifold pressure drift in a turbocharged engine. Less severe than bootstrapping, this condition is called overshoot. While overshoot is not a dangerous condition, it can be a source of concern to the pilot or operator who selects a particular manifold pressure setting only to find it has changed in a few seconds and must be reset. Since the automatic controls cannot respond rapidly enough to abrupt changes in throttle settings to eliminate the inertia of turbocharger speed changes, overshoot must be controlled by the operator. This can best be accomplished by slowly making changes in throttle setting, accompanied by a few seconds' wait for the system to reach a new equilibrium. Such a procedure is effective with turbocharged engines, regardless of the degree of throttle sensitivity.

Turbocharger Controllers and System Descriptions

Turbocharger system engines contain many of the same components mentioned with the previous systems. [Figure 3-19] Some systems use special lines and fittings that are connected to the upper-deck pressure for air reference to the fuel injection system and in some cases for pressurizing the magnetos. Basic system operation is similar to other turbocharger systems with the main differences being in the controllers. The controller monitors deck pressure by sensing the output of the compressor. The controller controls the oil flow through the wastegate actuator, which opens or closes the exhaust bypass valve. When deck pressure is insufficient, the controller restricts oil flow thereby increasing oil pressure at the wastegate actuator. This pressure acts on the piston to close off the wastegate valve, forcing more exhaust gas pulses to turn the turbine faster and cause an increase in compressor output. When deck pressure is too great, the opposite occurs. The exhaust wastegate fully opens and bypasses some of the exhaust gases to decrease exhaust flow across the turbine. An aftercooler is installed in the induction air path between the compressor stage and the air throttle inlet. [Figure 3-20]

Most turbochargers are capable of compressing the induction air to the point at which it can raise the air temperature by a factor of five. This means that full power takeoff on a 100 °F day could produce induction air temperatures exiting the compressor at up to 500 °F. This would exceed the allowable throttle air inlet temperature on all reciprocating engine models. Typically, the maximum air throttle inlet temperature ranges from a low 230 °F to a high of 300 °F. Exceeding these maximums can place the combustion chambers closer to detonation. The function of the aftercooler is to cool the compressed air, which decreases the likelihood of detonation and increases the charge air density, which improves the turbocharger performance for that engine design. On engine start, the controller senses insufficient compressor discharge pressure (deck pressure) and restricts the flow of oil from the

Figure 3-19. *Components of a turbocharger system engine.*

Figure 3-20. *An aftercooler installation.*

wastegate actuator to the engine. This causes the wastegate butterfly valve to close. As the throttle is advanced, exhaust gas flows across the turbine increases, thereby increasing turbine/compressor shaft speed and compressor discharge pressure. The controller senses the difference between upper deck and manifold pressure. If either deck pressure or throttle differential pressure rises, the controller poppet valve opens, relieving oil pressure to the wastegate actuator. This decreases turbocharger compressor discharge pressure (deck pressure).

Variable Absolute Pressure Controller (VAPC)

The VAPC contains an oil control valve similar to the other controllers that were discussed. *[Figure 3-21]* The oil restrictor is actuated by an aneroid bellows that is referenced to upper deck pressure. A cam connected to the throttle mechanism applies pressure to the restrictor valve and aneroid. As the throttle is opened to greater values, the cam applies a greater pressure to the aneroid. This increases the amount of upper deck pressure necessary to compress the aneroid and thereby open the oil restrictor valve. This means that the scheduled absolute value of upper deck pressure that is required to overcome the aneroid is variable by throttle position. As the throttle is opened wide, the manifold pressure and upper deck pressure requirements greatly increase.

Sloped Controller

The sloped controller is designed to maintain the rated compressor discharge pressure at wide-open throttle and to reduce this pressure at part throttle settings. *[Figure 3-22]* A diaphragm, coupled with a spring-supported bellows for absolute pressure reference, is exposed to deck pressure and intake manifold pressure through ports located before and after the throttle, respectively. This arrangement constantly monitors deck pressure and the pressure differential between the deck and manifold pressure due to a partially closed throttle. If either deck pressure or throttle differential pressure rises, the controller poppet opens and decreases turbocharger discharge (deck) pressure. The sloped controller is more sensitive to the throttle differential pressure than to deck pressure, thereby accomplishing deck pressure reduction as the throttle is closed.

Figure 3-21. *A diagram of a variable absolute pressure controller (VAPC).*

Figure 3-22. *A diagram of a sloped controller used to maintain the rated compressor discharge pressure at wide-open throttle.*

Absolute Pressure Controller

One device used to control the speed and output of the turbocharger, but controls the system only at maximum output, is the absolute pressure controller. The absolute pressure controller contains an aneroid bellows that is referenced to upper deck pressure. It operates the wastegate, which diverts, more or less, exhaust gas over the turbine. As an absolute pressure setting is reached, it bypasses oil, and relieves the pressure on the waste gate actuator. This allows the absolute pressure controller to control the maximum turbocharger compressor discharge pressure. The turbocharger is completely automatic, requiring no pilot action up to the critical altitude.

Turbocharger System Troubleshooting

Figure 3-23 includes some of the most common turbocharger system malfunctions together with their cause and repair. These troubleshooting procedures are presented as a guide only and should not be substituted for applicable manufacturer's instructions or troubleshooting procedures.

Turbine Engine Inlet Systems

The engine inlet of a turbine engine is designed to provide a relatively distortion-free flow of air, in the required quantity, to the inlet of the compressor. *[Figure 3-24]* Many engines use inlet guide vanes (IGV) to help straighten the airflow and direct it into the first stages of the compressor. A uniform and steady airflow is necessary to avoid compressor stall (airflow tends to stop or reverse direction of flow) and excessive internal engine temperatures in the turbine section. Normally, the air-inlet duct is considered an airframe part and not a part of the engine. However, the duct is very important to the engine's overall performance and the engine's ability to produce an optimum amount of thrust.

A gas turbine engine consumes considerable more airflow than a reciprocating engine. The air entrance passage is correspondingly larger. Furthermore, it is more critical in determining engine and aircraft performance, especially at high airspeeds. Inefficiencies of the inlet duct result in successively magnified losses through other components of the engine. The inlet varies according to the type of turbine engine. Small turboprop and turboshaft engines have a lower airflow than large turbofan engines which require a completely different type of inlet. Many turboprop, auxiliary

Trouble	Probable Cause	Remedy
Aircraft fails to reach critical altitude	Damaged compressor or turbine wheel	Replace turbocharger
	Exhaust system leaks	Repair leaks
	Faulty turbocharger bearings	Replace turbocharge
	Wastegate will not close fully	Refer to wastegate in the trouble column
	Malfunctioning controller	Refer to differential controller in the trouble column
Engine surges	Bootstrapping	Ensure engine is operated in proper range
	Wastegate malfunction	Refer to wastegate in the trouble column
	Controller malfunction	Refer to differential controller in the trouble column
Wastegate will not close fully	Wastegate bypass valve bearing tight	Replace bypass valve
	Oil inlet orifice blocked	Clean orifice
	Differential controller malfunction	Refer to controller in the trouble column
	Broken wastegate linkage	Replace linkage and adjust waste gate for proper opening and closing
Wastegate will not open	Oil outlet obstructed	Clean and reconnect oil return line
	Broken wastegate linkage	Replace linkage and adjust waste gate opening and closing
	Controller malfunction	Refer to controller in the trouble column
Differential controller malfunctions	Seals leaking	Replace controller
	Diaphragm broken	Replace controller
	Controller valve stuck	Replace controller
Density controller malfunctions	Seals leaking	Replace controller
	Bellows damaged	Replace controller
	Valve stuck	Replace controller

Figure 3-23. *Common issues when troubleshooting turbocharger systems.*

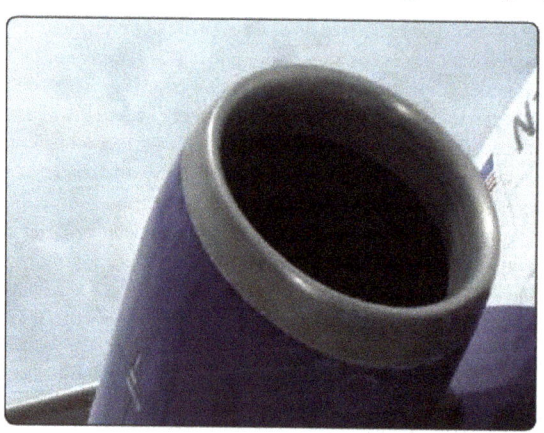

Figure 3-24. *An example of a turbine engine inlet.*

power units, and turboshaft engines use screens that cover the inlet to prevent foreign object damage (FOD).

As aircraft speed increases, thrust tends to decrease somewhat; as the aircraft speed reaches a certain point, ram recovery compensates for the losses caused by the increases in speed. The inlet must be able to recover as much of the total pressure of the free airstream as possible. As air molecules are trapped and begin to be compressed in the inlet, much of the pressure loss is recovered. This added pressure at the inlet of the engine increases the pressure and airflow to the engine. This is known as "ram recovery" or "total pressure recovery." The inlet duct must uniformly deliver air to the compressor inlet with as little turbulence and pressure variation as possible. The engine inlet duct must also hold the drag effect on the aircraft to a minimum.

Air pressure drop in the engine inlet is caused by the friction of the air along both sides of the duct and by the bends in the duct system. Smooth flow depends upon keeping the amount of turbulence to a minimum as the air enters the duct. On engines with low flow rates, turning the airflow allows the engine nacelle to be smaller and have less drag. On turbofan engines, the duct must have a sufficiently straight section to ensure smooth, even airflow because of the high airflows. The choice of configuration of the entrance to the duct is dictated by the location of the engine within the aircraft and the airspeed, altitude, and attitude at which the aircraft is designed to operate.

Divided-Entrance Duct

The requirements of high-speed, single- or twin-engine military aircraft, in which the pilot sits low in the fuselage and close to the nose, render it difficult to employ the older type single-entrance duct, which is not used on modern aircraft. Some form of a divided duct, which takes air from either side of the fuselage, has become fairly widely used. This divided duct can be either a wing-root inlet or a scoop at each side of the fuselage. *[Figure 3-25]* Either type of duct presents more problems to the aircraft designer than a single-entrance duct because of the difficulty of obtaining sufficient airscoop area without imposing prohibitive amounts of drag. Internally, the problem is the same as that encountered with the single-entrance duct: to construct a duct of reasonable length with as few bends as possible. Scoops at the sides of the fuselage are often used. These side scoops are placed as far forward as possible to permit a gradual bend toward the compressor inlet, making the airflow characteristics approach those of a single-entrance duct. A series of turning vanes is sometimes placed in the side-scoop inlet to assist in straightening the incoming airflow and to prevent turbulence.

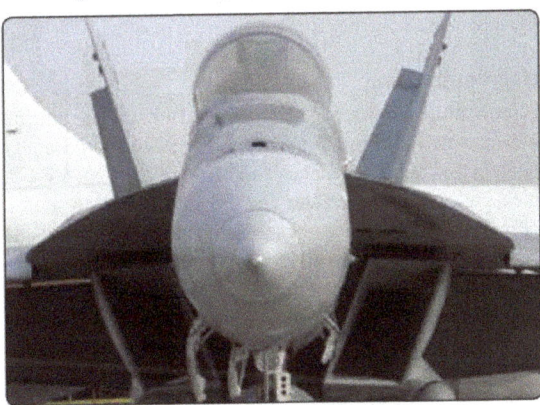

Figure 3-25. *An example of a divided-entrance duct.*

Variable-Geometry Duct

The main function of an inlet duct is to furnish the proper amount of air to the engine inlet. In a typical military aircraft using a turbojet or low bypass turbofan engine, the maximum airflow requirements are such that the Mach number of the airflow directly ahead of the face of the engine is less than Mach 1. Airflow through the engine must be less than Mach 1 at all times. Therefore, under all flight conditions, the velocity of the airflow as it enters the air-inlet duct must be reduced through the duct before the airflow is ready to enter the compressor. To accomplish this, inlet ducts are designed to function as diffusers, decreasing the velocity and increasing the static pressure of the air passing through them. *[Figure 3-26]*

Figure 3-26. *An inlet duct acts as a diffuser to decrease the airflow velocity and to increase the static pressure of air.*

As with military supersonic aircraft, a diffuser progressively decreases in area in the downstream direction. Therefore, a supersonic inlet duct follows this general configuration until the velocity of the incoming air is reduced to Mach 1. The aft section of the duct then increases in area, since this part must act as a subsonic diffuser. *[Figure 3-27]* In practice, inlet ducts for supersonic aircraft follows this general design only as much as practical, depending upon the design features of the aircraft. For very high speed aircraft, the inside area of configuration of the duct is changed by a mechanical device as the speed of the aircraft increases or decreases. A duct of this type is usually known as a variable-geometry inlet duct.

Figure 3-27. *The aft section of an inlet duct acting as a subsonic diffuser.*

Military aircraft use the three methods described above to diffuse the inlet air and slow the inlet airflow at supersonic flight speeds. One is to vary the area, or geometry, of the inlet duct either by using a movable restriction, such as a ramp or wedge, inside the duct. Another system is some sort of a variable airflow bypass arrangement, which extracts part of the inlet airflow from the duct ahead of the engine. In some cases, a combination of both systems is used.

The third method is the use of a shock wave in the airstream. A shock wave is a thin region of discontinuity in a flow of air or gas, during which the speed, pressure, density, and temperature of the air or gas undergo a sudden change. Stronger shock waves produce larger changes in the properties of the air or gas. A shock wave is willfully set up in the supersonic flow of the air entering the duct, by means of some restriction or small obstruction which automatically protrudes into the duct at high flight Mach numbers. The shock wave results in diffusion of the airflow, which, in turn, decreases the velocity of the airflow. In at least one aircraft installation, both the shock method and the variable-geometry method of causing diffusion are used in combination. The same device that changes the area of the duct also sets up a shock wave that further reduces the speed of the incoming air within the duct. The amount of change in duct area and the magnitude of the shock are varied automatically with the airspeed of the aircraft.

Compressor Inlet Screens

To prevent the engine from readily ingesting any items that can be drawn in the intake, a compressor inlet screen is sometimes placed across the engine air inlet at some location along the inlet duct. Engines that incorporate inlet screens, such as turboprops *[Figure 3-28]* and APUs *[Figure 3-29]* are not as vulnerable to FOD. The advantages and disadvantages of a screen vary. If the engine is readily subjected to internal damage, as would be the case for an engine having an axial compressor fitted with aluminum compressor blades, an inlet screen is almost a necessity. Screens, however, add appreciably to inlet duct pressure loss and are very susceptible to icing. Failure due to fatigue is also a problem. A failed

Figure 3-29. *An example of an inlet screen on an APU.*

screen can sometimes cause more damage than no screen at all. In some instances, inlet screens are made retractable and may be withdrawn from the airstream after takeoff or whenever icing conditions prevail. Such screens are subject to mechanical failure and add both weight and bulk to the installation. In large turbofan engines having steel or titanium compressor (fan) blades, which do not damage easily, the disadvantages of compressor screens outweigh the advantages, so they are not generally used.

Bellmouth Compressor Inlets

A bellmouth inlet is usually installed on an engine undergoing testing in a test cell. *[Figure 3-30]* It is generally equipped with probes that, with the use of instruments, can measure intake temperature and pressure (total and static). *[Figure 3-31]* During testing, it is important that the outside static air is allowed to flow into the engine with as little resistance as possible. The bellmouth is attached to the movable part of the test stand and moves with the engine. The

Figure 3-28. *An example of a turboprop engine that incorporates inlet screens.*

Figure 3-30. *A bellmouth inlet used during system tests.*

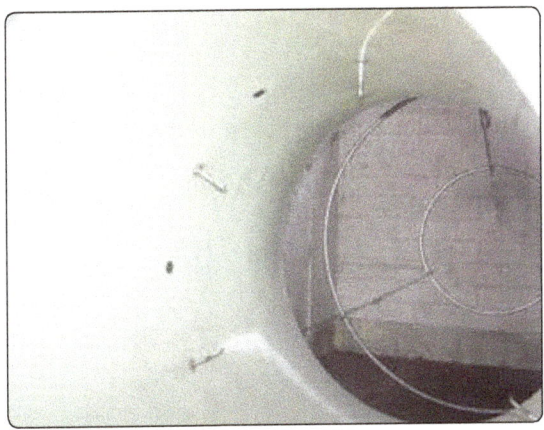

Figure 3-31. *Probes within a bellmouth inlet used to measure intake temperature and pressure.*

Figure 3-32. *An example of a ducted arrangement on a turboprop engine.*

thrust stand is made up of two components, one nonmoving and one moving. This is so the moving component can push against a load cell and measure thrust during the testing of the engine. The bellmouth is designed with the single objective of obtaining very high aerodynamic efficiency. Essentially, the inlet is a bell-shaped funnel having carefully rounded shoulders which offer practically no air resistance. *[Figure 3-30]* Duct loss is so slight that it is considered zero. The engine can, therefore, be operated without the complications resulting from losses common to an installed aircraft inlet duct. Engine performance data, such as rated thrust and thrust specific fuel consumption, are obtained while using a bellmouth inlet. Usually, the inlets are fitted with protective screening. In this case, the efficiency lost as the air passes through the screen must be taken into account when very accurate engine data are necessary.

Turboprop and Turboshaft Compressor Inlets

The air inlet on a turboprop is more of a problem than some other gas turbine engines because the propeller drive shaft, the hub, and the spinner must be considered in addition to other inlet design factors. The ducted arrangement is generally considered the best inlet design of the turboprop engine as far as airflow and aerodynamic characteristics are concerned. *[Figure 3-32]* The inlet for many types of turboprops are anti-iced by using electrical elements in the lip opening of the intake. Ducting either part of the engine or nacelle directs the airflow to the intake of the engine. Deflector doors are sometimes used to deflect ice or dirt away from the intake. *[Figure 3-33]* The air then passes through a screen and into the engine on some models. A conical spinner, which does not allow ice to build up on the surface, is sometimes used with turboprop and turbofan engines. In either event, the arrangement of the spinner and the inlet duct plays an important function in the operation and performance of the engine.

Figure 3-33. *Deflector doors used to deflect ice or dirt away from the intake.*

Turbofan Engine Inlet Sections

High-bypass turbofan engines are usually constructed with the fan at the forward end of the compressor. A typical turbofan intake section is shown in *Figure 3-34*. Sometimes, the inlet cowl is bolted to the front of the engine and provides the airflow path into the engine. In dual compressor (dual spool) engines, the fan is integral with the relatively slow-turning, low-pressure compressor, which allows the fan blades to rotate at low tip speed for best fan efficiency. The fan permits the use of a conventional air inlet duct, resulting in low inlet duct loss. The fan reduces engine damage from ingested foreign material because much of any material that may be ingested is thrown radially outward and passes through the fan discharge rather than through the core of the engine. Warm bleed air is drawn from the engine and circulated on the inside of the inlet lip for anti-icing. The fan hub or spinner is either heated by warm air or is conical

Figure 3-34. *A typical turbofan intake section.*

as mentioned earlier. Inside the inlet by the fan blade tips is an abraidable rub strip that allows the fan blades to rub for short times due to flightpath changes. *[Figure 3-35]* Also, inside the inlet are sound-reducing materials to lower the noise generated by the fan.

Figure 3-35. *Rubber stripping inside a turbofan engine inlet allows for friction for short periods of time during changes in the flightpath.*

The fan on high-bypass engines consists of one stage of rotating blades and stationary vanes that can range in diameter from less than 84 inches to more than 112 inches. *[Figure 3-36]* The fan blades are either hollow titanium or composite materials. The air accelerated by the outer part of the fan blades forms a secondary airstream, which is ducted overboard without passing through the main engine. This secondary air (fan flow) produces 80 percent of the thrust in high-bypass engines. The air that passes through the inner part of the fan blades becomes the primary airstream (core flow) through the engine itself. *[Figure 3-36]*

Figure 3-36. *The air that passes through the inner part of the fan blades becomes the primary airstream.*

The air from the fan exhaust, which is ducted overboard, may be discharged in either of two ways:

1. To the outside air through short ducts (dual exhaust nozzles) directly behind the fan. *[Figure 3-37]*

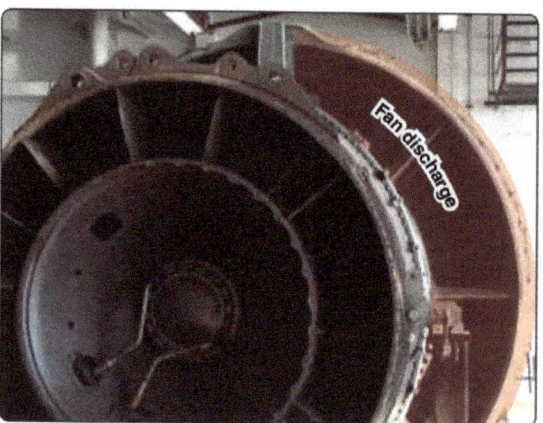

Figure 3-37. *Air from the fan exhaust can be discharged overboard through short ducts directly behind the fan.*

2. Ducted fan, which uses closed ducts all the way to the rear of the engine, where it is exhausted to the outside air through a mixed exhaust nozzle. This type engine is called a ducted fan and the core airflow and fan airflow mix in a common exhaust nozzle.

Reciprocating Engine Exhaust Systems

The reciprocating engine exhaust system is fundamentally a scavenging system that collects and disposes of the high temperature, noxious gases being discharged by the engine. Its main function is to dispose of the gases with complete safety to the airframe and the occupants of the aircraft. The exhaust system can perform many useful functions, but its first duty is to provide protection against the potentially destructive action of the exhaust gases. Modern exhaust systems, though comparatively light, adequately resist high temperatures, corrosion, and vibration to provide long, trouble-free operation with minimum maintenance.

There are two general types of exhaust systems in use on reciprocating aircraft engines: the short stack (open) system and the collector system. The short stack system is generally used on nonsupercharged engines and low-powered engines where noise level is not too objectionable. The collector system is used on most large nonsupercharged engines and on all turbosupercharged engines and installations on which it would improve nacelle streamlining or provide easier maintenance in the nacelle area. On turbosupercharged engines, the exhaust gases must be collected to drive the turbine compressor of the supercharger. Such systems have individual exhaust headers that empty into a common collector ring with only one outlet. From this outlet, the hot exhaust gas is routed via a tailpipe to the turbosupercharger that drives the turbine. Although the collector system raises the back pressure of the exhaust system, the gain in horsepower from turbosupercharging more than offsets the loss in horsepower that results from increased back pressure. The short stack system is relatively simple, and its removal and installation consists essentially of removing and installing the hold-down nuts and clamps. Short stack systems have limited use on most modern aircraft.

In *Figure 3-38*, the location of typical collector exhaust system components of a horizontally opposed engine is shown in a side view. The exhaust system in this installation consists of a down-stack from each cylinder, an exhaust collector tube on each side of the engine, and an exhaust ejector assembly protruding aft and down from each side of the firewall. The down-stacks are connected to the cylinders with high temperature locknuts and secured to the exhaust collector tube by ring clamps. A cabin heater exhaust shroud is installed around each collector tube. *[Figure 3-39]*

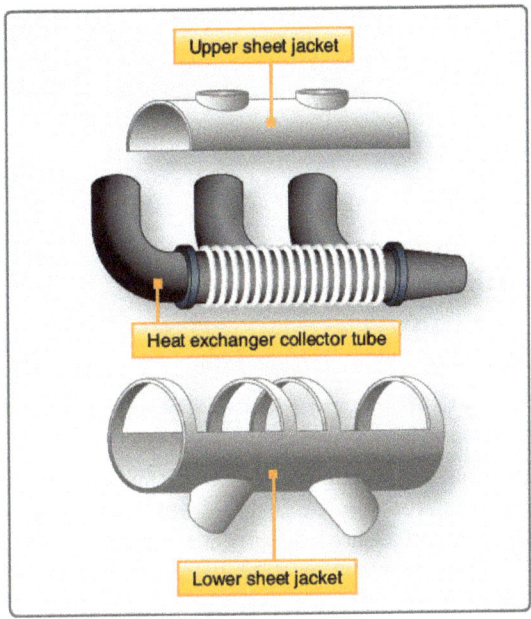

Figure 3-39. *A cabin heater exhaust shroud.*

The collector tubes terminate at the exhaust ejector openings at the firewall and are tapered to deliver the exhaust gases at the proper velocity to induce airflow through the exhaust ejectors. The exhaust ejectors consist of a throat-and-duct assembly that utilizes the pumping action of the exhaust gases to induce a flow of cooling air through all parts of the engine compartment (augmenter tube action).

Radial Engine Exhaust Collector Ring System

Figure 3-40 shows the exhaust collector ring installed on a 14-cylinder radial engine. The collector ring is a welded corrosion-resistant steel assembly manufactured in seven sections, with each section collecting the exhaust from two cylinders. The sections are graduated in size. *[Figure 3-41]* The small sections are on the inboard side, and the largest sections are on the outboard side at the point where the tailpipe connects to the collector ring. Each section of the collector ring is bolted to a bracket on the blower section of the engine and is partly supported by a sleeve connection between the collector ring ports and the short stack on the engine exhaust ports. The exhaust tailpipe is joined to the collector ring by a telescoping expansion joint, which allows enough slack for the removal of segments of the collector ring without removing the tailpipe. The exhaust tailpipe is a welded, corrosion-resistant steel assembly consisting of the exhaust tailpipe and, on some aircraft, a muff-type heat exchanger.

Figure 3-38. *Location of a typical collector exhaust system.*

Figure 3-40. *Elements of an exhaust collector ring installed on a radial engine.*

Manifold and Augmentor Exhaust Assembly

Some radial engines are equipped with a combination exhaust manifold and augmentor assembly. On a typical 18-cylinder engine, two exhaust assemblies and two augmentor assemblies are used. Each manifold assembly collects exhaust gases from nine cylinders and discharges the gases into the forward end of the augmentor assembly. The exhaust gases are directed into the augmentor bellmouths. The augmentors are designed to produce a venturi effect to draw an increased airflow over the engine to augment engine cooling. An augmentor vane is located in each tailpipe. When the vane is fully closed, the cross-sectional area of the tailpipe is reduced by approximately 45 percent. The augmentor vanes are operated by an electrical actuator, and indicators adjacent to the augmentor vane switches in the cockpit show vane positions. The vanes may be moved toward the "closed" position to decrease the velocity of flow through the augmentor to raise the engine temperature. This system is only used with older aircraft that generally use radial engines.

Reciprocating Engine Exhaust System Maintenance Practices

Any exhaust system failure should be regarded as a severe hazard. Depending on the location and type of failure, an exhaust system failure can result in carbon monoxide poisoning of crew and passengers, partial or complete loss of engine power, or an aircraft fire. Cracks in components, leaking gaskets, or complete failure can cause serious problems in flight. Often, these failures can be detected before complete failure. Black soot around an exhaust gasket shows the gasket has failed. The exhaust system should be inspected very thoroughly.

Figure 3-41. *A radial engine exhaust collector ring is graduated in size from the inboard side to the outboard side.*

Exhaust System Inspection

While the type and location of exhaust system components vary somewhat with the type of aircraft, the inspection requirements for most reciprocating engine exhaust systems are very similar. The following paragraphs include a discussion of the most common exhaust system inspection items and procedures for all reciprocating engines. *Figure 3-42* shows the primary inspection areas of three types of exhaust systems.

When performing maintenance on exhaust systems, never use galvanized or zinc-plated tools on the exhaust system. Exhaust system parts should never be marked with a lead pencil. The lead, zinc, or galvanized mark is absorbed by the metal of the exhaust system when heated, creating a distinct change in its molecular structure. This change softens the metal in the area of the mark, causing cracks and eventual failure.

After the installation of a complete exhaust system and all pieces of engine cowl are installed and secured, the engine should be operated to allow the exhaust system to heat up to normal operating temperatures. The engine is then shut down and the cowling removed to expose the exhaust system. Each clamped connection and each exhaust port connection should be inspected for evidence of exhaust gas leakage.

Figure 3-42. *Primary inspection areas of three types of exhaust systems.*

An exhaust leak is indicated by a flat gray or a sooty black streak on the pipes in the area of the leak. An exhaust leak is usually the result of poor alignment of two mated exhaust system members. When a leaking exhaust connection is discovered, the clamps should be loosened and the leaking units repositioned to ensure a gas-tight fit.

After repositioning, the system nuts should be retightened enough to eliminate any looseness without exceeding the specified torque. If tightening to the specified torque does not eliminate looseness, the bolts and nuts should be replaced since they have probably stretched. After tightening to the specified torque, all nuts should be safetied. With the cowling removed, all necessary cleaning operations can be performed. Some exhaust units are manufactured with a plain sandblast finish. Others may have a ceramic-coated finish. Ceramic-coated stacks should be cleaned by degreasing only. They should never be cleaned with sandblast or alkali cleaners.

During the inspection of an exhaust system, close attention should be given to all external surfaces of the exhaust system for cracks, dents, or missing parts. This also applies to welds, clamps, supports, support attachment lugs, bracing, slip joints, stack flanges, gaskets, and flexible couplings. Each bend should be examined, as well as areas adjacent to welds. Any dented areas or low spots in the system should be inspected for thinning and pitting due to internal erosion by combustion products or accumulated moisture. An ice pick or similar pointed instrument is useful in probing suspected areas.

The system should be disassembled as necessary to inspect internal baffles or diffusers. If a component of the exhaust system is inaccessible for a thorough visual inspection or is hidden by nonremovable parts, it should be removed and checked for possible leaks. This can often be accomplished best by plugging the openings of the component, applying a suitable internal pressure (approximately 2 psi), and submerging it in water. Any leaks cause bubbles that can readily be detected. The procedures required for an installation inspection are also performed during most regular inspections. Daily inspection of the exhaust system usually consists of checking the exposed exhaust system for cracks, scaling, excessive leakage, and loose clamps.

Muffler and Heat Exchanger Failures

Approximately half of all muffler and heat exchanger failures can be traced to cracks or ruptures in the heat exchanger surfaces used for cabin and carburetor heat sources. Failures in the heat exchanger surface (usually in the outer wall) allow exhaust gases to escape directly into the cabin heat system. These failures, in most cases, are caused by thermal and vibration fatigue cracking in areas of stress concentration. Failure of the spot-welds, which attach the heat transfer pins, can result in exhaust gas leakage. In addition to a carbon monoxide hazard, failure of heat exchanger surfaces can permit exhaust gases to be drawn into the engine induction system, causing engine overheating and power loss.

Exhaust Manifold and Stack Failures

Exhaust manifold and stack failures are usually fatigue failures at welded or clamped points (e.g., stack-to-flange, stack-to-manifold, and crossover pipe or muffler connections). Although these failures are primarily fire hazards, they also present carbon monoxide problems. Exhaust gases can enter the cabin via defective or inadequate seals at firewall openings, wing strut fittings, doors, and wing root openings.

Internal Muffler Failures

Internal failures (baffles, diffusers, etc.) can cause partial or complete engine power loss by restricting the flow of the exhaust gases. If pieces of the internal baffling breaks loose and partially or totally blocks the flow of exhaust gases, engine failure can occur. *[Figure 3-43]* As opposed to other failures, erosion and carburization caused by the extreme thermal conditions are the primary causes of internal failures. Engine backfiring and combustion of unburned fuel within the exhaust system are probable contributing factors. In addition, local hot-spot areas caused by uneven exhaust gas flow can result in burning, bulging, or rupture of the outer muffler wall.

Figure 3-43. *An example of internal muffler failure. Muffler failure can be caused by erosion and carbonization, which in turn can lead to breakage blocking exhaust flow.*

Exhaust Systems With Turbocharger

When a turbocharger or a turbosupercharger system is included, the engine exhaust system operates under greatly increased pressure and temperature conditions. Extra precautions should be taken in exhaust system care and maintenance. During high-pressure altitude operation, the exhaust system pressure is maintained at or near sea level values. Due to the pressure differential, any leaks in the system allow the exhaust gases to escape with torchlike intensity that can severely damage adjacent structures. A common cause of malfunction is coke deposits (carbon buildup) in the wastegate unit causing erratic system operation. Excessive deposit buildups may cause the wastegate valve to stick in the "closed" position, causing an overboost condition. Coke deposit buildup in the turbo itself causes a gradual loss of power in flight and low manifold pressure reading prior to takeoff. Experience has shown that periodic de-coking, or removal of carbon deposits, is necessary to maintain peak efficiency. Clean, repair, overhaul, and adjust the system components and controls in accordance with the applicable manufacturer's instructions.

Augmentor Exhaust System

On exhaust systems equipped with augmentor tubes, the augmentor tubes should be inspected at regular intervals for proper alignment, security of attachment, and general overall condition. Even where augmentor tubes do not contain heat exchanger surfaces, they should be inspected for cracks along with the remainder of the exhaust system. Cracks in augmentor tubes can present a fire or carbon monoxide hazard by allowing exhaust gases to enter the nacelle, wing, or cabin areas.

Exhaust System Repairs

It is generally recommended that exhaust stacks, mufflers, tailpipes, etc., be replaced with new or reconditioned components rather than repaired. Welded repairs to exhaust systems are complicated by the difficulty of accurately identifying the base metal so that the proper repair materials can be selected. Changes in composition and grain structure of the original base metal further complicate the repair. However, when welded repairs are necessary, the original contours should be retained; the exhaust system alignment must not be warped or otherwise affected. Repairs or sloppy weld beads that protrude internally are not acceptable as they cause local hot spots and may restrict exhaust gas flow. The proper hardware and clamps should always be used when repairing or replacing exhaust system components. Steel or low temperature, self-locking nuts should not be substituted for brass or special high temperature locknuts used by the manufacturer. Old gaskets should never be re-used. When disassembly is necessary, gaskets should be replaced with new ones of the same type provided by the manufacturer.

Turbine Engine Exhaust Nozzles

Turbine engines have several different types of exhaust nozzles depending upon the type of engine. Turboshaft engines in helicopters can have an exhaust nozzle that forms a divergent duct. This type of nozzle would not provide any thrust, all engine power going to rotate the rotors, improving helicopter hovering abilities. Turbofan engines tend to fall into either ducted fan of unducted fan engines. Ducted fan engines take the fan airflow and direct it through closed ducts along the engine. Then, it flows into a common exhaust nozzle. The core exhaust flow and the fan flow mix and flow from the engine through this mixed nozzle. The unducted fan has two nozzles, one for the fan airflow and one for the core airflow. These both flow to ambient air separate from each other and have separate nozzles. *[Figure 3-44]*

The unducted engine or the separate nozzle engine handles high amounts of airflow. The fan air which creates most of the thrust (80–85 percent total thrust) must be directed through

Figure 3-44. *Path of both core exhaust flow and fan flow from the engine to separate nozzles.*

the fan blades and exit vanes with little turbulence as possible. *[Figure 3-45]* The core airflow needs to be straightened as it comes from the turbine. Through the use of a converging nozzle, the exhaust gases increase in velocity before they are discharged from the exhaust nozzle. Increasing the velocity of the gases increases their momentum and increases the thrust produced (20–15 percent total thrust). Most of the energy of the gases have been absorbed to drive the fan through the low-pressure turbine stages.

Figure 3-45. *Fan air is directed through the fan blades and exit vanes.*

Turboprop exhaust nozzles provide small amounts of thrust (10–15 percent), but are mainly used to discharge the exhaust gases from the aircraft. Most of the energy has been transferred to the propeller. On some turboprop aircraft, an exhaust duct is often referred to as a tailpipe, although the duct itself is essentially a simple, stainless steel, conical or cylindrical pipe. The assembly also includes an engine tail cone and the struts inside the duct. The tail cone and the struts add strength to the duct, impart an axial direction to the gas flow, and smooth the gas flow. In a typical installation, the tailpipe assembly is mounted in the nacelle and attached at its forward end to the firewall. The forward section of the tailpipe is funnel shaped and surrounds but does not contact the turbine exhaust section. This arrangement forms an annular gap that serves as an air ejector for the air surrounding the engine hot section. As the high-velocity exhaust gases enter the tailpipe, a low-pressure effect is produced which causes the air around the engine hot section to flow through the annular gap into the tailpipe. The rear section of the tailpipe is secured to the airframe by two support arms, one on each side of the tailpipe. The support arms are attached to the upper surface of the wing in such a way that allow movement fore and aft to compensate for expansion. The tailpipe assembly is wrapped in an insulating blanket to shield the surrounding area from the high heat produced by the exhaust gases. Such blankets may be made of a stainless steel laminated sheet on the outside and fiberglass on the inside. This is used when the engine exhaust is located some distance from the edge of the wing or aircraft structure.

Immediately aft of the turbine outlet, and usually just forward of the flange to which the exhaust duct is attached, the engine is instrumented for turbine discharge pressure. One or more pressure probes are inserted into the exhaust duct to provide adequate sampling of the exhaust gases. In large engines, it is not practical to measure the internal temperature at the turbine inlet, so the engine is often also instrumented for exhaust gas temperature at the turbine outlet.

Convergent Exhaust Nozzle

As the exhaust gases exit the rear of the engine, they flow into the exhaust nozzle. *[Figure 3-46]* The very first part of the exhaust nozzle and the exhaust plug form a divergent duct to reduce turbulence in the airflow, then the exhaust gases flow into the convergent component of the exhaust nozzle where the flow is restricted by a smaller outlet opening. Since this forms a convergent duct, the gas velocity is increased providing increased thrust. The restriction of the opening of the outlet of the exhaust nozzle is limited by two factors. If the nozzle opening is too big, thrust is being wasted. If it is too little, the flow is choked in the other components of the engine. In other words, the exhaust nozzle acts as an orifice, the size of which determines the density and velocity of the gases as they emerge from the engine. This is critical to thrust performance. Adjusting the area of the exhaust nozzle changes both the engine performance and the exhaust gas temperature. When the velocity of the exhaust gases at the nozzle opening becomes Mach 1, the flow passes only at this speed—it does not increase or decrease. Sufficient flow to maintain Mach 1 at the nozzle opening and have extra flow (flow that is being restricted by the opening) creates what is called a choked nozzle. The extra flow builds up pressure in the nozzle, which is sometimes called pressure thrust. A differential in pressure exists between the inside of the nozzle and the ambient air. By multiplying this difference in pressure times the area of the nozzle opening, pressure thrust can be calculated. Many engines cannot develop pressure thrust because most of the energy is used to drive turbines that turn propellers, large fans, or helicopter rotors.

Figure 3-46. *Exhaust gases exit the rear of the engine through the exhaust nozzle.*

Convergent-Divergent Exhaust Nozzle

Whenever the engine pressure ratio is high enough to produce exhaust gas velocities which might exceed Mach 1 at the engine exhaust nozzle, more thrust can be gained by using a convergent-divergent type of nozzle. *[Figure 3-47]* The advantage of a convergent-divergent nozzle is greatest at high Mach numbers because of the resulting higher pressure ratio across the engine exhaust nozzle.

Figure 3-47. *A convergent-divergent nozzle can be used to help produce more thrust when exhaust gas velocities are greater than Mach 1.*

To ensure that a constant weight or volume of a gas flows past any given point after sonic velocity is reached, the rear part of a supersonic exhaust duct is enlarged to accommodate the additional weight or volume of a gas that flows at supersonic rates. If this is not done, the nozzle does not operate efficiently. This is the divergent section of the exhaust duct.

When a divergent duct is used in combination with a conventional exhaust duct, it is called a convergent-divergent exhaust duct. In the convergent-divergent, or C-D nozzle, the convergent section is designed to handle the gases while they remain subsonic, and to deliver the gases to the throat of the nozzle just as they attain sonic velocity. The divergent section handles the gases, further increasing their velocity, after they emerge from the throat and become supersonic. As the gas flows from the throat of the nozzle, it becomes supersonic (Mach 1 and above) and then passes into the divergent section of the nozzle. Since it is supersonic, it continues to increase in velocity. This type of nozzle is generally used on very high speed aerospace vehicles.

Thrust Reversers

As aircraft have increased in gross weights with higher landing airspeeds, the problem of stopping an aircraft after landing has greatly increased. In many instances, the aircraft brakes can no longer be relied upon solely to slow the aircraft within a reasonable distance, immediately after touchdown.

Most thrust reverser systems can be divided into two categories: mechanical-blockage and aerodynamic-blockage.

Mechanical blockage is accomplished by placing a removable obstruction in the exhaust gas stream, usually somewhat to the rear of the nozzle. The engine exhaust gases are mechanically blocked and diverted at a suitable angle in the reverse direction by an inverted cone, half-sphere, or clam shell. *[Figure 3-48]* This is placed in position to reverse the flow of exhaust gases. This type is generally used with ducted turbofan engines, where the fan and core flow mix in a common nozzle before exiting the engine. The clamshell-type or mechanical-blockage reverser operates to form a barrier in the path of escaping exhaust gases, which nullifies and reverses the forward thrust of the engine. The reverser system must be able to withstand high temperatures, be mechanically strong, relatively light in weight, reliable, and "fail-safe." When not in use, it must be streamlined into the configuration of the engine nacelle. When the reverser is not in use, the clamshell doors retract and nest neatly around the engine exhaust duct, usually forming the rear section of the engine nacelle.

In the aerodynamic blockage type of thrust reverser, used mainly with unducted turbofan engines, only fan air is used to slow the aircraft. A modern aerodynamic thrust reverser system consist of a translating cowl, blocker doors, and cascade vanes that redirect the fan airflow to slow the aircraft. *[Figure 3-49]* If the thrust levers are at idle position and the aircraft has weight on the wheels, moving the thrust levers aft activates the translating cowl to open closing the blocker doors. This action stops the fan airflow from going aft and redirects it through the cascade vanes, which direct the airflow forward to slow the aircraft. Since the fan can produce approximately 80 percent of the engine's thrust, the fan is the best source for reverse thrust. By returning the thrust levers (power levers) to the idle position, the blocker doors open and the translating cowl closes.

A thrust reverser must not have any adverse affect on engine operation either deployed or stowed. Generally, there is an indication in the flight deck with regard to the status of the reverser system. The thrust reverser system consists of several components that move either the clam shell doors or the blocker door and translating cowl. Actuating power is generally pneumatic or hydraulic and uses gearboxes, flexdrives, screwjacks, control valves, and air or hydraulic motors to deploy or stow the thrust reverser systems. The systems are locked in the stowed position until commanded to deploy by the flight deck. Since there are several moving parts, maintenance and inspection requirements are very important. While performing any type of maintenance, the reverser system must be mechanically locked out from deploying while personnel are in the area of the reverser system.

Afterburning/Thrust Augmentation

The terms afterburning and thrust augmentation generally pertain to military engine applications. The terms are used to describe the same system. Normally, this is used to increase the thrust of the engine up to double the original thrust. The required additions to the exhaust nozzle for this system are a flame stabilizer, fuel manifold, flame holder, igniter, and a variable area exhaust nozzle. *[Figure 3-50]* After the engine has reached full power under normal operation, the power lever can be advanced to activate the afterburner. This allows more fuel to flow into the exhaust nozzle where it is ignited and burned. As energy and mass is added to the gas flow, the exhaust nozzle must open wider to allow greater flow. As the power lever is moved back out of the afterburner, the exhaust nozzle closes down again. Some low-bypass turbofan engines used in military aircraft use bypass (fan air) to flow into the exhaust nozzle. Just as in a ducted fan, this air is used in the afterburner. It contains more oxygen and assists combustion in the afterburner. Since fuel is being burned in the exhaust nozzle, the heat buildup around the nozzle is a

Figure 3-48. *Engine exhaust gases are blocked and diverted in a reserve direction during thrust reversal.*

Figure 3-49. *Components of a thrust reverser system.*

Figure 3-50. *An example of a variable area exhaust nozzle used to increase or decrease exhaust flow during afterburn.*

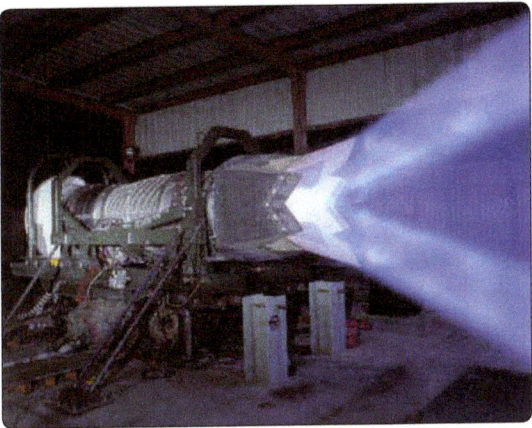

Figure 3-51. *A pilot can direct thrust via the vectoring nozzle 20° up or down to increase flight maneuverability.*

problem. A special type of liner is used around the nozzle to allow cooler air to circulate around the nozzle. This operates somewhat like a single burner can combustion chamber. Operation in the afterburner mode is somewhat limited by high fuel consumption, which can be almost double normal consumption.

Thrust Vectoring

Thrust vectoring is the ability of an aircraft's main engines to direct thrust other than parallel to the vehicle's longitudinal axis, allowing the exhaust nozzle to move or change position to direct the thrust in varied directions. Vertical takeoff aircraft use thrust vectoring as takeoff thrust and then change direction to propel the aircraft in horizontal flight. Military aircraft use thrust vectoring for maneuvering in flight to change direction. Thrust vectoring is generally accomplished by relocating the direction of the exhaust nozzle to direct the thrust to move the aircraft in the desired path. At the rear of a gas turbine engine, a nozzle directs the flow of hot exhaust gases out of the engine and afterburner. Usually, the nozzle points straight out of the engine. The pilot can move, or vector, the vectoring nozzle up and down by 20°. This makes the aircraft much more maneuverable in flight. *[Figure 3-51]*

Engine Noise Supression

Aircraft powered by gas turbine engines sometimes require noise suppression for the engine exhaust gases when operating from airports located in or near highly populated areas. Several types of noise suppressor are used. A common type of noise suppressor is an integral, airborne part of the aircraft engine installation or engine exhaust nozzle. Engine noise comes from several sources on the engine, the fan, or compressor and the air discharge from the core of the engine. There are three sources of noise involved in the operation of a gas turbine engine. The engine air intake and vibration from engine housing are sources of some noise, but the noise generated does not compare in magnitude with that produced by the engine exhaust. *[Figure 3-52]* The noise produced by the engine exhaust is caused by the high degree of turbulence of a high-velocity jet stream moving through a relatively quiet atmosphere. For a distance of a few nozzle diameters downstream behind the engine, the velocity of the jet stream is high, and there is little mixing of the atmosphere with the jet stream. In this region, the turbulence within the high speed jet stream is very fine grain turbulence, and produces relatively high-frequency noise. This noise is caused by violent, turbulent mixing of the exhaust gases with the atmosphere and is influenced by the shearing action caused by the relative speeds between the velocity and the atmosphere.

Farther downstream, as the velocity of the jet stream slows down, the jet stream mixes with the atmosphere and turbulence of a coarser type begins. Compared with noise from other portions of the jet stream, noise from this portion has a much lower frequency. As the energy of the jet stream finally is dissipated in large turbulent swirls, a greater portion of the energy is converted into noise. The noise generated as the exhaust gases dissipate is at a frequency near the low end of the audible range. The lower the frequency of the noise, the greater the distance the noise travels. This means that the low-frequency noises reach an individual on the ground in greater volume than the high-frequency noises, and hence are more objectionable. High-frequency noise is weakened more rapidly than low-frequency noise, both by distance and the interference of buildings, terrain, and atmospheric disturbances. A deep-voiced, low-frequency foghorn, for example, may be heard much farther than a shrill, high-frequency whistle, even though both may have the same overall volume (decibels) at their source.

Figure 3-52. *Engine noise from engine exhaust is created by the turbulence of a high velocity jet stream moving through the relatively quiet atmosphere.*

Noise levels vary with engine thrust and are proportional to the amount of work done by the engine on the air that passes through it. An engine having relatively low airflow but high thrust due to high turbine discharge (exhaust gas) temperature, pressure, and/or afterburning produces a gas stream of high velocity and, therefore, high noise levels. A larger engine, handling more air, is quieter at the same thrust. Thus, the noise level can be reduced considerably by operating the engine at lower power settings, and large engines operating at partial thrust are less noisy than smaller engines operating at full thrust. Compared with a turbojet, a turbofan version of the same engine is quieter during takeoff. The noise level produced by a fan-type engine is less, principally because the exhaust gas velocities ejected at the engine tailpipe are slower than those for a turbojet of comparative size.

Fan engines require a larger turbine to provide additional power to drive the fan. The large turbine, which usually has an additional turbine stage, reduces the velocity of the gas and, therefore, reduces the noise produced because exhaust gas noise is proportional to exhaust gas velocity. The exhaust from the fan is at a relatively low velocity and, therefore, does not create a noise problem. Because of the characteristic of low-frequency noise to linger at a relatively high volume, effective noise reduction for a turbojet aircraft must be achieved by revising the noise pattern or by changing the frequency of the noise emitted by the jet nozzle.

The noise suppressors in current use are either of the corrugated-perimeter type, or the multi-tube type. *[Figure 3-53]* Both types of suppressors break up the single, main jet exhaust stream into a number of smaller jet streams. This increases

Figure 3-53. *Noise suppressors currently in use are corrugated-perimeter type, or multi-tube type.*

the total perimeter of the nozzle area and reduces the size of the air stream eddies created as the gases are discharged into the open air. Although the total noise-energy remains unchanged, the frequency is raised considerably. The size of the air stream eddies scales down at a linear rate with the size of the exhaust stream. This has two effects: 1) the change in frequency may put some of the noise above the audibility range of the human ear, and 2) high frequencies within the audible range, while perhaps more annoying, are more highly attenuated by atmospheric absorption than are low frequencies. Thus, the falloff in intensity is greater and the noise level is less at any given distance from the aircraft.

In the engine nacelle, the area between the engine and the cowl has acoustic linings surrounding the engine. This noise-absorbing lining material converts acoustic energy into heat. These linings normally consist of a porous skin supported by a honeycomb backing and provide a separation between the fact sheet and the engine duct. For optimum suppression, the acoustic properties of the skin and the liner are carefully matched.

Turbine Engine Emissions

Engineers are introducing new combustion technology that has dramatically reduced emissions from gas turbine engines. Lowering exhaust emissions from gas turbine, especially oxides of nitrogen (NO_X), continue to require improvement. Most of the research has centered around the combustion section of the engine. New technology with unique combustor design has greatly reduced emissions. One manufacturer has a design called the Twin Annular, Pre-mixing Swirler (TAPS) combustor. Most advanced designs rely on a method of pre-mixing the fuel/air before it enters the combustion burner area. In the TAPS design, air from the high-pressure compressor is directed into the combustor through two high-energy swirlers adjacent to the fuel nozzles. This swirl creates a more thorough and leaner mix of fuel and air, which burns at lower temperatures than in previous gas turbine engine designs. Most of the NO_X is formed by the reaction of oxygen and nitrogen at high temperatures. The NO_X levels are higher if the burning fuel/air mixture stays at high temperatures for a longer time. Newly designed combustors also produce lower levels of carbon monoxide and unburned hydrocarbons. The increases in gas turbine engine component efficiencies have resulted in fewer emissions from gas turbine engines.

Chapter 4
Engine Ignition and Electrical Systems

Reciprocating Engine Ignition Systems

The basic requirements for reciprocating engine ignition systems are similar, regardless of the type of engine. All ignition systems must deliver a high-tension spark across the electrodes of each spark plug in each cylinder of the engine in the correct firing order. At a predetermined number of degrees ahead of the top dead center position of the piston, as measured by crankshaft travel in degrees of rotation, the spark occurs in the cylinder. The potential output voltage of the system must be adequate to arc the gap in the spark plug electrodes under all operating conditions. The spark plug is threaded into the cylinder head with the electrodes exposed to the combustion area of the engine's cylinder.

Ignition systems can be divided into two classifications: magneto-ignition systems or electronic Full Authority Digital Engine Control (FADEC) systems for reciprocating engines. Ignition systems can also be subclassified as either single or dual magneto-ignition systems. The single magneto-ignition system, usually consisting of one magneto and the necessary wiring, was used with another single magneto on the same engine. Dual magnetos generally use one rotating magnet that feeds two complete magnetos in one magneto housing. An example of each type is shown in *Figure 4-1*.

Figure 4-1. *Single and dual magnetos.*

Aircraft magneto-ignition systems can be classified as either high-tension or low-tension. The low-tension magneto system, covered in a later section of this chapter, generates a low-voltage that is distributed to a transformer coil near each spark plug. This system eliminates some problems inherent in the high-tension system that was containing the high-voltage until it passed through the spark plug. The materials that were used for ignition leads could not withstand the high-voltage and were prone to leak to ground before the spark would get to the cylinder. As new materials evolved and shielding was developed, the problems with high-tension magnetos were overcome. The high-tension magneto system is still the most widely used aircraft ignition system.

Some very old antique aircraft used a battery-ignition system. In this system, the source of energy is a battery or generator, rather than a magneto. This system was similar to that used in most automobiles at the time. *Figure 4-2* shows a simplified schematic of a battery-ignition system.

Magneto-Ignition System Operating Principles

The magneto, a special type of engine-driven alternate current (AC) generator, uses a permanent magnet as a source of energy. By the use of a permanent magnet (basic magnetic field), coil of wire (concentrated lengths of conductor), and

Figure 4-2. *Battery-ignition system.*

relative movement of the magnetic field, current is generated in the wire. At first, the magneto generates electrical power by the engine rotating the permanent magnet and inducing a current to flow in the coil windings. As current flows through the coil windings, it generates its own magnetic field that surrounds the coil windings. At the correct time, this current flow is stopped and the magnetic field collapses across a second set of windings in the coil and a high-voltage is generated. This is the voltage used to arc across the spark plug gap. In both cases, the three basic things needed to generate electrical power are present to develop the high-voltage that forces a spark to jump across the spark plug gap in each cylinder. Magneto operation is timed to the engine so that a spark occurs only when the piston is on the proper stroke at a specified number of crankshaft degrees before the top dead center piston position.

High-Tension Magneto System Theory of Operation

The high-tension magneto system can be divided, for purposes of discussion, into three distinct circuits: magnetic, primary electrical, and secondary electrical circuits.

The Magnetic Circuit

The magnetic circuit consists of a permanent multi-pole rotating magnet, a soft iron core, and pole shoes. *[Figure 4-3]* The magnet is geared to the aircraft engine and rotates in the gap between two pole shoes to furnish the magnetic lines of force (flux) necessary to produce an electrical voltage. The poles of the magnet are arranged in alternate polarity so that the flux can pass out of the north pole through the coil core and back to the south pole of the magnet. When the magnet is in the position shown in *Figure 4-3A*, the number of magnetic lines of force through the coil core is maximum because two magnetically opposite poles are perfectly aligned with the pole shoes.

Figure 4-3. *Magnetic flux at three positions of the rotating magnet.*

This position of the rotating magnet is called the full register position and produces a maximum number of magnetic lines of force, flux flow clockwise through the magnetic circuit and from left to right through the coil core. When the magnet is moved away from the full register position, the amount of flux passing through the coil core begins to decrease. This occurs because the magnet's poles are moving away from the pole shoes, allowing some lines of flux to take a shorter path through the ends of the pole shoes.

As the magnet moves farther from the full register position, more lines of flux are short circuited through the pole shoe ends. Finally, at the neutral position 45° from the full register position, all flux lines are short circuited, and no flux flows through the coil core. *[Figure 4-3B]* As the magnet moves from full register to the neutral position, the number of flux lines through the coil core decreases in the same manner as the gradual collapse of flux in the magnetic field of an ordinary electromagnet.

The neutral position of the magnet is where one of the poles of the magnet is centered between the pole shoes of the magnetic circuit. As the magnet is moved clockwise from this position, the lines of flux that had been short circuited through the pole shoe ends begin to flow through the coil core again. But this time, the flux lines flow through the coil core in the opposite direction. *[Figure 4-3C]* The flux flow reverses as the magnet moves out of the neutral position because the north pole of the rotating permanent magnet is opposite the right pole shoe instead of the left. *[Figure 4-3A]*

When the magnet is again moved a total of 90°, another full register position is reached with a maximum flux flow in the opposite direction. The 90° of magnet travel is shown in *Figure 4-4*, where a curve shows how the flux density in the coil core, without a primary coil around the core, changes as the magnet is rotated.

Figure 4-4. *Change in flux density as magnet rotates.*

Figure 4-4 shows that as the magnet moves from the full register position 0°, flux flow decreases and reaches a zero value as it moves into the neutral position 45°. While the magnet moves through the neutral position, flux flow reverses and begins to increase as indicated by the curve below the horizontal line. At the 90° position, another position of maximum flux is reached. Thus, for one revolution 360° of the four pole magnet, there are four positions of maximum flux, four positions of zero flux, and four flux reversals.

This discussion of the magnetic circuit demonstrates how the coil core is affected by the rotating magnet. It is subjected to an increasing and decreasing magnetic field and a change in polarity each 90° of magnet travel.

When a coil of wire as part of the magneto's primary electrical circuit is wound around the coil core, it is also affected by the varying magnetic field.

The Primary Electrical Circuit

The primary electrical circuit consists of a set of breaker contact points, a condenser, and an insulated coil. *[Figure 4-5]* The coil is made up of a few turns of heavy copper wire, one end is grounded to the coil core and the other end to the ungrounded side of the breaker points. *[Figure 4-5]* The primary circuit is complete only when the ungrounded breaker point contacts the grounded breaker point. The third unit in the circuit, the condenser (capacitor), is wired in parallel with the breaker points. The condenser prevents arcing at the points when the circuit is opened and hastens the collapse of the magnetic field about the primary coil.

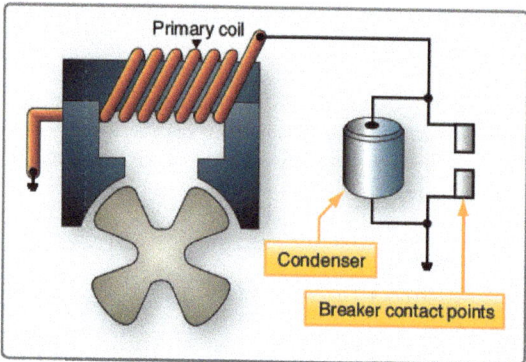

Figure 4-5. *Primary electrical circuit of a high-tension magneto.*

The primary breaker closes at approximately full register position. When the breaker points are closed, the primary electrical circuit is completed and the rotating magnet induces current flow in the primary circuit. This current flow generates its own magnetic field, which is in such a direction that it opposes any change in the magnetic flux of the permanent magnet's circuit.

While the induced current is flowing in the primary circuit, it opposes any decrease in the magnetic flux in the core. This is in accordance with Lenz's Law that states: "An induced current always flows in such a direction that its magnetism opposes the motion or the change that induced it." (For a review of Lenz's Law, refer to the Aviation Maintenance Technician—General Handbook, FAA-H-8083-30). Thus, the current flowing in the primary circuit holds the flux in the core at a high value in one direction until the rotating magnet has time to rotate through the neutral position to a point a few degrees beyond neutral. This position is called the E-gap position (E stands for efficiency).

With the magnetic rotor in E-gap position and the primary coil holding the magnetic field of the magnetic circuit in the opposite polarity, a very high rate of flux change can be obtained by opening the primary breaker points. Opening the breaker points stops the flow of current in the primary circuit and allows the magnetic rotor to quickly reverse the field through the coil core. This sudden flux reversal produces a high rate of flux change in the core, that cuts across the secondary coil of the magneto (wound over and insulated from the primary coil), inducing the pulse of high-voltage electricity in the secondary needed to fire a spark plug. As the rotor continues to rotate to approximately full register position, the primary breaker points close again and the cycle is repeated to fire the next spark plug in firing order.

The sequence of events can now be reviewed in greater detail to explain how the state of extreme magnetic stress occurs.

With the breaker points, cam, and condenser connected in the circuit as shown in *Figure 4-6*, the action that takes place as the magnetic rotor turns is depicted by the graph curve in *Figure 4-7*. At the top (A) of *Figure 4-7*, the original static flux curve of the magnets is shown. Shown below the static flux curve is the sequence of opening and closing the magneto breaker points. Note that opening and closing the breaker points is timed by the breaker cam. The points close when a maximum amount of flux is passing through the coil core and open at a position after neutral. Since there are four

Figure 4-6. *Components of a high-tension magneto circuit.*

Figure 4-7. *Magneto flux curves.*

lobes on the cam, the breaker points close and open in the same relation to each of the four neutral positions of the rotor magnet. Also, the point opening and point closing intervals are approximately equal.

Starting at the maximum flux position marked 0° at the top of *Figure 4-7*, the sequence of events in the following paragraphs occurs.

As the magnet rotor is turned toward the neutral position, the amount of flux through the core starts to decrease. *[Figure 4-7D]* This change in flux linkages induces a current in the primary winding. *[Figure 4-7C]* This induced current creates a magnetic field of its own that opposes the change of flux linkages inducing the current. Without current flowing in the primary coil, the flux in the coil core decreases to zero as the magnet rotor turns to neutral and starts to increase in the opposite direction (dotted static flux curve in *Figure 4-7D*). But, the electromagnetic action of the primary current prevents the flux from changing and temporarily holds the field instead of allowing it to change (resultant flux line in *Figure 4-7D*).

As a result of the holding process, there is a very high stress in the magnetic circuit by the time the magnet rotor has reached the position where the breaker points are about to open. The breaker points, when opened, function with the condenser to interrupt the flow of current in the primary coil, causing an extremely rapid change in flux linkages. The high-voltage in the secondary winding discharges across the gap in the spark plug to ignite the fuel/air mixture in the engine cylinder. Each spark actually consists of one peak discharge, after which a series of small oscillations takes place.

They continue to occur until the voltage becomes too low to maintain the discharge. Current flows in the secondary winding during the time that it takes for the spark to completely discharge. The energy or stress in the magnetic circuit is completely dissipated by the time the contacts close for the production of the next spark. Breaker assemblies, used in high-tension magneto-ignition systems, automatically open and close the primary circuit at the proper time in relation to piston position in the cylinder to which an ignition spark is being furnished. The interruption of the primary current flow is accomplished through a pair of breaker contact points made of an alloy that resists pitting and burning.

Most breaker points used in aircraft ignition systems are of the pivotless type in which one of the breaker points is movable and the other stationary. [Figure 4-8] The movable breaker point attached to the leaf spring is insulated from the magneto housing and is connected to the primary coil. [Figure 4-8] The stationary breaker point is grounded to the magneto housing to complete the primary circuit when the points are closed and can be adjusted so that the points can open at the proper time.

Figure 4-8. *Pivotless type breaker assembly and cam.*

Another part of the breaker assembly is the cam follower, which is spring-loaded against the cam by the metal leaf spring. The cam follower is a Micarta block or similar material that rides the cam and moves upward to force the movable breaker contact away from the stationary breaker contact each time a lobe of the cam passes beneath the follower. A felt oiler pad is located on the underside of the metal spring leaf to lubricate and prevent corrosion of the cam.

The breaker-actuating cam may be directly driven by the magneto rotor shaft or through a gear train from the rotor shaft. Most large radial engines use a compensated cam that is designed to operate with a specific engine and has one lobe for each cylinder to be fired by the magneto. The cam lobes are machine ground at unequal intervals to compensate for the elliptical path of the articulated connecting rods. This path causes the pistons top dead center position to vary from cylinder to cylinder with regard to crankshaft rotation. A compensated 14-lobe cam, together with a two-, four-, and eight-lobe uncompensated cam, is shown in *Figure 4-9*.

The unequal spacing of the compensated cam lobes, although it provides the same relative piston position for ignition to occur, causes a slight variation of the E-gap position of the rotating magnet and thus a slight variation in the high-voltage impulses generated by the magneto. Since the spacing between each lobe is tailored to a particular cylinder of a particular engine, compensated cams are marked to show the series of the engine, the location of the master rods, the lobe used for magneto timing, the direction of cam rotation, and the E-gap specification in degrees past neutral of magnet rotation. In addition to these markings, a step is cut across the face of the cam, that, when aligned with scribed marks on the magneto housing, places the rotating magnet in the E-gap position for the timing cylinder. Since the breaker points should begin to open when the rotating magnet moves into the E-gap position, alignment of the step on the cam with marks in the housing provides a quick and easy method of establishing the exact E-gap position to check and adjust the breaker points.

The Secondary Electrical Circuit

The secondary circuit contains the secondary windings of the coil, distributor rotor, distributor cap, ignition lead, and spark plug. The secondary coil is made up of a winding containing approximately 13,000 turns of fine, insulated wire; one end of which is electrically grounded to the primary coil or to the coil core and the other end connected to the distributor rotor. The primary and secondary coils are encased in a non-conducting material. The whole assembly is then fastened to the pole shoes with screws and clamps.

Figure 4-9. *Typical breaker assemblies.*

When the primary circuit is closed, the current flow through the primary coil produces magnetic lines of force that cut across the secondary windings, inducing an electromotive force. When the primary circuit current flow is stopped, the magnetic field surrounding the primary windings collapses, causing the secondary windings to be cut by the lines of force. The strength of the voltage induced in the secondary windings, when all other factors are constant, is determined by the number of turns of wire. Since most high-tension magnetos have many thousands of turns of wire in the secondary coil windings, a very high-voltage, often as high as 20,000 volts, is generated in the secondary circuit. The high-voltage induced in the secondary coil is directed to the distributor, which consists of two parts: revolving and stationary. The revolving part is called a distributor rotor and the stationary part is called a distributor block. The rotating part, which may take the shape of a disk, drum, or finger, is made of a non-conducting material with an embedded conductor. The stationary part consists of a block also made of non-conducting material that contains terminals and terminal receptacles into which the ignition lead wiring that connects the distributor to the spark plug is attached. This high-voltage is used to jump the air gap of electrodes of the spark plug in the cylinder to ignite the fuel/air mixture.

As the magnet moves into the E-gap position for the No. 1 cylinder and the breaker points just separate or open, the distributor rotor aligns itself with the No. 1 electrode in the distributor block. The secondary voltage induced as the breaker points open enters the rotor where it arcs a small air gap to the No. 1 electrode in the block.

Since the distributor rotates at one-half crankshaft speed on all four-stroke cycle engines, the distributor block has as many electrodes as there are engine cylinders, or as many electrodes as cylinders served by the magneto. The electrodes are located circumferentially around the distributor block so that, as the rotor turns, a circuit is completed to a different cylinder and spark plug each time there is alignment between the rotor finger and an electrode in the distributor block. The electrodes of the distributor block are numbered consecutively in the direction of distributor rotor travel. [*Figure 4-10*]

The distributor numbers represent the magneto sparking order rather than the engine cylinder numbers. The distributor electrode marked "1" is connected to the spark plug in the No. 1 cylinder; distributor electrode marked "2" to the second cylinder to be fired; distributor electrode marked "3" to the third cylinder to be fired, and so forth.

In *Figure 4-10*, the distributor rotor finger is aligned with the distributor electrode marked "3," which fires the No. 5

Figure 4-10. *Relation between distributor terminal numbers and cylinder numbers.*

cylinder of a nine-cylinder radial engine. Since the firing order of a nine-cylinder radial engine is 1-3-5-7-9-2-4-6-8, the third electrode in the magneto sparking order serves the No. 5 cylinder.

Magneto and Distributor Venting

Since magneto and distributor assemblies are subjected to sudden changes in temperature, the problems of condensation and moisture are considered in the design of these units. Moisture in any form is a good conductor of electricity. If absorbed by the nonconducting material in the magneto, such as distributor blocks, distributor fingers, and coil cases, it can create a stray electrical conducting path. The high-voltage current that normally arcs across the air gaps of the distributor can flash across a wet insulating surface to ground, or the high-voltage current can be misdirected to some spark plug other than the one that should be fired. This condition is called flashover and usually results in cylinder misfiring. This can cause a serious engine condition called pre-ignition, which can damage the engine. For this reason, coils, condensers, distributors, and distributor rotors are waxed so that moisture on such units stand in separate beads and do not form a complete circuit for flashover.

Flashover can lead to carbon tracking, which appears as a fine pencil-like line on the unit across which flashover occurs. The carbon trail results from the electric spark burning dirt particles that contain hydrocarbon materials. The water in the hydrocarbon material is evaporated during flashover, leaving carbon to form a conducting path for current. When moisture is no longer present, the spark continues to follow the carbon track to the ground. This prevents the spark from getting to the spark plug, so the cylinder does not fire.

Magnetos cannot be hermetically sealed to prevent moisture from entering a unit, because the magneto is subject to pressure and temperature changes in altitude. Thus, adequate drains and proper ventilation reduce the tendency of flashover and carbon tracking. Good magneto circulation also ensures that corrosive gases produced by normal arcing across the distributor air gap, such as ozone, are carried away. In some installations, pressurization of the internal components of the magnetos and other various parts of the ignition system is essential to maintain a higher absolute pressure inside the magneto and to eliminate flashover due to high altitude flight. This type of magneto is used with turbocharged engines that operate at higher altitudes. Flashover becomes more likely at high altitudes because of the lower air pressure, which makes it easier for the electricity to jump air gaps. By pressurizing the interior of the magneto, the normal air pressure is maintained and the electricity or the spark is held within the proper areas of the magneto even though the ambient pressure is very low.

Even in a pressurized magneto, the air is allowed to flow through and out of the magneto housing. By providing more air and allowing small amounts of air to bleed out for ventilation, the magneto remains pressurized. Regardless of the method of venting employed, the vent bleeds or valves must be kept free of obstructions. Further, the air circulating through the components of the ignition system must be free of oil since even minute amounts of oil on ignition parts result in flashover and carbon tracking.

Ignition Harness

The ignition lead directs the electrical energy from the magneto to the spark plug. The ignition harness contains an insulated wire for each cylinder that the magneto serves in the engine. *[Figure 4-11]* One end of each wire is connected to the magneto distributor block and the other end is connected to the proper spark plug. The ignition harness leads serve a

Figure 4-11. *A high-tension ignition harness.*

dual purpose. It provides the conductor path for the high-tension voltage to the spark plug. It also serves as a shield for stray magnetic fields that surround the wires as they momentarily carry high-voltage current. By conducting these magnetic lines of force to the ground, the ignition harness cuts down electrical interference with the aircraft radio and other electrically sensitive equipment.

A magneto is a high frequency radiation emanating (radio wave) device during its operation. The wave oscillations produced in the magneto are uncontrolled and cover a wide range of frequencies and must be shielded. If the magneto and ignition leads were not shielded, they would form antennas and pick up the random frequencies from the ignition system. The lead shielding is a medal mesh braid that surrounds the entire length of the lead. The lead shielding prevents the radiation of the energy into the surrounding area.

Capacitance is the ability to store an electrostatic charge between two conducting plates separated by a dielectric. Lead insulation is called a dielectric, meaning it can store electrical energy as an electrostatic charge. An example of electrostatic energy storage in a dielectric is the static electricity stored in a plastic hair comb. When shielding is placed around the ignition lead, capacitance increases by bringing the two plates closer together. Electrically, the ignition lead acts as a capacitor and has the ability to absorb and store electrical energy. The magneto must produce enough energy to charge the capacitance caused by the ignition lead and have enough energy left over to fire the plug.

Ignition lead capacitance increases the electrical energy required to provide a spark across the plug gap. More magneto primary current is needed to fire the plug with the shielded lead. This capacitance energy is discharged as fire across the plug gap after each firing of the plug. By reversing the polarity during servicing by rotating the plugs to new locations, the plug wear is equalized across the electrodes. The very center of the ignition lead is the high-voltage carrier surrounded by a silicone insulator material that is surrounded by a metal mesh, or shielding, covered with a thin silicone rubber coating that prevents damage by engine heat, vibration, or weather.

A sectional view of the typical ignition lead is shown in *Figure 4-12*. Ignition leads must be routed and clamped correctly to avoid hot spots on the exhaust and vibration points as the leads are routed from the magneto to the individual cylinders. Ignition leads are normally of the all-weather type and are hard connected at the magneto distributor and affixed to the spark plug by threads. The shielded ignition lead spark plug terminal is available in all-weather ¾ inch diameter and ⅝ inch diameter barrel ignition lead nut. *[Figure 4-13]* The ⅝ – 24 plug takes a ¾ wrench on the lead nut and the ¾ – 20 plug takes a ⅞ wrench on the lead nut. The ¾ inch all-weather design utilizes a terminal seal that results in greater terminal well insulation. This is recommended because the lead end of the spark plug is completely sealed from moisture.

Figure 4-13. *Ignition lead spark plug end.*

An older radial engine type of ignition harness is a manifold formed to fit around the crankcase of the engine with flexible extensions terminating at each spark plug. A typical high-tension ignition harness is shown in *Figure 4-14*. Many older single-row radial engine aircraft ignition systems employ a dual-magneto system, in which the right magneto supplies the electric spark for the front plugs in each cylinder, and the left magneto fires the rear plugs.

Ignition Switches

All units in an aircraft ignition system are controlled by an ignition switch. The type of switch used varies with the number of engines on the aircraft and the type of magnetos used. All switches, however, turn the system off and on in much the same manner. The ignition switch is different in at least one respect from all other types of switches: when the ignition switch is in the off position, a circuit is completed through the switch to ground. In other electrical switches, the off position normally breaks or opens the circuit.

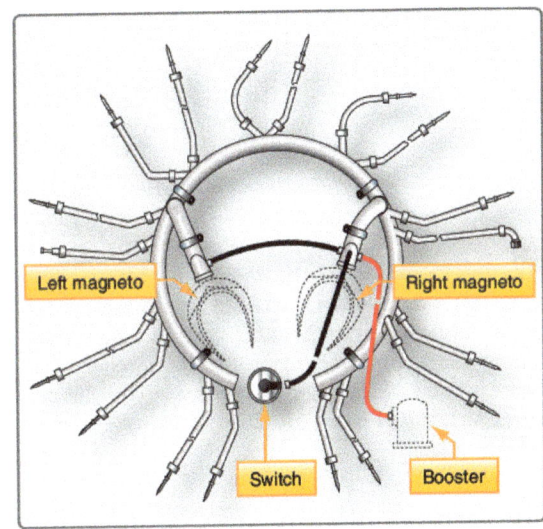

Figure 4-14. *Accessory-mounted nine cylinder engine ignition harness.*

Figure 4-12. *Ignition lead.*

The ignition switch has one terminal connected to the primary electrical circuit between the coil and the breaker contact points. The other terminal of the switch is connected to the aircraft ground structure. As shown in *Figure 4-15*, two ways to complete the primary circuit are:

1. Through the closed breaker points to ground and
2. Through the closed ignition switch to ground.

Figure 4-15. *Typical ignition switch in off position.*

Figure 4-15 shows that the primary current is not interrupted when the breaker contacts open since there is still a path to ground through the closed, or off, ignition switch. Since primary current is not stopped when the contact points open, there can be no sudden collapse of the primary coil flux field and no high-voltage induced in the secondary coil to fire the spark plug.

As the magnet rotates past the electrical gap (E-gap) position, a gradual breakdown of the primary flux field occurs. But that breakdown occurs so slowly that the induced voltage is too low to fire the spark plug. Thus, when the ignition switch is in the off position with the switch closed, the contact points are as completely short-circuited as if they were removed from the circuit, and the magneto is inoperative.

When the ignition switch is placed in the on position switch open, the interruption of primary current and the rapid collapse of the primary coil flux field is once again controlled or triggered by the opening of the breaker contact points. *[Figure 4-16]* When the ignition switch is in the on position, the switch has absolutely no effect on the primary circuit.

Figure 4-16. *Typical ignition switch in on position.*

The ignition/starter switch, or magneto switch, controls the magnetos on or off and can also connect the starter solenoid for turning the starter. When a starting vibrator, a box that emits pulsating direct current (DC), is used on the engine, the ignition/starter switch is used to control the vibrator and retard points. This system is explained in detail later in this chapter. Some ignition starter switches have a push to prime feature during the starting cycle. This system allows additional fuel to spray into the intake port of the cylinder during the starting cycle.

Single and Dual High-Tension System Magnetos
High-tension system magnetos used on aircraft engines are either single or dual type magnetos. The single magneto design incorporates the distributor in the housing with the magneto breaker assembly, rotating magnet, and coil. *[Figure 4-17]* The dual magneto incorporates two magnetos contained in a single housing. One rotating magnet and a cam are common to two sets of breaker points and coils. Two separate distributor units are mounted in the magneto. *[Figure 4-18]*

Magneto Mounting Systems
Flange-mounted magnetos are attached to the engine by a flange around the driven end of the rotating shaft of the magneto. *[Figure 4-19]* Elongated slots in the mounting flange permit adjustment through a limited range to aid in timing the magneto to the engine. Some magnetos mount by the flange and use clamps on each side to secure the magneto to the engine. This design also allows for timing adjustments. Base mounted magnetos are only used on very old or antique aircraft engines.

Figure 4-17. *Magneto cutaway.*

Figure 4-18. *A dual magneto with two distributors.*

Figure 4-19. *Magneto mounting flange.*

Low-Tension Magneto System

High-tension ignition systems have undergone many refinements and improvements in design. This includes new electronic systems that control more than just providing ignition to the cylinders. High-tension voltage presents certain problems with carrying the high-voltage from the magneto internally and externally to the spark plugs. In early years, it was difficult to provide insulators that could contain the high-voltage, especially at high altitudes when the air pressures were reduced. Another requirement of high-tension systems was that all weather and radio-equipped aircraft have ignition wires enclosed in shielding to prevent radio noise due to high-voltages. Many aircraft were turbosupercharged and operated at increased high altitudes. The low pressure at these altitudes would allow the high-voltage to leak out even more. To meet these problems, low-tension ignition systems were developed.

Electronically, the low-tension system is different from the high-tension system. In the low-tension system, low-voltage is generated in the magneto and flows to the primary winding of a transformer coil located near the spark plug. There, the voltage is increased to high by transformer action and conducted to the spark plug by very short high-tension leads. [Figure 4-20]

The low-tension system virtually eliminates flashover in both the distributor and the harness because the air gaps within the distributor have been eliminated by the use of a brush-type distributor, and high-voltage is present only in short leads between the transformer and spark plug.

Although a certain amount of electrical leakage is characteristic of all ignition systems, it is more pronounced on radio-shielded installations because the metal conduit is at ground potential and close to the ignition wires throughout their entire length. In low-tension systems, however, this leakage is reduced considerably because the current throughout most of the system is transmitted at a low-voltage potential. Although the leads between the transformer coils and the spark plugs of a low-tension ignition system are short, they are high-tension high-voltage conductor, and are subject to the same failures that occur in high-tension systems. Low-tension ignition systems have limited use in modern aircraft because of the excellent materials and shielding available to construct high-tension ignition leads and the added cost of a coil for each spark plug with the low-tension system.

FADEC System Description

A FADEC is a solid-state digital electronic ignition and electronic sequential port fuel injection system with only one moving part that consists of the opening and closing of the fuel injector. FADEC continuously monitors and controls ignition, timing, and fuel mixture/delivery/injection, and spark ignition as an integrated control system. FADEC monitors engine operating conditions (crankshaft speed, top

Figure 4-20. *Simplified low-tension ignition system schematic.*

dead center position, the induction manifold pressure, and the induction air temperature) and then automatically adjusts the fuel-to-air ratio mixture and ignition timing accordingly for any given power setting to attain optimum engine performance. As a result, engines equipped with FADEC require neither magnetos nor manual mixture control.

This microprocessor-based system controls ignition timing for engine starting and varies timing with respect to engine speed and manifold pressure. *[Figure 4-21]*

PowerLink provides control in both specified operating conditions and fault conditions. The system is designed to prevent adverse changes in power or thrust. In the event of loss of primary aircraft-supplied power, the engine controls continue to operate using a secondary power source (SPS). As a control device, the system performs self-diagnostics to determine overall system status and conveys this information to the pilot by various indicators on the health status annunciator (HSA) panel. PowerLink is able to withstand storage temperature extremes and operate at the same capacity as a non-FADEC-equipped engine in extreme heat, cold, and high humidity environments.

Low-Voltage Harness
The low-voltage harness connects all essential components of the FADEC System. *[Figure 4-22]* This harness acts as a signal transfer bus interconnecting the electronic control units (ECUs) with aircraft power sources, the ignition switch, speed sensor assembly (SSA), temperature and pressure sensors. The fuel injector coils and all sensors, except the SSA and fuel pressure and manifold pressure sensors, are hardwired to the low-voltage harness. This harness transmits sensor inputs to the ECUs through a 50-pin connector. The harness connects to the engine-mounted pressure sensors via cannon plug connectors. The 25-jpin connectors connect

Figure 4-22. *Typical six-cylinder engine electronic control and low-voltage harness.*

Figure 4-21. *PowerLink system components.*

the harness to the speed sensor signal conditioning unit. The low-voltage harness attaches to the cabin harness by a firewall-mounted data port through the same cabin harness/bulkhead connector assembly. The bulkhead connectors also supply the aircraft electrical power required to run the system.

The ECU is at the heart of the system, providing both ignition and fuel injection control to operate the engine with the maximum efficiency realizable. Each ECU contains two microprocessors, referred to as a computer, that control two cylinders. Each computer controls its own assigned cylinder and is capable of providing redundant control for the other computer's cylinder.

The computer constantly monitors the engine speed and timing pulses developed from the camshaft gear as they are detected by the SSA. Knowing the exact engine speed and the timing sequence of the engine, the computers monitor the manifold air pressure and manifold air temperature to calculate air density and determine the mass air flow into the cylinder during the intake stroke. The computers calculate the percentage of engine power based on engine revolutions per minute (rpm) and manifold air pressure.

From this information, the computer can then determine the fuel required for the combustion cycle for either best power or best economy mode of operation. The computer precisely times the injection event, and the duration of the injector should be on time for the correct fuel-to-air ratio. Then, the computer sets the spark ignition event and ignition timing, again based on percentage of power calculation. Exhaust gas temperature is measured after the burn to verify that the fuel-to-air ratio calculations were correct for that combustion event. This process is repeated by each computer for its own assigned cylinder on every combustion/power cycle.

The computers can also vary the amount of fuel to control the fuel-to-air ratio for each individual cylinder to control both cylinder head temperature (CHT) and exhaust gas temperature (EGT).

Electronic Control Unit (ECU)

An ECU is assigned to a pair of engine cylinders. *[Figure 4-23]* The ECUs control the fuel mixture and spark timing for their respective engine cylinders; ECU 1 controls opposing cylinders 1 and 2, ECU 2 controls cylinders 3 and 4, and ECU 3 controls cylinders 5 and 6. Each ECU is divided into upper and lower portions. The lower portion contains an electronic circuit board, while the upper portion houses the ignition coils. Each electronic control board contains two independent microprocessor controllers that serve as control channels. During engine operation, one control channel is assigned to operate a single engine cylinder. Therefore, one ECU can

Figure 4-23. *Electronic control unit.*

control two engine cylinders, one control channel per cylinder. The control channels are independent, and there are no shared electronic components within one ECU. They also operate on independent and separate power supplies. However, if one control channel fails, the other control channel in the pair within the same ECU is capable of operating both its assigned cylinder and the other opposing engine cylinder as backup control for fuel injection and ignition timing. Each control channel on the ECU monitors the current operating conditions and operates its cylinder to attain engine operation within specified parameters. The following transmit inputs to the control channels across the low-voltage harness:

1. Speed sensor that monitors engine speed and crank position
2. Fuel pressure sensors
3. Manifold pressure sensors
4. Manifold air temperature (MAT) sensors
5. CHT sensors
6. EGT sensors

All critical sensors are dually redundant with one sensor from each type of pair connected to control channels in different ECUs. Synthetic software default values are also used in the unlikely event that both sensors of a redundant pair fail. The control channel continuously monitors changes in engine speed, manifold pressure, manifold temperature, and fuel pressure based on sensor input relative to operating conditions to determine how much fuel to inject into the intake port of the cylinder.

PowerLink Ignition System

The ignition system consists of the high-voltage coils atop the ECU, the high-voltage harness, and spark plugs. Since there are two spark plugs per cylinder on all engines, a six-cylinder engine has 12 leads and 12 spark plugs. One end of each lead on the high-voltage harness attaches to a spark plug, and the other end of the lead wire attaches to the spark plug towers on each ECU. The spark tower pair is connected to opposite ends of one of the ECU's coil packs. Two coil packs are located in the upper portion of the ECU. Each coil pack generates a high-voltage pulse for two spark plug towers. One tower fires a positive polarity pulse and the other of the same coil fires a negative polarity pulse. Each ECU controls the ignition spark for two engine cylinders. The control channel within each ECU commands one of the two coil packs to control the ignition spark for the engine cylinders. *[Figure 4-24]* The high-voltage harness carries energy from the ECU spark towers to the spark plugs on the engine.

For both spark plugs in a given cylinder to fire on the compression stroke, both control channels must fire their coil packs. Each coil pack has a spark plug from each of the two cylinders controlled by that ECU unit.

The ignition spark is timed to the engine's crankshaft position. The timing is variable throughout the engine's operating range and is dependent upon the engine load conditions. The spark energy is also varied with respect to the engine load.

NOTE: Engine ignition timing is established by the ECUs and cannot be manually adjusted.

During engine starting, the output of a magneto is low because the cranking speed of the engine is low. This is understandable when the factors that determine the amount of voltage induced in a circuit are considered.

To increase the value of an induced voltage, the strength of the magnetic field must be increased by using a stronger magnet, by increasing the number of turns in the coil, or by increasing the rate of relative motion between the magnet and the conductor.

Since the strength of the rotating magnet and the number of turns in the coil are constant factors in magneto ignition systems, the voltage produced depends upon the speed at which the rotating magnet is turned. When the engine is being cranked for starting, the magnet is rotated at about 80 rpm. Since the value of the induced voltage is so low, a spark may not jump the spark plug gap. To facilitate engine starting, an auxiliary device is connected to the magneto to provide a high ignition voltage.

Ordinarily, such auxiliary ignition units are energized by the battery and connected to the left magneto. Reciprocating engine starting systems normally include one of the following types of auxiliary starting systems: booster coil (older style),

Figure 4-24. *Ignition control.*

starting vibrator (sometimes called shower of sparks), impulse coupling, or electronic ignition systems.

During the starting cycle, the engine is turning very slowly compared to normal speed. The ignition must be retarded or moved back to prevent kickback of the piston trying to rotate opposite normal rotation. Each starting system has a method of retarding the spark during starting of the engine.

Booster Coil

The booster coil assembly, used mainly with older radial engine ignition systems, consists of two coils wound on a soft iron core, a set of contact points, and a condenser. *[Figure 4-25]* The booster coil is separate from the magneto and can generate a series of sparks on its own. During the start cycle, these sparks are routed to the trailing finger on the distributor rotor and then to the appropriate cylinder ignition lead. The primary winding has one end grounded at the internal grounding strip and its other end connected to the moving contact point. The stationary contact is fitted with a terminal to which battery voltage is applied when the magneto switch is placed in the start position, or automatically applied when the starter is engaged. The secondary winding, which contains several times as many turns as the primary coil, has one end grounded at the internal grounding strip and the other terminated at a high-tension terminal. The high-tension terminal is connected to an electrode in the distributor by an ignition cable.

Since the regular distributor terminal is grounded through the primary or secondary coil of a high-tension magneto, the high-voltage furnished by the booster coil must be distributed by a separate circuit in the distributor rotor. This is accomplished by using two electrodes in one distributor rotor. The main electrode, or finger, carries the magneto output voltage; the auxiliary electrode or trailing finger, distributes only the output of the booster coil. The auxiliary electrode is always located so that it trails the main electrode, thus retarding the spark during the starting period.

Figure 4-26 illustrates, in schematic form, the booster coil components shown in *Figure 4-25*. In operation, battery voltage is applied to the positive (+) terminal of the booster coil through the start switch. This causes current to flow through the closed contact points to the primary coil and ground. *[Figure 4-26]* Current flow through the primary coil sets up a magnetic field about the coil that magnetizes the coil core. As the core is magnetized, it attracts the movable contact point, which is normally held against the stationary contact point by a spring.

As the movable contact point is pulled toward the iron core, the primary circuit is broken, collapsing the magnetic field that extended about the coil core. Since the coil core acts as an electromagnet only when current flows in the primary coil, it loses its magnetism as soon as the primary coil circuit is broken. This permits the action of the spring to close the contact points and again complete the primary

Figure 4-25. *Booster coil.*

Figure 4-26. *Booster coil schematic.*

coil circuit. This remagnetizes the coil core, and again attracts the movable contact point, which again opens the primary coil circuit. This action causes the movable contact point to vibrate rapidly, as long as the start switch is held in the closed, or on, position. The result of this action is a continuously expanding and collapsing magnetic field that links the secondary coil of the booster coil. With several times as many turns in the secondary as in the primary, the induced voltage that results from lines of force linking the secondary is high enough to furnish ignition for the engine.

The condenser, which is connected across the contact points, has an important function in this circuit. *[Figure 4-26]* As current flow in the primary coil is interrupted by the opening of the contact points, the high self-induced voltage that accompanies each collapse of the primary magnetic field surges into the condenser. Without a condenser, an arc would jump across the points with each collapse of the magnetic field. This would burn and pit the contact points and greatly reduce the voltage output of the booster coil. The booster coil generates a pulsating DC in the primary winding that induces a high-voltage spark in the secondary windings of the booster coil.

Impulse Coupling

Many opposed reciprocating engines are equipped with an impulse coupling as the auxiliary starting system. An impulse coupling gives one of the magnetos attached to the engine, generally the left, a brief acceleration, that produces an intense spark for starting. This device consists of a cam and flyweight assembly, spring, and a body assembly. *[Figure 4-27]* The assembled impulse coupling is shown installed on a typical magneto in *Figure 4-28*.

The magneto is flexibly connected through the impulse coupling by means of the spring so that at low speed the

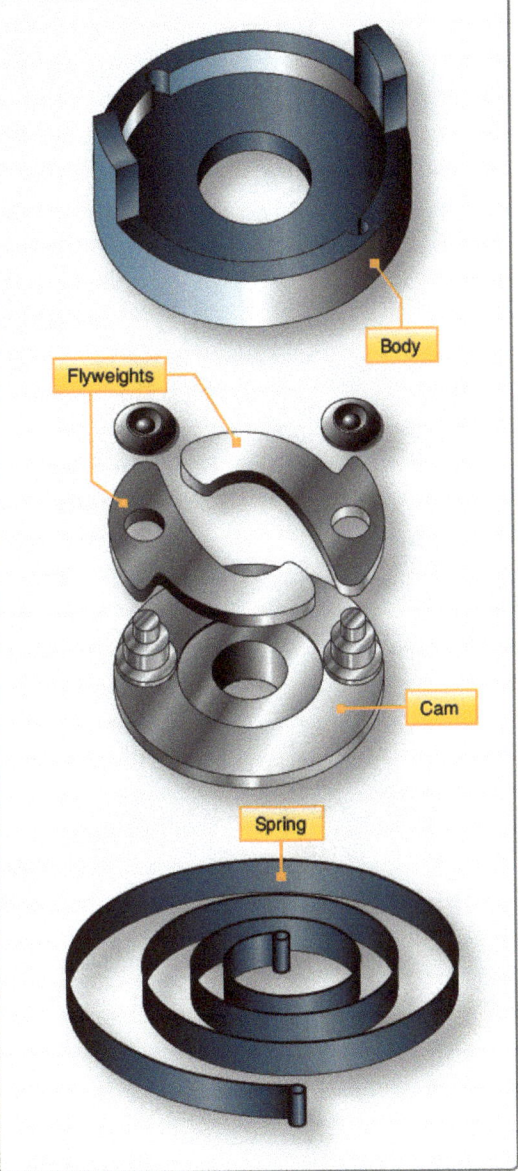

Figure 4-27. *Parts of an impulse coupling.*

magneto is temporarily held. *[Figure 4-29]* The flyweight, because of slow rotation, catches on a stud or stop pins, and the magneto spring is wound as the engine continues to turn. The engine continues to rotate until the piston of the cylinder to be fired reaches approximately a top dead center position. At this point, the magneto flyweight contacts the body of the impulse coupling and is released. The spring kicks back to its original position, resulting in a quick twist of the rotating magnet of the magneto. *[Figure 4-30]* This, being equivalent to high-speed magneto rotation, produces a spark that jumps

4-17

Figure 4-28. *Impulse coupling on a magneto.*

Figure 4-29. *Flyweights engage stop pins.*

the gap at the spark plug electrodes. The impulse coupling has performed two functions: rotating the magneto fast enough to produce a good spark and retarding the timing of the spark during the start cycle. After the engine is started and the magneto reaches a speed at which it furnishes sufficient current, the flyweights in the impulse coupling fly outward due to centrifugal force or rapid rotation. This action prevents the two flyweight coupling members from contact with the stop pin. That makes it a solid unit, returning the magneto to a normal timing position relative to the engine. The presence of an impulse coupling is identified by a sharp clicking noise as the crankshaft is turned at starter cranking speed past top center on each cylinder.

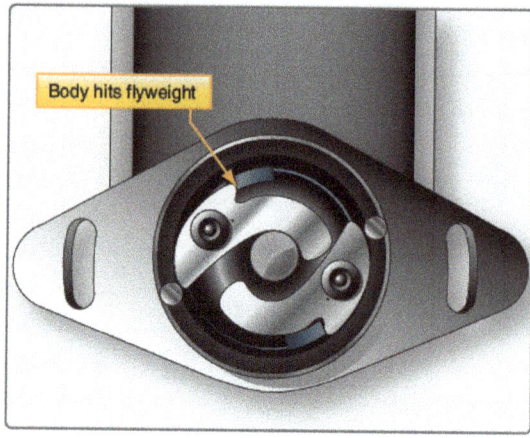

Figure 4-30. *Flyweight contacts body, releasing impulse coupling to spin.*

A problem that can arise from impulse couplings is that the flyweights can become magnetized and not engage the stop pins. Congealed oil or sludge on the flyweights during cold weather may produce the same results. This prevents the flyweight weights from engaging the stop pins, which results in no starting spark being produced. Wear can cause problems with impulse couplings. They should be inspected and any maintenance should be performed as set forth by the manufacturer. Another disadvantage of the impulse coupling is that it can produce only one spark for each firing cycle of the cylinder. This is a disadvantage, especially during adverse starting conditions. Even with these disadvantages, the impulse coupling is still in wide use.

High-Tension Retard Breaker Vibrator

To provide for more spark power during the starting cycle, the shower of sparks system was developed, which provides several sparks at the spark plug electrodes during starting. The starting vibrator, or shower of sparks, consists essentially of an electrically operated vibrator, a condenser, and a relay. *[Figure 4-31]* These units are mounted on a base plate and enclosed in a metal case.

The starting vibrator, unlike the booster coil, does not produce the high ignition voltage within itself. The function of this starting vibrator is to change the DC of the battery into a pulsating DC and deliver it to the primary coil of the magneto. Closing the ignition switch energizes the starter solenoid and causes the engine to rotate. At the same time, current also flows through the vibrator coil and its contact points. Current flow in the vibrator coil sets up a magnetic field that attracts and opens the vibrator points. When the vibrator points open, current flow in the coil stops, and the magnetic field that attracted the movable vibrator contact point disappears. This allows the vibrator points to close and

Figure 4-31. *High-tension retard breaker magneto and starting vibrator circuit.*

again permits battery current to flow in the vibrator coil. This completes a cycle of operation. The cycle, however, occurs many times per second, so rapidly that the vibrator points produce an audible buzz.

Each time the vibrator points close, current flows to the magneto as a pulsating DC. Since this current is being interrupted many times per second, the resulting magnetic field is building and collapsing across the primary and secondary coils of the magneto many times per second. The rapid successions of separate voltages induced in the secondary coil produces a shower of sparks across the selected spark plug air gap.

The retard breaker magneto and starting vibrator system is used as part of the high-tension starting system on many types of aircraft. Designed for four- and six-cylinder ignition systems, the retard breaker magneto eliminates the need for the impulse coupling in light aircraft. This system uses an additional breaker to obtain retarded sparks for starting. The starting vibrator is also adaptable to many helicopter ignition systems. A schematic diagram of an ignition system using the retard breaker magneto and starting vibrator concept is shown in *Figure 4-31*.

With the magneto switch in the both position and the starter switch S1 in the on position, starter solenoid L3 and coil L1 are energized, closing relay contacts R4, R1, R2, and R3. R3 connects the right magneto to ground, keeping it inoperative during starting operation. Electrical current flows from the battery through R1, vibrator points V1, coil L2, through both the retard breaker points, through R2, and the main breaker points of the left magneto to ground.

The energized coil L2 opens vibrator points V1, interrupting the current flow through L2. The magnetic field about L2 collapses, and vibrator points V1 close again. Once more, current flows through L2, and again V1 vibrator points open. This process is repeated continuously, and the interrupted battery current flows to ground through the main and retard breaker points of the left magneto.

Since relay R4 is closed, the starter is energized and the engine crankshaft is rotated. When the engine reaches its normal advance firing position, the main breaker points of the left magneto begin to open. The interrupted surges of current from the vibrator can still find a path to ground through the retard breaker points, which do not open until the retarded firing position of the engine is reached. At this point in crankshaft travel, the retard points open. Since the main breaker points are still open, the magneto primary coil is no longer shorted, and current produces a magnetic field around T1.

Each time the vibrator points V1 open, current flow through V1 is interrupted. The collapsing field about T1 cuts through the magneto coil secondary and induces a high-voltage surge of energy used to fire the spark plug. Since the V1 points are opening and closing rapidly and continuously, a shower of sparks is furnished to the cylinders when both the main and retard breaker points are open.

After the engine begins to accelerate, the manual starter switch is released, causing L1 and L3 to become deenergized. This action causes both the vibrator and retard breaker circuits to become inoperative. It also opens relay contact R3, which removes the ground from the right magneto. Both magnetos now fire at the normal advanced running degrees of crankshaft rotation before top dead center piston position.

Low-Tension Retard Breaker Vibrator

This system, which is in limited use, is designed for light aircraft reciprocating engines. A typical system consists of a retard breaker magneto, a single breaker magneto, a starting vibrator, transformer coils, and a starter and ignition switch. [Figure 4-32]

To operate the system, place the starter switch S3 in the on position. This energizes starter solenoid L3 and coil L1, closing relay contacts R1, R2, R3, and R4. With the magneto switch in the L position, current flows through R1, the vibrator points, L2, R2, and through the main breaker points to ground. Current also flows through R3 and the retard breaker points to ground. Current through L2 builds up a magnetic field that opens the vibrator points. Then, the current stops flowing through L2, reclosing the points. These surges of current flow through both the retard and main breaker points to ground.

Since the starter switch is closed, the engine crankshaft is turning. When it has turned to the normal advance or running ignition position, the main breaker points of the magneto open. However, current still flows to ground through the closed retard breaker points. As the engine continues to turn, the retard ignition position is reached, and the retard breaker points open. Since the main breaker points are still open, current must flow to ground through coil L4, producing a magnetic field around the coil L4.

As the engine continues to turn, the vibrator breaker points open, collapsing the L4 magnetic field through T1 primary, inducing a high-voltage in the secondary of T1 to fire the spark plug.

When the engine fires, the starter switch is released, de-energizing L1 and L3. This opens the vibrator circuit and retard breaker points circuit. The ignition switch is then turned to the both position, permitting the right magneto to operate in time with the left magneto.

Figure 4-32. *Low-tension retard breaker magneto and starting vibrator circuit.*

Spark Plugs

The function of the spark plug in an ignition system is to conduct a short impulse of high-voltage current through the wall of the combustion chamber. Inside the combustion chamber, it provides an air gap across which the impulse can produce an electric spark to ignite the fuel/air charge. While the aircraft spark plug is simple in construction and operation, it can be the cause of malfunctions in aircraft engines. Despite this fact, spark plugs provide a great deal of trouble-free operation when properly maintained and when correct engine operating procedures are practiced.

Spark plugs operate at extreme temperatures, electrical pressures, and very high cylinder pressures. A cylinder of an engine operating at 2,100 rpm must produce approximately 17 separate and distinct high-voltage sparks that bridge the air gap of a single spark plug each second. This would appear as a continuous spark across the spark plug electrodes at temperatures of over 3,000 °F. At the same time, the spark plug is subjected to gas pressures as high as 2,000 pounds per square inch (psi) and electrical pressure as high as 20,000 volts. Given the extremes that spark plugs must operate under, and the fact that the engine loses power if one spark does not occur correctly, proper function of a spark plug in the operation of the engine is imperative.

The three main components of a spark plug are the electrode, insulator, and outer shell. *[Figure 4-33]* The outer shell, threaded to fit into the cylinder, is usually made of finely machined steel and is often plated to prevent corrosion from engine gases and possible thread seizure. Close-tolerance screw threads and a copper gasket prevent cylinder gas pressure from escaping around the plug. Pressure that might escape through the plug is retained by inner seals between the outer metal shell and the insulator, and between the insulator and the center electrode assembly. The other end is threaded to receive the ignition lead from the magneto. All-weather plugs form a seal between the lead and the plug that is water proof to prevent moisture from entering this connection.

The insulator provides a protective core around the electrode. In addition to affording electrical insulation, the ceramic insulator core also transfers heat from the ceramic tip, or nose, to the cylinder. The insulator is made from aluminum oxide ceramic having excellent dielectric strength, high mechanical strength, and thermal conductivity. The types of spark plugs used in different engines vary in respect to heat range, reach, massive electrode, fine wire electrode (Iridium/platinum), or other characteristics of the installation requirements for different engines.

The electrodes can be of several designs from massive electrodes or Nickel-base alloy to fine wire electrodes.

Figure 4-33. *Spark plug cutaway.*

[Figure 4-33 and *4-34]* The massive electrode material has a lower melting point and is more susceptible to corrosion. The main differences include cost and length of service. Fine wire iridium and platinum electrodes have a very high

Figure 4-34. *Fine wire electrodes.*

4-21

melting point and are considered precious metals. Therefore, the cost of this type of spark plug is higher, but they have a longer service life with increased performance. Fine wire spark plugs are more effective than massive electrode plugs because the size shields its own spark from some of the fuel air mixture. Less than efficient combustion occurs due to uneven ignition. The iridium electrode allows for a larger spark gap, which creates a more intense spark that increases performance. The spark gap of any electrode is vulnerable to erosion and the melting point of the electrode material.

The heat range of a spark plug is a measure of its ability to transfer the heat of combustion to the cylinder head. The plug must operate hot enough to burn off carbon deposits, which can cause fouling, a condition where the plug no longer produces a spark across the electrodes, yet remain cool enough to prevent a preignition condition. Spark plug preignition is caused by plug electrodes glowing red hot as a glow plug, setting off the fuel-air mixture before the normal firing position. The length of the nose core is the principal factor in establishing the plug's heat range. *[Figure 4-35]* Hot plugs have a long insulator nose that creates a long heat transfer path; cold plugs have a relatively short insulator to provide a rapid transfer of heat to the cylinder head. *[Figure 4-35]*

Figure 4-35. *Hot and cold spark plugs.*

If an engine were operated at only one speed, spark plug design would be greatly simplified. Because flight demands impose different loads on the engine, spark plugs must be designed to operate as hot as possible at slow speeds and light loads, and as cool as possible at cruise and takeoff power.

The choice of spark plugs to be used in a specific aircraft engine is determined by the engine manufacturer after extensive tests. When an engine is certificated to use hot or cold spark plugs, the plug used is determined by the compression ratio, the degree of supercharging, and how the engine is to be operated. High-compression engines tend to use colder range plugs while low-compression engines tend to use hot range plugs.

A spark plug with the proper reach ensures that the electrode end inside the cylinder is in the best position to achieve ignition. The spark plug reach is the length of the threaded portion that is inserted in the spark plug bushing of the cylinder. *[Figure 4-36]* Spark plug seizure and/or improper combustion within the cylinder can occur if a plug with the wrong reach is used. In extreme cases, if the reach is too long, the plug may contact a piston or valve and damage the engine. If the plug threads are too long, they extend into the combustion chamber and carbon adheres to the threads making it almost impossible to remove the plug. This can also be a source of preignition. Heat of combustion can make some of the carbon a source for ignition, which can ignite the fuel-air mixture prematurely. It is very important to select the approved spark plugs for the engine.

Figure 4-36. *Spark plug reach.*

Reciprocating Engine Ignition System Maintenance and Inspection

An aircraft's ignition system is the result of careful design and thorough testing. The ignition system usually provides good, dependable service, provided it is maintained and inspected properly. However, difficulties can occur with normal wear, which affects ignition system performance, especially with magneto systems. Breakdown and deterioration of insulating materials, breaker point wear, corrosion, bearing and oil seal wear, and electrical connection problems are all possible defects that can be associated with magneto-ignition systems. The ignition timing requires precise adjustment and painstaking care so that the following four conditions occur at the same instant:

1. The piston in the No. 1 cylinder must be in a position a prescribed number of degrees before top dead center on the compression stroke.

2. The rotating magnet of the magneto must be in the E-gap position.

3. The breaker points must be just opening on the No. 1 cam lobe.
4. The distributor finger must be aligned with the electrode serving the No. 1 cylinder.

If one of these conditions is out of synchronization with any of the others, the ignition system is out of time. If the spark is out of time, it is not delivered to the cylinder at the correct time and engine performance decreases.

When ignition in the cylinder occurs before the optimum crankshaft position is reached, the timing is said to be early. If ignition occurs too early, the piston rising in the cylinder is opposed by the full force of combustion. This condition results in a loss of engine power, overheating, and possible detonation and preignition.

If ignition occurs at a time after the optimum crankshaft position is reached, the ignition timing is said to be late. If it occurs too late, not enough time is allowed to consume the fuel-air charge, and combustion is incomplete. As a result, the engine loses power and requires a greater throttle opening to carry a given propeller load.

Moisture forming on different parts of the ignition system causes more common irregularities. Moisture can enter ignition system units through cracks or loose covers, or it can result from condensation. Breathing, a situation that occurs during the readjustment of the system from low to high atmospheric pressure, can result in drawing in moisture-laden air. Ordinarily, the heat of the engine is sufficient to evaporate this moisture, but occasionally the moist air condenses as the engine cools. The result is an appreciable moisture accumulation which causes the insulation materials to lose electrical resistance. A slight amount of moisture contamination may cause reduction in magneto output by short-circuiting to ground a part of the high-voltage current intended for the spark plug. If the moisture accumulation is appreciable, the entire magneto output may be dissipated to ground by way of flashover and carbon tracking. Moisture accumulation during flight is extremely rare because the high operating temperature of the system is effective in preventing condensation. Difficulties from moisture accumulation are probably more evident during starting and ground operation.

Spark plugs are often diagnosed as being faulty when the real malfunction exists in a different system. Malfunctioning of the carburetor, poor fuel distribution, too much valve overlap, leaking primer system, or poor idle speed and mixture settings show symptoms that are the same as those for faulty ignition. Unfortunately, many of these conditions can be temporarily improved by a spark plug change, but the trouble recurs in a short time because the real cause of the malfunction has not been eliminated. A thorough understanding of the various engine systems, along with meticulous inspection and good maintenance methods, can substantially reduce such errors.

Magneto-Ignition Timing Devices

Built-In Engine Timing Reference Marks

Most reciprocating engines have timing reference marks built into the engine. The timing reference marks vary by manufacturer. *[Figure 4-37]* When the starter gear hub is installed correctly, the timing marks are marked on it that line up with the mark on the starter. On an engine that has no starter gear hub, the timing mark is normally on the propeller flange edge. *[Figure 4-38]* The top center (TC) mark stamped on the edge aligns with the crankcase split line below the crankshaft when the No. 1 piston is at top dead center. Other flange marks indicate degrees before top center.

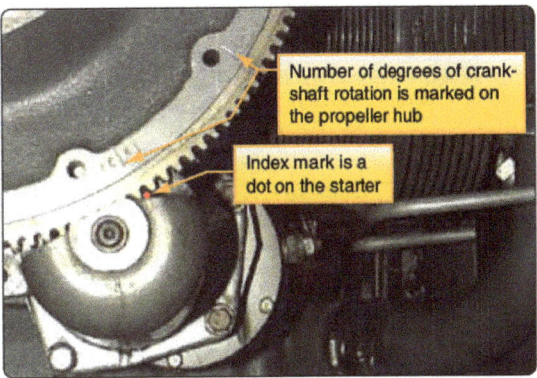

Figure 4-37. *Lycoming timing marks.*

Some engines have degree markings on the propeller reduction drive gear. To time these engines, the plug provided on the exterior of the reduction gear housing must be removed to view the timing marks. On other engines, the timing marks are on a crankshaft flange and can be viewed by removing a plug from the crankcase. In every case, the engine manufacturer's instructions give the location of built-in timing reference marks.

In using built-in timing marks to position the crankshaft, be sure to sight straight across the stationary pointer or mark on the nose section, the propeller shaft, crankshaft flange, or bell gear. *[Figure 4-39]* Sighting at an angle results in an error in positioning the crankshaft. Normally, the No. 1 cylinder is used to time or check the timing of the magnetos. When installing magnetos, the timing marks must be lined up and the No. 1 cylinder must be on the compression stroke.

The amount of gear backlash in any system of gears varies between installations because there is clearance between the gear teeth. Always take timing when reading, or stop

Figure 4-38. *Propeller flange timing marks.*

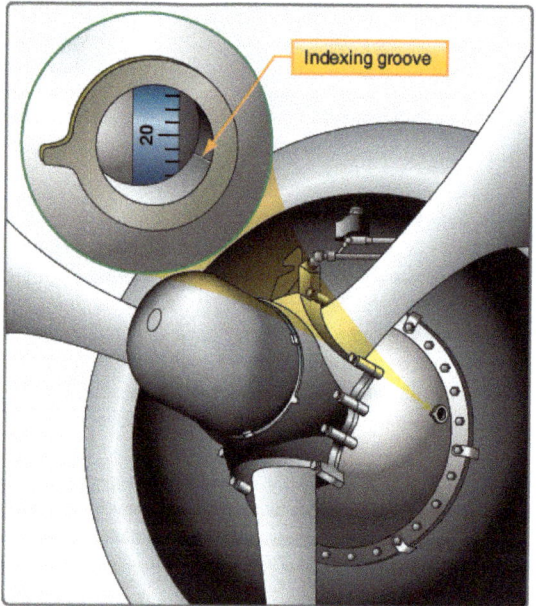

Figure 4-39. *Typical built-in timing mark on propeller reduction gear.*

movement of the engine for timing set up, in the direction of rotation. Another unfavorable aspect in the use of timing marks on the reduction gear is the small error that exists when sighting down the reference mark to the timing mark inside the housing on the reduction gear. This can occur because there is depth between the two reference marks.

Timing Disks

Most timing disk devices are mounted to the crankshaft flange and use a timing plate. *[Figure 4-40]* The markings vary according to the specifications of the engine. This plate is temporarily installed on the crankshaft flange with a scale numbered in crankshaft degrees and the pointer attached to the timing disk.

Figure 4-40. *A timing plate and pointer.*

Piston Position Indicators

Any given piston position, whether it is to be used for ignition, valve, or injection pump timing, is referenced to a piston position called top dead center. This piston position is not to be confused with a piston position called top center. A piston in top center has little value from a timing standpoint because the corresponding crankshaft position may vary from 1° to 5° for this piston position. This is illustrated in *Figure 4-41*, which is exaggerated to emphasize the no-travel zone of the piston. Notice that the piston does not move while the crankshaft describes the small arc from position A to position B. This no-travel zone occurs between the time the crankshaft and connecting rod stop pushing the piston upward, and continues until the crankshaft has swung the lower end of the connecting rod into a position where the crankshaft can start pulling the piston downward. Top dead center is a piston and crankshaft position from which all other piston and crankshaft locations are referenced. When a piston is in the top dead center position of the crankshaft, it is also in the center of the no-travel zone. The piston is in a position where a straight line can be drawn through the center of the crankshaft journal, the crankpin, and the piston pin. This is shown on the right of *Figure 4-41*.

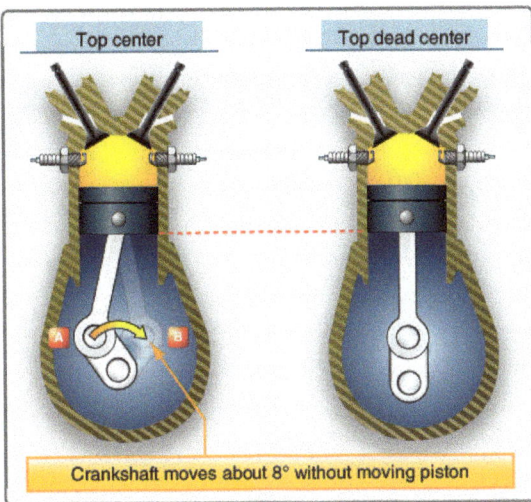

Figure 4-41. *Difference between top center and top dead center.*

With such an alignment, a force applied to the piston could not move the crankshaft.

Timing Lights

Timing lights are used to help determine the exact instant that the magneto points open. There are two general types of timing lights in common use. Both have two lights and three external wire connections. Although both have internal circuits that are somewhat different, their function is very much the same. *[Figure 4-42]*

Figure 4-42. *Timing light.*

Three wires plug into the light box. *[Figure 4-42]* There are two lights on the front face of the unit, one green and one red, and a switch to turn the unit on and off. To use the timing light, the center lead, which is black, marked "ground lead" is connected to the case of the magneto being tested. The other leads are connected to the primary leads of the breaker point assembly of the magnetos being timed. The color of the lead corresponds to the color of the light on the timing light.

With the leads connected in this manner, it can be easily determined whether the points are open or closed by turning on the switch and observing the two lights. If the points are closed, most of the current flows through the breaker points and not through the transformers, and the lights do not come on. If the points are open, the current flows through the transformer and the lights glow. Some models of timing lights operate in the reverse manner (i.e., the light goes out when the points open). Each of the two lights is operated separately by the set of breaker points to which it is connected. This makes it possible to observe the time, or point in reference to magneto rotor rotation, that each set of points opens.

Most timing lights use batteries that must be replaced after long use. Attempts to use a timing light with weak batteries may result in erroneous readings because of low current flow in the circuits.

Checking the Internal Timing of a Magneto

When replacing or preparing a magneto for installation, the first concern is with the internal timing of the magneto. For each magneto model, the manufacturer determines how many degrees beyond the neutral position a pole of the rotor magnet should be to obtain the strongest spark at the instant of breaker point separation. This angular displacement from the neutral position, known as the E-gap angle, varies with different magneto models. On one model, a step is cut on the end of the breaker cam to check internal timing of the magneto. When a straightedge is laid along this step and it coincides with the timing marks on the rim of the breaker housing, the magneto rotor is then in the E-gap position, and the breaker contact points should just begin to open.

Another method for checking E-gap is to align a timing mark with a pointed chamfered tooth. *[Figure 4-43]* The breaker points should be just starting to open when these marks line up.

In a third method, the E-gap is correct when a timing pin is in place and red marks visible through a vent hole in the side of the magneto case are aligned. *[Figure 4-44]* The contact points should be just opening when the rotor is in the position just described.

Bench timing the magneto, or setting the E-gap, involves positioning the magneto rotor at the E-gap position and setting the breaker points to open when the timing lines or marks provided for that purpose are perfectly aligned.

Figure 4-43. *Timing marks indicate the number one firing position of a magneto.*

Figure 4-44. *Checking magneto E-gap.*

High-Tension Magneto E-Gap Setting (Bench Timing)

The following steps are taken to check and adjust the timing of the breaker points for the S-200 magneto, which does not have timing marks in the breaker compartment:

1. Remove the timing inspection plug from the top of the magneto. Turn the rotating magnet in its normal direction of rotation until the painted, chamfered tooth on the distributor gear is approximately in the center of the inspection window. Then, turn the magnet back a few degrees until it is in its neutral position. Because of its magnetism, the rotating magnet holds itself in the neutral position.

2. Install the timing kit and place the pointer in the zero position. *[Figure 4-45]*

Figure 4-45. *Installing timing kit.*

3. Connect a suitable timing light across the main breaker points and turn the magnet in its normal direction of rotation 10° as indicated by the pointer. This is the E-gap position. The main breaker points should be adjusted to open at this point.

4. Turn the rotating magnet until the cam follower is at the highpoint on the cam lobe, and measure the clearance between the breaker points. This clearance must be 0.018 inch ± 0.006 inch [0.46 millimeter (mm) ± 0.15 mm]. If the breaker point clearance is not within these limits, the points must be adjusted for correct setting. It is then necessary to recheck and readjust the timing for breaker opening. If the breaker points cannot be adjusted to open at the correct time, they should be replaced.

Timing the High-tension Magneto to the Engine

When replacing magnetos on aircraft engines, two factors must be considered:

1. The internal timing of the magneto, including breaker point adjustment, which must be correct to obtain maximum potential voltage from the magneto.

2. The engine crankshaft position where the spark occurs. The engine is usually timed by using the No. 1 cylinder on the compression stroke.

The magneto must be timed by first adjusting or checking the internal timing with the magneto off the engine. This is done by checking and adjusting the ignition points to open at the E-gap position. The chamfered tooth should line up (reference timing mark for the magneto) in the middle of the timing window. The magneto is set to fire the No. 1 cylinder. Remove the most accessible spark plug from the No. 1 cylinder. Pull the propeller through in the direction of rotation until the No. 1 piston is coming up on the compression stroke. This can be determined by holding a thumb over the spark plug hole until the compression air is felt. Set the engine crankshaft at the prescribed number of degrees ahead of true top dead center as specified in the applicable manufacturer's instruction, usually using the timing marks on the engine. With the engine set at a prescribed number of degrees ahead of true top dead center on the compression stroke and with final movement of the engine stopped in the direction of normal rotation, the magneto can be installed on the engine. *[Figure 4-46]*

Figure 4-46. *Timing marks aligned.*

While holding the magneto drive in the firing position for the No. 1 cylinder as indicated by the alignment of the reference marks for the magneto, install the magneto drive into the engine drive. It should be installed in the middle of its slotted flange to allow for fine timing of the magneto to the engine. Attach a timing light to both magnetos. With the engine still in the firing position, the magnetos should be timed by moving them in the flange slots until the breaker points in the magneto just open. If the slots in the mounting flange of the magneto do not permit sufficient movement to effect breaker point opening for the No. 1 cylinder, move the magneto out of position far enough to permit turning the magneto drive shaft. Then, install the magneto in position again and repeat the previous check for point opening.

Install the magneto attaching nuts on the studs and tighten slightly. The nuts must not be tight enough to prevent the movement of the magneto assembly when the magneto mounting flange is tapped with a mallet. Reconnect the timing light to the magneto and breaker points. With the light and ignition switch turned on, rotate the magneto assembly first in the direction of rotation and then in the opposite direction. This is done to determine that the points just opened. After completing this adjustment, tighten the mounting nuts. Move the propeller one blade opposite the direction of rotation and then, while observing the timing light, move the propeller in the direction of rotation until the prescribed number of degrees ahead of top dead center is reached. Be sure that the lights for both sets of points come on points open, within the prescribed timing position.

Both right and left sets of breaker points should open at the same instant, proper magneto-to-engine timing exists, and all phases of magneto operation are synchronized. Some early engines had what was referred to as staggered timing where one magneto would fire at a different number of degrees before top dead center on the compression stroke. In this case, each magneto had to be timed separately.

In the following example, a timing light is used for timing the magneto to the engine. The timing light is designed in such a way that one of two lights come on when the points open. The timing light incorporates two lights. When connecting the timing light to the magneto, the leads should be connected so that the light on the right side of the box represents the breaker points on the right magneto, and the light on the left side represents the left magneto breaker points. The black lead or ground lead must be attached to the engine or an effective ground. When using the timing light to check a magneto in a complete ignition system installed on the aircraft, the ignition switch for the engine must be turned to both. Otherwise, the lights do not indicate breaker point opening.

Performing Ignition System Checks

The ignition system has checks performed on it during the aircraft engine run-up, which is the engine check before each flight. The magneto check, as it is usually referred to, is performed during the engine run-up check list.

One other check is accomplished prior to engine shutdown. The ignition system check is used to check the individual magnetos, harnesses, and spark plugs. After reaching the engine rpm specified for the ignition system check, allow the rpm to stabilize. Place the ignition switch in the right position and note the rpm drop on the tachometer. Return the switch to the both position. Allow the switch to remain in the both position for a few seconds so that the rpm stabilizes again. Place the ignition switch in the left position and again note the rpm drop. Return the ignition switch to the both position. Note the amount of total rpm drop that occurs for each magneto position. The magneto drop should be even for both magnetos and is generally in the area of a 25–75 rpm drop for each magneto. Always refer to the aircraft operating manual for specific information. This rpm drop is because operating on one magneto combustion is not as efficient as it is with two magnetos providing sparks in the cylinder.

Remember, this tests not only the magnetos but also the ignition leads and spark plugs. If either magneto has excessive rpm drop while operating by itself, the ignition system needs to be checked for problems. If only one magneto has a high magneto drop, the problem can be isolated and corrected by operating on that magneto. This ignition system check is usually performed at the beginning of the engine run-up because rpm drops not within the prescribed limits affect later checks.

Ignition Switch Check

The ignition switch check is performed to see that all magneto ground leads are electrically grounded. The ignition switch check is usually made at 700 rpm. On those aircraft engine installations that do not idle at this low rpm, set the engine speed to the lowest possible to perform this check. When the speed to perform this check is obtained, momentarily turn the ignition switch to the off position. The engine should completely quit firing. After a drop of 200–300 rpm is observed, return the switch to the both position as rapidly as possible. Do this quickly to eliminate the possibility of afterfire and backfire when the ignition switch is returned to both.

If the ignition switch is not returned quickly enough, the engine rpm drops off completely and the engine stops. In this case, leave the ignition switch in the off position and place the mixture control in the idle-cutoff position to avoid overloading the cylinders and exhaust system with raw fuel. When the engine has completely stopped, allow it to remain inoperative for a short time before restarting.

If the engine does not cease firing in the off position, the magneto ground lead, more commonly referred to as the P lead, is open, and the trouble must be corrected. This means that one or more of the magnetos are not being shut off even when the ignition switch is in the off position. Turning the propeller of this engine can result in personnel injury or death. If the propeller is turned in this condition, the engine can start with personnel in the propeller arch.

Maintenance and Inspection of Ignition Leads

Inspection of ignition leads should include both a visual and an electrical test. During the visual test, the lead cover should be inspected for cracks or other damage, abrasions, mutilated braid, or other physical damage. Inspect leads for overheating if routed close to exhaust stacks. Disconnect the harness coupling nuts from the top of the spark plugs and remove the leads from the spark plug lead well. Inspect the contact springs and compression springs for any damage or distortion and the sleeves for cracks or carbon tracking. The coupling nut that connects to the spark plug should be inspected for damaged threads or other defects.

Each lead should be checked for continuity using a high-tension lead tester by connecting the black lead to the contact spring and the red lead to the eyelet of the same lead in the cover. The continuity lamp on the tester should illuminate when tested. The insulation resistance test of each lead is accomplished using the high-tension lead tester by attaching the red, or high-voltage, lead to the spring of the harness lead. Then, attach the black lead to the ferrule of the same lead. Depress the press-to-test push button switch on the lead tester. Observe that the indictor lamp flashes and gap fires simultaneously as long as the press-to-test switch is held in the depressed position.

If the indicator lamp flashes and the gap fails to fire, the lead under test is defective and must be replaced. The indicator lamp flashes to show that a high-voltage impulse was sent out. If it fails to pass through the tester, then the electrical pulse leaked through the wire showing it to be defective.

When defective leads are revealed by an ignition harness test, continue the test to determine whether the leads or distributor block are defective. If the difficulty is in an individual ignition lead, determine whether the electrical leak is at the spark plug elbow or elsewhere. Remove the elbow, pull the ignition lead out of the manifold a slight amount, and repeat the harness test on the defective lead. If this stops the leakage, cut away the defective portion of the lead and reinstall the elbow assembly, integral seal, and terminal (sometimes referred to as cigarette). *[Figure 4-47]*

If the lead is too short to repair in the manner described, or the electrical leak is inside the harness, replace the defective lead. Single ignition lead replacement procedures are as follows:

1. Disassemble the magneto or distributor so that the distributor block is accessible.

2. Loosen the piercing screw in the distributor block for the lead to be replaced, and remove the lead from the distributor block.

3. Remove approximately 1 inch of insulation from the distributor block end of the defective lead and approximately 1 inch of insulation from the end of the replacement cable. Splice this end to the end of the lead to be replaced and solder the splice.

4. Remove the elbow adapter from the spark plug end of the defective lead, then pull the old lead out and put the new lead into the harness. While pulling the

Figure 4-47. *Replacement procedure for ignition lead terminals.*

leads through the harness, have someone push the replacement lead into the ignition manifold at the distributor end to reduce the force required to pull the lead through the ignition manifold.

5. When the replacement lead has been pulled completely through the manifold, force the ignition lead up into the manifold from the distributor block end to provide extra length for future repairs, which may be necessary because of chafing at the spark plug elbow.

6. Remove approximately ⅜ inch of insulation from the distributor block end. Bend the ends of the wire back and prepare the ends of the cable for installation into the distributor block well. Insert the lead in the distributor and tighten the piercing screw.

7. Remove approximately ¼ inch of insulation from the spark plug end of the lead and install the elbow, integral seal, and cigarette. *[Figure 4-47]*

8. Install a marker on the distributor end of the cable to identify its cylinder number. If a new marker is not available, use the marker removed from the defective cable.

Replacement of Ignition Harness

Replace a complete ignition harness only when the shielding of the manifold is damaged or when the number of defective leads makes it more practical to replace the harness than to replace the individual leads. Replace a cast-filled harness only when leakage in the cast-filled portion is indicated. Before replacing any harness to correct engine malfunctioning, make extensive ignition harness tests. Typical procedures for installing an ignition harness are detailed in the following paragraphs.

Install the ignition harness on the engine. Tighten and safety the hold down nuts and bolts and install and tighten the individual lead brackets according to instructions. The ignition harness is then ready for connection of the individual leads to the distributor block. A band is attached to each lead at the distributor end of the harness to identify the cylinder for the lead. However, each lead should be checked individually with a continuity or timing light prior to connecting it.

Check for continuity by grounding the lead at the cylinder and then checking at the distributor block end to establish that the lead grounded is as designated on the band for the lead.

After checking all leads for proper identification, cut them to the proper length for installation into the distributor block. Before cutting the leads, however, force them back into the manifold as far as possible to provide surplus wire in the ignition manifold. This extra wire may be needed at a later date in the event that chafing of a lead at the spark plug elbow necessitates cutting a short section of wire from the spark plug end of the harness. After cutting each lead to length, remove approximately ⅜ inch of insulation from the end and prepare the lead for insertion into the distributor block. Before installing the lead, back out the set screw in the distributor block far enough to permit slipping the end of the wire into the hole without force. Insert the lead into the block and tighten the set screw. Connect the wires in firing order (the first cylinder to fire No. 1 location on the block, the second in the firing order to No. 2 location, etc).

After connecting each lead, check continuity between the lead and its distributor block electrode with continuity light or timing light. To perform one test lead, touch the other test lead to the proper distributor block electrode. If the light does not indicate a complete circuit, the set screw is not making contact with the ignition wire or the lead is connected to the wrong block location. Correct any faulty connections before installing the distributor block.

Checking Ignition Induction Vibrator Systems

To check the induction vibrator, ensure that the manual mixture control is in idle cutoff, the fuel shutoff valve and booster pump for that engine are in the off position, and the battery switch is on. Since the induction vibrator buzzes whether the ignition switch is on or off, leave the switch off during the check. If the engine is equipped with an inertia or combination starter, make the check by closing the engage mesh switch; if the engine is equipped with a direct-cranking starter, see that the propeller is clear and close the start switch. An assistant stationed close to the induction vibrator should listen for an audible buzzing sound. If the unit buzzes when the starter is engaged or cranked, the induction vibrator is operating properly.

Spark Plug Inspection and Maintenance

Spark plug operation can often be a major source of engine malfunctions because of lead, oil, graphite, carbon fouling, and spark plug gap erosion. Most of these failures, which usually accompany normal spark plug operation, can be minimized by good operational and maintenance practices. A spark plug is considered fouled if it has stopped allowing the spark to bridge the gap either completely of intermittently.

Carbon Fouling of Spark Plugs

Carbon fouling from fuel is associated with mixtures that are too rich to burn or mixtures that are so lean they cause intermittent firing. *[Figure 4-48]* Each time a spark plug does not fire, raw fuel and oil collect on the nonfiring electrodes and nose insulator. These difficulties are almost invariably associated with an improper idle mixture adjustment, a leaking primer, or carburetor malfunctions that cause too rich a mixture in the idle range. A rich fuel-air mixture is detected by soot or black smoke coming from the exhaust and by an increase in rpm when the idling fuel-air mixture is leaned to best power. The soot that forms as a result of overly rich

Figure 4-48. *Carbon fouled spark plug.*

idle fuel-air mixtures settles on the inside of the combustion chamber because the heat of the engine and the turbulence in the combustion chamber are slight. At higher engine speeds and powers, however, the soot is swept out and does not condense out of the charge in the combustion chamber.

Oil Fouling of Spark Plugs

Even though the idling fuel-air mixture is correct, there is a tendency for oil to be drawn into the cylinder past the piston rings, valve guides, and impeller shaft oil seal rings. At low engine speeds, the oil combines with the soot in the cylinder to form a solid that is capable of shorting out the spark plug. Spark plugs that are wet or covered with lubricating oil are usually grounded out during the engine start. In some cases, these plugs may clear up and operate properly after a short period of engine operation.

Engine oil that has been in service for any length of time holds in suspension minute carbon particles that are capable of conducting an electric current. Thus, a spark plug will not arc the gap between the electrodes when the plug is full of oil. Instead, the high-voltage impulse flows through the oil from one electrode to the other without a spark as though a wire conductor were placed between the two electrodes. Combustion in the affected cylinder does not occur until, at a higher rpm, increased airflow has carried away the excess oil. Then, when intermittent firing starts, combustion assists in emitting the remaining oil. In a few seconds, the engine is running clean with white fumes of evaporating and burning oil coming from the exhaust.

Lead Fouling of Spark Plugs

Lead fouling of aviation spark plugs is a condition likely to occur in any engine using leaded fuels. Lead is added to aviation fuel to improve its anti-knock qualities. The lead, however, has the undesirable effect of forming lead oxide during combustion. This lead oxide forms as a solid with varying degrees of hardness and consistency. Lead deposits on combustion chamber surfaces are good electrical conductors at high temperatures and cause misfiring. At low temperatures, the same deposits may be good insulators. In either case, lead formations on aircraft spark plugs prevent their normal operation. *[Figure 4-49]* To minimize the formation of lead deposits, ethylene dibromide is added to the fuel as a scavenging agent that combines with the lead during combustion.

Figure 4-49. *Lead fouled spark plug.*

Lead fouling may occur at any power setting, but perhaps the power setting most conducive to lead fouling is cruising with lean mixtures. At this power, the cylinder head temperature is relatively low and there is more oxygen than needed to consume all the fuel in the fuel-air mixture. Oxygen, when hot, is very active and aggressive. When all the fuel has been consumed, some of the excess oxygen unites with some of the lead and some of the scavenger agent to form oxygen compounds of lead or bromine or both. Some of these undesirable lead compounds solidify and build up in layers as they contact the relatively cool cylinder walls and spark plugs. Although lead fouling may occur at any power setting, experience indicates that the lead buildup is generally confined to a specific combustion temperature range. Combustion temperatures outside this specific range minimize the lead fouling tendency.

If lead fouling is detected before the spark plugs become completely fouled, the lead can usually be eliminated or reduced by either a sharp rise or a sharp decrease in combustion temperature. This imposes a thermal shock on cylinder parts, causing them to expand or contract. Since there is a different rate of expansion between deposits and metal parts on which they form, the deposits chip off or are loosened and then scavenged from the combustion chamber by the exhaust or are burned in the combustion process.

Several methods of producing thermal shock to cylinder parts are used. The method used depends on the accessory equipment installed on the engine. A sharp rise in combustion temperatures can be obtained on all engines by operating them at full takeoff power for approximately 1 minute. When using this method to eliminate fouling, the propeller control must be placed in low pitch, or high rpm, and the throttle advanced slowly to produce takeoff rpm and manifold pressure. Slow movement of the throttle control provides reasonable freedom from backfiring in the affected cylinders during the application of power.

Another method of producing thermal shock is the use of excessively rich fuel-air mixtures. This method suddenly cools the combustion chamber because the excess fuel does not contribute to combustion; instead, it absorbs heat from the combustion area. Some carburetor installations use two-position manual mixture controls that provide a lean mixture setting for cruising economy and a richer mixture setting for all powers above cruising. Neither manual mixture control setting in this type of configuration is capable of producing an excessively rich fuel-air mixture. Even when the engine is operated in auto-rich at powers where an auto-lean setting would be entirely satisfactory, the mixture is not rich enough.

Graphite Fouling of Spark Plugs

As a result of careless and excessive application of thread lubricant, called antiseize compound, to the spark plug, the lubricant flows over the electrodes and causes shorting. Shorting occurs because graphite is a good electrical conductor. The elimination of service difficulties caused by graphite is up to the aircraft technician. Use care when applying the lubricant to make certain that smeared fingers, shop towels, or brushes do not contact the electrodes or any part of the ignition system except the spark plug threads. Never apply to the first set of threads.

Gap Erosion of Spark Plugs

Erosion of the electrodes takes place in all aircraft spark plugs as the spark jumps the air gap between the electrodes. *[Figure 4-50]*

Figure 4-50. *Spark plug gap erosion.*

The spark carries with it a portion of the electrode, part of which is deposited on the other electrode. The remainder is blown off in the combustion chamber. As the airgap is enlarged by erosion, the resistance that the spark must overcome in jumping the air gap also increases. This means that the magneto must produce a higher voltage to overcome the higher resistance. With higher voltages in the ignition system, a greater tendency exists for the spark to discharge at some weak insulation point in the ignition system. Since the resistance of an air gap also increases as the pressure in the engine cylinder increases, a double danger exists at takeoff and during sudden acceleration with enlarged airgaps. Insulation breakdown, premature flashover, and carbon tracking result in misfiring of the spark plug and go hand in hand with excessive spark plug gap. Wide gap settings also raise the coming in speed of a magneto and therefore cause hard starting.

Spark plug manufacturers have partially overcome the problem of gap erosion by using a hermetically sealed resistor in the center electrode of spark plugs. This added resistance in the high-tension circuit reduces the peak current at the instant of firing. This reduced current flow helps prevent metal disintegration in the electrodes. Also, due to the high erosion rate of steel or any of its known alloys, spark plug manufacturers are using tungsten or an alloy of nickel for their massive electrode plugs and iridium/platinum plating for their fine wire electrode plugs.

Spark Plug Removal

Spark plugs should be removed for inspection and servicing at the intervals recommended by the manufacturer. Since the rate of gap erosion varies with different operating conditions, engine models, and type of spark plug, engine malfunction traceable to faulty spark plugs may occur before the regular servicing interval is reached. Normally, in such cases, only the faulty plugs are replaced.

Since spark plugs can be easily damaged, careful handling of the used and replacement plugs during installation and removal of spark plugs from an engine cannot be overemphasized. To prevent damage, spark plugs should always be handled individually and new and reconditioned plugs should be stored in separate cartons. A common method of storage is illustrated in *Figure 4-51*. This is a drilled tray, which prevents the plugs from bumping against one another and damaging the fragile insulators and threads. If a plug is dropped on the floor or other hard surface, it should not be installed in an engine, since the shock of impact usually causes small, invisible cracks in the insulators. A dropped spark plug should be discarded.

Figure 4-51. *Spark plug tray.*

Before a spark plug can be removed, the ignition harness lead must be disconnected. Using the special spark plug coupling elbow wrench, loosen and remove the spark plug to elbow coupling nut from the spark plug. Take care to pull the lead straight out and in line with the centerline of the plug barrel. If a side load is applied, damage to the barrel insulator and the ceramic lead terminal may result. *[Figure 4-52]* If the lead cannot be removed easily in this manner, the neoprene collar may be stuck to the shielding barrel. Break loose the neoprene collar by twisting the collar as though it were a nut being unscrewed from a bolt.

After the lead has been disconnected, select the proper size deep socket for spark plug removal. Apply steady pressure with one hand on the hinge handle, holding the socket in alignment with the other hand. Failure to hold the socket in correct alignment causes the socket to tilt to one side and damage the spark plug. *[Figure 4-53]*

Figure 4-52. *Improper lead removal technique.*

Figure 4-53. *Proper spark plug removal technique.*

In the course of engine operation, carbon and other products of combustion are deposited across the spark plug and cylinder, and some carbon may even penetrate the lower threads of the shell. As a result, a high torque is generally required to break the spark plug loose. This factor imposes a shearing load on the shell section of the plug. After removing the plugs, they should be placed in a spark plug tray. *[Figure 4-51]*

Spark Plug Reconditioning Service

A visual inspection should be the first step in servicing spark plugs. The threads on the shielding barrel and on the shell that screws into the cylinder should be inspected for damaged or nicked threads. Inspect the lead shielding barrel for corrosion, nicks, and cracks. The firing end should be checked for insulator cracks, chips, and excessive electrode wear. The shell hex or wrench hex should be checked to see if it is rounded off or mutilated. If the spark plug passes the visual check, then it should be degreased using petroleum solvent. Take care to keep solvent out of the shielding barrel. Never soak the plugs in solvent. After drying the firing end of the plugs, remove the lead compound deposits using a vibrator cleaner. *[Figure 4-54]* The firing end can now be cleaned by using an abrasive blaster. This is usually done using a spark plug cleaner tester. *[Figure 4-55]* As the firing end is subjected to the abrasive blast, the plug should be rotated so all the area of the firing end is cleaned. After the abrasive blast, the firing end gets a thorough air blast to remove the abrasive material. The shielding barrel insulators may be cleaned with a cotton cloth or felt swab saturated with solvent, wood alcohol, or other approved cleaner. The firing end should be inspected using a light and a magnifying glass. If the plug passes the firing end visual and cleaning checks, then the spark gap should be set using a round thickness gauge. The spark plug should be tested by using a tester as shown in *Figure 4-55*, which passes a high-voltage through the spark plug and fire the gap. As this test takes place, the firing end of the plug is subjected to air pressure to simulate the pressure in the engine's cylinder. If the firing pattern is good, the plug should be returned to its holder ready for installation in the engine.

Figure 4-54. *Spark plug vibrator cleaner.*

Figure 4-55. *Spark plug cleaner tester.*

Inspection Prior to Installation

Before installing new or reconditioned spark plugs in the engine cylinders, clean the spark plug bushings or Heli-Coil inserts.

Brass or stainless steel spark plug bushings are usually cleaned with a spark plug bushing cleanout tap. Before inserting the cleanout tap in the spark plug hole, fill the flutes of the tap, or channels between threads, with clean grease to prevent hard carbon or other material removed by the tap from dropping into the inside of the cylinder. Align the tap with the bushing threads by sight where possible, and start the tap by hand until there is no possibility of it being cross-threaded in the bushing. To start the tap on installations where the spark plug hole is located deeper than can be reached by a clenched hand, it may be necessary to use a short length of hose slipped over the square end of the tap to act as an extension. When screwing the tap into the bushing, be sure that the full tap cutting thread reaches the bottom thread of the bushing. This removes carbon deposits from the bushing threads without removing bushing metal, unless the pitch diameter of the threads has contracted as the result of shrinkage or some other unusual condition. Replace the cylinder if, during the thread-cleaning process, the bushing is found to be loose, loosened in the cylinder, or the threads are cross-threaded or otherwise seriously damaged.

Spark plug Heli-Coil inserts are cleaned with a round wire brush, preferably one having a diameter slightly larger than the diameter of the spark plug hole. A brush considerably larger than the hole may cause removal of material from the Heli-Coil proper or from the cylinder head surrounding the insert. Also, the brush should not disintegrate with use, allowing wire bristles to fall into the cylinder. Clean the insert by carefully rotating the wire brush with a power tool. When using the power brush, be careful that no material is removed from the spark plug gasket seating surface, since this may cause a change in the spark plug's heat range, combustion leakage, and eventual cylinder damage. Never clean the Heli-Coil inserts with a cleaning tap, since permanent damage to the insert results. If a Heli-Coil insert is damaged as a result of normal operation or while cleaning it, replace it according to the applicable manufacturer's instructions.

Using a lint-free rag and cleaning solvent, wipe the spark plug gasket seating surface of the cylinder to eliminate the possibility of dirt or grease being accidentally deposited on the spark plug electrodes at the time of installation.

Before the new or reconditioned plugs are installed, they must be inspected for each of the following conditions:

1. Ensure that the plug is of the approved type, as indicated by the applicable manufacturer's instructions.

2. Check for evidence of rust-preventive compound on the spark plug exterior and core insulator and on the inside of the shielding barrel. Rust-preventive compound accumulations are removed by washing the plug with a brush and cleaning solvent. It must then be dried with a dry air blast.

3. Check both ends of the plug for nicked or cracked threads and any indication of cracks in the nose insulator.

4. Inspect the inside of the shielding barrel for cracks in the barrel insulator, and the center electrode contact for rust and foreign material that might cause poor electrical contact.

5. Install a new spark plug gasket. When the thermocouple gasket is used, do not use an additional gasket.

The gap setting should be checked with a round wire-thickness gauge. *[Figure 4-56]* A flat-type gauge gives an incorrect clearance indication because the massive ground electrodes are contoured to the shape of the round center electrode. When using the wire thickness gauge, insert the gauge in each gap parallel to the centerline of the center electrode. If the gauge is tilted slightly, the indication is incorrect. Do not install a plug that does not have an air gap within the specified clearance range.

Spark Plug Installation

Prior to spark plug installation, carefully coat the first two or three threads from the electrode end of the shell with a graphite base antiseize compound. Prior to application, stir the antiseize compound to ensure thorough mixing. When applying the antiseize compound to the threads, be extremely careful that none of the compound gets on the ground,

Figure 4-56. *Wire gap gauge.*

center electrodes, or on the nose of the plug, where it can spread to the ground or center electrode during installation. This precaution is mentioned because the graphite in the compound is an excellent electrical conductor and could cause permanent fouling.

To install a spark plug, start it into the cylinder without using a wrench of any kind, and turn it until the spark plug is seated on the gasket. If you can screw the plug into the cylinder with comparative ease using your fingers, this indicates good, clean threads. In this case, only a small amount of additional tightening torque is needed to compress the gasket to form a gastight seal. If a high torque is needed to install the plug, dirty or damaged threads on either the plug or plug bushing are indicated. The use of excessive torque might compress the gasket out of shape and distort and stretch the plug shell to a point where breakage would result during the next removal or installation. Shell stretching occurs as excessive torque continues to screw the lower end of the shell into the cylinder after the upper end has been stopped by the gasket shoulder. As the shell stretches, the seal between the shell and core insulator is opened, creating a loss of gas tightness or damage to the core insulator. After a spark plug has been seated with the fingers, use a torque wrench and tighten to the specified torque. *[Figure 4-57]*

Spark Plug Lead Installation

Before installing the spark plug lead, carefully wipe the terminal sleeve and the integral seal with a cloth moistened with acetone or an approved solvent. After the plug lead is cleaned, inspect it for cracks and scratches. If the terminal sleeve is damaged or heavily stained, replace it.

Figure 4-57. *Effect of excessive torque in installing a spark plug.*

Application of a light coating of an insulating material to the outer surface of the terminal sleeve, as well as filling the space occupied by the contact spring, is sometimes recommended. By occupying the space in the electrical contact area of the shielding barrel, the insulating material prevents moisture from entering the contact area and shorting the spark plug. Some manufacturers recommend the use of such insulating compounds only when moisture in the ignition system becomes a problem, and others have discontinued the use of such materials.

After inspection of the spark plug lead, slip the lead into the shielding barrel of the plug with care. Then, tighten the spark plug coupling elbow nut with the proper tool. Most manufacturers' instructions specify the use of a tool designed to help prevent an overtorque condition. After the coupling nut is tightened, avoid checking for tightness by twisting the body of the elbow.

After all plugs have been installed, torqued, and the leads properly installed, start the engine and perform a complete ignition system operational check.

Breaker Point Inspection

Inspection of the magneto consists essentially of a periodic breaker point and dielectric inspection. After the magneto has been inspected for security of mounting, remove the magneto cover, or breaker cover, and check the cam for proper lubrication. Under normal conditions, there is usually ample oil in the felt oiler pad of the cam follower to keep the cam lubricated between overhaul periods. However, during the regular routine inspection, examine the felt pad on the cam follower to be sure it contains sufficient oil for cam lubrication. Make this check by pressing the thumbnail against the oiler pad. If oil appears on the thumbnail, the pad contains sufficient oil for cam lubrication. If there is no evidence of oil on the fingernail, apply one drop of a light aircraft engine oil to the bottom felt pad and one drop to the upper felt pad of the follower assembly. [Figure 4-58]

Figure 4-58. *Felt lubricator.*

After application, allow at least 15 minutes for the felt to absorb the oil. At the end of 15 minutes, blot off any excess oil with a clean, lint-free cloth. During this operation, or any time the magneto cover is off, use extreme care to keep the breaker compartment free of oil, grease, or engine cleaning solvents, since each of these have an adhesiveness that collects dirt and grime that could foul an otherwise good set of breaker contact points.

After the felt oiler pad has been inspected, serviced, and found to be satisfactory, visually inspect the breaker contacts for any condition that may interfere with proper operation of the magneto. If the inspection reveals an oily or gummy substance on the sides of the contacts, swab the contacts with a flexible wiper, such as a pipe cleaner dipped in acetone or other approved solvent. By forming a hook on the end of the wiper, ready access can be gained to the back side of the contacts.

To clean the contact mating surfaces, force open the breaker points enough to admit a small swab. Whether spreading the points for purposes of cleaning or checking the surfaces for condition, always apply the opening force at the outer end of the mainspring and never spread the contacts more than $1/16$ inch. If the contacts are spread wider than recommended, the mainspring, the spring carrying the movable contact point, is likely to take a permanent set. If the mainspring takes a permanent set, the movable contact point loses some of its closing tension and the points then either bounce or float, preventing the normal induction buildup of the magneto.

A swab can be made by wrapping a piece of linen tape or a small piece of lint-free cloth over one of the leaves of a clearance gauge and dipping the swab in an approved solvent. Pass the swab between the carefully separated contact surfaces until the surfaces are clean. During this entire operation, take care that drops of solvent do not fall on lubricated parts, such as the cam, follower block, or felt oiler pad.

To inspect the breaker contact surfaces, it is necessary to know what a normal operating set of contacts looks like, what surface condition is considered as permissible wear, and what surface condition is cause for dressing or replacement. The probable cause of an abnormal surface condition can be determined from the contact appearance. The normal contact surface has a dull gray, sandblasted, almost rough appearance over the area where electrical contact is made. [Figure 4-59] This gray, sandblasted appearance indicates that the points have worn in and have mated to each other and are providing the best possible electrical contact. This does not imply that this is the only acceptable contact surface condition. Slight, smooth-surfaced irregularities, without deep pits or high peaks, such as shown in Figure 4-60, are considered normal wear and are not cause for replacement.

Figure 4-59. *Normal contact surface.*

However, when wear advances to a point where the slight, smooth irregularities develop into well-defined peaks extending noticeably above the surrounding surface, the breaker contacts must be replaced. [Figure 4-61]

Unfortunately, when a peak forms on one contact, the mating contact has a corresponding pit or hole. This pit is more

Figure 4-60. *Points with normal irregularities.*

Figure 4-61. *Points with well-defined peaks.*

of the points, producing the coarse, crystalline, or frosted appearance. Properly operating points have a fine-grained, frosted, or silvery appearance and should not be confused with the coarse-grained and sooty point caused by faulty condenser action.

Figure 4-62. *Examples of contact surface conditions.*

Figure 4-62B and *C* illustrate badly pitted points. In the early stage, these points are identified by a fairly even contact edge and minute pits or pocks in or near the center of the contact surface with an overall smoky appearance. In more advanced stages, the pit may develop into a large, jagged crater, and eventually the entire contact surface takes on a burned, black, and crumpled appearance. Pitted points, as a general rule, are caused by dirt and impurities on the contact surfaces. If points are excessively pitted, a new breaker assembly must be installed.

Figure 4-62E illustrates a built-up point that can be recognized by the mound of metal that has been transferred from one point to another. Buildup, like the other conditions mentioned, results primarily from the transfer of contact material by means of the arc as the points separate. But, unlike the others, there is no burning or oxidation in the process because of the closeness of the pit of one point and the buildup of the other. This condition may result from excessive breaker point spring tension that retards the opening of the points or causes a slow, lazy break. It can also be caused by a poor primary condenser or a loose connection at the primary coil. If excessive buildup has occurred, a new breaker assembly must be installed.

Figure 4-62F illustrates oily points that can be recognized by their smoked and smudged appearance and by the lack of any of the previously mentioned irregularities. This condition may be the result of excessive cam lubrication or of oil

troublesome than the peak because it penetrates the platinum pad of the contact surface. It is sometimes difficult to judge whether a contact surface is pitted deeply enough to require replacement because this depends on how much of the original platinum is left on the contact surface. The danger arises from the possibility that the platinum pad may already be thin as a result of long service life and previous dressings.

At overhaul facilities, a gauge is used to measure the remaining thickness of the pad, and no difficulty in determining the condition of the pad exists. But at line maintenance activities, this gauge is generally unavailable. Therefore, if the peak is quite high or the pit quite deep, remove and replace them with a new assembly. A comparison between *Figures 4-60* and *4-61* will help to draw the line between minor irregularities and well-defined peaks.

Some examples of possible breaker contact surface conditions are illustrated in *Figure 4-62*. Item A illustrates an example of erosion or wear called frosting. This condition results from an open-circuited condenser and is easily recognized by the coarse, crystalline surface and the black "sooty" appearance of the sides of the points. The lack of effective condenser action results in an arc of intense heat being formed each time the points open. This, together with the oxygen in the air, rapidly oxidizes and erodes the platinum surface vapors that may come from within or outside the magneto. A smoking or fuming engine, for example, could produce the oil vapors. These vapors then enter the magneto through the magneto ventilator and pass between and around the points. These conductive vapors produce arcing and burning on the contact surfaces. The vapors also adhere to the other surfaces of the breaker assembly and form the sooty deposit. If so, install new breaker assembly.

Dielectric Inspection

Another phase of magneto inspection is the dielectric inspection. This inspection is a visual check for cleanliness and cracks. If inspection reveals that the coil cases, condensers, distributor rotor, or blocks are oily or dirty or have any trace of carbon tracking, they require cleaning and possibly waxing to restore their dielectric qualities.

Clean all accessible condensers and coil cases that contain condensers by wiping them with a lint-free cloth moistened with acetone. Many parts of this type have a protective coating. This protective coating is not affected by acetone, but it may be damaged by scraping or by the use of other cleaning fluids. Never use unapproved cleaning solvents or improper cleaning methods. Also, when cleaning condensers or parts that contain condensers, do not dip, submerge, or saturate the parts in any solution because the solution used may seep inside the condenser and short out the plates.

Coil cases, distributor blocks, distributor rotors, and other dielectric parts of the ignition system are treated with a wax coating when they are new and again at overhaul. The waxing of dielectrics aids their resistance to moisture absorption, carbon tracking, and acid deposits. When these parts become dirty or oily, some of the original protection is lost, and carbon tracking may result.

If any hairline carbon tracks or acid deposits are present on the surface of the dielectric, immerse the part in approved cleaning solvent and scrub it vigorously with a stiff bristle brush. When the carbon track or acid deposits have been removed, wipe the part with a clean, dry cloth to remove all traces of the solvent used for cleaning. Then, coat the part with a special ignition-treating wax. After wax treating the part, remove excess wax deposits and reinstall the part in the magneto.

Ignition Harness Maintenance

Although the ignition harness is simple, it is a vital link between the magneto and spark plug. Because the harness is mounted on the engine and exposed to the atmosphere, it is vulnerable to heat, moisture, and the effects of changing altitude. These factors, plus aging insulation and normal gap erosion, work against efficient engine operation. The insulation may break down on a wire inside the harness and allow the high-voltage to leak through the insulation to the harness shielding instead of going to the spark plug. Open circuits may result from broken wires or poor connections. A bare wire may be in physical contact with the shielding, or two wires may be shorted together.

Any serious defect in an individual lead prevents the high-tension impulse from reaching the spark plug to which the lead is connected. As a result, this plug will not fire. When only one spark plug is firing in a cylinder, the charge is not consumed as quickly as it would be if both plugs were firing. This factor causes the peak pressure of combustion to occur later on in the power stroke. If the peak pressure in the cylinder occurs later, a loss of power in that cylinder results. However, the power loss from a single cylinder becomes a minor factor when the effects of a longer burning time is considered. A longer burning time overheats the affected cylinder, causing detonation, possible preignition, and perhaps permanent damage to the cylinder.

High-Tension Ignition Harness Faults

Perhaps the most common and most difficult high-tension ignition system faults to detect are high-voltage leaks. This is leakage from the core conductor through insulation to the ground of the shielded manifold. A certain small amount of leakage exists even in brand new ignition cable during normal operation. Various factors combine to produce first a high rate of leakage and then complete breakdown. Of these factors, moisture in any form is probably the worst.

Under high-voltage stress, an arc forms and burns a path across the insulator where the moisture exists. If there is gasoline, oil, or grease present, it breaks down and forms carbon. The burned path is called a carbon track, since it is actually a path of carbon particles. With some types of insulation, it may be possible to remove the carbon track and restore the insulator to its former useful condition. This is generally true of porcelain, ceramics, and some of the plastics because these materials are not hydrocarbons and any carbon track forming on them is the result of a dirt film that can be wiped away.

Differences in location and amount of leakage produce different indications of malfunction during engine operation. Indications are generally misfiring or crossfiring. The indication may be intermittent, changing with manifold pressure or with climate conditions. An increase in manifold pressure increases the compression pressure and the resistance of the air across the air gap of the spark plugs. An increase in the resistance at the air gap opposes the spark discharge and produces a tendency for the spark to discharge at some weak point in the insulation. A weak spot in the harness may be aggravated by moisture collecting in the harness manifold.

With moisture present, continued engine operation causes the intermittent faults to become permanent carbon tracks. Thus, the first indication of ignition harness unserviceability may be engine misfiring or roughness caused by partial leakage of the ignition voltage.

Figure 4-63 demonstrates four faults that may occur. Fault A shows a short from one cable conductor to another. This fault usually causes misfiring, since the spark is short circuited to a plug in a cylinder where the cylinder pressure is low. Fault B illustrates a cable with a portion of its insulation scuffed away. Although the insulation is not completely broken down, more than normal leakage exists, and the spark plug to which this cable is connected may be lost during takeoff when the manifold pressure is quite high. Fault C is the result of condensation collecting in the lowest portion of the ignition manifold. This condensation may completely evaporate during engine operation, but the carbon track that is formed by the initial flashover remains to allow continued flashover whenever high manifold pressure exists. Fault D may be caused by a flaw in the insulation or the result of a weak spot in the insulation that is aggravated by the presence of moisture. However, since the carbon track is in direct contact with the metal shielding, it probably results in flashover under all operating conditions.

Figure 4-64. *Harness tester.*

a guide to the condition or serviceability of the cable. As mentioned earlier, there is a gradual deterioration of flexible insulating material. When new, the insulation has a low rate of conductivity; so low that, under several thousand volts of electrical pressure, the current leakage is only a very few millionths of an ampere. Natural aging causes an extremely slow, but certain, change in the resistance of insulating material, allowing an ever-increasing rate of current leakage. The procedures for testing ignition harness and leads were discussed earlier in this chapter.

Turbine Engine Ignition Systems

Since turbine ignition systems are operated mostly for a brief period during the engine-starting cycle, they are, as a rule, more trouble-free than the typical reciprocating engine ignition system. The turbine engine ignition system does not need to be timed to spark during an exact point in the operational cycle. It is used to ignite the fuel in the combustor and then it is switched off. Other modes of turbine ignition system operation, such as continuous ignition that is used at a lower voltage and energy level, are used for certain flight conditions.

Figure 4-63. *Cross section of an ignition harness.*

Harness Testing

The electrical test of the ignition harness checks the condition or effectiveness of the insulation around each cable in the harness. *[Figure 4-64]* This test involves application of a definite voltage to each lead, and then measurement with a very sensitive meter of the amount of current leakage between the lead and the grounded harness manifold. This reading, when compared with known specifications, becomes

4-39

Continuous ignition is used in case the engine were to flame out. This ignition could relight the fuel and keep the engine from stopping. Examples of critical flight modes that use continuous ignition are takeoff, landing, and some abnormal and emergency situations.

Most gas turbine engines are equipped with a high-energy, capacitor-type ignition system and are air cooled by fan airflow. Fan air is ducted to the exciter box, and then flows around the igniter lead and surrounds the igniter before flowing back into the nacelle area. Cooling is important when continuous ignition is used for some extended period of time. Gas turbine engines may be equipped with an electronic-type ignition system, which is a variation of the simpler capacitor-type system.

The typical turbine engine is equipped with a capacitor-type, or capacitor discharge, ignition system consisting of two identical independent ignition units operating from a common low-voltage (DC) electrical power source: the aircraft battery, 115AC, or its permanent magnet generator. The generator is turned directly by the engine through the accessory gear box and produces power any time the engine is turning. The fuel in turbine engines can be ignited readily in ideal atmospheric conditions, but since they often operate in the low temperatures of high altitudes, it is imperative that the system be capable of supplying a high heat intensity spark. Thus, a high-voltage is supplied to arc across a wide igniter spark gap, providing the ignition system with a high degree of reliability under widely varying conditions of altitude, atmospheric pressure, temperature, fuel vaporization, and input voltage.

A typical ignition system includes two exciter units, two transformers, two intermediate ignition leads, and two high-tension leads. Thus, as a safety factor, the ignition system is actually a dual system designed to fire two igniter plugs. [Figure 4-65]

Figure 4-66 is a functional schematic diagram of a typical older style capacitor-type turbine ignition system. A 24-volt DC input voltage is supplied to the input receptacle of the exciter unit. Before the electrical energy reaches the exciter unit, it passes through a filter that prevents noise voltage from being induced into the aircraft electrical system. The low-voltage input power operates a DC motor that drives one multilobe cam and one single-lobe cam. At the same time, input power is supplied to a set of breaker points that are actuated by the multilobe cam.

From the breaker points, a rapidly interrupted current is delivered to an auto transformer. When the breaker closes, the flow of current through the primary winding of the

Figure 4-65. *Turbine ignition system components.*

transformer establishes a magnetic field. When the breaker opens, the flow of current stops, and the collapse of the field induces a voltage in the secondary of the transformer. This voltage causes a pulse of current to flow into the storage capacitor through the rectifier, which limits the flow to a single direction. With repeated pulses, the storage capacitor assumes a charge, up to a maximum of approximately 4 joules. (Note: 1 joule per second equals 1 watt.) The storage capacitor is connected to the spark igniter through the triggering transformer and a contactor, normally open.

When the charge on the capacitor has built up, the contactor is closed by the mechanical action of the single-lobe cam. A portion of the charge flows through the primary of the triggering transformer and the capacitor connected with it. This current induces a high-voltage in the secondary, which ionizes the gap at the spark igniter.

When the spark igniter is made conductive, the storage capacitor discharges the remainder of its accumulated energy along with the charge from the capacitor in series with the primary of the triggering transformer. The spark rate at the spark igniter varies in proportion to the voltage of the DC power supply that affects the rpm of the motor. However, since both cams are geared to the same shaft, the storage capacitor always accumulates its store of energy from the same number of pulses before discharge. The employment of the high-frequency triggering transformer, with a low-reactance secondary winding, holds the time duration of the discharge to a minimum. This concentration of maximum energy in minimum time achieves an optimum spark for ignition purposes, capable of blasting carbon deposits and vaporizing globules of fuel.

Figure 4-66. *Capacitor-type ignition system schematic.*

All high-voltage in the triggering circuits is completely isolated from the primary circuits. The complete exciter is hermetically sealed, protecting all components from adverse operating conditions, eliminating the possibility of flashover at altitude due to pressure change. This also ensures shielding against leakage of high-frequency voltage interfering with the radio reception of the aircraft.

Capacitor Discharge Exciter Unit

This capacity-type system provides ignition for turbine engines. Like other turbine ignition systems, it is required only for starting the engine; once combustion has begun, the flame is continuous. *[Figure 4-67]*

The energy is stored in capacitors. Each discharge circuit incorporates two storage capacitors; both are located in the exciter unit. The voltage across these capacitors is stepped up by transformer units. At the instant of igniter plug firing, the resistance of the gap is lowered sufficiently to permit the larger capacitor to discharge across the gap. The discharge of the second capacitor is of low-voltage, but of very high energy. The result is a spark of great heat intensity, capable of not only igniting abnormal fuel mixtures but also burning away any foreign deposits on the plug electrodes.

The exciter is a dual unit that produces sparks at each of the two igniter plugs. A continuous series of sparks is produced until the engine starts. The power is then cut off, and the plugs do not fire while the engine is operating other than on continuous ignition for certain flight conditions. This is why the exciters are air cooled to prevent overheating during long use of continuous ignition.

Figure 4-67. *Fan air-cooled exciter.*

Igniter Plugs

The igniter plug of a turbine engine ignition system differs considerably from the spark plug of a reciprocating engine ignition system. *[Figure 4-68]* Its electrode must be capable of withstanding a current of much higher energy than the electrode of a conventional spark plug. This high energy current can quickly cause electrode erosion, but the short periods of operation minimize this aspect of igniter maintenance. The electrode gap of the typical igniter plug is designed much larger than that of a spark plug since the operating pressures are much lower and the spark can arc more easily than in a spark plug. Finally, electrode fouling, common to the spark plug, is minimized by the heat of the high-intensity spark.

Figure 4-69 is a cutaway illustration of a typical annular-gap igniter plug, sometimes referred to as a long reach igniter because it projects slightly into the combustion chamber liner to produce a more effective spark.

Another type of igniter plug, the constrained-gap plug, is used in some types of turbine engines. *[Figure 4-70]* It operates at a much cooler temperature because it does not project into the combustion-chamber liner. This is possible because the spark does not remain close to the plug, but arcs beyond the face of the combustion chamber liner.

Turbine Ignition System Inspection and Maintenance

Maintenance of the typical turbine engine ignition system consists primarily of inspection, test, troubleshooting, removal, and installation.

Inspection

Inspection of the ignition system normally includes the following:

- Ignition lead terminal inspection; ceramic terminal should be free of arcing, carbon tracking and cracks.
- The grommet seal should be free of flashover and carbon tracking. *[Figure 4-71]*
- The wire insulation should remain flexible with no evidence of arcing through the insulation.
- Inspect the complete system for security of component mounting, shorts or high-voltage arcing, and loose connections.

Figure 4-68. *Ignitor plugs.*

Check System Operation

The igniter can be checked by listening for a snapping noise as the engine begins to turn, driven by the starter. The igniter can also be checked by removing it and activating the start cycle, noting the spark across the igniter.

CAUTION: The high energy level and voltage associated with turbine ignition systems can cause injury or death to personnel coming into contact with the activated system.

Repair

Tighten and secure as required and replace faulty components and wiring. Secure, tighten, and safety as required.

Removal, Maintenance, and Installation of Ignition System Components

The following instructions are typical procedures suggested by many gas turbine manufacturers. These instructions are applicable to the engine ignition components. Always consult the applicable manufacturer's instructions before performing any ignition system maintenance.

Figure 4-69. *Typical annular gap igniter plug.*

Ignition System Leads

1. Remove clamps securing ignition leads to engine.
2. Remove safety wire and disconnect electrical connectors from exciter units.
3. Remove safety wire and disconnect lead from igniter plug.
4. Discharge any electrical charge stored in the system by grounding and remove ignition leads from engine.
5. Clean leads with approved dry cleaning solvent.
6. Inspect connectors for damaged threads, corrosion, cracked insulators, and bent or broken connector pins.
7. Inspect leads for worn or burned areas, deep cuts, fraying, and general deterioration.
8. Perform continuity check of ignition leads.
9. Reinstall leads, reversing the removal procedure.

Figure 4-70. *Constrained gap igniter plug.*

Figure 4-71. *Flashover inspection.*

Igniter Plugs

1. Disconnect ignition leads from igniter plugs. A good procedure to perform before disconnecting the ignition lead is to disconnect the low-voltage primary lead from the ignition exciter unit and wait at least one minute to permit the stored energy to dissipate before disconnecting the high-voltage cable from the igniter.

2. Remove igniter plugs from mounts.

3. Inspect igniter plug gap surface material. Before inspection, remove residue from the shell exterior using a dry cloth. Do not remove any deposits or residue from the firing end of the low-voltage igniters. High-voltage igniters can have the firing end cleaned to aid in inspection. *[Figure 4-72]*

Gap Description	Typical Firing End Configuration	Clean Firing End
High-voltage air surface gap		Yes
High-voltage surface gap		Yes
High-voltage recessed surface gap		Yes
Low-voltage shunted surface gap		No

Figure 4-72. *Firing end cleaning.*

4. Inspect for fretting of igniter plug shank.

5. Replace an igniter plug whose surface is granular, chipped, or otherwise damaged.

6. Replace dirty or carbonized igniter plugs.

7. Install igniter plugs in mounting pads.

8. Check for proper clearance between chamber liner and igniter plug.

9. Tighten igniter plugs to manufacturer's specified torque.
10. Safety wire igniter plugs.

Powerplant Electrical Systems

The satisfactory performance of any modern aircraft depends to a great degree on the continuing reliability of electrical systems and subsystems. Improperly or carelessly installed or maintained wiring can be a source of both immediate and potential danger. The continued proper performance of electrical systems depends upon the knowledge and technique of the mechanic who installs, inspects, and maintains the electrical wire and cable of the electrical systems.

The procedures and practices outlined in this section are general recommendations and are not intended to replace the manufacturer's instructions in approved practices.

For the purpose of this discussion, a wire is described as a single solid conductor, or a stranded conductor, covered with an insulating material. *[Figure 4-73]* The term "cable," as used in aircraft electrical installations, includes the following:

Figure 4-73. *Two types of aircraft wire.*

1. Multiconductor cable—two or more separately insulated conductors in the same jacket.
2. Twisted pair—two or more separately insulated conductors twisted together.
3. Shielded cable—one or more insulated conductors, covered with a metallic braided shield.
4. Radio frequency cable—a single, insulated center conductor with a metallic braided outer conductor. The concentricity of the center conductor and the outer conductor is carefully controlled during manufacture to ensure that they are coaxial.

Wire Size

Wire is manufactured in sizes according to a standard known as the American wire gauge (AWG). The wire diameters become smaller as the gauge numbers become larger. The largest wire size shown in *Figure 4-74* is number 0000, and the smallest is number 40. Larger and smaller sizes are manufactured but are not commonly used.

Wire size may be determined by using a wire gauge. *[Figure 4-75]* This type of gauge measures wires ranging in size from number 0 (zero) to number 36. The wire to be measured is inserted in the smallest slot that just accommodates the bare wire. The gauge number corresponding to that slot indicates the wire size. The slot has parallel sides and should not be confused with the semicircular opening at the end of the slot. The opening simply permits the free movement of the wire all the way through the slot.

Gauge numbers are useful in comparing the diameter of wires, but not all types of wire or cable can be accurately measured with a gauge. Large wires are usually stranded to increase their flexibility. In such cases, the total area can be determined by multiplying the area of one strand, usually computed in circular mils (commonly used as a reference to wire size) when diameter or gauge number is known by the number of strands in the wire or cable.

Factors Affecting the Selection of Wire Size

Several factors must be considered in selecting the size of wire for transmitting and distributing electric power. One factor is the allowable power loss (PR loss) in the line. This loss represents electrical energy converted into heat. The use of large conductors reduces the resistance and therefore the PR loss. However, large conductors are more expensive initially than small ones; they are heavier and require more substantial supports.

A second factor is the permissible voltage drop (IR drop) in the line. If the source maintains a constant voltage at the input to the line, any variation in the load on the line causes a variation in line current and a consequent variation in the IR drop in the line. A wide variation in the IR drop in the line causes poor voltage regulation at the load. The obvious remedy is to reduce either current or resistance. A reduction in load current lowers the amount of power being transmitted, whereas a reduction in line resistance increases the size and weight of conductors required. A compromise is generally reached whereby the voltage variation at the load is within tolerable limits and the weight of line conductors is not excessive.

4-45

Gauge Number	Cross Section			Ohms per 1,000 ft	
	Diameter (mils)	Circular (mils)	Square inches	25 °C (77 °F)	65 °C (149 °F)
0000	460.0	212,000.0	0.166	0.0500	0.0577
000	410.0	168,000.0	0.132	0.0630	0.0727
00	365.0	133,000.0	0.105	0.0795	0.0917
0	325.0	106,000.0	0.0829	0.100	0.166
1	289.0	83,700.0	0.0657	0.126	0.146
2	258.0	66,400.0	0.0521	0.159	0.184
3	229.0	52,600.0	0.0413	0.201	0.232
4	204.0	41,700.0	0.0328	0.253	0.292
5	182.0	33,100.0	0.0260	0.319	0.369
6	162.0	26,300.0	0.0206	0.403	0.465
7	144.0	20,800.0	0.0164	0.508	0.586
8	128.0	16,500.0	0.0130	0.641	0.739
9	114.0	13,100.0	0.0103	0.808	0.932
10	102.0	10,400.0	0.00815	1.02	1.18
11	91.0	8,230.0	0.00647	1.28	1.48
12	81.0	6,530.0	0.00513	1.62	1.87
13	72.0	5,180.0	0.00407	2.04	2.36
14	64.0	4,110.0	0.00323	2.58	2.97
15	57.0	3,260.0	0.00256	3.25	3.75
16	51.0	2,580.0	0.00203	4.09	4.73
17	45.0	2,050.0	0.00161	5.16	5.96
18	40.0	1,620.0	0.00128	6.51	7.51
19	36.0	1,290.0	0.00101	8.21	9.48
20	32.0	1,020.0	0.000802	10.40	11.90
21	28.5	810.0	0.000636	13.10	15.10
22	25.3	642.0	0.000505	16.50	19.00
23	22.6	509.0	0.000400	20.80	24.00
24	20.1	404.0	0.000317	26.20	30.20
25	17.9	320.0	0.000252	33.00	38.10
26	15.9	254.0	0.000200	41.60	48.00
27	14.2	202.0	0.000158	52.50	60.60
28	12.6	160.0	0.000126	66.20	76.40
29	11.3	127.0	0.0000995	83.40	96.30
30	10.0	101.0	0.0000789	105.00	121.00
31	8.9	79.7	0.0000626	133.00	153.00
32	8.0	63.2	0.0000496	167.00	193.00
33	7.1	50.1	0.0000394	211.00	243.00
34	6.3	39.8	0.0000312	266.00	307.00
35	5.6	31.5	0.0000248	335.00	387.00
36	5.0	25.0	0.0000196	423.00	488.00
37	4.5	19.8	0.0000156	533.00	616.00
38	4.0	15.7	0.0000123	673.00	776.00
39	3.5	12.5	0.0000098	848.00	979.00
40	3.1	9.9	0.0000078	1,070.00	1,230.00

Figure 4-74. *American wire gauge for standard annealed solid copper wire.*

Figure 4-75. *Wire gauge.*

conductor is insulated, the heat generated in the conductor is not so readily removed as it would be if the conductor were not insulated. Thus, to protect the insulation from too much heat, the current through the conductor must be maintained below a certain value.

When electrical conductors are installed in locations where the ambient temperature is relatively high, the heat generated by external sources constitutes an appreciable part of the total conductor heating. Allowance must be made for the influence of external heating on the allowable conductor current, and each case has its own specific limitations. The maximum allowable operating temperature of insulated conductors varies with the type of conductor insulation being used.

Tables are available that list the safe current ratings for various sizes and types of conductors covered with various types of insulation. The chart in *Figure 4-76* shows the current carrying capacity and resistance of copper wire continuous duty wire in bundles at various temperature ratings.

A third factor is the current carrying ability of the conductor. When current is drawn through the conductor, heat is generated. The temperature of the wire rises until the heat radiated, or otherwise dissipated, is equal to the heat generated by the passage of current through the line. If the

Factors Affecting Selection of Conductor Material

Although silver is the best conductor, its cost limits its use to special circuits where a substance with high conductivity is needed. The two most generally used conductors are copper

Wire Size	Continuous Duty Current (Amps)-Wires in Bundles, Groups, Harnesses, or Conduits (See Note #1)			Max. Resistance ohms/1,000 ft@20 °C Tin Plated Conductor (See Note #2)	Nominal Conductor Area (circ.mils)
	Wire Conductor Temperature Rating				
	105 °C	150 °C	200 °C		
24	2.5	4	5	28.40	475
22	3	5	6	16.20	755
20	4	7	9	9.88	1,216
18	6	9	12	6.23	1,900
16	7	11	14	4.81	2,426
14	10	14	18	3.06	3,831
12	13	19	25	2.02	5,874
10	17	26	32	1.26	9,354
8	38	57	71	0.70	16,983
6	50	76	97	0.44	26,818
4	68	103	133	0.28	42,615
2	95	141	179	0.18	66,500
1	113	166	210	0.15	81,700
0	128	192	243	0.12	104,500
00	147	222	285	0.09	133,000
000	172	262	335	0.07	166,500
0000	204	310	395	0.06	210,900

Note 1: Rating is for 70 °C ambient, 33 or more wires in the bundle for sizes 24 through 10, and 9 wires for size 8 and larger, with no more than 20 percent of harness current carrying capacity being used, at an operating altitude of 60,000 feet.

Note 2: For resistance of silver or nickel-plated conductors, see wire specifications.

Figure 4-76. *Current-carrying capacity and resistance of copper wire.*

and aluminum. Each has characteristics that make its use advantageous under certain circumstances; also, each has certain disadvantages.

Copper has a higher conductivity; it is more ductile, can be drawn out, has relatively high tensile strength, and can be easily soldered. It is more expensive and heavier than aluminum.

Although aluminum has only about 60 percent of the conductivity of copper, it is used extensively. Its light weight makes possible long spans, and its relatively large diameter for a given conductivity reduces corona, the discharge of electricity from the wire when it has a high potential. The discharge is greater when smaller diameter wire is used than when larger diameter wire is used. Some bus bars are made of aluminum which has a greater radiating surface than copper for the same conductance. The characteristics of copper and aluminum are compared in *Figure 4-77*.

Characteristic	Copper	Aluminum
Tensile strength (lb/in²)	55,000	25,000
Tensile strength for same conductivity (lb)	55,000	40,000
Weight for same conductivity (lb)	100	48
Cross section for same conductivity (CM)	100	160
Specific resistance (Ω/mil ft)	10.6	17

Figure 4-77. *Characteristics of copper and aluminum.*

Voltage Drop in Aircraft Wire and Cable

The voltage drop in the main power cables from the aircraft generation source or the battery to the bus should not exceed 2 percent of the regulated voltage when the generator is carrying rated current or the battery is being discharged at a 5-minute rate. The 5-minute rate in this case means that the battery should last a minimum of 5 minutes in an emergency, with all battery operated equipment running. *Figure 4-78* shows the recommended maximum voltage drop in the load circuits between the bus and the utilization equipment.

Nominal System Voltage	Allowable Voltage Drop	
	Continuous Operation	Intermittent Operation
14	0.5	1
28	1	2
115	4	8
200	7	14

Figure 4-78. *Recommended voltage drop in load circuits.*

The resistance of the current return path through the aircraft structure is always considered negligible. However, this is based on the assumption that adequate bonding of the structure or a special electric current return path has been provided that is capable of carrying the required electric current with a negligible voltage drop. A resistance measurement of 0.005 ohms from ground point of the generator or battery to ground terminal of any electrical device is considered satisfactory.

Another satisfactory method of determining circuit resistance is to check the voltage drop across the circuit. If the voltage drop does not exceed the limit established by the aircraft or product manufacturer, the resistance value for the circuit is considered satisfactory. When using the voltage drop method of checking a circuit, the input voltage must be maintained at a constant value.

The graph in *Figure 4-79* applies to copper conductors carrying direct current. To select the correct size of conductor, two major requirements must be met. First, the size must be sufficient to prevent an excessive voltage drop while carrying the required current over the required distance. Second, the size must be sufficient to prevent overheating of the cable while carrying the required current. The graphs in *Figures 4-79* and *4-80* can simplify these determinations. To use this graph to select the proper size of conductor, the following must be known:

1. The conductor length in feet
2. The number of amperes of current to be carried
3. The amount of voltage drop permitted
4. Whether the current to be carried is intermittent or continuous
5. The estimated or measured temperature of the conductor
6. Whether the wire to be installed is in a conduit or in a bundle
7. Whether it is a single conductor in free air

Suppose that you want to install a 50-foot conductor from the aircraft bus to the equipment in a 28-volt system. For this length, a 1-volt drop is permissible for continuous operation with a conductor temperature of 20 °C or less. By referring to the chart in *Figure 4-79*, the maximum number of feet a conductor may be run carrying a specified current with a 1-volt drop can be determined. In this example, the number 50 is selected.

Assuming the current required by the equipment is 20 amperes, the line indicating the value of 20 amperes should be selected from the diagonal lines. Follow this diagonal line downward until it intersects the horizontal line number 50. From this point, drop straight down to the bottom of the graph to find that a conductor between size No. 8 and No. 10 is required to prevent a greater drop than 1 volt. Since the

Figure 4-79. *Conductor graph—continuous flow.*

indicated value is between two numbers, the larger size, No. 8, should be selected. This is the smallest size that should be used to avoid an excessive voltage drop.

If the installation is for equipment having only an intermittent (maximum 2 minutes) requirement for power, the graph in *Figure 4-80* is used in the same manner.

Conductor Insulation

Two fundamental properties of insulation materials (e.g., rubber, glass, asbestos, and plastic) are insulation resistance and dielectric strength. These are entirely different and distinct properties.

Insulation resistance is the resistance to current leakage through and over the surface of insulation materials. Insulation resistance can be measured with a megger without damaging the insulation. This serves as a useful guide in determining the general condition of insulation. However, the data obtained in this manner may not give a true picture of the condition of the insulation. Clean, dry insulation having cracks or other faults may show a high value of insulation resistance but would not be suitable for use.

Dielectric strength is the ability of the insulator to withstand potential difference and is usually expressed in terms of the voltage at which the insulation fails due to electrostatic stress. Maximum dielectric strength values can be measured by raising the voltage of a test sample until the insulation breaks down.

Because of the expense of insulation, its stiffening effect, and the great variety of physical and electrical conditions under which the conductors are operated, only the necessary minimum insulation is applied for any particular type of cable designed to do a specific job.

The type of conductor insulation material varies with the type of installation. Rubber, silk, and paper insulation are no longer used extensively in aircraft systems. More common today are such materials as vinyl, cotton, nylon, Teflon, and Rockbestos.

Figure 4-80. *Conductor graph—intermittent flow.*

Identifying Wire and Cable

To aid in testing and repair operations, many maintenance activities mark wire or cable with a combination of letters and numbers that identify the wire, the circuit it belongs to, the gauge number, and other information necessary to relate the wire or cable to a wiring diagram. Such markings are the identification code.

There is no standard procedure for marking and identifying wiring; each manufacturer normally develops its own identification code. *Figure 4-81* illustrates one identification system and shows the usual spacing in marking a wire. Some system components, especially plugs and jacks, are identified by a letter or group of letters and numbers added to the basic identification number. These letters and numbers may indicate the location of the component in the system. Interconnected cables are also marked in some systems to indicate location, proper termination, and use. In any system, the marking should be legible, and the stamping color should contrast with the color of the wire insulation. For example, use black stamping with light-colored backgrounds, or white stamping on dark-colored backgrounds.

Most manufacturers mark the wires at intervals of not more than 15 inches lengthwise and within 3 inches of each junction or terminating point. *[Figure 4-82]*

Coaxial cable and wires at terminal blocks and junction boxes are often identified by marking or stamping a wiring sleeve rather than the wire itself. For general purpose wiring, flexible vinyl sleeving, either clear or white opaque, is commonly used. For high-temperature applications, silicone rubber or silicone fiberglass sleeving is recommended. Where resistance to synthetic hydraulic fluids or other solvents is necessary, either clear or white opaque nylon sleeving can be used.

Figure 4-81. *Spacing of printed identification marks.*

Figure 4-82. *Wire identification at a terminal block.*

While the preferred method is to stamp the identification marking directly on the wire or on sleeving, other methods are often employed. One method uses a marked sleeve tied in place. The other uses a pressure-sensitive tape. *[Figure 4-83]*

Figure 4-83. *Alternate methods of identifying wire bundles.*

Electrical Wiring Installation

The following recommended procedures for installing aircraft electrical wiring are typical of those used on most types of aircraft. For purposes of this discussion, the following definitions are applicable:

1. Open wiring—any wire, wire group, or wire bundle not enclosed in conduit.
2. Wire group—two or more wires in the same location, tied together to identity the group.
3. Wire bundle—two or more wire groups tied together because they are going in the same direction at the point where the tie is located. The bundle facilitates maintenance.
4. Electrically protected wiring—wires that include in the circuit protections against overloading, such as fuses, circuit breakers, or other limiting devices.
5. Electrically unprotected wiring—wires, generally from generators to main bus distribution points, that do not have protection, such as fuses, circuit breakers, or other current-limiting devices.

Wire Groups and Bundles

Grouping or bundling certain wires, such as electrically unprotected power wiring and wiring to duplicate vital equipment, should be avoided. Wire bundles should generally be limited in size to a bundle of 75 wires, or 2 inches in diameter where practicable. When several wires are grouped at junction boxes, terminal blocks, panels, etc., the identity of the group within a bundle can be retained. *[Figure 4-84]*

Figure 4-84. *Group and bundle ties.*

Twisting Wires

When specified on the engineering drawing, parallel wires must be twisted. The most common examples are:

1. Wiring in the vicinity of magnetic compass or flux valve,
2. Three-phase distribution wiring, and
3. Certain other wires (usually radio wiring).

Twist the wires so that they lie snugly against each other, making approximately the number of twists per foot as listed in *Figure 4-85*. Always check wire insulation for damage after twisting. If the insulation is torn or frayed, replace the wire.

	#22	#20	#18	#16	#14	#12	#10	#8	#6	#4
2 Wires	10	10	9	8	7 1/2	7	6 1/2	6	5	4
3 Wires	10	10	8 1/2	7	6 1/2	6	5 1/2	5	4	3

Figure 4-85. *Recommended number of twists per foot.*

Spliced Connections in Wire Bundles

Spliced connections in wire groups or bundles should be located so that they can be easily inspected. Splices should also be staggered so that the bundle does not become excessively enlarged. *[Figure 4-86]* All noninsulated splices should be covered with plastic, securely tied at both ends.

Slack in Wiring Bundles

Single wires or wire bundles should not be installed with excessive slack. Slack between supports should normally not exceed ½ inch. This is the maximum it should be possible to deflect the wire with normal hand force. However, this may be exceeded if the wire bundle is thin and the clamps are far apart. But the slack should never be so great that the wire bundle can abrade against any surface it touches. *[Figure 4-87]* A sufficient amount of slack should be allowed near each end of a bundle to:

1. Permit easy maintenance;
2. Allow replacement of terminals;
3. Present mechanical strain on the wires, wire junctions, or supports;
4. Permit free movement of shock and vibration-mounted equipment; and
5. Permit shifting of equipment for purposes of maintenance.

Bend Radii

Bends in wire groups or bundles should not be less than ten times the outside diameter of the wire group or bundle. However, at terminal strips, where wire is suitably supported at each end of the bend, a minimum radius of three times the outside diameter of the wire, or wire bundle, is usually acceptable. There are exceptions to these guidelines in the case of certain types of cable; for example, coaxial cable should never be bent to a smaller radius than six times the outside diameter.

Routing and Installation

All wiring should be installed so that it is mechanically and electrically sound and neat in appearance. Whenever practicable, wires and bundles should be routed parallel with, or at right angles to, the stringers or ribs of the area involved. An exception to this general rule is the coaxial cables, which are routed as directly as possible.

The wiring must be adequately supported throughout its length. A sufficient number of supports must be provided to prevent undue vibration of the unsupported lengths. All wires and wire groups should be routed and installed to protect them from:

1. Chafing or abrasion;
2. High temperature;
3. Being used as handholds, or as support for personal belongings and equipment;
4. Damage by personnel moving within the aircraft;
5. Damage from cargo stowage or shifting;
6. Damage from battery acid fumes, spray, or spillage; and
7. Damage from solvents and fluids.

Figure 4-86. *Staggered splices in wire bundle.*

Figure 4-87. *Slack in wire bundle between supports.*

Protection Against Chafing

Wires and wire groups should be installed so that they are protected against chafing or abrasion in those locations where contact with sharp surfaces or other wires would damage the insulation. Damage to the insulation can cause short circuits, malfunctions, or inadvertent operation of equipment. Cable clamps should be used to support wire bundles at each hole through a bulkhead. *[Figure 4-88]* If wires come closer than ¼ inch to the edge of the hole, a suitable grommet is used in the hole. *[Figure 4-89]*

Figure 4-88. *Cable clamp at bulkhead hole.*

Figure 4-89. *Cable clamp and grommet at bulkhead hole.*

Sometimes, it is necessary to cut nylon or rubber grommets to facilitate installation. In these instances, after insertion, the grommet can be secured in place with general purpose cement. The slot should be at the top of the hole, and the cut should be made at an angle of 45° to the axis of the wire bundle hole.

Protection Against High Temperature

To prevent insulation deterioration, wires should be kept separate from high-temperature equipment, such as resistors, exhaust stacks, heating ducts. The amount of separation is usually specified by engineering drawings. Some wires must be run through hot areas. These wires must be insulated with high-temperature rated material, such as asbestos, fiberglass, or Teflon. Additional protection is also often required in the form of conduits. A low-temperature insulated wire should never be used to replace a high-temperature insulated wire.

Many coaxial cables have soft plastic insulation, such as polyethylene, that is especially subject to deformation and deterioration at elevated temperatures. All high-temperature areas should be avoided when installing these cables.

Additional abrasion protection should be given to asbestos wires enclosed in conduit. Either conduit with a high temperature rubber liner should be used or asbestos wires can be enclosed individually in high-temperature plastic tubes before being installed in the conduit.

Protection Against Solvents and Fluids

Avoid installing wires in areas where they are subjected to damage from fluids. Wires should not be placed in the lowest four inches of the aircraft fuselage, except those that must terminate in that area. If there is a possibility that wiring without a protective nylon outer jacket may be soaked with fluids, plastic tubing should be used to protect it. This tubing should extend past the exposure area in both directions and should be tied at each end. If the wire has a low point between the tubing ends, provide a ⅛-inch drainage hole. *[Figure 4-90]* This hole should be punched into the tubing after the installation is complete and the low point definitely established by using a hole punch to cut a half circle. Care should be taken not to damage any wires inside the tubing when using the punch.

Wire should never be routed below a battery. All wires in the vicinity of a battery should be inspected frequently. Wires discolored by battery fumes should be replaced.

4-53

Figure 4-90. *Drainage hole in low point of tubing.*

Protection of Wires in Wheel Well Area

Wires located in wheel wells are subject to many additional hazards, such as exposure to fluids, pinching, and severe flexing in service. All wire bundles should be protected by sleeves of flexible tubing securely held at each end. There should be no relative movement at points where flexible tubing is secured. These wires and the insulating tubing should be inspected carefully at very frequent intervals, and wires or tubing should be replaced at the first sign of wear. There should be no strain on attachments when parts are fully extended, but slack should not be excessive.

Routing Precautions

When wiring must be routed parallel to combustible fluid or oxygen lines for short distances, as much separation as possible should be maintained. The wires should be on a level with, or above, the plumbing lines. Clamps should be spaced so that if a wire is broken at a clamp, it will not contact the line. Where a 6-inch separation is not possible, both the wire bundle and the plumbing line can be clamped to the same structure to prevent any relative motion. If the separation is less than 2 inches but more than ½ inch, two cable clamps back to back can be used to maintain a rigid separation only and not for support of the bundle. *[Figure 4-91]* No wire should be routed so that it is located nearer than ½ inch to a plumbing line, nor should a wire or wire bundle be supported from a plumbing line that carries flammable fluids or oxygen. Wiring should be routed to maintain a minimum clearance of at least 3 inches from control cables. If this cannot be accomplished, mechanical guards should be installed to prevent contact between wiring and control cables.

Figure 4-91. *Separation of wires from plumbing lines.*

Installation of Cable Clamps

Cable clamps should be installed with regard to the proper mounting angle. *[Figure 4-92]* The mounting screw should be above the wire bundle. It is also desirable that the back of the cable clamp rest against a structural member where practicable. *Figure 4-93* shows some typical mounting hardware used in installing cable clamps. Be sure that wires are not pinched in cable clamps. Where possible, mount them directly to structural members. *[Figure 4-94]*

Figure 4-92. *Proper mounting angle for cable clamps.*

Clamps can be used with rubber cushions to secure wire bundles to tubular structures. *[Figure 4-95]* Such clamps must fit tightly but should not be deformed when locked in place.

Figure 4-93. *Typical mounting hardware for cable clamps.*

Figure 4-94. *Mounting cable clamps to structure.*

Lacing and Tying Wire Bundles

Wire groups and bundles are laced or tied with cord to provide ease of installation, maintenance, and inspection. This section describes and illustrates recommended procedures for lacing and tying wires with knots that hold tightly under all conditions. For the purposes of this discussion, the following terms are defined:

1. Tying is the securing together of a group or bundle of wires by individual pieces of cord tied around the group or bundle at regular intervals.
2. Lacing is the securing together of a group or bundle of wires by a continuous piece of cord forming loops at regular intervals around the group or bundle.

Figure 4-95. *Installing cable clamps to tubular structure.*

The material used for lacing and tying is either cotton or nylon cord. Nylon cord is moisture- and fungus-resistant, but cotton cord must be waxed before using to give it these necessary protective characteristics.

Single-Cord Lacing

Figure 4-96 shows the steps in lacing a wire bundle with a single cord. The lacing procedure is started at the thick end of the wire group or bundle with a knot consisting of a clove hitch with an extra loop. The lacing is then continued at regular intervals with half hitches along the wire group or bundle and at each point where a wire or wire group branches off. The half hitches should be spaced so that the bundle is neat and secure.

4-55

Figure 4-96. *Single cord lacing.*

The lacing is ended by tying a knot consisting of a clove hitch with an extra loop. After the knot is tied, the free ends of the lacing cord should be trimmed to approximately ⅜ inch.

Double-Cord Lacing

Figure 4-97 illustrates the procedure for double-cord lacing. The lacing is started at the thick end of the wire group or bundle with a bowline-on-a-bight knot. *[Figure 4-97A]* At regular intervals along the wire group or bundle, and at each point where a wire branches off, the lacing is continued using half hitches, with both cords held firmly together. The half hitches should be spaced so that the group or bundle is neat and secure. The lacing is ended with a knot consisting of a half hitch, continuing one of the cords clockwise and the other counterclockwise and then tying the cord ends with a square knot. The free ends of the lacing cord should be trimmed to approximately ⅜ inch.

Lacing Branch-Offs

Figure 4-98 illustrates a recommended procedure for lacing a wire group that branches off the main wire bundle. The branch-off lacing is started with a knot located on the main bundle just past the branch-off point. Continue the lacing along the branched-off wire group using regularly spaced half hitches. If a double cord is used, both cords should be held snugly together. The half hitches should be spaced to lace the bundle neatly and securely. End the lacing with the regular terminal knot used in single- or double-cord lacing, as applicable, and trim the free ends of the lacing cord neatly.

Tying

All wire groups or bundles should be tied where supports are more than 12 inches apart. Ties are made using waxed cotton cord, nylon cord, or fiberglass cord. Some manufacturers permit the use of pressure-sensitive vinyl electrical tape. When permitted, the tape should be wrapped three turns around the bundle and the ends heat sealed to prevent unwinding of the tape. *Figure 4-99* illustrates a recommended procedure for tying a wire group or bundle. The tie is started by wrapping the cord around the wire group to tie a clove-hitch knot. Then, a square knot with an extra loop is tied and the free ends of the cord trimmed.

Temporary ties are sometimes used in making up and installing wire groups and bundles. Colored cord is normally used to make temporary ties, since they are removed when the installation is complete.

Whether lacing or tying, bundles should be secured tightly enough to prevent slipping, but not so tightly that the cord cuts into or deforms the insulation. This applies especially to coaxial cable, which has a soft dielectric insulation between the inner and outer conductor. Coxial cables have been damaged by the use of lacing materials or by methods of lacing or tying wire bundles that cause a concentrated force on the cable insulation. Elastic lacing materials, small-diameter lacing cord, and excessive tightening deform the interconductor insulation and result in short circuits or impedance changes. Flat nylon braided waxed lacing tape

Figure 4-97. *Double cord lacing.*

Figure 4-98. *Lacing a branch off.*

should be used for lacing or tying any wire bundles containing coaxial cables.

The part of a wire group or bundle located inside a conduit is not tied or laced; however, wire groups or bundles inside enclosures, such as junction boxes, should be laced only.

Cutting Wire and Cable

To make installation, maintenance, and repair easier, runs of wire and cable in aircraft are broken at specified locations by junctions, such as connectors, terminal blocks, or buses.

Figure 4-99. *Tying a wire group of bundle.*

Before assembly to these junctions, wires and cables must be cut to length.

All wires and cables should be cut to the lengths specified on drawings and wiring diagrams. The cut should be made clean and square, and the wire or cable should not be deformed. If necessary, large diameter wire should be reshaped after cutting. Good cuts can be made only if the blades of cutting tools are sharp and free from nicks. A dull blade deforms and extrudes wire ends.

Stripping Wire and Cable

Nearly all wire and cable used as electrical conductors are covered with some type of insulation. In order to make electrical connections with the wire, a part of this insulation must be removed to expose the bare conductor. Copper wire can be stripped in a number of ways depending on the size and insulation. *Figure 4-100* lists some types of stripping tools recommended for various wire sizes and types of insulation. Aluminum wire must be stripped using extreme care, since individual strands break very easily after being nicked.

Stripper	Wire Size	Insulations
Hot blade	#26–#4	All except asbestos
Rotary, electric	#26–#4	All
Bench	#20–#6	All
Hand pliers	#26–#8	All
Knife	#2–#0000	All

Figure 4-100. *Wire strippers for copper wire.*

The following general precautions are recommended when stripping any type of wire:

1. When using any type of wire stripper, hold the wire so that it is perpendicular to the cutting blades.
2. Adjust automatic stripping tools carefully; follow the manufacturer's instructions to avoid nicking, cutting, or otherwise damaging strands. This is especially important for aluminum wires and for copper wires smaller than No. 10. Examine stripped wires for damage. Cut off and restrip, if length is sufficient, or reject and replace any wires with more than the allowable number of nicked or broken strands listed in the manufacturer's instructions.
3. Make sure insulation is clean cut with no frayed or ragged edges. Trim, if necessary.
4. Make sure all insulation is removed from stripped area. Some types of wires are supplied with a transparent layer of insulation between the conductor and the primary insulation. If this is present, remove it.
5. When using hand wire strippers to remove lengths of insulation longer than ¾ inch, it is easier to accomplish in two or more operations.
6. Retwist copper strands by hand or with pliers, if necessary, to restore natural lay and tightness of strands.

A pair of hand wire strippers is shown in *Figure 4-101*.

Figure 4-101. *Light duty hand wire strippers.*

This tool is commonly used to strip most types of wire. The following general procedures describe the steps for stripping wire with a hand stripper. *[Figure 4-102]*

1. Insert wire into exact center of correct cutting slot for wire size to be stripped. Each slot is marked with wire size.
2. Close handles together as far as they will go.
3. Release handles allowing wire holder to return to the open position.
4. Remove stripped wire.

Solderless Terminals and Splices

Splicing of electrical cable should be kept to a minimum and avoided entirely in locations subject to extreme vibrations. Individual wires in a group or bundle can usually be spliced if the completed splice is located where it can be inspected periodically. The splices should be staggered so that the bundle does not become excessively enlarged. Many types of aircraft splice connectors are available for splicing individual wires. Self-insulated splice connectors are usually preferred; however, a noninsulated splice connector can be used if the splice is covered with plastic sleeving secured at both ends. Solder splices may be used, but they are particularly brittle and not recommended.

Electric wires are terminated with solderless terminal lugs to permit easy and efficient connection to and disconnection from terminal blocks, bus bars, or other electrical equipment. Solderless splices join electric wires to form permanent

Figure 4-102. *Stripping wire with hand strippers.*

continuous runs. Solderless terminal lugs and splices are made of copper or aluminum and are preinsulated or uninsulated, depending on the desired application.

Terminal lugs are generally available in three types for use in different space conditions. These are the flag, straight, and right-angle lugs. Terminal lugs are crimped, sometimes called staked or swaged, to the wires by means of hand or power crimping tools.

Copper Wire Terminals

Copper wires are terminated with solderless, preinsulated straight copper terminal lugs. The insulation is part of the terminal lug and extends beyond its barrel so that it covers a portion of the wire insulation, making the use of an insulation sleeve unnecessary. *[Figure 4-103]*

Figure 4-103. *Preinsulated terminal lug.*

In addition, preinsulated terminal lugs contain an insulation grip (a metal reinforcing sleeve) beneath the insulation for extra gripping strength on the wire insulation. Preinsulated terminals accommodate more than one size of wire; the insulation is usually color coded to identify the wire sizes that can be terminated with each of the terminal lug sizes.

Crimping Tools

Hand, portable power, and stationary power tools are available for crimping terminal lugs. These tools crimp the barrel of the terminal lug to the conductor and simultaneously crimp the insulation grip to the wire insulation.

Hand crimping tools all have a self-locking ratchet that prevents opening the tool until the crimp is complete. Some hand crimping tools are equipped with a nest of various size inserts to fit different size terminal lugs. Others are used on one terminal lug size only. All types of hand crimping tools are checked by gauges for proper adjustment of crimping jaws.

Figure 4-104 shows a terminal lug inserted into a hand tool. The following general guidelines outline the crimping procedure:

1. Strip the wire insulation to proper length.
2. Insert the terminal lug, tongue first, into the hand tool barrel crimping jaws until the terminal lug barrel butts flush against the tool stop.

Figure 4-104. *Inserting terminal lug into hand tool.*

3. Insert the stripped wire into the terminal lug barrel until the wire insulation butts flush against the end of the barrel.
4. Squeeze the tool handles until the ratchet releases.
5. Remove the completed assembly and examine it for proper crimp.

Some types of uninsulated terminal lugs are insulated after assembly to a wire by means of pieces of transparent flexible tubing called sleeves. The sleeve provides electrical and mechanical protection at the connection. When the size of the sleeves used is such that it fits tightly over the terminal lug, the sleeves need not be tied; otherwise, it should be tied with lacing cord *[Figure 4-105]*

Figure 4-105. *Insulating sleeves.*

Aluminum Wire Terminals

Aluminum wire is being used increasingly in aircraft systems because of its weight advantage over copper. However, bending aluminum causes "work hardening" of the metal, making it brittle. This results in failure or breakage of strands much sooner than in a similar case with copper wire. Aluminum also forms a high-resistant oxide film immediately upon exposure to air. To compensate for these disadvantages, it is important to use the most reliable installation procedures. Only aluminum terminal lugs are used to terminate aluminum wires.

All aluminum terminals incorporate an inspection hole that permits checking the depth of wire insertion. *[Figure 4-106]* The barrel of aluminum terminal lugs is filled with a petrolatum-zinc dust compound. This compound removes the oxide film from the aluminum by a grinding process during the crimping operation. The compound also minimizes later oxidation of the completed connection by excluding moisture and air. The compound is retained inside the terminal lug barrel by a plastic or foil seal at the end of the barrel.

Splicing Copper Wires Using Preinsulated Wires

Preinsulated permanent copper splices join small wires of sizes 22 through 10. Each splice size can be used for more than one wire size. Splices are usually color coded in the same manner as preinsulated, small copper terminal lugs. Some splices are insulated with white plastic. Splices are also used to reduce wire sizes *[Figure 4-107]*

Crimping tools are used to accomplish this type of splice. The crimping procedures are the same as those used for terminal lugs, except that the crimping operation must be done twice, one for each end of the splice.

Emergency Splicing Repairs

Broken wires can be repaired by means of crimped splices, by using terminal lugs from which the tongue has been cut off, or by soldering together and potting broken strands. These repairs are applicable to copper wire. Damaged aluminum wire must not be temporarily spliced. These repairs are for temporary emergency use only and should be replaced as soon as possible with permanent repairs. Since some manufacturers prohibit splicing, the applicable manufacturer's instructions should always be consulted.

Splicing with Solder and Potting Compound

When neither a permanent splice nor a terminal lug is available, a broken wire can be repaired as follows *[Figure 4-108]*:

1. Install a piece of plastic sleeving about 3 inches long and of the proper diameter to fit loosely over the insulation on one piece of the broken wire.
2. Strip approximately 1½ inches from each broken end of the wire.

Figure 4-106. *Inserting aluminum wire into aluminum terminal lugs.*

Figure 4-107. *Reducing wire size with a permanent splice.*

3. Lay the stripped ends side by side and twist one wire around the other with approximately four turns.

4. Twist the free end of the second wire around the first wire with approximately four turns. Solder the wire turns together using $^{60}/_{40}$ tin-lead resin-core solder.

5. When solder is cool, draw the sleeve over the soldered wires and tie at one end. If potting compound is available, fill the sleeve with potting material and tie securely.

Figure 4-108. *Repairing broken wire by soldering and potting.*

6. Allow the potting compound to set without touching for 4 hours. Full cure and electrical characteristics are achieved in 24 hours.

Connecting Terminal Lugs to Terminal Blocks

Terminal lugs should be installed on terminal blocks in such a manner that they are locked against movement in the direction of loosening. *[Figure 4-109]*

Figure 4-109. *Connecting terminals to terminal block.*

Terminal blocks are normally supplied with studs secured in place by a plain washer, an external tooth lockwasher, and a nut. In connecting terminals, a recommended practice is to place copper terminal lugs directly on top of the nut, followed with a plain washer and elastic stop nut, or with a plain washer, split steel lockwasher, and plain nut.

Aluminum terminal lugs should be placed over a plated brass plain washer, followed with another plated brass plain washer, split steel lockwasher, and plain nut or elastic stop nut. The plated brass washer should have a diameter equal to the tongue width of the aluminum terminal lug. Consult the manufacturer's instructions for recommended dimensions of these plated brass washers. Do not place any washer in the current path between two aluminum terminal lugs or between two copper terminal lugs. Also, do not place a lockwasher directly against the tongue or pad of the aluminum terminal.

To join a copper terminal lug to an aluminum terminal lug, place a plated brass plain washer over the nut that holds the stud in place; follow with the aluminum terminal lug, a plated brass plain washer, the copper terminal lug, plain washer, split steel lockwasher and plain nut or self-locking, all metal nut. As a general rule, use a torque wrench to tighten nuts to ensure sufficient contact pressure. Manufacturer's instructions provide installation torques for all types of terminals.

Bonding and Grounding

Bonding is the electrical connecting of two or more conducting objects not otherwise connected adequately. Grounding is the electrical connecting of a conducting object to the primary structure for return of current. Primary structure is the main frame, fuselage, or wing structure of the aircraft. Bonding and grounding connections are made in aircraft electrical systems to:

1. Protect aircraft and personnel against hazards from lightning discharge,
2. Provide current return paths,
3. Prevent development of radio-frequency potentials,
4. Protect personnel from shock hazard,
5. Provide stability of radio transmission and reception, and
6. Prevent accumulation of static charge.

General Bonding and Grounding Procedures

The following general procedures and precautions are recommended when making bonding or grounding connections.

1. Bond or ground parts to the primary aircraft structure, where practicable.
2. Make bonding or grounding connections in such a manner that no part of the aircraft structure is weakened.
3. Bond parts individually, if possible.
4. Install bonding or grounding connections against smooth, clean surfaces.
5. Install bonding or grounding connections so that vibration, expansion or contraction, or relative movement in normal service does not break or loosen the connection.
6. Install bonding and grounding connections in protected areas whenever possible.

Bonding jumpers should be kept as short as practicable, and installed so that the resistance of each connection does not exceed 0.003 ohm. The jumper should not interfere with the operation of movable aircraft elements, such as surface controls; normal movement of these elements should not result in damage to the bonding jumper.

To be sure a low resistance connection has been made, nonconducting finishes, such as paint and anodizing films, should be removed from the surface to be contacted by the bonding terminal.

Electrolytic action can rapidly corrode a bonding connection if suitable precautions are not observed. Aluminum alloy jumpers are recommended for most cases; however, copper jumpers can be used to bond together parts made of stainless steel, cadmium-plated steel, copper, brass, or bronze. Where contact between dissimilar metals cannot be avoided, the choice of jumper and hardware should be such that corrosion is minimized, and the part most likely to corrode is the jumper or associated hardware. Parts A and B of *Figure 4-110* illustrate some proper hardware combinations for making bonding connections. At locations where finishes are removed, a protective finish should be applied to the completed connection to prevent corrosion.

The use of solder to attach bonding jumpers should be avoided. Tubular members should be bonded by means of clamps to which the jumper is attached. The proper choice of clamp material minimizes the probability of corrosion. When bonding jumpers carry a substantial amount of ground return current, the current rating of the jumper should be adequate, and it should be determined that a negligible voltage drop is produced.

Bonding and grounding connections are normally made to flat surfaces by means of through-bolts or screws where there is easy access for installation. The general types of bolted connections are:

1. In making a stud connection, a bolt or screw is locked securely to the structure becoming a stud. *[Figure 4-111]* Grounding or bonding jumpers can be removed or added to the shank of the stud without removing the stud from the structure.

2. Nutplates are used where access to the nut for repairs is difficult. Nutplates are riveted or welded to a clean area of the structure. *[Figure 4-112]*

Bonding and grounding connections are also made to a tab riveted to a structure. *[Figure 4-113]* In such cases, it is important to clean the bonding or grounding surface and make the connection as though the connection were being made to the structure. If it is necessary to remove the tab for any reason, the rivets should be replaced with rivets one size larger, and the mating surfaces of the structure and the tab should be clean and free of anodic film.

Bonding or grounding connections can be made to aluminum alloy, magnesium, or corrosion-resistant steel tubular structure. *Figure 4-114* shows the arrangement of hardware for bonding with an aluminum jumper. Because of the ease with which aluminum is deformed, it is necessary to distribute screw and nut pressure by means of plain washers.

Figure 4-110. *Hardware combinations used in making bonding connections.*

Hardware used to make bonding or grounding connections should be selected on the basis of mechanical strength, current to be carried, and ease of installation. If connection is made by aluminum or copper jumpers to the structure of

Figure 4-111. *Stud bonding or grounding to a flat surface.*

Figure 4-112. *Nut plate bonding or grounding to flat surface.*

Figure 4-113. *Bonding or grounding tab riveted to structure.*

Figure 4-114. *Bonding or grounding connections to a cylindrical structure.*

a dissimilar material, a washer of suitable material should be installed between the dissimilar metals so that any corrosion occurs on the washer.

Hardware material and finish should be selected on the basis of the material of the structure to which attachment is made and on the material of the jumper and terminal specified for the bonding or grounding connection. Either a screw or bolt of the proper size for the specified jumper terminal should be used. When repairing or replacing existing bonding or grounding connections, the same type of hardware used in the original connection should always be used.

Connectors

Connectors (plugs and receptacles) facilitate maintenance when frequent disconnection is required. Since the cable is soldered to the connector inserts, the joints should be individually installed and the cable bundle firmly supported to avoid damage by vibration. Connectors have been particularly vulnerable to corrosion in the past, due to condensation within the shell. Special connectors with waterproof features have been developed that may replace nonwaterproof plugs in areas where moisture causes a problem. A connector of the same basic type and design should be used when replacing a connector. Connectors that are susceptible to corrosion difficulties may be treated with a chemically inert waterproof jelly. When replacing connector assemblies, the socket-type insert should be used on the half that is "live" or "hot" after the connector is disconnected to prevent unintentional grounding.

Types of Connectors

Connectors are identified by Air Force Navy (AN) numbers and are divided into classes with the manufacturer's variations in each class. The manufacturer's variations are differences in appearance and in the method of meeting a specification. Some commonly used connectors are shown in *Figure 4-115*. There are five basic classes of AN connectors used in most aircraft. Each class of connector has slightly different construction characteristics. Classes A, B, C, and D are made of aluminum, and class K is made of steel.

1. Class A—solid, one-piece back shell general-purpose connector.

2. Class B—connector back shell separates into two parts lengthwise. Used primarily where it is important that the soldered connectors are readily accessible. The back shell is held together by a threaded ring or by screws.

3. Class C—a pressurized connector with inserts that are not removable. Similar to a class A connector in appearance, but the inside sealing arrangement is sometimes different. It is used on walls or bulkheads of pressurized equipment.

4. Class D—moisture and vibration resistant connector that has a sealing grommet in the back shell. Wires are

Figure 4-115. *AN connectors.*

threaded through tight fitting holes in the grommet, sealing against moisture.

5. Class K—a fireproof connector used in areas where it is vital that the electric current is not interrupted, even though the connector may be exposed to continuous open flame. Wires are crimped to the pin or socket contacts and the shells are made of steel. This class of connector is normally longer than other connectors.

Connector Identification

Code letters and numbers are marked on the coupling ring or shell to identify a connector. This code provides all the information necessary to obtain the correct replacement for a defective or damaged part. *[Figure 4-116]*

Figure 4-116. *AN connector markings.*

Many special-purpose connectors have been designed for use in aircraft applications. These include subminiature and rectangular shell connectors, and connectors with short body shells, or of split-shell construction.

Installation of Connectors

The following procedures outline one recommended method of assembling connectors to receptacles:

1. Locate the proper position of the plug in relation to the receptacle by aligning the key of one part with the groove or keyway of the other part.
2. Start the plug into the receptacle with a slight forward pressure and engage the threads of the coupling ring and receptacle.
3. Alternately push in the plug and tighten the coupling ring until the plug is completely seated.
4. Use connector pliers to tighten coupling rings one-sixteenth to one-eighth turn beyond finger tight if space around the connector is too small to obtain a good finger grip.
5. Never use force to mate connectors to receptacles.

Do not hammer a plug into its receptacle and never use a torque wrench or pliers to lock coupling rings.

A connector is generally disassembled from a receptacle in the following manner:

1. Use connector pliers to loosen coupling rings that are too tight to be loosened by hand.
2. Alternately pull on the plug body and unscrew the coupling ring until the connector is separated.
3. Protect disconnected plugs and receptacles with caps or plastic bags to keep debris from entering and causing faults.
4. Do not use excessive force and do not pull on attached wires.

Conduit

Conduit is used in aircraft installations for the mechanical protection of wires and cables. It is available in metallic and nonmetallic materials and in both rigid and flexible form.

When selecting conduit size for a specific cable bundle application, it is common practice to allow for ease in maintenance and possible future circuit expansion by specifying the conduit inner diameter about 25 percent larger than the maximum diameter of the conductor bundle. The nominal diameter of a rigid metallic conduit is the outside diameter. Therefore, to obtain the inside diameter, subtract twice the tube wall thickness.

From the abrasion standpoint, the conductor is vulnerable at the ends of the conduit. Suitable fittings are affixed to conduit ends in such a manner that a smooth surface comes in contact with the conductor within the conduit. When fittings are not used, the conduit end should be flared to prevent wire insulation damage. The conduit is supported by clamps along the conduit run.

Many of the common conduit installation problems can be avoided by proper attention to the following details:

1. Do not locate conduit where it can be used as a handhold or footstep.
2. Provide drain holes at the lowest point in a conduit run. Drilling burrs should be carefully removed from the drain holes.
3. Support the conduit to prevent chafing against the structure and to avoid stressing its end fittings.

Damaged conduit sections should be repaired to prevent injury to the wires or wire bundle. The minimum acceptable tube bend radii for rigid conduit as prescribed by the manufacturer's instructions should be carefully followed. Kinked or wrinkled bends in a rigid conduit are normally not considered acceptable.

Flexible aluminum conduit is widely available in two types: bare flexible and rubber-covered conduit. Flexible brass conduit is normally used instead of flexible aluminum where it is necessary to minimize radio interference. Flexible conduit may be used where it is impractical to use rigid conduit, such as areas that have motion between conduit ends or where complex bends are necessary. Transparent adhesive tape is recommended when cutting flexible conduit with a hacksaw to minimize fraying of the braid.

Electrical Equipment Installation

This section provides general procedures and safety precautions for installation of commonly used aircraft electrical equipment and components. Electrical load limits, acceptable means of controlling or monitoring electrical loads, and circuit protection devices are subjects with which mechanics must be familiar to properly install and maintain aircraft electrical systems.

Electrical Load Limits

When installing additional electrical equipment that consumes electrical power in an aircraft, the total electrical load must be safely controlled or managed within the rated limits of the affected components of the aircraft's power-supply system.

Before any aircraft electrical load is increased, the associated wires, cables, and circuit-protection devices, such as fuses or circuit breakers, should be checked to determine that the new electrical load—previous maximum load plus added load—does not exceed the rated limits of the existing wires, cables, or protection devices.

The generator or alternator output ratings prescribed by the manufacturer should be compared with the electrical loads that can be imposed on the affected generator or alternator by installed equipment. When the comparison shows that the probable total connected electrical load can exceed the output load limits of the generator(s) or alternator(s), the load should be reduced so that an overload cannot occur. When a storage battery is part of the electrical power system, ensure that the battery is continuously charged in flight, except when short intermittent loads are connected, such as a radio transmitter, a landing gear motor, or other similar devices that may place short-time demand loads on the battery.

Controlling or Monitoring the Electrical Load

Placards are recommended to inform crewmembers of an aircraft about the combinations of loads that can safely be connected to the power source.

In installations where the ammeter is in the battery lead and the regulator system limits the maximum current that the generator or alternator can deliver, a voltmeter can be installed on the system bus. As long as the ammeter does not read discharge, except for short intermittent loads such as operating the gear and flaps, and the voltmeter remains at system voltage, the generator or alternator is not overloaded.

The ammeter can be redlined at 100 percent of the generator or alternator rating in installations with the ammeter in the generator or alternator lead, and the regulator system does not limit the maximum current that the generator or alternator can deliver. If the ammeter reading is never allowed to exceed the red line, except for short, intermittent loads, the generator or alternator is not overloaded.

Where the use of placards or monitoring devices is not practical or desired, and where assurance is needed that the battery in a typical small aircraft generator or battery power source is charged in flight, the total continuous connected electrical load may be held to approximately 80 percent of the total rated generator output capacity. When more than one generator is used in parallel, the total rated output is the combined output of the installed generators.

Means must be provided for quickly coping with the sudden overloads that can be caused by generator or engine failure if two or more generators are operated in parallel and the total connected system load can exceed the rated output of one generator. A quick load-reduction system can be employed or a specified procedure where the total load is reduced to a quantity that is within the rated capacity of the remaining operable generator or generators.

Electrical loads should be connected to inverters, alternators, or similar aircraft electrical power sources in such a manner that the rated limits of the power source are not exceeded, unless some type of effective monitoring means is provided to keep the load within prescribed limits.

Circuit Protection Devices

Conductors should be protected with circuit breakers or fuses located as close as possible to the electrical power source bus. Normally, the manufacturer of the electrical equipment specifies the fuse or circuit breaker to be used when installing the equipment.

The circuit breaker or fuse should open the circuit before the conductor emits smoke. To accomplish this, the time/current characteristic of the protection device must fall below that of the associated conductor. Circuit protector characteristics should be matched to obtain the maximum utilization of the connected equipment.

Figure 4-117 shows an example of the table used in selecting the circuit breaker and fuse protection for copper conductors. This limited table is applicable to a specific set of ambient temperatures and wire bundle sizes and is presented as a typical example only. It is important to consult such guides before selecting a conductor for a specific purpose. For example, a wire run individually in the open air may be protected by the circuit breaker of the next higher rating to that shown in the table.

Wire AN Gauge Copper	Circuit Breaker Amperage	Fuse Amperage
22	5.0	5
20	7.5	5
18	10.0	10
16	15.0	10
14	20.0	15
12	30.0	20
10	40.0	30
8	50.0	50
6	80.0	70
4	100.0	70
2	125.0	100
1		150
0		150

Figure 4-117. *Wire and circuit protector table.*

All resettable circuit breakers should open the circuit in which they are installed, regardless of the position of the operating control when an overload or circuit fault exists. Such circuit breakers are referred to as trip-free. Automatic reset circuit breakers automatically reset themselves periodically. They should not be used as circuit protection devices in aircraft.

Switches

A specifically designed switch should be used in all circuits in which a switch malfunction would be hazardous. Such switches are of rugged construction and have sufficient contact capacity to break, make, and carry continuously the connected load current. Snap-action design is generally preferred to obtain rapid opening and closing of contacts regardless of the speed of the operating toggle or plunger, thereby minimizing contact arcing.

The nominal current rating of the conventional aircraft switch is usually stamped on the switch housing. This rating represents the continuous current rating with the contacts closed. Switches should be derated from their nominal current rating for the following types of circuits:

1. High rush-in circuits—circuits containing incandescent lamps can draw an initial current that is 15 times greater than the continuous current. Contact burning or welding may occur when the switch is closed.

2. Inductive circuits—magnetic energy stored in solenoid coils or relays is released and appears as an arc as the control switch is opened.

3. Motors—direct current motors draw several times their rated current during starting, and magnetic energy stored in their armature and field coils is released when the control switch is opened.

Figure 4-118 is typical of those tables available for selecting the proper nominal switch rating when the continuous load current is known. This selection is essentially a derating to obtain reasonable switch efficiency and service life.

Nominal System Voltage	Type of Load	Derating Factor
24 VDC	Lamp	8
24 VDC	Inductive (Relay-Solenoid)	4
24 VDC	Resistive (Heater)	2
24 VDC	Motor	3
12 VDC	Lamp	5
12 VDC	Inductive (Relay-Solenoid)	2
12 VDC	Resistive (Heater)	1
12 VDC	Motor	2

Figure 4-118. *Switch derating factors.*

Hazardous errors in switch operation can be avoided by logical and consistent installation. Two position on-off switches should be mounted so that the on position is reached by an upward or forward movement of the toggle. When the switch controls movable aircraft elements, such as landing gear or flaps, the toggle should move in the same direction as the desired motion. Inadvertent operation of a switch can be prevented by mounting a suitable guard over the switch.

Relays

Relays are used as switching devices in which a weight reduction can be achieved or electrical controls can be simplified. A relay is an electrically operated switch and is therefore subject to dropout under low system voltage conditions. The previous discussion of switch ratings is generally applicable to relay contact ratings.

Chapter 5
Engine Starting Systems

Introduction

Most aircraft engines, reciprocating or turbine, require help during the starting process. Hence, this device is termed the starter. A starter is an electromechanical mechanism capable of developing large amounts of mechanical energy that can be applied to an engine, causing it to rotate. Reciprocating engines need only to be turned through at a relatively slow speed until the engine starts and turns on its own. Once the reciprocating engine has fired and started, the starter is disengaged and has no further function until the next start. In the case of a turbine engine, the starter must turn the engine up to a speed that provides enough airflow through the engine for fuel to be ignited. Then, the starter must continue to help the engine accelerate to a self-sustaining speed. Turbine engine starters have a critical role in starting of the engine.

If the starter turns the turbine engine up to a self sustaining speed, the engine start process will not be successful. There are only a few types or methods used to turn the engine. Almost all reciprocating engines use a form of electric motor geared to the engine. Modern turbine engines use electric motors, starter/generators (electric motor and a generator in the same housing), and air turbine starters. Air turbine starters are driven by compressed air through a turbine wheel that is mechanically connected through reduction gears to one of the engine's compressors, generally the highest pressure compressor.

Reciprocating Engine Starting Systems

In the early stages of aircraft development, relatively low powered reciprocating engines were started by pulling the propeller through a part of a revolution by hand. Difficulty was often experienced in cold weather starting when lubricating oil temperatures were near the congealing point. In addition, the magneto systems delivered a weak starting spark at the very low cranking speeds. This was often compensated for by providing a hot spark using such ignition system devices as the booster coil, induction vibrator, or impulse coupling.

Some small, low-powered aircraft which use hand cranking of the propeller, or propping, for starting are still being operated. For general instructions on starting this type of aircraft, refer to the Aviation Maintenance Technician—General Handbook, Chapter 11, Safety, Ground Operations, and Servicing. Throughout the development of the aircraft reciprocating engine from the earliest use of starting systems to the present, a number of different starter systems have been used. Most reciprocating engine starters are the direct cranking electric type. A few older model aircraft are still equipped with inertia starters. Thus, only a brief description of these starting systems is included in this section.

Inertia Starters

There are three general types of inertia starters: hand, electric, and combination hand and electric. The operation of all types of inertia starters depends on the kinetic energy stored in a rapidly rotating flywheel for cranking ability. Kinetic energy is energy possessed by a body by virtue of its state of motion, which may be movement along a line or spinning action.

In the inertia starter, energy is stored slowly during an energizing process by a manual hand crank or electrically with a small motor. The flywheel and movable gears of a combination hand electric inertia starter are shown in *Figure 5-1*. The electrical circuit for an electric inertia starter is shown in *Figure 5-2*. During the energizing of the starter, all movable parts within it, including the flywheel, are set in motion. After the starter has been fully energized, it is engaged to the crankshaft of the engine by a cable pulled manually or by a meshing solenoid that is energized electrically. When the starter is engaged, or meshed, flywheel energy is transferred to the engine through sets of reduction gears and a torque overload release clutch. *[Figure 5-3]*

Direct Cranking Electric Starter

The most widely used starting system on all types of reciprocating engines utilizes the direct cranking electric starter. This type of starter provides instant and continual cranking when energized. The direct cranking electric starter consists basically of an electric motor, reduction gears, and an automatic engaging and disengaging mechanism that is operated through an adjustable torque overload release clutch. A typical circuit for a direct cranking electric starter is shown in *Figure 5-4*. The engine is cranked directly when the starter solenoid is closed. As shown in *Figure 5-4*, the main cables leading from the starter to the battery are heavy duty to carry the high current flow, which may be in a range from as high as 350 amperes to 100 amperes (amps), depending on the starting torque required. The use of solenoids and heavy

Figure 5-1. *Combination hand and electric inertia starter.*

Figure 5-2. *Electric inertia starting circuit.*

Figure 5-3. *Torque overload release clutch.*

wiring with a remote control switch reduces overall cable weight and total circuit voltage drop.

The typical starter motor is a 12- or 24-volt, series-wound motor that develops high starting torque. The torque of the motor is transmitted through reduction gears to the overload release clutch. Typically, this action actuates a helically splined shaft moving the starter jaw outward to engage the engine cranking jaw before the starter jaw begins to rotate. After the engine reaches a predetermined speed, the starter automatically disengages. The schematic in *Figure 5-5* provides a pictorial arrangement of an entire starting system for a light twin-engine aircraft.

Direct Cranking Electric Starting System for Large Reciprocating Engines

In a typical high horsepower reciprocating engine starting system, the direct cranking electric starter consists of two basic components: a motor assembly and a gear section. The gear section is bolted to the drive end of the motor to form a complete unit.

The motor assembly consists of the armature and motor pinion assembly, the end bell assembly, and the motor housing assembly. The motor housing also acts as the magnetic yoke for the field structure.

The starter motor is a nonreversible, series interpole motor. Its speed varies directly with the applied voltage and inversely with the load. The starter gear section consists of an external housing with an integral mounting flange, planetary gear reduction, a sun and integral gear assembly, a torque-limiting

Figure 5-4. *Typical starting circuit using a direct cranking electric starter.*

5-3

Figure 5-5. *Engine starting schematic for a light twin-engine aircraft.*

clutch, and a jaw and cone assembly. *[Figure 5-6]* When the starter circuit is closed, the torque developed in the starter motor is transmitted to the starter jaw through the reduction gear train and clutch. The starter gear train converts the high speed low torque of the motor to the low speed high torque required to crank the engine. In the gear section, the motor pinion engages the gear on the intermediate countershaft. *[Figure 5-6]* The pinion of the countershaft engages the internal gear. The internal gear is an integral part of the sun gear assembly and is rigidly attached to the sun gear shaft. The sun gear drives three planet gears that are part of the planetary gear assembly. The individual planet gear shafts are supported by the planetary carrying arm, a barrel-like part shown in *Figure 5-6*. The carrying arm transmits torque from the planet gears to the starter jaw as follows:

1. The cylindrical portion of the carrying arm is splined longitudinally around the inner surface.

2. Mating splines are cut on the exterior surface of the cylindrical part of the starter jaw.

3. The jaw slides fore and aft inside the carrying arm to engage and disengage with the engine.

The three planet gears also engage the surrounding internal teeth on the six steel clutch plates. *[Figure 5-6]* These plates are interleaved with externally splined bronze clutch plates that engage the sides of the housing, preventing them from turning. The proper pressure is maintained upon the clutch pack by a clutch spring retainer assembly. A cylindrical traveling nut inside the starter jaw extends and retracts the jaw. Spiral jaw-engaging splines around the inner wall of the nut mate with similar splines cut on an extension of the sun gear shaft. *[Figure 5-6]*

Being splined in this fashion, rotation of the shaft forces the nut out and the nut carries the jaw with it. A jaw spring around the traveling nut carries the jaw with the nut and tends to keep a conical clutch surface around the inner wall of the jaw head seated against a similar surface around the underside of the nut head. A return spring is installed on the sun gear shaft extension between a shoulder, formed by the

Figure 5-6. *Starter gear section.*

splines around the inner wall of the traveling nut, and a jaw stop retaining nut on the end of the shaft. Because the conical clutch surfaces of the traveling nut and the starter jaw are engaged by jaw spring pressure, the two parts tend to rotate at the same speed. However, the sun gear shaft extension turns six times faster than the jaw. The spiral splines on it are cut left hand, and the sun gear shaft extension, turning to the right in relation to the jaw, forces the traveling nut and the jaw out from the starter its full travel (about 5/16 inches) in approximately 12° of rotation of the jaw.

The jaw moves out until it is stopped either by engagement with the engine or by the jaw stop retaining nut. The travel nut continues to move slightly beyond the limit of jaw travel, just enough to relieve some of the spring pressure on the conical clutch surfaces. As long as the starter continues to rotate, there is just enough pressure on the conical clutch surfaces to provide torque on the spiral splines that balance most of the pressure of the jaw spring. If the engine fails to start, the starter jaw does not retract since the starter mechanism provides no retracting force. However, when the engine fires and the engine jaw overruns the starter jaw, the sloping ramps of the jaw teeth force the starter jaw into the starter against the jaw spring pressure. This disengages the conical clutch surfaces entirely, and the jaw spring pressure forces the traveling nut to slide in along the spiral splines until the conical clutch surfaces are again in contact.

When the starter and engine are both running, there is an engaging force keeping the jaws in contact that continue until the starter is de-energized. However, the rapidly moving engine jaw teeth, striking the slowly moving starter jaw teeth, hold the starter jaw disengaged. As soon as the starter comes to rest, the engaging force is removed and the small return spring throws the starter jaw into its fully retracted position where it remains until the next start. When the starter jaw first engages the engine jaw, the motor armature has had time to reach considerable speed because of its high starting torque. The sudden engagement of the moving starter jaw with the stationary engine jaw would develop forces sufficiently high enough to severely damage the engine or the starter were it not for the plates in the clutch pack that slip when the engine torque exceeds the clutch-slipping torque.

In normal direct cranking action, the internal steel gear clutch plates are held stationary by the friction of the bronze plates with which they are interleaved. When the torque imposed by the engine exceeds the clutch setting, however, the internal gear clutch plates rotate against the clutch friction, allowing the planet gears to rotate while the planetary carrying arm and the jaw remain stationary. When the engine reaches the speed that the starter is trying to achieve, the torque drops off to a value less than the clutch setting, the internal gear clutch plates are again held stationary, and the jaw rotates at the speed that the motor is attempting to drive it. The starter control switches are shown schematically in *Figure 5-7*.

The engine selector switch must be positioned and the starter switch and the safety switch—wired in series—must be closed before the starter can be energized. Current is supplied to the starter control circuit through a circuit breaker labeled "Starter, Primer, and Induction Vibrator." *[Figure 5-7]* When the engine selector switch is in position for the engine start, closing the starter energizes the starter relay located in the engine nacelle area. Energizing the starter relay completes the power circuit to the starter motor. The current necessary for this heavy load is taken directly from the master bus through the starter bus cable.

All starting systems have operating time limits because of the high energy used during cranking or rotation of the engine. These limits are referred to as starter limits and must be observed, or overheating and damage of the starter occurs. After energizing the starter for 1 minute, it should be allowed to cool for at least 1 minute. After a second or subsequent cranking period of 1 minute, it should cool for 5 minutes.

Direct Cranking Electric Starting System for Small Aircraft

Most small, reciprocating engine aircraft employ a direct cranking electric starting system. Some of these systems are automatically engaged starting systems, while others are manually engaged.

Manually engaged starting systems used on many older, small aircraft employ a manually operated overrunning clutch drive pinion to transmit power from an electric starter motor to a crankshaft starter drive gear. *[Figure 5-8]* A knob or handle on the instrument panel is connected by a flexible control to a lever on the starter. This lever shifts the starter drive pinion into the engaged position and closes the starter switch contacts when the starter knob or handle is pulled.

Figure 5-7. *Starter control circuit.*

The starter lever is attached to a return spring that returns the lever and the flexible control to the off position. When the engine starts, the overrunning action of the clutch protects the starter drive pinion until the shift lever can be released to disengage the pinion. For the typical unit, there is a specified length of travel for the starter gear pinion. *[Figure 5-8]* It is important that the starter lever move the starter pinion gear this proper distance before the adjustable lever stud contacts the starter switch.

The automatic, or remote solenoid engaged, starting systems employ an electric starter mounted on an engine adapter. A starter solenoid is activated by either a push button or turning the ignition key on the instrument panel. When the solenoid is activated, its contacts close and electrical energy energizes the starter motor. Initial rotation of the starter motor engages the starter through an overrunning clutch in the starter adapter, which incorporates worm reduction gears.

Some engines incorporate an automatic starting system that employs an electric starter motor mounted on a right angle drive adapter. As the starter motor is electrically energized, the adapter worm shaft and gear engage the starter shaft gear by means of a spring and clutch assembly. The shaft gear, in turn, rotates the crankshaft. When the engine begins to turn on its own power, the clutch spring disengages from the shaft gear. The starter adapter uses a worm drive gear shaft and worm gear to transfer torque from the starter motor to the clutch assembly. *[Figure 5-9]* As the worm gear rotates the worm wheel and clutch spring, the clutch spring is tightened around the drum of the starter shaft gear. As the shaft gear turns, torque is transmitted directly to the crankshaft gear.

Figure 5-8. *Starter level controls and adjustment.*

Figure 5-9. *Starter adapter.*

Other engines use a starter that drives a ring gear mounted to the propeller hub. *[Figure 5-10]* It uses an electric motor and a drive gear that engages as the motor is energized and spins the gear, which moves out and engages the ring gear on the propeller hub cranking the engine for start. *[Figure 5-11]* As the engine starts, the starter drive gear is spun back by the engine turning, which disengages the drive gear. *[Figure 5-12]* The starter motors on small aircraft also have operational limits with cool down times that should be observed.

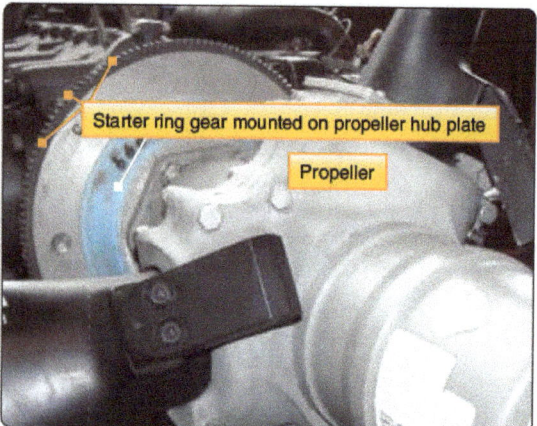

Figure 5-10. *Starter ring gear mounted on the propeller hub.*

Reciprocating Engine Starting System Maintenance Practices

Most starting system maintenance practices include replacing the starter motor brushes and brush springs, cleaning dirty commutators, and turning down burned or out-of-round starter commutators. As a rule, starter brushes should be replaced when worn down to approximately one-half the original length. Brush spring tension should be sufficient to give brushes a good firm contact with the commutator. Brush leads should be unbroken and lead terminal screws tight.

A glazed or dirty starter commutator can be cleaned by holding a strip of double-0 sandpaper or a brush seating stone against the commutator as it is turned. The sandpaper or stone should be moved back and forth across the commutator to avoid wearing a groove. Emery paper or carborundum should never be used for this purpose because of their possible shorting action.

Roughness, out-of-roundness, or high-mica conditions are reasons for turning down the commutator. In the case of a high-mica condition, the mica should be undercut after the turning operation is accomplished. Refer to FAA-H-8083-30, Aviation Maintenance Technician—General for a review of high-mica commutators in motors.

The drive gear should be checked for wear along with the ring gear. The electrical connections should be checked for looseness and corrosion. Also, check the security of the mounting of the housing of the starter.

Troubleshooting Small Aircraft Starting Systems

The troubleshooting procedures listed in *Figure 5-13* are typical of those used to isolate malfunctions in small aircraft starting systems.

Gas Turbine Engine Starters

Gas turbine engines are started by rotating the high-pressure compressor. On dual-spool, axial flow engines, the high-

Figure 5-11. *Starter drive gear mounting holes and electrical connector.*

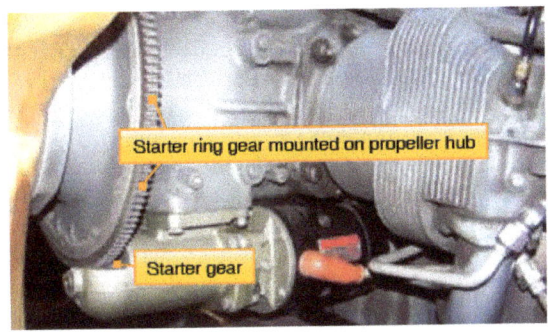

Figure 5-12. *Engine starter mounted on the engine.*

pressure compressor and N1 turbine system is only rotated by the starter. To start a gas turbine engine, it is necessary to accelerate the compressor to provide sufficient air to support combustion in the combustion section, or burners. Once ignition and fuel has been introduced and the lite-off has occured, the starter must continue to assist the engine until the engine reaches a self sustaining speed. The torque supplied by the starter must be in excess of the torque required to overcome compressor inertia and the friction loads of the engine's compressor. *Figure 5-14* illustrates a typical starting sequence for a gas turbine engine, regardless of the type of starter employed. As soon as the starter has accelerated the compressor sufficiently to establish airflow through the engine, the ignition is turned on followed by the fuel. The exact sequence of the starting procedure is important since there must be sufficient airflow through the engine to support combustion before the fuel-air mixture is ignited. At low engine cranking speeds, the fuel flow rate is not sufficient to enable the engine to accelerate; for this reason, the starter continues to crank the engine until after self-accelerating speed has been attained. If assistance from the starter were cut off below the self-accelerating speed, the engine would either fail to accelerate to idle speed or might even decelerate because it could not produce sufficient energy to sustain rotation or to accelerate during the initial phase of the starting cycle. The starter must continue to assist the engine considerably above the self-accelerating speed to avoid a delay in the starting cycle, which would result in a hot or hung false start or a combination of both. At the proper points in the sequence, the starter and ignition are automatically cut off. The basic types of starters that are in current use for gas turbine engines are direct current (DC) electric motor, starter/generators, and the air turbine type of starters.

	Small Aircraft Troubleshooting Procedures		
	Probable Cause	**Isolation Procedure**	**Remedy**
Starter will not operate	• Defective master switch or circuit • Defective starter switch or switch circuit • Starter lever does not activate switch • Defective starter	• Check master circuit. • Check switch circuit continuity. • Check starter lever adjustment. • Check through items above. If another cause is not apparent, starter is defective.	• Repair circuit. • Replace switch or wires. • Adjust starter lever in accordance with manufacturer's instructions. • Remove and repair or replace starter.
Starter motor runs, but does not turn crankshaft	• Starter lever adjusted to activate switch without engaging pinion with crankshaft gear • Defective overrunning clutch or drive • Damaged starter pinion gear or crankshaft gear	• Check starter lever adjustment. • Remove starter and check starter drive and overrunning clutch. • Remove and check pinion gear and crankshaft gear.	• Adjust starter lever in accordance with manufacturer's instructions. • Replace defective parts. • Replace defective parts.
Starter drags	• Low battery • Starter switch or relay contacts burned or dirty • Defective starter	• Check battery. • Check contacts. • Check starter brushes, brush spring tension for solder thrown on brush cover.	• Charge or replace battery. • Replace with serviceable unit. • Repair or replace starter.
Starter excessively noisy	• Dirty, worn commutator • Worn starter pinion • Worn or broken teeth on crankshaft gears	• Clean and check visually. • Remove and examine pinion. • Remove starter and turn over engine by hand to examine crankshaft gear.	• Turn down commutator. • Replace starter drive. • Replace crankshaft gear.

Figure 5-13. *Small aircraft troubleshooting procedures.*

Figure 5-14. *Typical gas turbine engine starting sequence.*

Many types of turbine starters have included several different methods for turning the engine for starting. Several methods have been used but most of these have given way to electric or air turbine starters. An air impingement starting system, which is sometimes used on small engines, consists of jets of compressed air piped to the inside of the compressor or turbine case so that the jet air blast is directed onto the compressor or turbine rotor blades, causing them to rotate.

A typical cartridge/pneumatic turbine engine starter may be operated as an ordinary air turbine starter from a ground-operated air supply or an engine cross-bleed source. It may also be operated as a cartridge starter. *[Figure 5-15]* To accomplish a cartridge start, a cartridge is first placed in the breech cap. The breech is then closed on the breech chamber by means of the breech handle and then rotated a partial turn to engage the lugs between the two breech sections. The cartridge is ignited by applying voltage through the connector at the end of the breech handle. Upon ignition, the cartridge begins to generate gas. The gas is forced out of the breech to the hot gas nozzles that are directed toward the buckets on the turbine rotor, and rotation is produced via the overboard exhaust collector. Before reaching the nozzle, the hot gas passes an outlet leading to the relief valve. This valve directs hot gas to the turbine, bypassing the hot gas nozzle, as the pressure rises above the preset maximum. Thus, the pressure of the gas within the hot gas circuit is maintained at the optimum level.

The fuel/air combustion starter was used to start gas turbine engines by using the combustion energy of jet A fuel and compressed air. The starter consists of a turbine-driven power unit and auxiliary fuel, air, and ignition systems. Operation of this type starter is, in most installations, fully automatic; actuation of a single switch causes the starter to fire and accelerate the engine from rest to starter cutoff speed.

Figure 5-15. *Cartridge/pneumatic starter schematic.*

Hydraulic pumps and motors have also been used for some smaller engines. Many of these systems are not often used on modern commercial aircraft because of the high power demands required to turn the large turbofan engines during the starting cycle on transport aircraft.

Electric Starting Systems and Starter Generator Starting System

Electric starting systems for gas turbine aircraft are of two general types: direct cranking electrical systems and starter generator systems. Direct cranking electric starting systems are used mostly on small turbine engines, such as Auxiliary Power Units (APUs), and some small turboshaft engines. Many gas turbine aircraft are equipped with starter generator systems. Starter generator starting systems are also similar to direct cranking electrical systems except that after functioning as a starter, they contain a second series of windings that allow it to switch to a generator after the engine has reached a self-sustaining speed. This saves weight and space on the engine.

The starter generator is permanently engaged with the engine shaft through the necessary drive gears, while the direct cranking starter must employ some means of disengaging the starter from the shaft after the engine has started. The starter generator unit is basically a shunt generator with an additional heavy series winding. *[Figure 5-16]* This series winding is electrically connected to produce a strong field and a resulting high torque for starting. Starter generator units are desirable from an economical standpoint, since one unit performs the functions of both starter and generator. Additionally, the total weight of starting system components is reduced and fewer spare parts are required.

Figure 5-16. *Typical starter generator.*

The starter generator internal circuit has four field windings: a series field (C field), a shunt field, a compensating field, and an interpole or commutating winding. *[Figure 5-17]* During starting, the C field, compensating, and commutating windings are used. The unit is similar to a direct cranking starter since all of the windings used during starting are in series with the source. While acting as a starter, the unit makes no practical use of its shunt field. A source of 24 volts and 1,500 peak amperes is usually required for starting.

Figure 5-17. *Starter generator internal circuit.*

When operating as a generator, the shunt, compensating, and commutating windings are used. The C field is used only for starting purposes. The shunt field is connected in the conventional voltage control circuit for the generator. Compensating and commutating or interpole windings provide almost sparkless commutation from no load to full load. *Figure 5-18* illustrates the external circuit of a starter generator with an undercurrent controller. This unit controls the starter generator when it is used as a starter. Its purpose is to assure positive action of the starter and to keep it operating until the engine is rotating fast enough to sustain combustion. The control block of the undercurrent controller contains two relays. One is the motor relay that controls the input to the starter; the other, the undercurrent relay, controls the operation of the motor relay.

5-11

The sequence of operation for the starting system is discussed in the following paragraphs. *[Figure 5-18]* To start an engine equipped with an undercurrent relay, it is first necessary to close the engine master switch. This completes the circuit from the aircraft's bus to the start switch, to the fuel valves, and to the throttle relay. Energizing the throttle relay starts the fuel pumps, and completing the fuel valve circuit gives the necessary fuel pressure for starting the engine. As the battery and start switch is turned on, three relays close: the motor relay, ignition relay, and battery cutout relay. The motor relay closes the circuit from the power source to the starter motor; the ignition relay closes the circuit to the ignition units; the battery cutout relay disconnects the battery. Opening the battery circuit is necessary because the heavy drain of the starter motor would damage the battery. Closing the motor relay allows a very high current to flow to the motor. Since this current flows through the coil of the undercurrent relay, it closes. Closing the undercurrent relay completes a circuit from the positive bus to the motor relay coil, ignition relay coil, and battery cutout relay coil. The start switch is allowed to return to its normal off position, and all units continue to operate.

As the motor builds up speed, the current draw of the motor begins to decrease. As it decreases to less than 200 amps, the undercurrent relay opens. This action breaks the circuit from the positive bus to the coils of the motor, ignition, and battery cutout relays. The de-energizing of these relay coils halts the start operation.

After these procedures are completed, the engine should be operating efficiently and ignition should be self-sustaining. If, however, the engine fails to reach sufficient speed to halt the starter operation, the stop switch may be used to break the circuit from the positive bus to the main contacts of the undercurrent relay.

Troubleshooting a Starter Generator Starting System

The procedures listed in *Figure 5-19* are typical of those used to repair malfunctions in a starter generator starting system similar to the system described in this section. These procedures are presented as a guide only. The appropriate manufacturer's instructions and approved maintenance directives should always be consulted for the aircraft involved.

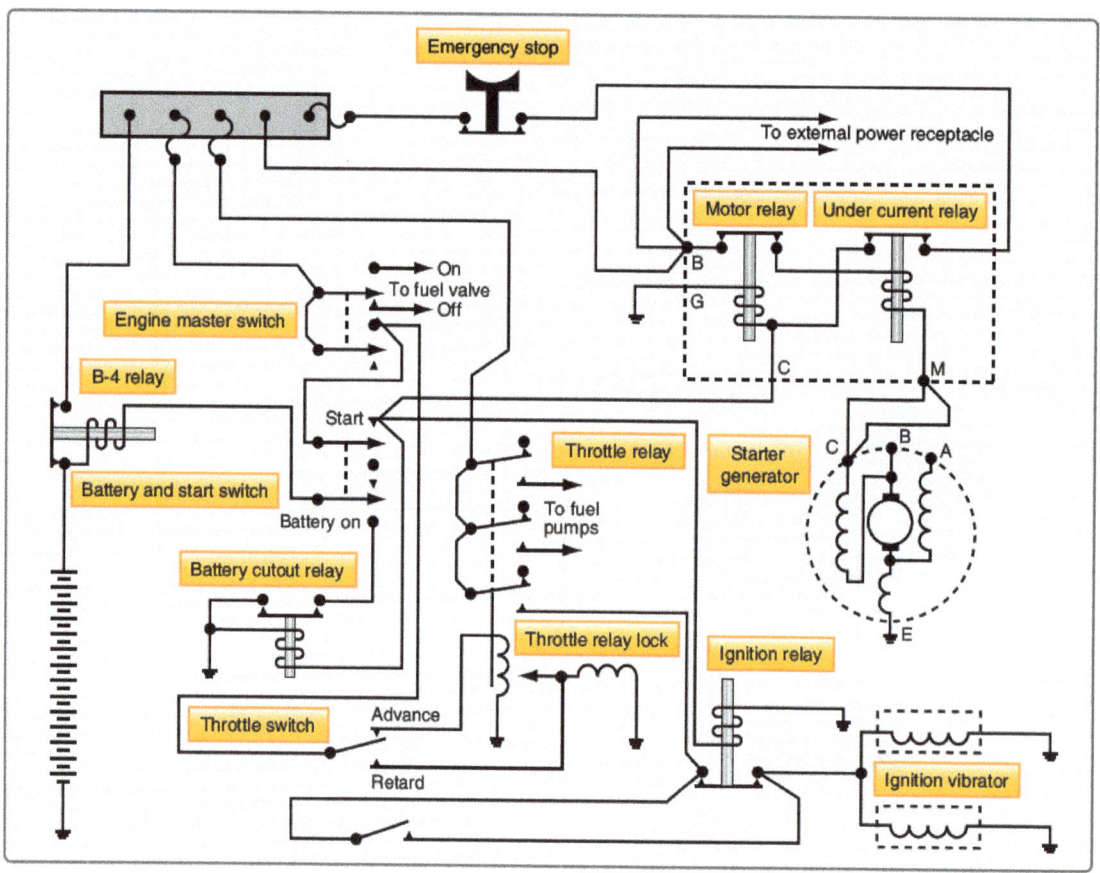

Figure 5-18. *Starter generator circuit.*

Starter Generator Starting System Troubleshooting Procedures		
Probable Cause	Isolation Procedure	Remedy
Engine does not rotate during start attempt		
• Low supply voltage to the starter • Power switch is defective • Ignition switch in throttle quadrant • Start-lockout relay is defective • Battery series relay is defective • Starter relay is defective • Defective starter • Start lock-in relay defective • Starter drive shaft in component drive gearbox is sheared	• Check voltage of the battery or external power source. • Check switch for continuity. • Check switch for continuity. • Check position of generator control switch. • With start circuit energized, check for 48 volts DC across series relay coil. • With start circuit energized, check for 48 volts DC across starter relay coil. • With start circuit energized, check for proper voltage at the starter. • With start circuit energized, check for 28 volts DC across the relay coil. • Listen for sounds of starter rotation during an attempted start. If the starter rotates but the engine does not, the drive shaft is sheared.	• Adjust voltage of the external power source or charge batteries. • Replace switch. • Replace switch. • Place switch in OFF position. • Replace relay if no voltage is present. • Replace relay if no voltage is present. • Replace the starter if voltage is present. • Replace relay if voltage is not present. • Replace the engine.
Engine starts but does not accelerate to idle		
• Insufficient starter voltage	• Check starter terminal voltage.	• Use larger capacity ground power unit or charge batteries.
Engine fails to start when throttle is placed in idle		
• Defective ignition system	• Turn on system and listen for spark-igniter operation.	• Clean or replace spark igniters, or replace exciters or leads to igniters.

Figure 5-19. *Starter generator starting system troubleshooting procedures.*

Air Turbine Starters

Air turbine starters are designed to provide high starting torque from a small, lightweight source. The typical air turbine starter weighs from one-fourth to one-half as much as an electric starter capable of starting the same engine. It is capable of developing considerable more torque than the electric starter.

The typical air turbine starter consists of an axial flow turbine that turns a drive coupling through a reduction gear train and a starter clutch mechanism. The air to operate an air turbine starter is supplied from either a ground-operated air cart, the APU, or a cross-bleed start from an engine already operating. *[Figure 5-20]* Only one source of around 30–50 pounds per square inch (psi) is used at a time to start the engines. The pressure in the ducts must be high enough to provide for a complete start with a normal limit minimum of about 30 psi. When starting engines with an air turbine starter, always check the duct pressure prior to the start attempt.

Figure 5-21 is a cutaway view of an air turbine starter. The starter is operated by introducing air of sufficient volume and pressure into the starter inlet. The air passes into the starter turbine housing where it is directed against the rotor blades by the nozzle vanes causing the turbine rotor to turn. As the rotor turns, it drives the reduction gear train and clutch arrangement, which includes the rotor pinion, planet gears and carrier, sprag clutch assembly, output shaft assembly, and drive coupling. The sprag clutch assembly engages automatically as soon as the rotor starts to turn, but disengages as soon as the drive coupling turns more rapidly than the rotor side. When the starter reaches this overrun speed, the action of the sprag clutch allows the gear train to coast to a halt. The output shaft assembly and drive coupling continue to turn as long as the engine is running. A rotor switch actuator, mounted in the turbine rotor hub, is set to open the turbine switch when the starter reaches cutout speed. Opening the turbine switch interrupts an electrical signal to the start valve. This closes the valve and shuts off the air supply to the starter.

Figure 5-20. *Air turbine starters are supplied by ground cart, APU, or another operating onboard engine.*

The turbine housing contains the turbine rotor, the rotor switch actuator, and the nozzle components that direct the inlet air against the rotor blades. The turbine housing incorporates a turbine rotor containment ring designed to dissipate the energy of blade fragments and direct their discharge at low energy through the exhaust duct in the event of rotor failure due to excessive turbine overspeed.

The transmission housing contains the reduction gears, the clutch components, and the drive coupling. The transmission housing also provides a reservoir for the lubricating oil. *[Figure 5-22]* Normal maintenance for air turbine starters includes checking the oil level, inspecting the magnetic chip detector for metal particles, and checking for leaks. Oil can be added to the transmission housing sump through a port in the starter. This port is closed by a vent plug containing a ball valve that allows the sump to be vented to the atmosphere during normal flight. The housing also incorporates a sight gauge that is used to check the oil quantity. A magnetic drain plug in the transmission drain opening attracts any ferrous particles that may be in the oil. The starter uses turbine oil, the same as the engine, but this oil does not circulate through the engine.

The ring gear housing, which is internal, contains the rotor assembly. The switch housing contains the turbine switch and bracket assembly. To facilitate starter installation and removal, a mounting adapter is bolted to the mounting pad on the engine. Quick-detach clamps join the starter to the mounting adapter and inlet duct. *[Figure 5-22]* Thus, the starter is easily removed for maintenance or overhaul by disconnecting the electrical line, loosening the clamps, and carefully disengaging the drive coupling from the engine starter drive as the starter is withdrawn.

The air path is directed through a combination pressure-regulating and shutoff valve, or bleed valve, that controls all duct pressure flowing to the starter inlet ducting. This valve

Figure 5-21. *Cutaway view of an air turbine starter.*

Figure 5-22. *Air turbine starter.*

5-15

regulates the pressure of the starter operating air and shuts off the air supply to the engine when selected off. Downstream from the bleed valve is the start valve, which is used to control air flow into the starter. *[Figure 5-23]*

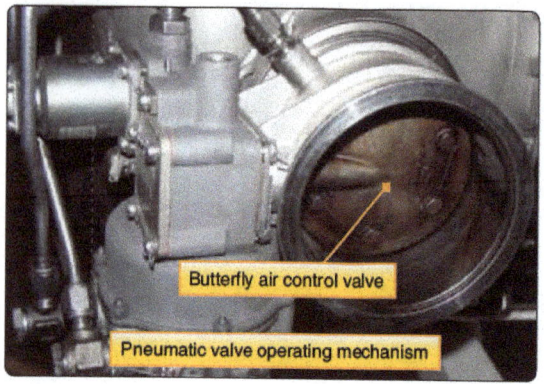

Figure 5-23. *Regulating and shutoff bleed valve.*

The pressure-regulating and shutoff valve consists of two subassemblies: pressure-regulating valve and pressure-regulating valve control. *[Figure 5-24]* The regulating valve assembly consists of a valve housing containing a butterfly-type valve. *[Figure 5-24]* The shaft of the butterfly valve is connected through a cam arrangement to a servo piston. When the piston is actuated, its motion on the cam causes rotation of the butterfly valve. The slope of the cam track is designed to provide small initial travel and high initial torque when the starter is actuated. The cam track slope also provides more stable action by increasing the opening time of the valve.

The control assembly is mounted on the regulating valve housing and consists of a control housing in which a solenoid is used to stop the action of the control crank in the off position. *[Figure 5-24]* The control crank links a pilot valve that meters pressure to the servo piston, with the bellows connected by an air line to the pressure-sensing port on the starter.

Turning on the starter switch energizes the regulating valve solenoid. The solenoid retracts and allows the control crank to rotate to the open position. The control crank is rotated by the control rod spring moving the control rod against the closed end of the bellows. Since the regulating valve is closed and downstream pressure is negligible, the bellows can be fully extended by the bellows spring.

As the control crank rotates to the open position, it causes the pilot valve rod to open the pilot valve, allowing upstream air, which is supplied to the pilot valve through a suitable filter and a restriction in the housing, to flow into the servo piston chamber. The drain side of the pilot valve, which bleeds the servo chamber to the atmosphere, is now closed by the pilot valve rod and the servo piston moves inboard. *[Figure 5-24]* This linear motion of the servo piston is translated to rotary motion of the valve shaft by the rotating cam, thus opening the regulating valve. As the valve opens, downstream pressure increases. This pressure is bled back to the bellows through the pressure-sensing line and compresses the bellows. This action moves the control rod, thereby turning the control crank, and moving the pilot valve rod gradually away from the servo chamber to vent to the

Figure 5-24. *Pressure-regulating and shutoff valve in on position.*

atmosphere. *[Figure 5-24]* When downstream (regulated) pressure reaches a preset value, the amount of air flowing into the servo through the restriction equals the amount of air being bled to the atmosphere through the servo bleed; the system is in a state of equilibrium.

When the bleed valve and the start valve are open, the regulated air passing through the inlet housing of the starter impinges on the turbine causing it to turn. As the turbine turns, the gear train is activated and the inboard clutch gear, which is threaded onto a helical screw, moves forward as it rotates; its jaw teeth engage those of the outboard clutch gear to drive the output shaft of the starter. The clutch is an overrunning type to facilitate positive engagement and minimize chatter. When starter cut-out speed is reached, the start valve is closed. When the air to the starter is terminated, the outboard clutch gear, driven by the engine, begins to turn faster than the inboard clutch gear; the inboard clutch gear, actuated by the return spring, disengages the outboard clutch gear allowing the rotor to coast to a halt. The outboard clutch shaft continues to turn with the engine.

Air Turbine Starter Troubleshooting Guide

The troubleshooting procedures listed in *Figure 5-25* are applicable to air turbine starting systems equipped with a combination pressure-regulating and shutoff valve. These procedures should be used as a guide only, and are not intended to replace the manufacturer's instructions.

Air Turbine Starter System Troubleshooting Procedures		
Trouble	**Probable Cause**	**Remedy**
• Starter does not operate (no rotation).	• No air supply • Electrical open in cutout switch • Sheared starter drive coupling • Internal starter discrepancy	• Check air supply. • Check switch continuity. If no continuity, remove starter and adjust or replace switch. • Remove starter and replace drive coupling. • Remove and replace starter.
• Starter will not accelerate to normal cutoff speed.	• Low starter air supply • Starter cutout switch set improperly • Valve pressure regulated too low • Internal starter malfunction	• Check air source pressure. • Adjust rotor switch actuator. • Replace valve. • Remove and replace starter.
• Starter will not not cut off.	• Low air supply • Rotor switch actuator set too high • Starter cutout switch shorted	• Check air supply. • Adjust switch actuator assembly. • Replace switch and bracket assembly.
• External oil leakage.	• Oil level too high • Loose vent, oil filler, or magnetic plugs • Loose clamp band assembly	• Drain oil and re service properly. • Tighten magnetic plug to proper torque. • Tighten vent and oil filler plugs as necessary and lock wire. Tighten clamp band assembly to higher torque.
• Starter runs, but engine does not turn over.	• Sheared drive coupling	• Remove starter and replace the drive coupling. If couplings persist in breaking in unusually short periods of time, remove and replace starter.
• Starter inlet will not line up with supply ducting.	• Improper installation of starter on engine, or improper indexing of turbine housing on starter	• Check installation and/or indexing for conformance with manufacturer's installation instructions and the proper index position of the turbine housing specified for the aircraft.
• Metallic particles on magnetic drain plug.	• Small fuzzy particles indicate normal wear • Particles coarser than fuzzy (chips, slivers, etc.) indicate internal difficulty	• No remedial action required. • Remove and replace starter.
• Broken nozzle vanes.	• Large foreign particles in air supply	• Remove and replace starter and check air supply filter.
• Oil leakage from vent plug assembly.	• Improper starter installation position	• Check installed position for levelness of oil plugs and correct as required in accordance with manufacturer's installation instructions.
• Oil leakage at drive coupling.	• Leaking rear seal assembly	• Remove and replace starter.

Figure 5-25. *Air turbine starter system troubleshooting procedures.*

Glossary

Abradable strip. A strip of material in the compressor housing of some axial-flow gas turbine engines. The tip of the compressor blade touches the abradable strip, and wears, or abrades a groove in it. This groove ensures the minimum tip clearance.

Abradable tip (compressor blade tip). The tip of some axial-flow compressor blades constructed so that it will abrade, or wear away, upon contact with the compressor housing, which ensures the minimum tip clearance between the blade and the housing.

Absolute pressure. Pressure referenced from zero pressure or a vacuum.

AC. Alternating current. Electrical current in which the electrons continually change their rate of flow and periodically reverse their direction.

ACC. Active clearance control. A system for controlling the clearance between tips of the compressor and turbine blades and the case of high-performance turbofan engines. When the engine is operating at maximum power, the blade tip clearance should be minimum, and the ACC system sprays cool fan discharge air over the outside of the engine case. This causes the case to shrink enough to decrease the tip clearance. For flight conditions that do not require such close clearance, the cooling air is turned off, and the case expands to its normal dimensions. The control of the ACC system is done by the FADEC, or full-authority digital electronic control.

Acceleration. The amount the velocity of an object is increased by a force during each second it is acted upon by that force. Acceleration is usually measured and expressed in terms of feet per second, per second (fps^2).

Accessory end. The end of a reciprocating engine on which many of the accessories are mounted. Also, called the anti-propeller end.

Accumulator. A hydraulic component that stores a non-compressible fluid, such as oil, under pressure. An accumulator has two compartments separated by a flexible or movable partition with one compartment containing compressed air. When oil is pumped into the other compartment, the partition moves over, further compressing the air which holds pressure on the oil.

AD (ashless dispersant) oil. A mineral-based lubricating oil used in reciprocating engines. This oil does not contain any metallic ash-forming additives, but has additives that disperse the contaminants and hold them in suspension until they can be removed by filters.

ADC. Air data computer. An electronic computer in an aircraft that senses pitot pressure, static pressure, and total air temperature. It produces an indication of altitude, indicated airspeed, true airspeed, and Mach number. The output of ADC is usable by any of the engine or flight control computers.

ADI (antidetonation injection) system. A system used with some large reciprocating engines in which a mixture of water and alcohol is sprayed into the engine with the fuel when operating at extremely high power. The fuel-air mixture is leaned to allow the engine to develop its maximum power, and the ADI fluid absorbs excessive heat when it vaporizes.

Adiabatic change. A physical change that takes place within a material in which heat energy is neither added to the material, nor taken away. If a container of gas is compressed, with no heat energy added to or taken from it, the gas will become hotter; its temperature will rise.

Aerodrome. The name given by Dr. Samuel Langley to the flying machines built under his supervision between the years of 1891 and 1903.

Aeromatic propeller. A patented variable-pitch propeller that has counterweights around the blade shanks and the blades angled back from the hub to increase the effects of aerodynamic and centrifugal twisting forces. This propeller automatically maintains a relatively constant rpm for any throttle setting.

Aft-fan engine. A turbofan engine with the fan mounted behind the compressor section. The blades of an aft-fan are normally extensions of the free turbine blades.

Afterburner. A component in the exhaust system of a turbojet or turbofan engine used to increase the thrust for takeoff and for special flight conditions. Since much of the air passing through a gas turbine engine is used only for cooling, it still contains a great deal of oxygen. Fuel is sprayed into the hot, oxygen-rich exhaust in the afterburner, where it is ignited and burned to produce additional thrust.

Air bleed (carburetor component). A small hole in the fuel passage between the float bowl and the discharge nozzle of a float carburetor. Air drawn into the liquid fuel through the air bleed breaks the fuel up into an emulsion, making it easy to atomize and vaporize.

Air cooling. The removal of unwanted heat from an aircraft engine by transferring the heat directly into the air flowing over the engine components.

Air-fuel mixture ratio. The ratio of the weight of the air to that of the fuel in the mixture fed into the cylinders of an engine.

Air impingement starter. A turbine engine starter that basically consists of a nozzle that blows a stream of compressed air against the turbine blades to rotate the compressor for starting the engine.

Air-oil separator. A component in a turbine engine lubrication system that removes the air from the scavenged oil before it is returned to the oil tank.

Airworthiness Directive. A regulatory notice sent out by the FAA to the registered owner of an aircraft informing him or her of the discovery of a condition that keeps the aircraft from continuing to meet its conditions for airworthiness. Also called AD notes, they are covered by Federal Aviation Regulations part 39 Airworthiness Directives. They must be complied with within the specified time, and the fact, date, and method of compliance must be recorded in the aircraft maintenance records.

All-weather spark plug. A shielded spark plug designed for high altitude operation. The ceramic insulator is recessed into the shell to allow a resilient grommet on the ignition harness to provide a watertight seal. All weather spark plugs, also called high-altitude spark plugs, are identified by their 3/4-20 shielding threads.

Alpha control range (alpha mode). The flight operating mode from takeoff through landing for a turbo-prop engine. Alpha mode includes operations from 95% to 100% of the engine's rated rpm.

Altitude engine. An aircraft reciprocating engine equipped with a supercharger that allows it to maintain its rated sea-level horsepower to an established higher altitude.

Amateur-built aircraft. Aircraft built by individuals as a hobby rather than by factories as commercial products. Amateur-built or homebuilt aircraft do not fall under the stringent requirements imposed by the FAA on commercially built aircraft.

Ambient air pressure. The pressure of the air that surrounds an object.

Analog indicator. An indicator that shows the value of the parameter being measured by a number marked on a graduated dial aligned with a movable pointer.

Angle of attack. The acute angle between the chord line of a propeller blade and the relative wind. The angle of attack is affected by both the engine rpm and the forward speed of the aircraft.

Annual inspection. A complete inspection of the air-frame and powerplant required for FAA-certificated aircraft operating under 14 CFR part 91 General Operating and Flight Rules, and not on one of the authorized special inspection programs. An annual inspection must be conducted every 12 calendar months, and it must be conducted by an aviation maintenance technician who holds an Airframe and Powerplant rating and an Inspection Authorization. The scope of an annual inspection is the same as that of a 100-hour inspection.

Annular duct. A duct, or passage, that surrounds an object. The annular fan-discharge duct surrounds the core engine.

Annular orifice. A ring-shaped orifice, normally one that surrounds another orifice.

Annulus. A ring or groove around the outside of a circular body or shaft, or around the inside of a cylindrical hole.

Annunciator panel. A panel of warning lights visible to the flight crew. The lights are identified by the name of the system they represent and are often covered with colored lenses. Red lights indicate a dangerous condition, amber indicates a system is armed, and green indicate a safe condition.

Anodizing. A hard, airtight, unbroken oxide film electrolytically deposited on an aluminum alloy surface to protect it from corrosion.

Anti-icing. Prevention of the formation of ice on a surface. anti-propeller end. The end of a reciprocating engine that does not attach to the propeller. Also called the accessory end.

APC. Absolute pressure controller.

APU. Auxiliary power unit. A small turbine- or reciprocating-engine-powered generator, hydraulic pump, and air pump. APUs are installed in the aircraft and are used to supply electrical power, air, and hydraulic pressure when the main engines are not running.

Aramid fiber. Fiber made from an organic compound of carbon, hydrogen, oxygen, and nitrogen. It has high strength and low density. It is flexible under load and is able to withstand impact, shock, and vibration. Kevlar is a well-known aramid fiber.

Aromatic compound. A chemical compound such as toluene, xylene, and benzene that is blended with gasoline to improve its anti-detonation characteristics.

Articulating rod. See link rod.

Aspect ratio. The ratio of the length of an airfoil, such as a compressor blade, to its width.

Asymmetrical loading. The loading of a propeller disk that causes one side to produce more thrust than the other side.

ATF. Aerodynamic twisting force. The aerodynamic force that acts on a rotating propeller blade to increase its blade angle. The axis of rotation of a blade is near the center of its chord line, and the center of pressure is between the axis and the leading edge. Aerodynamic lift acting through the center of pressure tries to rotate the blade to a higher pitch angle.

Atomize. The process of breaking a liquid down into tiny droplets or a fine spray. Atomized liquids vaporize easily.

Augmentor tube. A long, specially shaped stainless steel tube mounted around the exhaust tail pipe of a reciprocating engine. As exhaust gases flow through the augmentor tube, they produce a low pressure in the engine compartment that draws in cooling air through the cylinder fins.

Automatic intake valve. An intake valve opened by low pressure created inside the cylinder as the piston moves down. There is no mechanical means of opening it.

Automatic mixture control (AMC). The device in a fuel metering system, such as a carburetor or fuel injection system, that keeps the fuel-air mixture ratio constant as the density of air changes with altitude.

Autosyn system. The registered trade name of a remote indicating instrument system. An Autosyn system uses an electromagnet rotor, excited with 400-hertz AC, and a three-phase distributed-pole stator.

Axial bearing load. The load on a bearing parallel to the shaft on which the bearing is mounted. Thrust produces an axial load on a bearing.

Axial turbine. A turbine that is turned by a fluid flowing through it in a direction that is approximately parallel to the shaft on which the turbine wheel is mounted.

Axial-flow compressor. A type of compressor used in gas turbine engines. Air passes through the compressor in essentially a straight line, parallel to the axis of the compressor. The compressor is made of a number of stages of rotating compressor blades between stages of stationary stator vanes.

Axis of rotation. The center line about which a propeller rotates.

Babbitt. A soft silvery metal used for main bearing inserts in aircraft reciprocating engines. Babbitt is made of tin with small amounts of copper and antimony.

Back (propeller nomenclature). The curved surface of a propeller blade. The back of a propeller blade corresponds to the upper surface of an airplane wing.

Back-suction mixture control. A type of mixture control used in some float carburetors that regulates the fuel-air mixture by varying the air pressure above the fuel in the float bowl.

Baffle. A thin sheet metal shroud or bulkhead used to direct the flow of cooling air between and around the cylinder fins of an air-cooled reciprocating engine.

Bayonet stack. An exhaust stack with an elongated and flattened end. The gases leave the stack through a slot perpendicular to its length. Bayonet stacks decrease both exhaust back pressure and noise.

BDC. Bottom dead center. The position of a piston in a reciprocating engine when the piston is at the bottom of its stroke, and the wrist pin, crankpin, and center of the crankshaft are all in line.

Bell mouth. The shape of the inlet of an augmentor tube that forms a smooth converging duct. The bell mouth shape allows the maximum amount of air to be drawn into the tube.

Bell mouth inlet duct. A form of convergent inlet-air duct used to direct air into the compressor of a gas turbine engine. It is extremely efficient, and is used where there is little ram pressure available to force air into the engine. Bell mouth ducts are used in engine test cells and on engines installed in helicopters.

Benzene. A colorless, volatile, flammable, aromatic hydrocarbon liquid which has the chemical formula C_6H_6. Benzene, which is sometimes called benzoil, is used as a solvent, a cleaning fluid, and a fuel for some special types of reciprocating engines.

Bernoulli's principle. A physical principle that explains the relationship between kinetic and potential energy in a stream of moving fluid. When energy is neither added to nor taken from the fluid, any increase in its velocity (kinetic energy) will result in a corresponding decrease in its pressure (potential energy).

Beta control range (Beta mode). The range of operation of a turboprop powerplant used for in-flight approach and ground handling of the engine and aircraft. Typically, the Beta mode includes operations from 65% to 95% of the engine's rated rpm.

Beta tube. A tube in a Garrett TPE331 turboprop powerplant that extends into the propeller pitch control to act as a follow-up device. It provides movement of the propeller blades in proportion to movement of the power lever.

Bezel. The rim which holds the glass cover in the case of an aircraft instrument.

BHP. Brake horsepower. The actual horsepower delivered to the propeller shaft of a reciprocating or turboprop engine.

Bidirectional fibers. Fibers in a piece of composite material arranged to sustain loads in two directions.

Bimetallic hairspring. A flat, spiral-wound spring made of two strips of metal laid side-by-side and welded together. The two metals have different coefficients of expansion, and as the temperature changes, the spiral either tightens or loosens. A bimetallic hair spring is used in a thermocouple temperature changes at the reference junction.

Bimetallic strip. A metal strip made of two different types of metal fastened together side by side. When heated, the two metals expand different amounts and the strip warps or bends.

BITE. Built-in test equipment. A troubleshooting system installed in many modern jet aircraft. BITE equipment monitors engine and airframe systems, and when a fault is found, isolates it and provides maintenance personnel with a code that identifies the LRU (line replaceable unit) that contains the fault.

Blade. The component of a propeller that converts the rotation of the propeller shaft into thrust. The blade of a propeller corresponds to the wing of an airplane.

Blade angle. The acute angle between the chord line of a propeller blade and the plane of rotation.

Blade butt. The end of a propeller blade that fits into the hub.

Blade root. The ridges or upset portion of a propeller blade that holds it in the hub.

Blade shank. The rounded portion of a propeller blade between the root and the airfoil section.

Blade station. A reference position on a propeller blade that is a specified number of inches from the center of the propeller hub.

Blade tip. The opposite end from the root of a propeller blade.

Blending. A method of repairing damaged compressor and turbine blades. The damage is removed and the area is cleaned out with a fine file to form a shallow depression with generous radii. The file marks are then removed with a fine abrasive stone so the surface of the repaired area will match the surface of the rest of the blade.

Blisk. A turbine wheel machined from a single slab of steel. The disk and blades are an integral unit.

Blow-in doors. Spring-loaded doors in the inlet duct of some turbojet or turbofan engine installations that are opened by differential air pressure when inlet air pressure drops below that of the ambient air. Air flowing through the doors adds to the normal inlet air passing through the engine and helps prevent compressor stall.

Bluckets. The portions of aft-fan blades that are in the exhaust of the core engine. Bluckets drive the fan from energy received from hot gases leaving the core engine.

BMEP. Brake mean effective pressure. The average pressure inside the cylinder of a reciprocating engine during the power stroke. BMEP, measured in pounds per square inch, relates to the torque produced by the engine and can be calculated when you know the brake horsepower.

Boost. A term for manifold pressure that has been increased above the ambient atmospheric pressure by a supercharger.

Bootstrapping. An action that is self-initiating or self-sustaining. In a turbocharger system, bootstrapping describes a transient increase in engine power that causes the turbocharger to speed up, which in turn causes the engine to produce more power.

Bore. The diameter of a reciprocating engine cylinder.

Borescope. An inspection tool for viewing the inside of a turbine engine without disassembling it. The instrument consists of a light, mirror, and magnifying lens mounted inside a small-diameter tube that is inserted into a turbine engine through borescope inspection ports.

Boss. An enlarged area in a casting or machined part. A boss provides additional strength to the part where holes for mounting or attaching parts are drilled.

Bottom. (verb) A condition in the installation of a propeller on a splined shaft when either the front or rear cone contacts an obstruction that prevents the cone from properly seating inside the propeller hub.

Bourdon tube. The major component in a gage-pressure measuring instrument. It is a thin-wall metal tube that has an elliptical cross section and is formed into a curve. One end of the tube is sealed and connected to an arm that moves the pointer across the instrument dial, and the open end is anchored to the instrument case. The pressure to be measured is directed into the open end, which causes the elliptical cross section to become more circular. As the cross section changes, the curve straightens and moves the pointer over the dial by an amount proportional to the amount of pressure.

Brayton cycle. The constant-pressure cycle of energy transformation used by gas turbine engines. Fuel is sprayed into the air passing through the engine and burned. Heat from the burning fuel-air mixture expands the air and accelerates it as it moves through the engine. The Brayton cycle is an open cycle in that the intake, compression, combustion, expansion, and exhaust events all take place at the same time, but in different locations within the engine.

British thermal unit (Btu). The basic unit of heat energy in the English system. One Btu is the amount of heat energy needed to raise the temperature of one pound of pure water from 60 °F to 61 °F.

BSFC. Brake specific fuel consumption. A measure of the amount of fuel used for a given amount of power produced by a heat engine. BSFC is expressed in pounds of fuel burned per hour for each brake horse-power the engine is producing.

Bungee cord. An elastic cord made of small strips of rubber encased in a loosely braided cloth tube that holds and protects the rubber, yet allows it to stretch. The energy in a stretched bungee cord may be used to crank a large aircraft engine.

Burner. See combustor.

Burnish. To smooth the surface of a metal part that has been damaged by a deep scratch or gouge. Metal piled at the edge of the damage is pushed back into the damage with a smooth, hard steel burnishing tool.

Butterfly valve. A flat, disk-shaped valve used to control the flow of fluid in a round pipe or tube. When the butterfly valve is across the tube, the flow is shut off, and when it is parallel with the tube, the obstruction caused by the valve is minimum, and the flow is at its greatest. Butterfly-type throttle valves are used to control the airflow through the fuel metering system.

Bypass engine. Another name for a turbofan engine. See turbofan engine.

Bypass ratio. The ratio of the mass of air moved by the fan to the mass of air moved by the core engine.

Calendar month. The measurement of time used by the FAA for inspection and certification purposes. One calendar month from a given date extends from that date until midnight of the last day of that month.

Cam. An eccentric, or lobe, on a rotating shaft that changes rotary motion into linear motion. A cam is mounted on the magnet shaft in a magneto to push upward on the insulated breaker point to separate, or open, the points when the magnet is in a particular location.

Cam engine. A reciprocating engine with axial cylinders arranged around a central shaft. Rollers on the pistons in the cylinders press against a sinusoidal cam mounted on the shaft to produce rotation of the shaft.

Cam-ground piston. A reciprocating engine piston that is not round, but is ground so that its diameter parallel to the wrist pin is slightly smaller than its diameter perpendicular to the pin. The mass of metal used in the wrist pin boss, the enlarged area around the wrist pin hole, expands when heated, and when the piston is at its operating temperature, it is perfectly round.

Can-annular combustor. A type of combustor used in some large turbojet and turbofan engines. It consists of individual cans into which fuel is sprayed and ignited. These cans mount on an annular duct which collects the hot gases and directs them uniformly into the turbine.

Capacitance afterfiring. The continuation of the spark across the gap in a shielded spark plug after the fuel-air mixture in the cylinder is ignited. Afterfiring is caused by the return of electrical energy stored in the capacitance of the shielded ignition leads. Capacitance afterfiring is eliminated by the use of a resistor in the spark plug.

Capacitor. An electrical component, formerly called a condenser, that consists of two large-area conductors, called plates, separated by an insulator. Electrons stored on one of the plates produces an electrostatic pressure difference between the plates.

Capillary tube. A glass or metal tube with a tiny inside diameter. Capillary action causes the fluid to move within the tube.

Carbon pile voltage regulator. A voltage regulator for a high output DC generator that uses a stack of pure carbon disks for the variable resistance element. A spring holds pressure on the stack to reduce its resistance when the generator output voltage is low. This allows maximum field current to flow. The field from an electro-magnet, whose strength varies directly with the generator voltage, opposes the spring to loosen the stack and increase its resistance when the generator voltage needs to be decreased. The increased resistance decreases the field current and reduces the output voltage.

Carbon track. A trail of carbon deposited by an arc across a high-voltage component such as a distributor block. Carbon tracks have a relatively low resistance to the high voltage and can cause misfiring and loss of engine power.

Cartridge starter. A self-contained starter used on some military aircraft. A cartridge similar in size to a shotgun shell is ignited in the starter breech. The expanding gases drive a piston attached to a helical spline that converts the linear movement of the piston into rotary motion to rotate the crankshaft.

Cascade effect. The cumulative effect that occurs when the output of one series of components serves as the input to the next series.

Catalyst. A substance used to change the speed, or rate, of a chemical action without being chemically changed itself.

Cavitating. The creation of low pressure in an oil pump when the inlet system is not able to supply all of the oil the pump requires. Prolonged cavitation can damage pump components.

Center of pressure. The point on the chord line of an airfoil where all aerodynamic forces are concentrated.

Center-line thrust airplane. A twin-engine airplane with both engines mounted in the fuselage. One is installed as a tractor in the front of the cabin. The empennage is mounted on booms.

Centrifugal compressor. A type of compressor that uses a vaned plate like impeller. Air is taken into the center, or eye, of the impeller and slung outward by centrifugal force into a diffuser where its velocity is decreased and its pressure increased.

Ceramic. Any of several hard, brittle, heat-resistant, noncorrosive materials made by shaping and then firing a mineral, such as clay, at a high temperature.

Channel-chromed cylinders. Reciprocating engine cylinders with hard chromium-plated walls. The surface of this chrome plating forms a spider web of tiny stress cracks. Deplating current enlarges the cracks and forms channels that hold lubricating oil on the cylinder wall.

Cheek (crankshaft). The offset portion of a crankshaft that connects the crankpin to the main bearing journals.

Chip detector. A component in a lubrication system that attracts and holds ferrous metal chips circulating with the engine oil. Some chip detectors are part of an electrical circuit. When metal particles short across the two contacts in the detector, the circuit is completed, and an annunciator light is turned on to inform the flight crew that metal particles are loose in the lubrication system.

Choke of a cylinder. The difference in the bore diameter of a reciprocating engine cylinder in the area of the head and in the center of the barrel.

Choke-ground cylinder. A cylinder of a reciprocating engine that is ground so that its diameter at the top of the barrel is slightly smaller than the diameter in the center of the stroke. The large mass of metal in the cylinder head absorbs enough heat to cause the top end of the barrel to expand more than the rest of the barrel. At normal operating temperature, the diameter of a choke-ground cylinder is uniform throughout.

Choke nozzle. A nozzle in a gas turbine engine that limits the speed of gases flowing through it. The gases accelerate until they reach the speed of sound, and a normal shock wave forms that prevents further acceleration.

Chord line. An imaginary line, passing through a propeller blade, joining the leading and trailing edges.

Cigarette. A commonly used name for a spark plug terminal connector used with a shielded spark plug.

Circular magnetism. A method of magnetizing a part for magnetic particle inspection. Current is passed through the part, and the lines of magnetic flux surround it. Circular magnetism makes it possible to detect faults that extend lengthwise through the part.

Circumferential coil spring (garter spring). A coil spring formed into a ring. This type of spring is used to hold segmented ring-type carbon seals tightly against a rotating shaft.

Claret red. A dark purplish pink to a dark gray purplish red color.

Class A fire. A fire with solid combustible materials such as wood, paper, and cloth as its fuel.

Class B fire. A fire that has combustible liquids as its fuel.

Class C fire. A fire which involves energized electrical equipment.

Class D fire. A fire in which a metal such as magnesium burns.

Closed-loop control. A type of control in which part of the output is fed back to the input. This allows the input to continually compare the command signals with the output to determine the extent to which the commands have been complied with.

Coke. The solid carbon residue left when all volatile parts of a mineral oil have been evaporated by heat.

Cold-cranking simulation. A method used for specifying the characteristics of a lubricating oil at low temperature. Oils rated by this test have the letter W (standing for Winter) in their designation. For example, SAE 15W50.

Cold section. The portion of a gas turbine engine ahead of the combustion section. The cold section includes the inlet, compressor, and diffuser.

Cold-tank lubrication system. A turbine engine lubricating system in which the oil cooler is in the scavenge subsystem.

Collector ring. A ring made of thin corrosion-resistant steel tubing that encircles a radial engine and collects exhaust gases from each cylinder. The ring ends with a connection to the exhaust tail pipe.

Combustor (combustion chamber). The section of a gas turbine engine in which fuel is injected. This fuel mixes with air from the compressor and burns. The intense heat from the combustion expands the air flowing through the combustor and directs it our through the turbine. Combustors are also called burners.

Commutator. A mechanical rectifier mounted on the armature shaft of a DC generator or motor. It consists of a cylindrical arrangement of insulated copper bars connected to the armature coils. Carbon brushes ride on the copper bars to carry current into or out of the commutator, providing a unidirectional current from a generator or a reversal of current in the motor coils.

Compensating winding. A series winding in a compound-wound DC generator. The compensating windings are embedded in the faces of the field poles and their varying magnetic field works with the fields from the interpoles to effectively cancel the field distortion caused by armature current.

Composite propeller blade. A propeller blade made from several materials such as metal, graphite, glass or aramid fibers, and foam.

Compression ratio (reciprocating engine). The ratio of the volume of a cylinder of a reciprocating engine with the piston at the bottom of its stroke engine to the volume of the cylinder with the piston at the top of its stroke.

Compression ratio (turbine engine). The ratio of the pressure of the air at the discharge of a turbine engine compressor to the pressure of the air at its inlet.

Compressor bleed air. Air that is tapped off from a turbine engine compressor. Compressor bleed air is used for anti-icing the inlet ducts and for cooling the turbine inlet guide vanes and first stage turbine blades. Bleed air is also used for certain airframe functions. See customer bleed air.

Compressor pressure ratio. See compression ratio (turbine engine).

Compressor stall. A condition in a turbine engine axial-flow compressor in which the angle of attack of one or more blades is excessive and the smooth airflow through the compressor is disrupted.

Compressor surge. A stall that affects the entire compressor and seriously restricts the airflow through the engine.

Con-di ducts. The British name for a convergent-divergent duct. See convergent-divergent duct.

Condenser. See capacitor.

"Contact." The term used between a person hand-propping an aircraft engine and the person in the flightdeck. When the person is ready to spin the propeller, he calls "contact". The person in the flightdeck turns on the fuel, slightly opens the throttle, applies the brakes, and replies "contact", and then turns the ignition switch to BOTH. The propeller is then pulled through to start the engine.

Constant-displacement pump. A fluid pump that moves a specific volume of fluid each time it rotates.

Constant-pressure cycle of energy release. The cycle of energy transformation of a gas turbine engine. See Brayton cycle.

Constant-volume cycle of energy release. The cycle of energy transformation of a reciprocating engine. See Otto cycle.

Continuous magnetic particle inspection. A method of magnetic particle inspection in which the part is inspected by flowing a fluid containing particles of iron oxide over the part while the magnetizing current is flowing.

Contrarotating. Rotating in opposite directions. Turbine rotors are contrarotating when the different stages have a common center, but turn in opposite directions.

Convergent-divergent duct. A duct that has a decreasing cross section in the direction of flow (convergent) until a minimum area is reached. After this point, the cross section increases (divergent). Convergent-divergent ducts are called CD ducts or con-di ducts.

Convergent duct. A duct that has a decreasing cross section in the direction of flow.

Core engine. The gas generator portion of a turboshaft, turboprop, or turbofan engine. The core engine consists of the portion of the compressor used to supply air for the engine operation, diffuser, combustors, and turbine(s) used to drive the compressor. The core engine provides the high-velocity gas to drive the fan and/or any free turbines that provide power for propellers, rotors, pumps, or generators.

Cowling. The removable cover that encloses an aircraft engine.

Crankcase. The housing that encloses the crankshaft, camshaft, and many of the accessory drive gears of a reciprocating engine. The cylinders are mounted on the crankcase, and the engine attaches to the airframe by the crankcase.

Crankshaft. The central component of a reciprocating engine. This high-strength alloy steel shaft has hardened and polished bearing surfaces that ride in bearings in the crankcase. Offset throws, formed on the crankshaft, have ground and polished surfaces on which the connecting rods ride. The connecting rods change the in-and-out motion of the pistons into rotation of the crankshaft.

Creep. The deformation of a metal part that is continually exposed to high centrifugal loads and temperatures.

Critical altitude. The altitude above which a reciprocating engine will no longer produce its rated horsepower with its throttle wide open.

Critical engine. The engine of a twin-engine airplane whose loss would cause the greatest yawing effect.

Critical Match number. The flight match number at which there is the first indication of air flowing over any part of the structure at a speed of Mach one, the local speed of sound.

CRT. Cathode ray tube. An electronic display tube in which a stream of electrons is attracted to the charged inner surface of the tube face. Acceleration grids and inner surface of the tube face. Acceleration grids and focusing grids speed the movement of the electrons and shape the beam to a pinpoint size. Electrostatic or electromagnetic forces caused by deflection plates or coils move the beam over the face of the tube. The inside of the tube face is treated with a phosphor material that emits light when the electrons strike it.

Cryogenic fluid. A liquid which boils at a temperature lower than about 110 °K (-163 °C) under normal atmospheric pressure.

CSD. Constant-speed drive. A component used with either aircraft gas turbine or reciprocating engines to drive AC generators. The speed of the output shaft of the CSD is held constant while the speed of its input shaft caries. The CSD holds the speed of the generator, and the frequency of the AC constant as the engine speed varies through its normal operating range.

CTF. Centrifugal twisting force. The force acting about the longitudinal axis of a propeller blade, and which tries to rotate the blade to a low-pitch angle. As the propeller rotates, centrifugal force tries to flatten the blade so all of its mass rotates in the same plane.

Curtiss Jenny (Curtiss JN4-D). A World War I training airplane powered by a Curtiss OX-5 engine. It was widely available after the war and helped introduce aviation to the general public.

Customer bleed air. Air that is tapped off a turbine engine compressor and used for such airframe functions as the operation of air conditioning and pressurization systems.

Cylinder. The component of a reciprocating engine which houses the piston, valves, and spark plugs and forms the combustion chamber.

Data. The input for computer processing in the form of numerical information that represents characters or analog quantities.

Dataplate specifications. Specification of each gas turbine engine determined in the manufacturer's test cell when the engine was calibrated. This data includes the engine serial number with the EPR that produced a specific RPM. The technician refers to this information when trimming the engine.

Dataplate performance. The performance specifications of a turbine engine observed and recorded by the engine manufacturer or overhauler and recorded on the engine dataplate. This data includes the engine speed at which a specified EPR is attained. When trimming the engine, the technician uses this data as the goal.

DC. Direct current. Electrical current in which the electrons always flow in the same direction.

Deaerator. A component in a turbine engine lubrication system that removes air from the scavenged oil before it is returned to the tank.

Deceleration. The amount the velocity of an object, measured in feet per second, is decreased by a force during each second it is acted upon by that force. Deceleration is usually expressed in terms of feet per second, per second (fps^2).

DeHaviland DH-4. An English designed observation airplane built in large quantities in the united States during World War I. After the war, surplus DH-4s were used for carrying the U.S. Mail.

Deicing. The removal of ice that has formed on a surface.

Density altitude. The altitude in standard air at which the density is the same as that of the existing air.

Detergent oil. A type of mineral oil with metallic-ash-forming additives that protects the inside of an engine from sludge and varnish buildup. Used in automotive engines, it has proven unsuitable for use in aircraft engines.

Detonation. An uncontrolled explosion inside the cylinder of a reciprocating engine. Detonation occurs when the pressure and temperature of the fuel inside the cylinder exceeds the critical pressure and temperature of the fuel. Detonation may be caused by using fuel that has a lower octane rating or performance number than is specified for the engine.

Dewar bottle. A special container used to store liquid oxygen and liquid nitrogen. A Dewar bottle has an inner and an outer container, and the space between them forms a vacuum. The two surfaces within the vacuum are silvered to reflect heat away from the container walls.

Differential pressure. A single pressure that is the difference between two opposing pressures.

Diffuser. A component in a gas turbine engine that decreases the velocity of air flowing through it and increases its pressure.

Digitized image. A modified image picked up by the miniature TV camera in the end of a fiber-optic probe. This image is converted into a digital electronic signal that eliminates unwanted portions of the viewed area and allows the desired image to be enhanced for a clearer view of the inside of a turbine engine.

Dipstick. A gage, in the form of a thin metal rod, used to measure the level of liquid in a reservoir. The dipstick is pushed into the reservoir until it contacts a built-in stop; then it is removed and visually inspected. The level of liquid in the reservoir is indicated by the amount of the dipstick wet by the liquid.

Dirigible. A large, cigar shaped, lighter-than-air flying machine. Dirigibles differ from balloons in that they are powered and can be steered.

Distributed pole stator winding. Alternator stator windings wound in a series of slots in the stator frame. A distributed pole stator is distinguished from a salient pole stator whose coils are wound around separate pole shoes that project inward from the field frame toward the rotor.

Distributor. A high-voltage selector switch that is gear-driven from the shaft of the rotating magnet in a magneto. The distributor rotor picks up the high voltage from the secondary winding of the coil and directs it to high-voltage terminals. From here, it is carried by high-tension ignition leads to the spark plugs.

Divergent duct. A duct that has an increased cross-sectional area in the direction of flow.

Downdraft carburetor. A carburetor that mounts on the top of a reciprocating engine. Air entering the engine flows downward through the carburetor.

ΔP (delta P). Differential pressure.

Droop. A progressive decrease in RPOM with load in a gas turbine engine whose speed is governed with a fly-weight-type governor in the fuel control. As the load increases, the pilot valve drops down to meter more fuel. The lower position of the valve decreases the compression of the speeder spring and allows the flyweights to assume an on-speed position at a lower rpm.

Dry-sump engine. An engine that carries its lubricating oil supply in a tank external to the engine.

Dual ignition. An ignition system of an aircraft reciprocating engine that has two of every critical unit, including two spark plugs in each cylinder. Dual ignition provides safety in the event of one system malfunctioning, but more important, igniting the fuel-air mixture inside the cylinder at two locations provides more efficient combustion of the fuel-air mixture in the cylinder.

Dual-spool gas turbine engine. An axial-flow turbine engine that has two compressors, each driven by its own stage or stages of turbines.

Duct heater. A thrust augmentation system, similar to an afterburner, where fuel is added to the fan-discharge air and burned.

Duct losses. A decrease in pressure of the air flowing into a gas turbine engine caused by friction.

Durability. A measure of engine life. Durability is usually measured in TBO hours.

Duty cycle. A schedule that allows a device to operate for a given period of time, followed by a cooling down period before the device can be operated again.

Dwell chamber. A chamber in a turbine engine into which the scavenged oil is returned. Entrained air separates from the oil in the dwell chamber before it is picked up by the pressure pump.

Dynamometer. A device used to measure the amount of torque being produced by an engine. The drive shaft of the engine is loaded with either an electric generator or a fluid pump, and the output of the generator or pump is measured and converted into units of torque. Torque at a specific rpm can be converted into brake horsepower.

Dyne. The unit of force that imparts an acceleration of one centimeter per second, per second to a mass of one gram. One dyne is equal to $2.248 \cdot 10^{-6}$ pounds.

Eddy current. Current induced into a conductor due to a mobbing or non-uniform magnetic field.

EEC. Electronic engine control. An electronic fuel control for a gas turbine engine. The EEC senses the power-lever angle (PLA), engine RPM, bleed valve, and variable stator vane position, and the various engine pressures and temperatures. It meters the correct amount of fuel to the nozzles for all flight conditions, to prevent turbine over-speed and over-temperature.

Effective pitch. The actual distance a propeller advances in one revolution through the air.

E-gap angle. The position of the rotating magnet in a magneto when the breaker points are timed to open. The E-gap (efficiency gap) angle is several degrees of magnet rotation beyond the magnet's neutral position. At this point, the magnetic field stress is the greatest, and the change in flux is the greatest, inducing the maximum voltage in the secondary winding.

EGT. Exhaust gas temperature. The temperature of the gases as they leave the cylinder of a reciprocating engine or the turbine of a gas turbine engine.

EICAS. Engine indicating and crew alerting system. An electronic instrumentation system that monitors airframe and engine parameters and displays the essential information on a video display on the instrument panel. Only vital information is continually displayed, but when any sensed parameters fall outside of their allowable range of operation, they are automatically displayed.

Elastic limit. The maximum amount of tensile load, in pounds per square inch, that a material is able to withstand without permanent deformation.

Electrical potential. The electrical force caused by a deficiency of electrons in one location and an excess of electrons in another. Electrical potential is measured in volts.

Electrical steel. A low-carbon iron alloy that contains some silicon It is used as the core for transformers, field frames for generators and alternators, and the magnetic circuit of magnetos.

Electromagnet. A magnet produced by an electrical current flowing through a coil of wire. The coil is normally wound around a core of soft iron which has an extremely low retentivity, allowing it to lose its magnetism as soon as the current stops flowing.

Electromagnetic radiation. A method of transmitting energy from one location to another. Current caused by high voltage in the secondary winding of a magneto produces electric and magnetic fields which oscillate back and forth at a high frequency and extend out into space in the form of waves. These waves of electromagnetic radiation are received as interference by the radio receivers in the aircraft.

Electromotive force. A force that causes electrons to move from one atom to another within an electrical circuit. An electromotive force, or EMF, is the difference in the electrical pressure, or potential, that exists between two points. An EMF may be produced by converting mechanical movement, pressure, chemical, light, or heat energy into electrical energy. The basic unit of EMF is the volt.

Emulsion. A suspension of small globules of one material in another when the two materials will not mix. Oil and water will not mix, but they can be formed into an emulsion. An emulsion will separate into its components when it is allowed to sit.

Engine trimming. A maintenance procedure in which the fuel control on a gas turbine engine is adjusted to cause the engine to produce the required EGT or EPR at a specified rpm.

Entrained water. Water suspended in jet fuel. The amount of entrained water that can be held in the fuel is determined by the temperature of the fuel. When the fuel becomes cold, the water precipitates out and forms ice crystals on the fuel filter element.

Epicyclic reduction gears. A gear train in which a series of small planetary gears rotate around a central gear. More commonly called a planetary gear train.

EPR. Engine pressure ratio. The ratio of the turbine discharge total pressure to the compressor inlet total pressure. EPR is normally used as the parameter to determine the amount of thrust an axial-flow turbojet or turbofan engine is producing.

ESHP. Equivalent shaft horsepower. A measure of the power produced by a turboprop engine. ESHP takes into consideration both the shaft horsepower delivered to the propeller and the thrust developed at the engine exhaust. Under static conditions, one shaft horsepower is approximately equal to 2.5 pounds of thrust.

Ethanol. Alcohol made from cereal grains such as corn.

Ether. A volatile, highly flammable liquid that may be used to prime the cylinders of an aircraft engine when starting under extremely cold conditions.

Ethylene dibromide. A colorless, poisonous liquid $BrCH_2CH_2Br$ that is blended with leaded gasoline to help scavenge lead oxides.

Ethylene glycol. A form of alcohol used as a coolant for liquid-cooled aircraft engines. It is also used in automobile engines as a permanent antifreeze.

Eutectic. An alloy or solution that has the lowest possible constant melting point.

Evaporative cooling. See steam cooling.

Exceedance condition. A condition in which a parameter sensed by the EICAS exceeds the limits for which it is programmed.

Exhaust cone. The fixed conical fairing centered in the turbine wheel. The exhaust cone straightens the flow and prevents the hot gases from circulating over the rear face of the turbine wheel.

Exhaust nozzle. The opening at the rear of the exhaust pipe.

Expansion wave. The change in pressure and velocity of supersonic air as it passes over a surface that drops away from the flow. As the surface drops away, the air tries to follow it, and in changing its direction, the air speeds up to a higher supersonic speed, and its static pressure decreases. There is no change in the total amount of energy as air passes through an expansion wave.

External-combustion engine. A form of heat engine in which the fuel releases its energy outside of the engine. This released heat expands air which is used to perform useful work. Steam engines are a popular type of external combustion engine.

Extreme pressure (EP) lubricant. A lubricant that reacts with iron to form iron chlorides, sulfides, or phosphides on the surface of a steel part. These compounds reduce wear and damage to surfaces in heavy rubbing contact. EP lubricants are specially suited for lubricating gear trains.

FAA Form 337. The *Major Repair and Alteration* form that must be completed when an FAA-certificated aircraft or engine has been given a major repair or major alteration.

Face (propeller nomenclature). The flat surface of a propeller that strikes the air as the propeller rotates. The face of a propeller corresponds to the bottom of an airplane wing.

FADEC. Full-authority digital electronic control. A digital electronic fuel control for a gas turbine engine that is functioning during all engine operations, hence full authority. It includes the EEC (see EEC) and functions with the flight management computer. FADEC schedules the fuel to the nozzles in such a way that prevents overshooting power changes and over-temperature conditions. FADEC furnishes information to the EICAS (engine indication and crew alerting system).

Fan pressure ratio. The ratio of the fan-discharge pressure to the fan inlet pressure.

Feathering propeller. A controllable-pitch propeller whose blades can be moved into a high pitch angle of approximately 90°. Feathering the propeller of an inoperative engine prevents it from wind-milling and greatly decreases drag.

Feeler gages. A type of measuring tool consisting of strips of precision-ground steel of accurately measured thickness. Feeler gages are used to measure the distance between close-fitting parts, such as the clearances of a mechanical system or the distance by which moving contacts are separated.

FHP. Friction horsepower. The amount of horsepower used to turn the crankshaft, pistons, gears, and accessories in a reciprocating engine and to compress the air inside the cylinders.

Fiber optics. The technique of transmitting light or images through long, thin, flexible fibers of plastic or glass. Bundles of fibers are used to transmit complete images.

Fire sleeve. A covering of fire-resistant fabric used to protect flexible fluid lines that are routed through areas subject to high temperature.

Flame tubes. Small-diameter metal tubes that connect can-type combustors in a turbine engine to carry the ignition flame to all of the combustion chambers. The British call combustion liners flame tubes.

Flameout. A condition of turbine engine operation when the fire unintentionally goes out. Improper fuel-air mixture or interruption of the air flow through the engine can cause a flameout.

Flash point. The temperature to which a liquid must be raised for it to ignite, but not continue to burn when a flame is passed above it.

Flashing the field. A maintenance procedure for a DC generator that restores residual magnetism to the field frame. A pulse of current from a battery is sent through the field coils in the direction in which current normally flows. The magnetic field produced by this current magnetizes the steel frame of the generator.

Flashover. An ignition system malfunction in which the high voltage in the magneto distributor jumps to the wrong terminal. Flashover causes the wrong spark plug to fire. This reduces the engine power and produces vibration and excessive heat.

Flat-rated engine. A turboprop engine whose allowable output power is less than the engine is physically capable of producing.

Float carburetor. A fuel metering device that uses a float-actuated needle valve to maintain fuel level slightly below the edge of the discharge nozzle.

Flock. Pulverized wood or cotton fibers mixed with an adhesive. Flock, attached to a wire screen, acts as an effective induction air filter for small reciprocating engines.

Flow divider (reciprocating engine). The valve in an RSA fuel injection system that divides the fuel from the fuel control unit and distributes it to all of the cylinders. It compares with the manifold valve in a Teledyne-Continental fuel injection system.

Flow divider (turbine engine). A component in a turbine engine fuel system that routes all of the fuel to the primary nozzles or primary orifices when starting the engine or when the rpm is low. When the engine speed builds up, the flow divider shifts and opens a passage to send the majority of the fuel to the secondary nozzles or orifices.

FMC. Flight management computer. An electronic flight instrumentation system that enables the flight crew to initiate and implement a given flight plan and monitor its execution.

FOD. Foreign object damage. Damage to components in the gas path of a turbine engine, caused by ingested objects. Debris from the runway or ramp cause FOD on the ground. Ice and birds cause most in-flight FOD.

Four-stroke cycle. A constant-volume cycle of energy transformation that has separate strokes for intake, compression, power, and exhaust.

Fractional distillation. Procedure used for separating various components from a physical mixture of liquids. Crude oil is a mixture of many different types of hydrocarbon fuels which can be separated by carefully raising its temperature. The first products to be released, those having the lowest boiling points, are some of the gaseous fuels; next are gasoline, kerosene, diesel fuel, heavy fuel oils, lubricating oils, and finally, tar and asphalt.

Frangible. Capable of being broken.

Free-turbine engine. A gas turbine engine with a turbine stage on a shaft independent of the shaft used to drive the compressor. Free turbines are used to drive the propeller reduction gear in a turboprop engine and the rotor transmission in a helicopter.

Freezing point. The temperature at which solids, such as wax crystals, separate from a hydrocarbon fuel as it is cooled.

Fuel-air mixture ratio. Ratio of the number of pounds of fuel to the number of pounds of air in the mixture burned in cylinders of a reciprocating engine.

Full-register position. The position of a magnet in a magneto when its poles are aligned with the pole shoes and the maximum amount of magnetic flux is flowing through the magnetic circuit.

Gauge pressure. Pressure referenced from existing atmospheric pressure.

Gas generator. The basic gas turbine engine. It consists of the compressor, diffuser, combustor, and turbine. The gas generator is also called the core engine.

Gas turbine engine. An internal combustion engine that burns its fuel in a constant-pressure cycle and uses the expansion of the air to drive a turbine which, in turn, rotates a compressor. Energy beyond that needed to rotate the compressor is used to produce torque or thrust.

General Aviation Airworthiness Alerts. Documents published by the FAA as Advisory Circulars 43.16. These are used to alert technicians of problems that have been found in specific models of aircraft, and reported on Malfunction and Defect Reports. Airworthiness Alerts suggest corrective action, but compliance with the suggestion is not mandatory.
general aviation. A term used to describe the total field of aviation operation except the military and airlines.

Geometric pitch. The distance a propeller would advance in one revolution if it were rotating in a solid.

Geopotential of the tropopause. The point in the standard atmosphere where the temperature stops dropping and becomes constant. This is the tropopause, or the dividing line between the troposphere and the stratosphere.

Gerotor pump. A form of constant-displacement pump that uses an external-tooth drive gear that meshes with and drives an internal-tooth gear that has one more space for a tooth than there are teeth on the drive gear. Both gears turn inside a close-tolerance housing. As the gears rotate, fluid flows between the teeth that are beginning to un-mesh, and is carried around the pump as the space continues to open up. On the discharge side of the pump, the teeth becomes smaller, fluid is forced out of the pump.

Glass cockpit. An aircraft instrument system that uses a few color cathode-ray-tube displays to replace a large number of mechanically actuated instruments.

Governor. A control used to automatically change the pitch of a constant speed propeller to maintain a constant engine rpm as air loads vary in flight.

GPU. Ground power unit. A service component used to supply electrical power and compressed air to an aircraft when it is operating on the ground.

Gross thrust. The thrust produced by a turbojet or turbofan engine when the engine is static or not moving. The air is considered to have no inlet velocity, and the velocity of the gas leaving the engine is considered to be the acceleration factor.

Ground-boosted engine. An aircraft reciprocating engine with a built-in supercharger that boosts the sea-level rated horsepower of the engine.

Gudgeon pin. The British name for a wrist pin, or piston pin. See wrist pin.

Half-wave rectifier. An electrical rectifier circuit that converts AC into pulsating DC. Only one alternation of each cycle is present in the output.

Halogenated hydrocarbon. A hydrocarbon compound in which one or more hydrogen atoms have been replaced with atoms of one of the halogen elements such as fluorine, chlorine, or bromine.

Head of pressure. Pressure exerted by a column of fluid and created by the height of the column.

Heat engine. A mechanical device that converts the chemical energy in a fuel into heat energy. The heat energy is then converted into mechanical energy and useful work.

Heli-Coil insert. The registered trade name of a special helical insert used to restore threads stripped from a bolt hole, or to reinforce the threads in an aluminum casting. The damaged threads are drilled out and new threads are cut with a special oversize tap. A coil of stainless steel wire, with a cross section in the shape of a diamond, is screwed into the hole and serves as the new threads. Heli-Coil inserts are also used to provide durable threads in soft metal castings. Some spark plug holes in aluminum alloy cylinder heads are fitted with Heli-Coil inserts to minimize the wear caused by repeated removal and installation of the spark plugs.

Helical spline. A spline that twists, or winds, around the periphery of a shaft. Helical splines are used to change linear motion into rotary motion of the shaft on which the splines are cut.

Helical spring. A spring wound in the form of a helix, or coil.

Helix. A spiral.

Heptanes. An organic compound, $CH_3(CH_2)_5CH_3$, that is used as the low reference fuel for rating the antidetonation characteristics of aviation gasoline.

Hermetically sealed. A complete seal, especially against the escape or entry of air.

Hertz. A unit of frequency equal to one cycle per second.

High-bypass ratio engine. A turbofan engine whose bypass ratio is 4:1 or greater.

High-pressure compressor. The second-stage compressor in a dual-spool gas turbine engine. The high pressure compressor is called the N2 compressor and is the one that is rotated by the starter for starting, and the one whose rpm is controlled by the fuel control.

High unmetered fuel pressure. Pressure in a Teledyne-Continental fuel injector pump that is adjusted by the variable orifice.

Homebuilt aircraft. See amateur-built aircraft.

Honing (cylinder wall treatment). Scratching the surface of the cylinder wall with an abrasive to produce a series of grooves of microscopic depth and uniform pattern. The honed pattern holds oil to lubricate the cylinder walls.

Horsepower. The most commonly used unit of mechanical power. One horsepower is equal to 33,000 foot-pounds of work done in one second.

Hot section. The portion of a gas turbine engine that operates at a high temperature. The hot section includes the combustion, turbine, and exhaust sections.

Hot-tank lubricating system. A turbine engine lubricating system in which the oil cooler is located in the pressure subsystem. The oil is returned to the tank without being cooled.

HRD fire extinguisher. A fire extinguisher that carries the extinguishing agent in a sealed sphere or cylinder. When the agent-discharged switch is closed, an ignited powder charge drives a cutter through a frangible disk which releases the agent. The entire contents of the container is emptied in much less than a second.

Hub (propeller component). The high-strength component inside a propeller that attaches the blades to the engine propeller shaft.

Hybrid compressor engine. A gas turbine engine that has both centrifugal and axial-flow compressors.

Hybrid spark plug. A fine-wire spark plug that has a platinum center electrode and iridium ground electrodes.

Hydraulic lock. A condition in which oil drains into the lower cylinders of a reciprocating engine and leaks past the piston rings to fill the combustion chamber. If the oil is not removed before the engine is started, it can cause serious damage.

Hydromechanical. Any device that combines fluid pressures with mechanical actions to achieve a desired result. In a hydromechanical fuel control used for a turbine engine, hydraulic servos are used in conjunction with the mechanical linkages.

Ice bridging. A spark plug failure that occurs when starting a reciprocating engine in extremely cold weather. When a cylinder fires, the fuel-air mixture is converted into carbon dioxide and water vapor. The water vapor condenses on the spark plug electrodes and forms ice that bridges the electrode gap and prevents the plug firing until the ice is melted. This normally requires removing the spark plugs from the engine.

IDG. Integrated drive generator. An AC generator installed on turbine engines. An IDG incorporates a brushless, three-phase AC generator and a constant-speed drive in a single component.

Igniter. The component in a turbine-engine ignition system that provides a high-energy spark for igniting the fuel-air mixture in the combustion chamber for starting.

IHP. Indicated horsepower. The theoretical horse-power a reciprocating engine develops.

IMEP. Indicated mean effective pressure. The average pressure existing inside the cylinder of a reciprocating engine during its power stroke.

Impulse coupling. A spring-loaded coupling between a magneto shaft and the drive gear inside the engine. When the engine is rotated for starting, the impulse coupling locks the magnet so it cannot turn. The spring in the coupling winds up as the crankshaft continues to turn, and when the piston is near top center, the coupling releases and spins the magnet, producing a hot and retarded spark.

In-line engine. A reciprocating engine with all of the cylinders arranged in a straight line.

Incandescent. Glowing because of intense heat.

Inconel. The registered trade name for an alloy of chromium, iron, and nickel. Inconel is similar to stainless steel, but cannot be hardened by heat treatment.

Inductive reactance. An opposition to the flow of AC or changing DC caused by inductance in the circuit. Inductive reactance, whose symbol is X_L, causes a voltage drop, but it does not use power nor produce heat.

Inertia. The tendency of a body to resist acceleration. A body at rest will remain at rest or a body in motion will stay in motion in a straight line unless acted on by an outside force.

Inertia starter. A starter for a large reciprocating engine that uses energy stored in a rapidly spinning flywheel to turn the crankshaft.

Inlet guide vanes. A set of stator vanes in front of the first stage of compression in a gas turbine engine. The inlet guide vanes deflect the air entering the compressor in the correct direction for optimum operation. Inlet guide vanes may be fixed, or their angle may be controlled hydraulically by fuel from the fuel control.

Integral fuel tank. An aircraft fuel tank made by sealing off part of the structure so fuel can be carried in the structure itself.

Intercooler. An air-to-air heat exchanger installed between a turbosupercharger and the carburetor. Intercoolers decrease the temperature of compressed air to prevent detonation.

Interference angle (poppet valve dimension). The difference between the valve seat and the valve face angles. Normally, the valve seats are ground with between 0.5° and 1° greater angle than the valve face. This allows the face to touch the seat with a line contact that provides the best sealing.

Interference fit. A type of fit used when assembling certain mechanical devices. The hole is made smaller than the part that fits into it. The material containing the hole is heated to expand the hole, and the part that fits into the hole is chilled to shrink it. The parts are assembled, and when they reach the same temperature their fit is so tight they will not loosen in service.

Internal-combustion engine. A form of heat engine in which the fuel and air mixture is burned inside the engine to heat and expand the air so it can perform useful work.

Internal timing. The adjustment of the breaker points of a magneto so they will begin to open at the time the magnet is in its E-gap position.

Interpole. A field pole in a compound-wound DC generator used to minimize armature reaction. Interpoles are located between each of the regular field poles, and their coils are in series with the armature winding so all of the armature current flows through them. The magnetic field produced by the interpole coils cancels the distortion caused by the armature field and allows the brushed to remain in the neutral plane where there is no potential difference between the commutator segments. Keeping the brushes in the neutral plane minimizes sparking.

Inverted engine. An in-line or V-engine in which the cylinders are mounted below the crankshaft.

Iridium. A very hard, brittle, highly corrosion-resistant, whitish-yellow, metallic chemical element. Iridium is used for the fine-wire electrodes in spark plugs that must operate in engines using fuel with an exceptionally high lead content. iso-octane. An organic compound used as the high reference fuel for rating the antidetonation characteristics of aviation gasoline $(CH_3)_2CHCH_2C(CH_3)_3$.

Isothermal change. A physical change that takes place within a material in which heat energy is added to or taken from the material as needed to keep its temperature constant.

Jet fuel. Fuel designed and produced to be used in aircraft gas turbine engines.

Jet propulsion. A method of propulsion by accelerating a relatively small mass of air through a large change in velocity.

Jeweler's file. A small, fine-cut, metalworking file used by jewelry manufacturers.

Joule. A measure of energy. In terms of electrical energy, one joule is equal to one watt-second.

Journal (bearing). A hardened and polished surface on a rotating shaft that rides in a plain bearing.

Kerosene. A light, almost colorless, hydrocarbon liquid obtained from crude oil through the fractional distillation process. Kerosene is the base for turbine engine fuel.

Kevlar. The registered trade name by DuPont for a patented aramid fiber.

Kinematic viscosity. The ratio of the absolute viscosity of a fluid to its density. Kinematic viscosity is measured in centistokes.

Labyrinth seal. A type of air and/or seal used around the main –shaft bearings in a gas turbine engine. The seal consists of a series of rotating blades that almost contact the seal land. A small amount of air flows between the seal and the land to prevent oil flowing past the seal.

Land (piston) The portion of a piston between the ring grooves.

Land (splined shaft). The portion of a splined shaft between the grooves.

Laser tachometer. A highly accurate tachometer that shines a laser beam on a rotating element that has reflective tape or a contrasting mark. The reflected laser beam is converted into electrical pulses which are counted and displayed on a monitoring instrument.

Last-chance oil filter. A small filter installed in the oil line to the bearing jet in a gas turbine engine. This filter traps any contaminants that have passed the main filter and holds them until the engine is disassembled for overhaul.

LCD. Liquid crystal display. A digital display that consists of two sheets of glass separated by a sealed-in, normally transparent liquid crystal material. The outer surface of each glass sheet has a transparent conductive coating with the viewing side etched into character-forming segments with leads going to the edges of the display. A voltage applied between the front and back coatings disrupts the orderly arrangement of molecules and causes the liquid to darken so that light cannot pass through it. The segment to which the voltage is applied appears as black against a reflected background.

Leading edge. The thick edge at the front of a propeller blade.

Lean die-out. A condition in which the fire in a gas turbine engine goes out because the fuel-air mixture ratio is too lean to sustain combustion.

Lean mixture. A fuel-air mixture that contains more than 15 parts of air to 1 part of fuel, by weight.

Liaison aircraft. A type of light military aircraft made popular during World War II because of its ability to land and takeoff from unimproved terrain. Liaison aircraft have been replaced with helicopters.

Line boring. A method of assuring concentricity of bored holes. A boring bar extends through all of the holes and cuts the inside diameters so they all have the same center.

Link rod. The rod in a radial engine that connects one of the piston wrist pins to a knuckle pin on the master rod. Also called articulating rods.

Liquid cooling. The removal of unwanted heat from an aircraft engine by transferring the heat into a liquid and then passing the heated liquid through a liquid-to-air heat exchanger (radiator) to transfer the heat into the ambient air.

Longitudinal magnetism. A method of magnetizing through a solenoid, or coil, that encircles the part so the lines of magnetic flux pass lengthwise through the part. Longitudinal magnetism makes it possible to detect faults that extend across the part.

Low bypass ratio engine. A turbofan engine whose bypass ratio is less than 2:1.

Low-pressure compressor. The first-stage compressor in a dual-spool gas turbine engine. The low-pressure compressor is called the N1 compressor and its speed is not governed. It seeks its own best speed as the atmospheric conditions change so it can furnish a relatively constant mass of air to the inlet of the second-stage compressor.

Low unmetered fuel pressure. Pressure in a Teledyne-Continental fuel injector pump that is adjusted by the relief valve.

LRU. Line replaceable unit. Aircraft components designed to be replaced as a unit while the aircraft is on the flight line.

M&D (Malfunction and Defect) report. A small postcard-like form (FAA Form 8330) used by repair stations, maintenance shops, and technicians to report an unacceptable condition to the FAA. Information on these forms provides the basis for the General Airworthiness Alerts and subsequent Airworthiness Directives.

Mach number. The ratio of the speed of an object through the air to the speed of sound under the same atmospheric conditions. An object traveling at the speed of sound is traveling at Mach one (M1.0).

Magnesyn system. The registered trade name of a remote indicating instrument system. A Magnesyn system uses a permanent magnet as its rotor and a toroidal coil excited by 400-hertz AC as its stator. A small magnet in the center of the indicator coil follows the movement of a larger magnet in the transmitter coil.

Magnetic field. The invisible, but measurable, force surrounding a permanent magnet or current-carrying conductor. This field is produced when the orbital axes of the electrons of the atoms in the material are all in alignment.

Magnetic flux. Lines of magnetic force that are assumed to leave a magnet at its north end and return to its south end. Lines of flux tend to be as short as possible and cannot cross each other.

Magnetic particle inspection. A method of non-destructive inspection for ferrous metal components. The part being inspected is magnetized and then flooded with a solution of iron oxide suspended in a light oil, much like kerosene. Any flaw, either on the surface or just below the surface, forms a north and south pole, and the iron oxide attracted to these poles helps locate the flaw. The iron oxide is normally treated with a fluorescent dye, and the inspection is conducted in a darkened booth. When an ultraviolet light (black light) is shone on the part, the treated iron oxide shows up as a brilliant line.

Major alteration. An alteration not listed in the aircraft, aircraft engine, or propeller specifications that might appreciably affect weight, balance, structural strength, powerplant operation, flight characteristics, or other qualities affecting airworthiness; an alteration not done according to accepted practices, or one that cannot be done by elementary operations.

Major overhaul. The disassembly, cleaning, and inspection of an engine and the repair and replacement of all parts that do not meet the manufacturer's specification.

Major repair. A repair to a component that if improperly done might appreciably affect weight, balance, structural strength, performance, powerplant operation, flight characteristics, or other qualities affecting airworthiness; a repair not done according to accepted practices, or one that cannot be done by elementary operations.

Mandrel. A precision steel bar on which a propeller is mounted for balancing. The mandrel is placed across two perfectly level knife-edge plates, and the propeller is allowed to rotate until it stops with its heavy point at the bottom.

Manifold pressure. The absolute pressure of the air inside the induction system of a reciprocating engine.

Manifold valve. See flow divider (reciprocating engine).

MAP. Manifold absolute pressure. The absolute pressure that exists within the induction system of a reciprocating engine. It is the MAP that forces air into the cylinders of the engine. MAP is commonly called manifold pressure.

Mass. A measure of the amount of matter in an object. For the purpose of measuring the mass of air flowing through a turbine engine, the weight of the air, in pounds per second, is divided by the acceleration due to gravity (32.3 feet per second).

Matrix (advanced composites). The material that bonds the fibers together in an advanced composite structure. The matrix carries the stresses into the fibers.

Matter. Something that has mass, takes up space, and exists as a solid, liquid, or gas.

Medium-bypass ratio engine. A turbofan engine whose bypass ratio is between 2:1 and 4:1.

MEK. Methul ethyl ketone. A volatile, water soluble, organic chemical compound that is used as a solvent to remove oily contaminants from ignition system components.

Methanol. Alcohol made from wood.

MFD. Multifunction display. A liquid crystal or CRT display that shows a number of parameters and replaces several analog-type indicators.

Microinches rms. A measure used for cylinder wall surface roughness. Twenty microinches rms means that the highest and lowest deviation from the average surface is 20 millionths of an inch.

Micron. A measurement used to identify the size of particles trapped by filters. One micron is a micro meter, or one millionth of a meter. It is 0.000039 inch.

Microprocessor. A single silicon chip that contains the arithmetic and logic functions of a computer.

Milliammeter. An instrument that measures electrical current in units of thousandths of an ampere.

Millibar. A unit of pressure in the metric system. One bar is a pressure of 14.5 psi, or 29.52 in. Hg. One millibar is one thousandth of a bar, or 0.01469 psi, or 0.02952 in. Hg.

Minor alteration. Any alteration that does not fit the definition of a major repair. See major repair.

Module (modular engine construction). The method of construction for mast modern gas turbine engine. The engine is made of several modules, or units, that can be removed and replaced or serviced independent of the rest of the engine.

Momentum. A force caused by the inertia of a moving body as it tries to keep the object moving in the same direction, at the same speed.

Motor. (verb) The act of rotating a turbine engine using the starter, with the ignition system deactivated. An engine is motored to force air through it to purge fuel fumes.

Multiple-can combustor. A combustor used in a gas turbine engine that consists of a series of individual burner cans, each made of an inner liner and an outer case. The individual cans are arranged around the periphery of a centrifugal compressor. Hot gases flow directly from the cans into the turbine.

N1. A symbol representing the rotational speed of the low-pressure compressor in a dual-spool gas turbine engine.

N2. A symbol representing the rotational speed of the high-pressure compressor in a dual-spool gas turbine engine.

NACA. National Advisory Committee for Aeronautics. This organization, dedicated to the technical development of aviation, has been superseded by NASA.

NACA cowling. A long-chord cowling used over a radial engine. The forward portion of this cowling has an aerodynamic shape that produces a forward pull, and the rear portion extends back to fair in with the fuselage. There is a narrow peripheral gap between the rear of the cowling and the fuselage for the cooling air to escape. Some NACA cowlings have controllable flaps over this opening to control the amount of cooling air that flows through the engine.

Nacelle. An enclosed compartment, normally in the leading edge of the wing, in which an aircraft engine is mounted.

Naphtha. A volatile, flammable liquid distilled from petroleum. It is used as a cleaning agent and solvent, and is present in some blended turbine-engine fuels.

NASA. National Aeronautics and Space Administration.

Naturally aspirated engine. A reciprocating engine that depends upon atmospheric pressure to force the fuel-air mixture into the cylinders. Naturally aspirated engines are neither supercharged nor turbocharged.

Net thrust. The thrust produced by a turbojet or turbofan engine in which the acceleration factor is the difference between the velocity of the incoming air and the velocity of the exhaust gases leaving the engine.

Neutral position. The position of the magnet in a magneto when its poles are between the pole shoes and no lines of flux are flowing through the magnetic circuit.

Newton. The unit of force needed to accelerate a mass of one kilogram one meter per second per second. One newton is equal to 1000,000 dynes, or 2.248×10^{-1} pound.

Nichrome. The registered trade name for an alloy of nickel and chromium. Nichrome wire is used for making electrical heater elements and precision wire-wound resistors. Nichrome's resistance is approximately 65 times that of copper.

Nitriding. A method of case hardening steel. Steel is placed in a retort (a sealed, high-temperature furnace), and heated to a specified temperature while surrounded by ammonia gas (NH_3). The ammonia breaks down into nitrogen and hydrogen, and the nitrogen unites with some of the alloying elements in the steel to form an extremely hard surface. Nitriding hardens crankshaft bearing surfaces and cylinder walls in reciprocating engines. It takes place at a lower temperature than other forms of case hardening, and does not cause warping.

Normal category airplane. An aircraft that is certificated under 14 CFR part 23 that is not certificated under the acrobatic, utility, or commuter category.

Normal shock wave. A type of pressure wave that forms at right angles to a surface when air moves at the speed of sound.

Notch sensitivity. A measure of the loss of strength of a material caused by the presence of a notch, or a V-shaped cut.

Nozzle guide vanes. See turbine inlet guide vanes.

Oblique shock wave. A pressure wave that forms on a sharp-pointed object when air flows past it at a supersonic speed.

Octane rating. A system used to rate the antidetonation characteristics of a reciprocating engine fuel. Fuel with an octane rating of 80 performs in a laboratory test engine the same as the fuel made of a mixture of 80% iso-octane and 20% heptanes.

Odometer. The portion of an automobile speedometer that indicates the distance traveled.

Offset throw (crankshaft design). Crank arms on a reciprocating engine crankshaft. The arms, or throws, to which the connecting rods and pistons are attached are offset from the center of the crankshaft to move the pistons in and out of the cylinder. The amount of the offset determines the stroke of the engine.

Oil analysis. A method of measuring the contents in parts per million of various chemical elements in oil. A sample of the oil is burned in an electric arc, and the resulting light is analyzed with a spectroscope which identifies the chemical elements in the oil and gives an indication of the amount of each element. This type of oil analysis is called a spectrometric oil analysis program, or SOAP.

Oil dilution. A method of temporarily decreasing the viscosity of the lubricating oil to make it possible to start a reciprocating engine when the temperature is very low. Before shutting the engine down, enough gasoline from the fuel system is mixed with the lubricating oil in the engine to dilute it so the starter can turn the engine over when the oil is cold and viscous. When the engine starts and the oil warms up, the gasoline evaporates.

Oil-damped bearing. A type of roller bearing installation in a gas turbine engine in which the outer race is installed in an oil damper compartment whose inside diameter is a few thousandths of an inch larger than the outside diameter of the outer race. Oil under pressure fills the oil damper compartment and allows the bearing to compensate for sight misalignment and to absorb vibrations of the shaft.

On-condition maintenance. A maintenance program that closely monitors the operating condition of an engine and allows major repairs or replacements to be made when engine performance deteriorates to a specific level.

On-speed condition. The speed condition in which the engine is turning at the rpm for which the propeller governor is set.

One-hundred-hour inspection. An inspection required by 14 CFR part 91, section 91.409 for FAA-certificated aircraft operated for hire or used for flight instruction for hire. A 100-hour inspection is identical in content to an annual inspection, but can be conducted by an aviation maintenance technician who holds an Airframe and Powerplant rating, but does not have an Inspection Authorization. See 14 CFR part 43, Appendix D for list of the items that must be included in an annual or 100-hour inspection.

Operating cycle. One complete series of events in the operation of a turbine engine that consists of starting the engine, taking off, landing, and shutting the engine down.

Optoelectronic device. An electronic device that produces, modulates, or senses electromagnetic radiation in the ultraviolet, visible light, or infrared portions of the energy spectrum.

Otto cycle. The constant-volume cycle of energy transformation used by reciprocating engines. A mixture of fuel and air is drawn into the cylinder as the piston moves to the bottom of its stroke. The mixture is compressed as the piston moves upward in the cylinder, and when the piston is near the top of its stroke, the mixture is electrically ignited and burns. The burning mixture heats and expands the air inside the cylinder and forces the piston down, performing useful work. The piston then moves back up, forcing the burned gases out of the cylinder.

Overboost. A condition of excessive manifold pressure in a reciprocating engine. Overboosting occurs when the supercharger is operated at too high a speed.

Overrunning clutch. A type of clutch that couples an input shaft with an output shaft. When the input shaft is driven, the output shaft rotates with it. When the output shaft is driven, the output shaft rotates with it. But when the output shaft is driven, the input shaft does not turn.

Overspeed condition. A speed condition in which the engine is turning at an rpm higher than that for which the propeller governor is set.

P-lead. Primary lead. The wire that connects the primary winding of a magneto to the ignition switch. The magneto is turned off by grounding its P-lead.

Pascal. The unit of pressure produced when one newton of force acts uniformly over an area of one square meter. One pascal is equal to $14.503 \cdot 10^{-5}$ (0.00014503) psi. The kilopascal (kPa) is easier to manipulate. 1 kPa = 1,000 Pa = 0.14503 psi.

PCB. Plenum chamber burning. A method of thrust augmentation used on engines with vectored nozzles. Fuel injected into the fan-discharge air is burned to increase thrust.

Peak voltage. The voltage of AC electricity that is measured from zero voltage to the peak of either alternation.

Penetrant dwell time. The length of time a part is left in the penetrant when preparing it for inspection by the fluorescent or dye penetrant method. The hotter the part and the longer the penetrant dwell time, the smaller the fault that will be detected.

Performance number. The rating of antidetonation characteristics of a reciprocating engine fuel that is better than the high rating reference fuel, iso-octane. Performance numbers are greater than 100.

Permanent magnet. A piece of hardened steel that has been exposed to a strong magnetizing force which has aligned the spin axes of the electrons surrounding its atoms. The high retentivity of the material causes the electrons to retain their magnetic orientation.

Permanent-mold casting. A casting made in a reusable metal mold. The walls of permanent-mold castings can be made thinner than similar walls made by sand casting.

Permeability. A measure of the ease with which lines of magnetic flux can pass through a material.

Phase sequence, or phase rotation. The sequence with which the output phases of a three-phase generator are connected to the load. Reversing the phase sequence of a generator from A-B-C to A-C-B prevents the generator from being synchronized with the others on the bus.

Pi (π) filter. An electronic filter used to prevent radio frequency energy produced in the ignition exciter from feeding back into the aircraft electrical system. The filter is made of an inductor with a capacitor on its input and output. The name is derived from the resemblance of the three components on a schematic diagram to the Greek letter pi (π).

Pinion. A small gear that meshes with and drives a larger gear.

Piston (reciprocating engine component). The movable plug inside the cylinder of a reciprocating engine. The piston moves in and out to compress the fuel-air mixture and to transmit the force from the expanding gas in the cylinder to the crankshaft.

Piston pin. See wrist pin.

Pitch angle. The angle between the chord line of a propeller blade and the plane of rotation. See blade angle.

Pitch distribution. The gradual change in pitch angle of a propeller blade from the root to the tip.

Plane of rotation. The plane in which a propeller blade rotates. The plane of rotation is perpendicular to the propeller shaft.

Planetary gears. A type of large-ratio reduction gearing. A series of small planetary gears are mounted on a spider attached to the output shaft. The planetary gears rotate between a fixed sun gear and a driven ring gear.

Plenum chamber. An enclosed chamber in which air can be held at a pressure slightly higher than that of the surrounding air. Plenum chambers are used to stabilize the pressure of the air before it enters a double entry centrifugal compressor.

POH. Pilot's Operating Handbook. A document published by the airframe manufacturer and approved by the FAA that lists the operating conditions for a particular model of aircraft. Engine operating parameters are included in the POH.

Pole shoe. Inward extensions from the field frame of a generator around which the field coils are wound.

Poppet valve. A T-shaped valve with a circular head. Poppet valves are used to cover the intake and exhaust openings in the cylinder head of a reciprocating engine. The valves are held closed by one or more coil springs and are opened by a cam lobe or a rocker arm pushing on the end of the valve stem.

Porcelain. A hard, white, translucent ceramic material that was used as the insulator in some of the early aircraft spark plugs.

Positive-displacement pump. A fluid pump that moves a specific volume of fluid each time it rotates. Spur-gear pumps, gerotor pumps, and vane pumps are all positive-displacement pumps.

Power. The time rate of doing work. Power is found by dividing the amount of work done, measured in floor-pounds, by the time in seconds or minutes used to do the work. Power may be expressed in foot-pounds of work per minute or in horsepower. One horsepower is 33,000 foot-pounds of work done in one minute, or 550 foot pounds of work done in one second.

Power-assurance check. A test run made of a gas turbine engine to determine how its performance compares with its precious performance as new or freshly overhauled.

Powerplant. The complete installation of an aircraft engine, propeller, and all accessories needed for its proper function.

Preignition. Ignition of the fuel-air mixture inside the cylinder of an engine before the time for normal ignition. Preignition is often caused by incandescent objects inside the cylinder.

Prepreg. Preimpregnated fabric. A type of composite material in which the reinforcing fibers are encapsulated in an uncured resin. Prepreg materials are cut to size and shape and laid up with the correct ply orientation, and the entire component is cured with heat and pressure.

Pressure. A measure of force applied uniformly over a given unit of surface area.

Pressure altitude. The altitude in standard atmosphere at which the pressure is the same as the existing pressure.

Pressure carburetor. A carburetor installed on some aircraft reciprocating engines that uses the pressure difference between air inside the venture and ram air entering the carburetor to produce a fuel-metering force. Pressure carburetors have generally been replaced with continuous-flow fuel injection systems.

Pressure cooling. A method of air cooling a reciprocating engine in which the cylinders are enclosed in tight-fitting shrouds. The cowling is divided into two compartments by baffles and seals, with half of each cylinder in each compartment. Ram air is directed into one compartment, and the pressure in the other is decreased by air flowing over a flared exit or adjustable cowl flaps. The pressure difference across the cylinders causes cooling air to be drawn through the fins to remove the unwanted heat.

Pressure-injection carburetor. A multibarrel pressure carburetor used on large radial and V-engines. Fuel is metered on the basis of air mass flowing into the engine and is sprayed under pressure into the eye, or center, of the internal supercharger impeller.

Precailing torque. The torque required to turn a threaded fastener before it contacts the surface it is intended to hold.

Primary winding. The winding in a magneto or ignition coil that is between the source of voltage and the breaker points. The primary winding is normally made of comparatively large diameter wire, and has a small number of turns, typically about 200.

Profile tip (compressor blade tip). The tip of an axial-flow compressor bladed whose thickness is reduced to give it a higher resonant frequency so it will not be subject to the vibrations that would affect a blade with a squared tip. The profile tip also provides a more aerodynamically efficient shape for the high velocity air that is moved by the blade. Profile tips often touch the housing and make a squealing noise as the engine is shut down. For this reason profile tips are often called squealer tips.

Profilometer. A precision measuring instrument used to measure the depth of the hone marks in the surface of a cylinder wall.

Prony brake. An instrument used to measure the amount of horsepower an engine is delivering to its output shaft. The engine is operated at a specific rpm, and a brake is applied to its output shaft. The amount of torque applied to the brake is measured, and this, with the rpm, is converted into brake horsepower.

Propeller end. The end of a reciprocating engine to which the propeller is attached.

PropFan engine. The registered trade name by Hamilton Standard of an ultra-high-bypass turbine engine. See UHB engine.

Propulsive efficiency. A measure of the effectiveness with which an aircraft engine converts the fuel it burns into useful thrust. It is the ratio of the thrust horsepower produced by a propeller to the torque horsepower of the shaft turning the propeller. The nearer the speed of the aircraft is to the speed of the exhaust jet or propeller wake, the less kinetic energy is lost in the jet or wake, and the higher the propulsive efficiency.

PRT. Power recovery turbine. A turbine driven by exhaust gases from several cylinders of a reciprocating engine. Energy extracted from exhaust gases by the turbine is coupled, through a fluid clutch, to the engine crankshaft.

Pulsating DC. Direct current whose voltage periodically changes, but whose electrons flow in the same direction all of the time.

Pulse-jet engine. A type of air-breathing reaction engine used during World War II to power jet-propelled missiles. Fuel is sprayed into the combustion chamber and ignited. As the heated air expands, it closes the one-way shutter valve in the front of the engine and exits the engine through the nozzle at the rear. As soon as the pressure inside the combustion chamber decreases, air enters through the shutter valve and more fuel is ignited. The thrust is produced in a series of pulses.

Push fit. A fit between pieces in a mechanical assembly that is close enough to require the parts to be pushed together. A push fit is looser than a press fit, but closer than a free fit.

Pusher engine. An engine installed with the propeller facing the rear of the aircraft. Thrust produced by the propeller mounted on a pusher engine pushes rather than pulls the aircraft.

Pusher propeller. A propeller installed on an aircraft engine so that it faces the rear of the aircraft. Thrust from the propeller pushes rather than pulls the aircraft.

PV diagram. A diagram showing the relationship between the volume of a cylinder and the pressure during a cycle of engine operation.

Quill shaft. A type of shaft used to couple parts of an engine that are subject to torsional loads. A quill shaft is a long, hardened steel shaft with splines on each end. One end splines into the drive shaft and the other end splines into the device being driven. Torsional vibrations are absorbed by the quill shaft twisting.

Radial bearing load. The load on a bearing perpendicular to the shaft on which the bearing is mounted. Centrifugal loads are radial loads.

Radial engine (static radial). A form of reciprocating engine in which the cylinders radiate out from a small central crankcase. The pistons in the cylinders drive a central crankshaft which in turn drives the propeller.

Radial-inflow turbine. A turbine, similar in appearance to a centrifugal compressor rotor. Radial-inflow turbines are used to drive the compressor in reciprocating engine turbochargers and some of the smaller APU turbine engines. Hot gases flow into the turbine from its outside rim, then radially inward through the vanes and out of the turbine at its center.

Radiation. See electromagnetic radiation.

Ram air. Air whose pressure has been increased by the forward motion of the aircraft. Ram air pressure is the same as pitot pressure.

Ram drag. The loss of thrust produced by a turbojet or turbofan engine caused by the increase of velocity of air entering the engine. Ram drag is the difference between gross thrust and net thrust.

Ram pressure. Pressure produced when a moving fluid is stopped.

Ram-recovery speed. The speed of an aircraft at which the ram effect caused by the forward movement increases the air pressure at the compressor inlet so that it is the same as that of the ambient air.

Ramjet engine. The simplest type of air-breathing reaction engine. Air entering the front of the engine at a high velocity has fuel sprayed into it and ignited. A barrier formed by the incoming air forces the expanding gases to leave through the nozzle at the rear. The energy added by the burning fuel accelerates the air and produces a forward thrust. Ramjet engines are used in some military unmanned aircraft that are initially boosted to a speed high enough for the engine to function.

Ratiometer indicator. An analog temperature measuring instrument in which the pointer deflection is proportional to the ratio between the current flowing in an internal reference circuit and that flowing through the temperature-sensing probe.

Reach (spark plug specification). The length of the threads on the shell of a spark plug.

Reaction engine. A form of heat engine that produces thrust by heating a mass of air inside the engine and discharging it at a high velocity through a specially shaped nozzle. The amount of thrust is determined by the mass of the air and the amount it is accelerated.

Reactive power. Wattless power in an AC circuit. It is the power consumed in the inductive and capacitive reactances. Reactive power is expressed in volt-amps reactive (var) or in kilovolt-amps reactive (kvar).

Reamed fir. The fit of a shaft in a hole in which the hole is drilled undersize and cut with a reamer to the correct diameter. Reamed holes have smooth walls and a consistent diameter.

Rebuilt engine. A used engine that has been completely disassembled, inspected, repaired as necessary, and reassembled, tested, and approved in the same manner and to the same tolerances and limits as a new engine, using either new or used parts. However, all parts used must conform to all production drawings, tolerances, and limits for new parts, or be of approved oversize or undersize dimensions for a new engine. According to 14 CFR part 91, section 91.421, a rebuilt engine is considered to have no precious operating history and may be issued a zero-time logbook. Only the engine manufacturer can rebuild an engine and issue a zero-time record.

Reciprocating engine. A type of heat engine that changes the reciprocating (back-and-forth) motion of pistons inside the cylinders into rotary motion of a crank-shaft.

Rectifier. A device that allows electrons to flow in one direction while preventing their flow in the opposite direction. Rectifiers are used to change AC into DC.

Reheat system. The British name for an afterburner. See afterburner.

Reid vapor pressure. The amount of pressure that must be exerted on a liquid to keep it from vaporizing. Reid vapor pressure is measured at 100 °F.

Reliability. The ability of an aircraft engine to perform its designed functions under widely varying operating conditions.

Residual magnetic particle inspection. A form of magnetic particle inspection for small steel parts that have a high degree of retentivity. The part is magnetized, removed, and inspected away from the magnetizing machine.

Residual magnetism. The magnetism that remains in the field frame of a generator when no current is flowing in the field coils.

Residual voltage. The voltage produced in a generator armature when the armature is rotated in the residual magnetism.

Resistor spark plug. A shielded spark plug with a resistor between the ignition lead terminal and the center electrode. The resistor stops the flow of secondary current when its voltage drops to a specified value. The resistor prevents capacitive afterfiring.

Retarded sparks. The timing of the firing of the spark plugs used to start a reciprocating engine. The sparks for starting occur later in terms of crankshaft rotation than those used for normal operation. Retarding the sparks prevent the engine from kicking back when it is being started.

Retentivity. The ability of a magnetizable material to retain the alignment of the magnetic domains after the magnetizing force has been removed. Hard steel normally has a high retentivity, while soft iron and electrical steel both have very low retentivity.

Reverse-flow combustor. A type of combustor in which the air from the compressor enters the combustor outer case and reverses its direction as it flows into the inner liner. It again reverses its direction as it flows into the inner liner. It again reverses its direction before it flows through the turbine. Reverse-flow combustors are used where engine length is critical.

RF energy. Electromagnetic energy with a frequency high enough to radiate from any conductor through which it is flowing.

Rich blowout. A condition in which the fire in a gas turbine engine goes out because the fuel-air mixture ratio is too rich to sustain combustion.

Rich mixture. A fuel-air mixture that contains less than 15 parts of air to 1 part of fuel, by weight.

Riffle file. A hand file with its teeth formed on a curved surface that resembles a spoon.

Rms. Root mean square. A dimension that is the square root of the average of an infinite number of varying values. An rms dimension is used to indicate the allowable surface roughness of a reciprocating engine cylinder wall.

Rocker arm. A pivoted arm on the cylinder head of a reciprocating engine. The pushrod forces one end of the rocker arm up, and as the other end moves down, it forces the poppet valve off of its seat.

Rocker box. The enclosed part of a reciprocating engine cylinder that houses the rocker arm and valve mechanism.

Rocket engine. A form of reaction engine whose fuel and oxidizer contain all of the oxygen needed for the release of heat energy. The released heat expands the gases which are ejected at a high velocity from a nozzle at the rear of the rocket. Because rocket engines carry their own oxygen, they can operate in outer space where there is no atmosphere.

Rotary radial engine. A form of reciprocating engine used in some early aircraft. The crankshaft is rigidly attached to the airframe, and the propeller, crankcase, and cylinders all revolve as a unit.

Rotating combustion (RC) engine. A form of internal combustion engine in which a rounded, triangular-shaped rotor with sliding seals at the apexes forms the combustion space inside an hourglass-shaped chamber. Expanding gases from the burning fuel-air mixture push the rotor around and turn a geared drive shaft in its center. The RC engine was conceived in Germany by Felix Wankel in 1955.

RPM. Revolutions per minute. A measure of rotational speed. One rpm is one revolution made in one minute.

Run in. A time of controlled operation of a new or freshly overhauled engine that allows the moving parts to wear together.

Run up. A procedure in which an aircraft engine is operated on the ground to determine its condition and performance.

Runout. A measure of the amount a shaft, flange, or disk is bent or fails to run true. Runout is normally measured with a dial indicator.

SAE. Society of Automotive Engineers. A professional organization that has formulated standards for the automotive and aviation industries.

Safety gap. A location in a magneto that allows a spark to jump to ground from the secondary circuit before the voltage rises high enough to damage the secondary insulation.

Sand casting. A method of molding metal parts in a mold made of sand. A pattern that duplicates the part to be molded is made of wood and is covered with a special casting sand that contains a resin to bind it. The mold is separated along a special parting line, and the pattern is removed. The mold is put back together, and molten metal is poured into the cavity. When the metal cools, the sand is broken away from the molded part. Sand casting is less expensive than permanent-mold casting.

Saybolt Seconds Universal (SSU) viscosity. A measurement of viscosity (resistance to flow)of a lubricating oil. The number of seconds needed for 60 milliliters of oil at a specified temperature to flow through a calibrated orifice. The viscosity number used for commercial aviation engine lubricating oil relates closely to the SSU viscosity of the oil at 210 °F.

Scavenge subsystem. The subsystem in the lubrication system of a gas turbine engine that collects oil after it has lubricated the bearings and gears and returns it to the oil tank.

Scimitar shape. The shape of the blades of the propellers mounted on UHB engines. The name is derived from the shape of a curved Asian sword that has its edge on the convex side. See UHB engine.

Scramjet. Supersonic combustion ramjet. A special type of ramjet engine whose fuel can be ignited while the vehicle is mobbing at a supersonic speed.

Scuffing. Severe damage to moving parts caused when one metal part moves across another without sufficient lubricant between them. Enough heat is generated by friction to cause the high points of the surfaces to weld together; continued movement tears, or scuffs, the metal.

Sea-level boosted engine. A reciprocating engine that has had its sea-level rated horsepower increased by supercharging. This is the same as a ground-boosted engine.

Secondary winding. The winding in a magneto or ignition coil that connects to the distributor rotor. The secondary winding is normally made of very small diameter wire and has a large number of turns, typically about 20,000.

Self-accelerating speed. The speed attained by a gas turbine engine during start-up that allows it to accelerate to its normal idling speed without assistance from the starter.

Semiconductor transducer. A piezoelectric crystal that converts input energy of one form, such as pressure, into output energy of another, such as an electrical signal.

Series-wound motor. An electric motor with field coils connected in series with the armature.

Serviceable limits. Limits included in a reciprocating engine overhaul manual. If a part measures outside of the new-parts limits, but within the serviceable limits, it will not likely wear to the point of causing engine failure within the next TBO interval.

Servo system. A type of automatic control system in which part of the output is fed back into the input.

Shaft horsepower. The horsepower actually available at a rotating shaft.

Shielding. The electrically conductive covering placed around an electrical component to intercept and conduct to ground any electromagnetic energy radiated from the device.

Short circuit. A low-resistance connection between two points in an electric circuit.

Shower of Sparks ignition system. A patented ignition system for reciprocating engines. An induction civrator sends pulsating DC into a set of retard breaker points on one of the magnetos. This provides a hot and retarded spark for starting the engine.

Single-shaft turbine engine. A turboprop engine in which the propeller reduction gears are driven by the same shaft that drives the compressor for the gas generator.

Single-spool gas-turbine engine. A type of axial-flow-compressor gas turbine engine that has only one rotating element.

Skin radiator. A type of radiator used on some early liquid-cooled racing airplanes. The radiator was made of two thin sheets of brass, slightly separated so the heated coolant could flow between them. Skin radiators were mounted on the surface of the wing, on the sides of the fuselage, or on the floats of seaplanes. Air flowing over the smooth surface of the radiator removed heat from the coolant.

Slip (propeller specification). The difference between the geometric and effective pitch of a propeller.

Slip ring. A smooth, continuous ring of brass or copper mounted on the rotor shaft of an electrical generator or alternator. Brushes riding on the smooth surface of the slip ring carry current into and out of the rotor coil.

Slow-blow ruse. A special type of electrical circuit protection device that allows a momentary flow of excess current, but opens the circuit if the excessive flow is sustained.

Sludge. A heavy contaminant that forms in an aircraft engine lubricating oil because of oxidation and chemical decomposition of the oil.

Sludge plugs. Spool-shaped sheet metal plugs installed in the hollow throws of some engine crankshafts.

Slug. The unit of mass equal to that which experiences an acceleration of one foot per second, per second when a force of one pound acts on it. It is equal to 32.174 pounds, or 14.5939 kilograms, of mass. Also called a G-pound.

SOAP. Spectrometric oil analysis program. An oil analysis program in which a sample of oil is burned in an electric arc and an analysis is made of the wavelength composition of the resulting light. Each chemical element in the oil, when burned, produces light containing a unique band of frequencies. A computer analyzes the amount of each band of frequencies and prints out the number of parts of the element per million parts of the entire sample. SOAP can predict engine problems by warning the engine operator of an uncharacteristic increase of any elements in the oil.

Sound suppressor. The airframe component that replaces the turbine engine tail pipe. It reduces the distance the sounds made by the exhaust gases propagate by converting low-frequency vibrations.

Specific gravity. The ratio of the density of a material to the density of pure water.

Specific weight. The ratio of the weight of an aircraft engine to the brake horsepower it develops.

Spline. Parallel slots cut in the periphery of a shaft, parallel to its length. Matching slots, cut into the hub or wheel that fits on the shaft, lock the shaft into the device to transmit torque.

Sprag clutch. A freewheeling, nonreversible clutch that allows torque to be applied to a driven unit in one direction only.

Springback. A condition in the rigging of an aircraft engine control in which the stop at the engine is reached before the stop in the flightdeck. The flightdeck control moves slightly after the stop in the engine is reached, and when it is released, it springs back slightly.

Spur-gear pump. A form of constant-displacement fluid pump that uses two meshing spur-gears mounted in a close fitting housing. Fluid is taken into the housing where it fills the space between the teeth of the gears and is carried around the housing as the gears rotate. On the discharge side of the pump, the teeth of the two gears mesh, and the fluid is forced out of the pump.

Squat switch. An electrical switch actuated by the landing gear scissors on the oleo strut. When no weight is on the landing gear, the oleo piston is extended and the switch is in one position; but when weight is on the gear, the oleo strut compresses and the switch changes its position.

Squealer tip (compressor blade tip). See profile tip.

Squeeze film bearings. Another name for oil-damped bearings. See oil-damped bearings.

Stage length. The distance between landing points in airline operation.

Stage of a compressor. One disk of rotor blades and the following set of stator vanes in an axial-flow compressor.

Staggered timing. Ignition timing that causes the spark plug nearest the exhaust valve to fire a few degrees of crankshaft rotation before the spark plug nearest the intake valve.

Standard day conditions. Conditions that have been decided upon by the ICAO for comparing all aircraft and engine performance. The most basic standard day conditions are: temperature, 15 °C or 52 °F; altitude, mean sea level; pressure, 29.92 inches of mercury.

Standard J-1. A World War I training airplane powered by a Curtiss OX-5 engine.

Standpipe. A pipe which protrudes upward from the base of an oil tank and through which oil used for normal engine lubrication is drawn. In the event of a catastrophic leak when all oil available to the engine-driven pump is lost overboard, enough oil is available from an outlet below the standpipe to feather the propeller.

Starter-generator. A single-component starter and generator used on many smaller gas-turbine engines. It is used to start the engine, and when the engine is running, its circuitry is shifted so that it acts as a generator.

Static pressure. The pressure of an unmoving fluid.

Static rpm. The number of revolutions per minute an aircraft engine can produce when the aircraft is not moving.

Steam cooling. A method of liquid cooling in which the coolant, normally water, is allowed to absorb enough heat that it boils. The steam gives up its heat when it condenses back into a liquid.

Satellite. A nonferrous alloy of cobalt, chromium, and tungsten. Stellite is hard, water resistant, and corrosion resistant, and it does not soften until its temperature is extremely high. Stellite is welded to the faces of many reciprocating engine exhaust valves that operate at very high temperatures.

Stepping motor. A precision electric motor whose output shaft position is changed in steps by pulses from the control device. Stepping motors can make high-torque changes in small angular increments to their output shaft.

Stoichiometric mixture. The fuel-air mixture ratio that, when burned, leaves no uncombined oxygen nor any free carbon. It releases the maximum amount of heat, and therefore produces the highest exhaust gas temperature. A stoichiometric mixture of gasoline and air contains 15 pounds of air for 1 pound of gasoline.

Straight-through combustor. A combustor in a gas turbine engine through which the air from the compressor to the turbine flows in an essentially straight line.

Stratosphere. The upper part of the Earth's atmosphere. The stratosphere extends upward from the tropopause, which is approximately 36,000 feet above the surface of the Earth, to approximately 85,000 feet. The temperature of the air in the stratosphere remains constant at -56.5 °C (-69.7 °F).

Stress. A force within an object that tries to prevent an outside force from changing its shape.

Stroboscopic tachometer. A tachometer used to measure the speed of any rotating device without physical contact. A highly accurate variable-frequency oscillator triggers a high-intensity strobe light. When the lamp is flashing at the same frequency the device is rotating, the device appears to stand still.

Stroke. The distance the piston moves inside the cylinder.

Sump (aircraft engine component). A low point in an aircraft engine in which lubricating oil collects and is stored or transferred to an external oil tank. A removable sump attached to the bottom of the crankcase of a reciprocating engine is often called an oil pan.

Sump (fuel tank component). A low point in an aircraft fuel tank in which water and other contaminants collect and are held until they can be drained out.

Supercharged engine. A reciprocating engine that uses a mechanically driven compressor to increase the air pressure before it enters the engine cylinders.

Supercharger. An air compressor used to increase the pressure of the air being taken into the cylinders of a reciprocating engine.

Surface roughness. The condition of the surface of a reciprocating engine cylinder wall that has been honed to make it hold lubricating oil. Surface roughness is measured in micro-inches rms.

Surge. A condition of unstable airflow, through the compressor of a gas turbine engine, in which the compressor blades have an excessive angle of attack. Surge usually affects an entire stage of compression.

Synthetic oil. Oil made by chemical synthesis of a mineral, animal, or vegetable base. Synthetic oils have appropriate additives that give them such characteristics as low volatility, low pour point, high viscosity index, good lubricating qualities, low coke and lacquer formation, and low foaming.

Tachometer. An instrument that measures the rotational speed of an object.

TAI. Thermal anti-ice. A system used to prevent the formation of ice on an aircraft by flowing heated air inside the structure.

Tail pipe. The portion of the exhaust system of a gas turbine engine through which the gases leave. The tail pipe is often called the exhaust duct, or exhaust pipe.

TBO. Time between overhauls. A time period specified by the manufacturer of an aircraft engine as the maximum length of time an engine should be operated between overhauls without normal wear causing parts of the engine to be worn beyond safe limits. TBO depends upon proper operation and maintenance in accordance with the engine manufacturer's recommendations. The overhaul of an engine when it reaches its TBO hours is not mandatory, except for certain commercial operators that have the requirement written into their operations manual.

TDC. Top dead center. The position of a piston in a reciprocating engine when the piston is at the top of its stroke and the wrist pin, crankpin, and center of the crankshaft are all in line.

TEL. Tetraethyl lead.

Test club. A wide-blade, short-diameter propeller used on a reciprocating engine when it is run in a test cell. A test club applies a specific load to the engine and forces the maximum amount of air through the engine cooling fins.

Thermal efficiency. The ratio of the amount of useful work produced by a heat engine, to the amount of work that could be done by all of the heat energy available in the fuel burned.

Thermal expansion coefficient. A number that relates to the change in the physical dimensions of a material as the temperature of the material changes. The thermal expansion coefficient of aluminum is approximately twice that of steel.

Thermal shock. The sudden change in engine operating temperature that occurs when engine power is suddenly reduced at the same time the airspeed, thus the cooling, is increased. Thermal shock occurs when an aircraft is required to rapidly descend to a lower altitude.

Thermistor. A semiconductor material whose electrical resistance varies with its temperature.

Thermocouple. A device used to generate an electrical current. A thermocouple is made of two dissimilar metal wires whose ends are welded together to form a loop. A voltage exists in the loop proportional to the difference in temperature of the junctions at which the wires are joined. The amount of current flowing in the loop is determined by the types of metals used for the wires, the temperature difference between the junctions, and the resistance of the wires.

Thermosetting resin. A plastic resin that, once it has been hardened by heat, cannot be softened by heating again.

Thermostatic valve. A temperature-sensitive valve that controls the temperature of oil in an aircraft engine. When the oil is cold, the valve shifts and directs the oil through the oil cooler.

Thermoswitch. An electrical switch that closes a circuit when it is exposed to a specified high temperature.

Three-dimensional cam. A drum-shaped cam in a hydromechanical fuel control whose outer surface is ground so that followers riding on the surface, as the cam is moved up and down and rotated, can move mechanical linkages to control the fuel according to a preprogrammed schedule.

Throttle. The control in an aircraft that regulates the power or thrust the pilot wants the engine to produce.

Throw (crankshaft design). See offset throw.

Thrust horsepower. The horsepower equivalent of the thrust produced by a turbojet engine. Thrust horsepower is found by multiplying the net thrust of the engine, measured in pounds, by the speed of the aircraft, measured in miles per hour, and then dividing this by 375.

Thrust. The aerodynamic force produced by a propeller or turbojet engine as it forces a mass of air to the rear, behind the aircraft. A propeller produces its thrust by accelerating a large mass of air by a relatively small amount. A turbojet engine produces its thrust by accelerating a smaller mass of air by a much larger amount.

Time-Rite indicator. A patented piston-position indicator used to find the position of the piston in the cylinder of a reciprocating engine. The body of the Time-Rite indicator screws into a spark plug hole, and as the piston moves outward in the cylinder, it contacts the arm of the indicator. A pointer contacted by the arm moves across a calibrated scale to show the location of the piston in degrees of crankshaft rotation before top center.

Timing light. An indicator light used when timing magnetos to an engine to indicate when the breaker points open. Some timing lights incorporate an oscillator or buzzer that changes its pitch when the points open.

TIT. Turbine inlet temperature. The temperature of the gases from the combustion section of a gas turbine engine as they enter the turbine inlet guide vanes or the first stage of the turbine.

Toggle. A T-shaped handle fitted onto the end of a cable used to engage a simple starter with an overrunning clutch.

Top overhaul. An overhaul of the cylinders of an aircraft engine. The valves, pistons, and cylinders are overhauled, but the crankcase is not opened.

Torque. A force that produces or tries to produce rotation.

Total pressure. The pressure a column of moving fluid would have if it were stopped from its motion. Total pressure is the sum of dynamic pressure and static pressure.

Total temperature. The temperature of moving fluid that has been stopped from its motion. Total temperature is the sum of static temperature and the temperature rise caused by the ram effect as the fluid was stopped.

Townend ring. A type of ring cowling used over a single-row radial engine. The cross section of the ring is in the form of an airfoil that produces enough forward thrust to compensate for the cooling drag of the engine. In the United States, townend rings are often called speed rings.

Track. The path followed by a blade segment of a propeller or helicopter rotor in one rotation.

Tractor engine. An engine installed with the propeller facing the front of the aircraft. Thrust produced by the propeller mounted on a tractor engine pulls the aircraft through the air. tractor propeller. A propeller mounted on an airplane in such a way that its thrust pulls the aircraft.

Trailing edge. The thin edge at the rear of a propeller blade.

Transducer. A device that changes energy from one form to another. Commonly used transducers change mechanical movement or pressures into electrical signals.

Transformer. An electrical component used to change the voltage and current in an AC circuit.

Transonic range. Flight at Mach numbers between 0.8 and 1.2. In this range, some air passing over the aircraft is subsonic, and some is supersonic.

Trend monitoring. A system for comparing engine performance parameters with a baseline of these same parameters established when the engine was new or newly overhauled. Parameters such as EGT, rpm, fuel flow, and oil consumption are monitored on every flight, and the baseline is plotted. Any deviation from a normal increase or decrease warns the technician of an impending problem.

Tricresyl phosphate (TCP). A colorless, combustible compound, $(CH_3C_6H_4O)_3PO$, that is used as a plasticizer in aircraft dope and an additive in gasoline and lubricating oil. TCP aids in scavenging lead deposits left in the cylinders when leaded fuel is burned.

TSFC. Thrust specific fuel consumption. A measure of efficiency of a turbojet or turbofan engine. It is a measure of the number of pounds of fuel burned per hour for each pound of thrust produced.

Turbine. A wheel fitted with vanes, or buckets, radiating outward from its circumference. The reactive or aerodynamic force caused by the fluid flowing through the vanes is converted into mechanical power that spins the shaft on which the wheel is mounted.

Turbine engine. See gas turbine engine.

Turbine inlet guide vanes. A series of stator vanes immediately ahead of the first-stage turbine. The function of the inlet guide vanes is to divert the hot gases in the proper direction to enter the turbine, and to provide a series of convergent ducts which increase the velocity of the gases.

Turbine nozzle. Another name for turbine inlet guide vanes.

Turbocharger. An exhaust-driven air compressor used to increase the power of a reciprocating engine. A turbocharger uses a small radial inflow turbine in the exhaust system to drive a centrifugal-type air compressor on the turbine shaft. The compressed air is directed into the engine cylinders to increase power.

Turbo-compound engine. A reciprocating engine that has power recovery turbines in its exhaust system. The power extracted from the exhaust by these turbines is directed into the engine crankshaft through a fluid coupling.

Turbofan engine. A type of gas turbine engine that has a set of lengthened blades on the low-pressure compressor or low-pressure turbine. Air moved by these special blades bypasses the core engine and produces between 30% and 75% of the total thrust.

Turbojet engine. A gas turbine engine that produces thrust by accelerating the air flowing through it. A minimum of energy is extracted by the turbine, with the majority used to produce an exhaust velocity much greater than the inlet velocity. The amount of thrust produced by the engine is determined by the amount the air is accelerated as it flows through the engine.

Turboprop engine. A turbine engine in which several stages of turbines are used to extract as much energy as possible. The turbines drive reduction gears which in turn drive a propeller.

Turboshaft engine. A turbine engine in which several stages of turbines are used to extract as much energy as possible. The turbines drive shafts which are used to drive helicopter rotors, generators, or pumps.

Turbosupercharger. A centrifugal air compressor driven by exhaust gases flowing through a turbine. The compressed air is used to increase the power produced by a reciprocating engine at altitude.

Two-spool engine. See dual-spool gas turbine engine.

Two-stroke cycle. A constant-volume cycle of energy transformation that completes its operating cycle in two strikes of the piston, one up and one down. When the piston moves up, fuel is pulled into the crankcase, and at the same time the fuel-air mixture inside the cylinder is compressed. When the piston is near the top of its stroke, a spark plug ignites the compressed fuel-air mixture, and the burning and expanding gases force the piston down. Near the bottom of the stroke, the piston uncovers an exhaust port and the burned gases leave the cylinder. When the piston moves further down, it uncovers the intake port, and a fresh charge of fuel and air are forced from the crankcase into the cylinder.

UDF engine. Un-ducted Fan™. The trade name registered by General Electric for a type of ultra-high-bypass turbofan engine that drives one or more wide-blade propellers that have between eight and twelve blades. These blades, which are not enclosed in a duct or shroud, are very thin, have wide chords, and are highly swept back in a scimitar shape that enables them to power airplanes flying in the speed range near Mach 0.8.

UHB (ultra-high-bypass) engine. A turbine that drives a pair of ducted or un-ducted contrarotating propellers which have eight to 12 variable-pitch blades. These blades are very thin, have wide chords, and are swept back with a scimitar shape that allows them to power airplanes flying in the speed range of Mach 0.8. The blades are made of advanced composites for high strength and light weight. USH engines may be of either the tractor or pusher type, and have a bypass ratio in excess of 30:1.

Underspeed condition. A speed condition in which the engine is turning at an RPM lower than that for which the propeller governor is set.

Unidirectional fibers. Fibers in a piece of composite material arranged so that they sustain loads in only one direction.

Updraft carburetor. A carburetor that mounts on the bottom of a reciprocating engine. Air entering the engine flows upward through the carburetor.

Upper-deck pressure. The absolute pressure of air at the inlet to the fuel metering system of a turbocharged engine. Upper-deck pressure is the same as the turbocharger discharge pressure.

V-blocks. A fixture that allows a shaft to be centered and rotated to measure any out-of-round condition.

V-engine. A form of reciprocating engine in which the cylinders are arranged in two banks. The banks are separated by an angle of between 45° and 90°. Pistons in two cylinders, one in each bank, are connected to each throw of the crankshaft.

Valence electrons. Electrons in the outer shell, or ring, around the nucleus of an atom. It is the valence electrons that give an atom its electrical characteristics and are the electrons that may be pulled loose from an atom to cause electrical current.

Valve overlap. The portion of the operating cycle of a four-stroke-cycle reciprocating engine during which both the intake and exhaust valves are off of their seats at the same time.

Vapor lock. A condition of fuel starvation that can occur in a reciprocating engine fuel system. If the fuel in the line between the tank and carburetor is heated enough for the fuel to vaporize, a bubble will form in the line. If the vapor pressure of the bubble is high enough, it will block the fuel and keep it from flowing to the engine.

Vapor pressure. The amount of pressure needed above a liquid to prevent it from evaporating.

Vaporize. The changing of a liquid into a vapor.

Vectored-thrust engine. A turbojet or turbofan engine with the fan and/or exhaust nozzles mounted in such a way that they may be rotated in flight to produce forward, vertically upward, or rearward thrust.

Velocity. A vector quantity that expresses both the speed an object is moving and the direction in which it is moving.

Velocity turbine. A turbine driven by forces produced by the velocity, rather than the pressure, of gases flowing through the vanes.

Venture. A specially shaped restrictor in a tube designed to speed up the flow of fluid passing through it. According to Bernoulli's principal, any time the flow of fluid speeds up without losing or gaining any energy from the outside, the pressure of the fluid decreases.

Vernier coupling. A timing coupling used with base-mounted magnetos. The vernier coupling allows the timing to be adjusted in increments of considerably less than one degree.

Vertical tape instrument. A tall rectangular instrument that displays the quantity of the parameter being measured by a movable strip of colored tape. The presentation resembles a vertical bar graph.

Vibration loop. A loop in a rigid fluid line used to prevent vibration from concentrating stresses that could cause the line to break.

VIFF. Vectoring in forward flight. A method of enhancing the maneuverability of an airplane by vectoring the exhaust gases and/or fan-discharge air to produce thrust components not parallel to the longitudinal axis of the aircraft.

Viscosimeter. An instrument used to measure the viscosity of a liquid. The time required for a given volume of liquid at a specified temperature to flow through a calibrated orifice is used to indicate the viscosity of the liquid.

Viscosity. The resistance of a fluid to flow. Viscosity is the stiffness of the fluid, or its internal friction.

Viscosity index (VI). A measure of change in viscosity of an oil as it changes temperature. The higher the viscosity index, the less the viscosity changes.

Viscosity index improver. An additive used to produce a multi-viscosity lubricating oil. The polymer additive expands as temperature increases and contracts as temperature decreases. VI improvers cause viscosity to increase as oil heats and decrease as it cools.

Volatile memory. Computer memory that is lost when the power to the computer is turned off.

Volatility. The characteristic of a liquid that relates to its ability to vaporize or change into a gas.

Volumetric efficiency. The ratio of the volume of the charge of the fuel and air inside the cylinder of a reciprocating engine to the total physical volume of the cylinder.

Von Ohain, Dr. Hans Pabst. The designer and developer of the first turbojet engine to power an airplane. His HeS3b engine was built in Germany by the Heinkel Company and it flew in a Heinkel He178 airplane on August 27, 1939.

Vortex. A whirling mass of air that sucks everything near it toward its center.

Vortex dissipater. A high-velocity stream of compressor bleed air blown from a nozzle into an area where vortices are likely to form. Vortex dissipaters destroy the vortices that would otherwise suck debris from the ground into engines mounted in pods that are low to the ground.

Wake. The high-velocity stream of turbulent air behind an operating aircraft engine.

Wankel engine. See rotating combustion (RC) engine.

Waste gate. A controllable butterfly valve in the exhaust pipe of a reciprocating engine equipped with an exhaust-driven turbocharger. When the waste gate is open, exhaust gases leave the engine through the exhaust pipe, and when it is closed, they leave through the turbine.

Watt. The basic unit of power in the metric system. One watt is the amount of power needed to do one joule (0.7376 foot-pound of work) in one second. One watt is $1/746$ horsepower.

Wet-sump engine. An engine that carries its lubricating oil supply in a reservoir that is part of the engine itself.

Wet-sump lubrication system. A lubrication system in which the oil supply is carried within the engine itself. Return oil drains into the oil reservoir by gravity.

Whittle, Sir Frank. The British Royal Air Force flying officer who in 1929 filed a patent application for a turbojet engine. Whittle's engine first flew in a Gloster E.28 on May 15, 1941. The first jet flight in America was made on October 2, 1942, in a Bell XP-59A that was powered by two Whittle-type General Electric I-A engines.

Windmilling propeller. A propeller that is rotated by air flowing over the blades rather than powered by the engine.
work. The product of a force times the distance the force is moved.

Worm gear. A helical gear mounted on a shaft. The worm meshes with a spur gear whose teeth are cut at an angle to its face. A worm gear is an irreversible mechanism. The rotation of the shaft, on which the worm gear locks the spur gear so its shaft cannot be rotated.

Wrist pin. The hardened steel pin that attaches a piston to the small end of a connecting rod.

Yaw. Rotation of an aircraft about its vertical axis.

Zero-lash valve lifter. A hydraulic valve lifter that maintains zero clearance in the valve actuating mechanism.

Index

A

Accelerating system 2-14
Accessory section 1-39
    Accessory case 1-39
    Gear train 1-39
Adjusting idle mixtures 2-30
Afterburning/thrust augmentation 3-29
Airblast nozzles 2-46
Air bleed 2-12
Air entrance 1-38
Air filter 3-1
Airflow section 2-22
Airframe fuel system 2-3
Air scoop 3-1
Air throttle assembly 2-27
Air turbine starters 5-13
    Air path 5-14
    Axial flow turbine 5-13
    Control assembly 5-16
    Drive coupling 5-13
    Output shaft assembly 5-13
    Pressure-regulating and shutoff valve 5-16
    Ring gear housing 5-14
    Rotor switch actuator 5-13
    Sprag clutch assembly 5-13
    Transmission housing 5-14
    Turbine housing 5-14
Air turbine starter troubleshooting guide 5-17
Aluminum wire terminals 4-60
American wire gauge (AWG) 4-45
Area of a circle 1-29
Atmospheric air 1-2
Augmentor exhaust system 3-26
Augmentors 3-24
Automatic mixture control (AMC) 2-19
Auxiliary ignition starting units 4-15

B

Ball bearings 1-23, 1-52
Basic fuel system 2-2

Bearings 1-22
Bellmouth compressor inlets 3-20
Bendix/precision fuel-injection system 2-22
Bend radii 4-52
Bernoulli's principle 1-58
Bonding 4-62
Booster coil 4-16
Brake horsepower 1-32
Brayton cycle 1-58
Breaker point inspection 4-35
Built-in engine timing reference marks 4-23

C

Cam rings 1-19
Camshaft 1-20
Capacitance 4-8
Capacitor discharge exciter unit 4-41
Carbon fouling of spark plugs 4-30
Carbon seal 1-53
Carburetion principles 2-6
    Application of venturi principle to carburetor 2-6
    Metering and discharge of fuel 2-7
    Venturi principles 2-6
Carburetor air filter 3-2
Carburetor fuel strainer 2-17
Carburetor icing 2-9
    Fuel evaporation ice 2-9
    Impact ice 2-9
    Throttle ice 2-9
Carburetor induction system 3-2
    Induction system filtering 3-5
    Induction system icing 3-4
    Induction system inspection and maintenance 3-5
    Induction system troubleshooting 3-5
Carburetor maintenance 2-28
Carburetor removal 2-28
Carburetor systems 2-8
    Accelerating system 2-8
    Idle cutoff system 2-8
    Idling system 2-8
    Main metering system 2-8

  Mixture control system..................................2-8
  Power enrichment system............................2-9
 Carburetor types..2-9
  Float-type carburetor 2-9
  Pressure-type carburetor...............................2-9
Checking ignition induction vibrator systems 4-30
Checking the internal timing of a magneto.................4-25
Circuit protection devices 4-67
Combustion drain valves..2-47
Combustion section..1-44
Compactness 1-3
Complete fuel system...2-32
Compression ratio 1-29
Compressor inlet screens 3-20
Compressors...1-40
 Axial-flow compressor 1-41
  Rotor 1-41
   Disk-type rotor......................................1-42
   Drum-type rotor....................................1-42
  Stator 1-41
 Centrifugal-flow compressors 1-40
  Compressor manifold.......................... 1-40,1-41
  Diffuser 1-40,1-41
  Impeller...1-40
Compressor section..1-39
Conductor insulation...4-49
 Dielectric strength 4-49
 Insulation resistance 4-49
Conduit..4-66
Connecting rods 1-10
Connecting terminal lugs to terminal blocks 4-62
Connectors 4-64,4-65
 Identification...4-66
Continental/TCM fuel-injection system 2-25
Continuous ignition...4-39
Controlling or monitoring the electrical load............4-67
Convergent-divergent exhaust nozzle....................3-28
Convergent exhaust nozzle 3-28
Copper wire terminals...4-59
Crankshafts 1-8
 Balance 1-10
Crimping tools 4-59
Cutting wire and cable 4-57
Cylinders..1-14
 Barrels 1-16
 Heads..1-15
 Numbering..1-16

D

Density altitude 3-6
Dielectric inspection 4-38

Differential pressure controller 3-14
Diffuser 1-44
Direct cranking electric starter..................................5-2
 Direct cranking electric starting system for
 large reciprocating engines.................................5-3
  Motor assembly 5-3
  Starter motor 5-3
 Direct cranking electric starting system for
 small aircraft..5-6
Discharge nozzle..2-7
Divided-entrance duct..3-19
Double-row radial engines 1-17
Duplex fuel nozzle 2-46
Durability...1-3
Dynamic dampers 1-10

E

Economizer system..2-14
EEC system..2-37
Efficiencies...1-35
E-gap..4-25
Electrical equipment installation.............................4-67
Electrical load limits 4-67
Electrical wiring installation....................................4-51
Electric starting systems and starter generator
starting system 5-11
Electronic control unit (ECU)..................... 4-13,4-14
Emergency splicing repairs....................................4-60
Engine fuel system components............................2-43
Engine noise supression..3-31
Engines..1-4
 Inline engines 1-4
 Opposed engines..1-4
 O-type engines..1-4
 Radial engines 1-5
 V-type engines..1-5
Exhaust leak 3-25
Exhaust manifold and stack failures 3-25
Exhaust section 1-51
 Exhaust cone...1-51
 Exhaust nozzle..1-52
 Insulation blanket 1-52
 Tailpipe..1-52
Exhaust system inspection....................................3-24
Exhaust system repairs...3-26
Exhaust systems with turbocharger 3-26

F

Factors affecting selection of conductor material........4-47
Factors affecting the selection of wire size.................4-45
FADEC for an auxiliary power unit.........................2-37

FADEC fuel control propulsion engine 2-39
FADEC fuel control systems 2-37
FADEC system description 4-12
Firing order 1-17
Fittings 2-33
Float chamber mechanism system 2-10
Float-type carburetors 2-10
Flow divider 2-23, 2-46
Fork-and-blade rod assembly 1-12
Friction and brake mean effective pressures 1-33
Friction horsepower 1-33
Fuel/air control unit 2-27
Fuel/air mixtures 2-4
Fuel control assembly 2-28
Fuel control maintenance 2-42
Fuel control unit 2-18
    Idle needle valve 2-18
    Manual mixture control 2-18
    Power enrichment valve 2-18
    Regulator fill valve 2-18
Fuel counter 2-48
Fuel discharge nozzle 2-24, 2-28
Fuel economy 1-3
Fuel filters 2-44
Fuel heater 2-43
Fuel-injection pump 2-25
Fuel-injection systems 2-22
Fuel injector 2-22
Fuel manifold valve 2-28
Fuel metering devices for reciprocating engines 2-3
Fuel metering section 2-23
Fuel metering system 2-3
Fuel pressure gauge 2-24, 2-34
Fuel pressurizing and dump valves 2-46
Fuel quantity gauges 2-33
Fuel quantity indicating units 2-48
Fuel spray nozzles and fuel manifolds 2-45
Fuel system inspection and maintenance 2-32
Fuel system operation 2-41
Fuel system requirements 2-1
Fuel tanks 2-33

G

Gap erosion of spark plugs 4-31
Gas turbine engines 1-37, 3-17
    Bearings and seals 1-52
    Performance 1-58
    Turbofan engines 1-37
    Turbojet 1-37
    Turboprop engine 1-37
    Turboshaft engine 1-38

Gas turbine engine starters 5-8
Govenor 1-7
Graphite fouling of spark plugs 4-31
Grounding 4-62

H

Harness testing 4-39
High-tension ignition harness faults 4-38
High-tension magneto E-gap setting (bench timing) 4-26
High-tension magneto system theory of operation 4-2
High-tension retard breaker vibrator 4-18
Horsepower 1-28
Hydraulic valve lifters 1-22
Hydraulic valve tappets 1-21

I

Identifying wire and cable 4-50
Idle speed adjustment 2-31
Idling system 2-12
Igniter plugs 4-41
Ignition harness 4-8
    Maintenance 4-38
Ignition switches 4-9
    Check 4-28
Impulse coupling 4-17
Indicated horsepower 1-31
Inertia starters 5-2
Inline engine cylinders 1-16
Installation 4-52
    Cable clamps 4-54
    Carburetor 2-30
    Connectors 4-66
Internal muffler failures 3-25

K

Knuckle pins 1-12

L

Lacing and tying wire bundles 4-55
    Double-cord lacing 4-56
    Lacing branch-offs 4-56
    Single-cord lacing 4-55
    Tying 4-56
Lead fouling of spark plugs 4-30
Lines 2-33
Low-tension magneto system 4-12
Low-tension retard breaker vibrator 4-20
Low-voltage harness 4-13

M

Magnetic circuit 4-2
Magneto 4-8
    Magneto and distributor venting 4-7
    Magneto-ignition system operating principles 4-2
    Magneto-ignition timing devices 4-23
    Magneto mounting systems 4-10
Main fuel pumps (engine driven) 2-43
Main line strainers 2-33
Main metering system 2-11
Maintenance and inspection of ignition leads 4-28
Manifold and augmentor exhaust assembly 3-24
Master-and-articulated rod assembly 1-11
Mechanical blockage 3-29
Mechanical efficiency 1-36
Mixture control system 2-12
Mounting lugs 1-7
Muffler and heat exchanger failures 3-25

N

Naturally aspirated induction systems 3-1
Newton's third law of motion 1-2

O

Oil fouling of spark plugs 4-30
Operating cycles 1-26
    Diesel cycle 1-28
    Four-stroke cycle 1-26
        Compression stroke 1-27
        Exhaust stroke 1-28
        Intake stroke 1-27
        Power stroke 1-27
    Rotary cycle 1-28
    Two-stroke cycle 1-28
Operating flexibility 1-3

P

Performing ignition system checks 4-27
Pistons 1-12
    Construction 1-12
    Displacement 1-29
    Pin 1-13
    Position indicators 4-24
    Rings 1-14
        Compression ring 1-14
        Construction 1-14
        Oil control rings 1-14
        Oil scraper ring 1-14
Plain bearings 1-23
Plain-type connecting rods 1-12
PLA potentiometer 2-37

Power 1-2
Powerlink ignition system 4-13, 4-14
Powerplant electrical systems 4-45
Powerplant selection 1-3
Pressure 3-1
    Injection carburetors 2-15
    Warning signal 2-34
Primary electrical circuit 4-4
Propeller reduction gearing 1-24
Propeller shafts 1-24
Propulsive efficiency 1-36
Protection against chafing 4-53
Protection against high temperature 4-53
Protection against solvents and fluids 4-53
Protection of wires in wheel well area 4-54
Pumps 2-33
Push rod 1-22

R

Radial engine exhaust collector ring system 3-23
Ram recovery 1-60
Reciprocating engines 1-5
    Accessory gear trains 1-7
    Accessory section 1-7
    Crankcase sections 1-5
    Design and construction 1-5
    Exhaust systems 3-22
        Collector system 3-23
        Maintenance practices 3-24
        Short stack system 3-23
    Ignition systems 4-1
        Maintenance and inspection 4-22
    Induction systems 3-1
    Operating principles 1-24
    Power and efficiencies 1-28
    Starting systems 5-2
        Maintenance practices 5-8
Regulator section 2-22
Regulator unit 2-16
Relays 4-68
Reliability 1-3
Removal, maintenance, and installation of
ignition system components 4-43
    Igniter plugs 4-44
    Ignition system leads 4-43
Replacement of ignition harness 4-29
Rigging carburetor controls 2-30
Rocker arms 1-22
Roller bearings 1-23
Routing 4-52
    Precautions 4-54

S

Secondary electrical circuit 4-6
Selector valves 2-33
Simplex fuel nozzle 2-45
Single and dual high-tension system magnetos 4-10
Single-row radial engine cylinders 1-17
Single-row radial engines 1-17
Slack in wiring bundles 4-52
Solderless terminals and splices 4-58
Solid lifters/tappets 1-21
Spark plugs 4-21
    Electrodes 4-21
    Inspection and maintenance 4-30
    Inspection prior to installation 4-33
    Installation 4-34
    Insulator 4-21
    Lead installation 4-35
    Outer shell 4-21
    Reconditioning service 4-33
    Removal 4-32
Spliced connections in wire bundles 4-52
Splicing copper wires using preinsulated wires 4-60
Splicing with solder and potting compound 4-60
Stripping wire and cable 4-57
Stromberg PS carburetor 2-20
    Accelerating pump 2-21
    Manual mixture control 2-21
Supercharged induction systems 3-5
    Absolute pressure controller 3-17
    Ground-boosted turbosupercharger system 3-11
    Internally driven superchargers 3-6
    Normalizer turbocharger 3-11
    Sloped controller 3-16
    Turbocharger controllers and system descriptions 3-15
    Turbocharger system troubleshooting 3-17
    Turbosuperchargers 3-8
        Compressor assembly 3-8
        Exhaust gas turbine assembly 3-10
    Typical turbosupercharger system 3-13
    Variable absolute pressure controller (VAPC) ... 3-16
Switches 4-68

T

Tappet assembly 1-20
    Cylindrical tappet 1-20
    Tappet ball 1-20
    Tappet roller 1-20
    Tappet spring 1-20
Thermal efficiency 1-35
Throttle body 2-16
Thrust 1-57
Thrust horsepower 1-35
Thrust reversers 3-28
Thrust vectoring 3-31
Timing disks 4-24
Timing lights 4-25
Timing the high-tension magneto to the engine 4-26
Total engine fuel and control system 2-36
    Filter bypass valve 2-36
    Flow divider and drain valve assembly 2-37
    Fuel manifold assembly 2-37
    Hydromechanical fuel control assembly 2-36
    Vane fuel pump assembly 2-36
Troubleshooting a starter generator starting system 5-12
Troubleshooting small aircraft starting systems 5-8
Turbine engine emissions 3-33
Turbine engine exhaust nozzles 3-26
Turbine engine fuel system—general requirements ... 2-34
Turbine engine ignition systems 4-39
Turbine engine inlet systems 3-17
Turbine engine operating principles 1-57
Turbine fuel controls 2-34
    FADEC-type control 2-34
    Hydromechanical/electronic fuel control 2-34, 2-35
    Hydromechanical fuel control 2-35
Turbine ignition system inspection and maintenance 4-42
    Check system operation 4-43
    Repair 4-43
Turbine section 1-47
    Disk rim 1-49
    Rotor element 1-48
    Turbine blades 1-50
    Turbine disk 1-48
    Turbine inlet nozzle assembly 1-48
Turbofan engines 1-55
    Inlet sections 3-21
Turboprop and turboshaft compressor inlets 3-21
Turbopropeller (turboprop) engine 1-54
    Accessory drive housing assembly 1-55
    Gearbox assembly 1-55
    Power section assembly 1-55
Turboprop exhaust nozzles 3-27
Turboshaft engines 1-55
Twisting wires 4-51
Typical injection carburetor 2-15

V

Valve construction 1-17
    valve head 1-18

valve stem 1-18
Valves 1-17
    Duration 1-18
    Lift 1-18
    Operating mechanism 1-18
    Springs 1-22
Vapor lock 2-2
Vapor vent system 2-17
Variable-geometry duct 3-19
Voltage drop (IR drop) 4-45
    In aircraft wire and cable 4-48
Volumetric efficiency 1-36
V-type engine cylinders 1-16

W

Water injection system 2-42
    For reciprocating engines 2-34
Weight 1-2
Wire groups and bundles 4-51
Wire size 4-45
Work 1-28

www.ingramcontent.com/pod-product-compliance
Ingram Content Group UK Ltd.
Pitfield, Milton Keynes, MK11 3LW, UK
UKHW051351180426
11947UKWH00014B/873